R.Burton, delt.
C.F.Kell, Lith.

THE PILGRIM.

PERSONAL NARRATIVE

OF A

PILGRIMAGE

TO

AL-MADINAH & MECCAH

BY

CAPTAIN SIR RICHARD F. BURTON,

K.C.M.G., F.R.G.S. &c., &c., &c.

EDITED BY HIS WIFE,

ISABEL BURTON.

"Our notions of Mecca must be drawn from the Arabians; as no unbeliever is permitted to enter the city, our travellers are silent."—*Gibbon*, chap. 50.

Memorial Edition.

———

IN TWO VOLUMES

VOLUME II.

DOVER PUBLICATIONS, INC.
NEW YORK

Published in Canada by General Publishing Company, Ltd., 30 Lesmill Road, Don Mills, Toronto, Ontario.

Published in the United Kingdom by Constable and Company, Ltd., 10 Orange Street, London WC 2.

This Dover edition, first published in 1964, is an unabridged republication of the Memorial Edition, as published by Tylston and Edwards in 1893.

Standard Book Number: 486-21218-1
Library of Congress Catalog Card Number: 64-18842

Manufactured in the United States of America
Dover Publications, Inc.
180 Varick Street
New York, N.Y. 10014

اَللَّيْلُ وَالْخَيْلُ وَالْبَيْدَآءُ تَعْرِفُنِي

وَالسَّيْفُ وَالضَّيْفُ وَالْقِرْطَاسُ وَالْقَلَمِ

Dark and the Desert and Destriers me ken,
And the Glaive and the Joust, and Paper and Pen.
Al-Mutanabbi.

CONTENTS

OF

THE SECOND VOLUME.

x   *Contents.*

APPENDICES.

LIST OF ILLUSTRATIONS
IN VOLUME II.

List of Illustrations.

TO

LIEUT.-GENERAL W. MONTEITH,

(MADRAS ENGINEERS)

K. L. S.   F. R. SOC.   F. R. G. SOC.

&c.   &c.   &c.

THIS VOLUME IS INSCRIBED

A FEEBLE EVIDENCE OF THE AUTHOR'S

GRATITUDE.

PART II.

—

AL-MADINAH.
(Continued.)

A PILGRIMAGE

TO

AL-MADINAH AND MECCAH.

CHAPTER XXI.

THE PEOPLE OF AL-MADINAH.

AL-MADINAH contains but few families descended from the Prophet's Auxiliaries. I heard only of four whose genealogy is undoubted. These were,—

1. The Bayt al-Ansari, or descendants of Abu Ayyub, a most noble race whose tree ramifies through a space of fifteen hundred years. They keep the keys of the Kuba Mosque, and are Imams in the Harim, but the family is no longer wealthy or powerful.

2. The Bayt Abu Jud : they supply the Harim with Imams and Mu'ezzins.[1] I was told that there are now but two surviving members of this family, a boy and a girl.

3. The Bayt al-Sha'ab, a numerous race. Some of the members travel professionally, others trade, and others are employed in the Harim.

4. The Bayt al-Karrani, who are mostly engaged in commerce.

There is also a race called Al-Nakhawilah,[2] who,

---

1 Ibn Jubayr relates that in his day a descendant of Belal, the original Mu'ezzin of the Prophet, practised his ancestral profession at Al-Madinah.

2 This word is said to be the plural of Nakhwali,—one who cultivates the date tree, a gardener or farmer. No one could tell me whether these heretics had not a peculiar name for themselves. I

according to some, are descendants of the Ansar, whilst
others derive them from Yazid, the son of Mu'awiyah :
the latter opinion is improbable, as the Caliph in question
was a mortal foe to Ali's family, which is inordinately
venerated by these people.   As far as I could ascertain,
they abuse the Shaykhayn (Abu Bakr and Omar): all my
informants agreed upon this point, but none could tell me
why they neglected to bedevil Osman, the third object of
hatred to the Shi'ah persuasion. They are numerous and
warlike, yet they are despised by the townspeople, because
they openly profess heresy, and are moreover of humble
degree.   They have their own priests and instructors,
although subject to the orthodox Kazi ; marry in their
own sect, are confined to low offices, such as slaughtering
animals, sweeping, and gardening, and are not allowed to
enter the Harim during life, or to be carried to it after
death.   Their corpses are taken down an outer street
called the Darb al-Janazah—Road of Biers—to their own
cemetery near Al-Bakia. They dress and speak Arabic,
like the townspeople ; but the Arabs pretend to distinguish
them by a peculiar look denoting their degradation : it is
doubtless the mistake of effect for cause, about all such

"Tribes of the wandering foot and weary breast."

A number of reports are current about the horrid

---

hazard a conjecture that they may be identical with the Mutawalli
(also written Mutawilah, Mutaalis, Metoualis, &c., &c.), the hardy,
courageous, and hospitable mountaineers of Syria, and Cœlesyria
Proper. This race of sectarians, about 35,000 in number, holds to
the Imamship or supreme pontificate of Ali and his descendants.
They differ, however, in doctrine from the Persians, believing in a
transmigration of the soul, which, gradually purified, is at last
"orbed into a perfect star."   They are scrupulous of caste, and will
not allow a Jew or a Frank to touch a piece of their furniture: yet
they erect guest-houses for Infidels.   In this they resemble the
Shi'ahs, who are far more particular about ceremonial purity than
the Sunnis.   They use ablutions before each meal, and herein remind
us of the Hindus.

customs of these people, and their community of women[1] with the Persian pilgrims who pass through the town. It need scarcely be said that such tales coming from the mouths of fanatic foes are not to be credited. I regret not having had an opportunity to become intimate with any of the Nakhawilah, from whom curious information might be elicited. Orthodox Moslems do not like to be questioned about such hateful subjects; when I attempted to learn something from one of my acquaintance, Shaykh Ula al-Din, of a Kurd family, settled at Al-Madinah, a man who had travelled over the East, and who spoke five languages to perfection, he coldly replied that he had never consorted with these heretics. Sayyids and Sharifs,[2] the descendants of the Prophet, here abound. The Benu Hosayn of Al-Madinah have their head-quarters at Suwayrkiyah:[3] the former place contains six or seven families; the latter, ninety-three or ninety-four. Anciently they were much more numerous, and such was their power, that for centuries they retained charge of the Prophet's tomb. They

---

1 The communist principles of Mazdak the Persian (sixth century) have given his nation a permanent bad fame in this particular among the Arabs.

2 In Arabia the Sharif is the descendant of Hasan through his two sons, Zaid and Hasan al-Musanna: the Sayyid is the descendant of Hosayn through Zayn al-Abidin, the sole of twelve children who survived the fatal field of Kerbela. The former devotes himself to government and war; the latter, to learning and religion. In Persia and India, the Sharif is the son of a Sayyid woman and a common Moslem. The Sayyid "Nejib al-Taraf" (noble on one side) is the son of a Sayyid father and a common Moslemah. The Sayyid "Nejib al-Tarafayn" (noble on both sides) is one whose parents are both Sayyids.

3 Burckhardt alludes to this settlement when he says, "In the Eastern Desert, at three or four days' journey from Medinah, lives a whole Bedouin tribe, called Beni Aly, who are all of this Persian creed." I travelled to Suwayrkiyah, and found it inhabited by Benu Hosayn. The Benu Ali are Badawin settled at the Awali, near the Kuba Mosque: they were originally slaves of the great house of Auf, and are still heretical in their opinions.

subsist principally upon their Amlak, property in land, for which they have title-deeds extending back to Moham- med's day, and Aukaf, religious bequests; popular rumour accuses them of frequent murders for the sake of succes- sion. At Al-Madinah they live chiefly at the Hosh Ibn Sa'ad, a settlement outside the town and south of the Darb al-Janazah. There is, however, no objection to their dwelling within the walls; and they are taken to the Harim after death, if there be no evil report against the individual. Their burial-place is the Bakia cemetery. The reason of this toleration is, that some are supposed to be Sunni, or orthodox, and even the most heretical keep their "Rafz[1]" (heresy) a profound secret. Most learned Arabs believe that they belong, like the Persians, to the sect of Ali: the truth, however, is so vaguely known, that I could find out none of the peculiarities of their faith, till I met a Shirazi friend at Bombay. The Benu Hosayn are spare dark men of Badawi appearance, and they dress in the old Arab style still affected by the Sharifs,—a Kufiyah (kerchief) on the head,[2] and a Banish, a long and wide-sleeved garment resembling our magi- cians' gown, thrown over the white cotton Kamis (shirt): in public they always carry swords, even when others leave weapons at home. There are about two hundred families of Sayyid Alawiyah,—descendants of Ali by any of his wives but Fatimah,—they bear no distinctive mark in dress or appearance, and are either employed at the

---

1 " Refusing, rejecting." Hence the origin of Ráfizi,—" a rejector, a heretic." " Inná rafaznáhum,"—" verily we have rejected *them*," (Abu Bakr, Omar, and Osman,) exclaim the Persians, glorying in the opprobrious epithet.

2 Sayyids in Al-Hijaz, as a general rule, do not denote their descent by the green turband. In fact, most of them wear a red Kashmir shawl round the head, when able to afford the luxury. The green turband is an innovation in Al-Islam. In some countries it is confined to the Sayyids; in others it is worn as a mark of dis- tinction by pilgrims. Khudabakhsh, the Indian, at Cairo generally dressed in a tender green suit like a Mantis.

temple or engage at trade. Of the Khalifiyah, or descendants of Abbas, there is, I am told, but one household, the Bayt Al-Khalifah, who act as Imams in the Harim, and have charge of Hamzah's tomb. Some declare that there are a few of the Siddikiyah, or descendants from Abu Bakr ; others ignore them, and none could give me any information about the Benu Najjar.

The rest of the population of Al-Madinah is a motley race composed of offshoots from every nation in Al-Islam. The sanctity of the city attracts strangers, who, purposing to stay but a short time, become residents ; after finding some employment, they marry, have families, die, and are buried there with an eye to the spiritual advantages of the place. I was much importuned to stay at Al-Madinah. The only known physician was one Shaykh Abdullah Sahib, an Indian, a learned man, but of so melancholic a temperament, and so ascetic in his habits, that his knowledge was entirely lost to the public. "Why dost thou not," said my friends, "hire a shop somewhere near the Prophet's Mosque ? There thou wilt eat bread by thy skill, and thy soul will have the blessing of being on holy ground." Shaykh Nur also opined after a short residence at Al-Madinah that it was *bara jannati Shahr*, a "very heavenly City," and little would have induced him to make it his home. The present ruling race at Al-Madinah, in consequence of political vicissitudes, is the "Sufat,[1]" sons of Turkish fathers by Arab mothers. These half-castes are now numerous, and have managed to secure the highest and most lucrative offices. Besides Turks, there are families originally from the Maghrib, Takruris, Egyptians in considerable numbers, settlers from Al-Yaman and other parts of Arabia, Syrians, Kurds, Afghans, Daghistanis from the Caucasus, and a few Jawis—Java Moslems. The Sindís, I was told, reckon about one hundred families, who are exceedingly despised for their

---

1 Plural of Suftah—a half-caste Turk.

cowardice and want of manliness, whilst the Baluch and
the Afghan are respected. The Indians are not so
numerous in proportion here as at Meccah; still Hindustani is by no means uncommonly heard in the streets.
They preserve their peculiar costume, the women persist-
ing in showing their faces, and in wearing tight, exceedingly tight, pantaloons. This, together with other reasons,
secures for them the contempt of the Arabs. At Al-
Madinah they are generally small shopkeepers, especially
druggists and sellers of Kumash (cloth), and they form a
society of their own. The terrible cases of misery and
starvation which so commonly occur among the improvi-
dent Indians at Jeddah and Meccah are here rare.

The Hanafi school holds the first rank at Al-Madinah,
as in most parts of Al-Islam, although many of the
citizens, and almost all the Badawin, are Shafe'is. The
reader will have remarked with astonishment that at one
of the fountain-heads of the faith, there are several races
of schismatics, the Benu Hosayn, the Benu Ali, and the
Nakhawilah. At the town of Safra there are said to be
a number of the Zuyud schismatics,[1] who visit Al-
Madinah, and have settled in force at Meccah, and some
declare that the Bayazi sect[2] also exists.

The citizens of Al-Madinah are a favoured race, although the city is not, like Meccah, the grand mart of the
Moslem world or the meeting-place of nations. They pay
no taxes, and reject the idea of a "Miri," or land-cess, with
extreme disdain. "Are *we*, the children of the Prophet,"
they exclaim, "to support or to be supported?" The
Wahhabis, not understanding the argument, taxed them,

1 Plural of Zaydi. These are well-known schismatics of the
Shi'ah persuasion, who abound in Southern Arabia.

2 The Bayazi sect flourishes near Maskat, whose Imam or
Prince, it is said, belongs to the heretical persuasion. It rejects
Osman, and advocates the superiority of Omar over the other two
Caliphs.

as was their wont, in specie and in materials, for which reason the very name of those Puritans is an abomination. As has before been shown, all the numerous attendants at the Mosque are paid partly by the Sultan, partly by Aukaf, the rents of houses and lands bequeathed to the shrine, and scattered over every part of the Moslem world. When a Madani is inclined to travel, he applies to the Mudir al-Harim, and receives from him a paper which entitles him to the receipt of a considerable sum at Constantinople. The " Ikram " *(honorarium)*, as it is called, varies with the rank of the recipient, the citizens being divided into these four orders, viz.

First and highest, the Sádát (Sayyids),[1] and Imans, who are entitled to twelve purses, or about £60. Of these there are said to be three hundred families.

The Khanahdan, who keep open house and receive poor strangers gratis. Their Ikram amounts to eight purses, and they number from a hundred to a hundred and fifty families.

The Ahali[2] (burghers) or Madani properly speaking, who have homes and families, and were born in Al-Madinah. They claim six purses.

The Mujawirin, strangers, as Egyptians or Indians, settled at, though not born in, Al-Madinah. Their honorarium is four purses.

The Madani traveller, on arrival at Constantinople, reports his arrival to his Consul, the Wakil al-Haramayn. This " Agent of the two Holy Places " applies to the Nazir al-Aukaf, or " Intendant of Bequests "; the latter,

---

1 Sadat is the plural of Sayyid. This word in the Northern Hijaz is applied indifferently to the posterity of Hasan and Hosayn.

2 The plural of Ahl, an inhabitant (of a particular place). The reader will excuse my troubling him with these terms. As they are almost all local in their application, and therefore are not explained in such restricted sense by lexicographers, the specification may not be useless to the Oriental student.

after transmitting the demand to the different officers of
the treasury, sends the money to the Wakil, who delivers
it to the applicant.   This gift is sometimes squandered in
pleasure, more often profitably invested either in merchandise or in articles of home-use, presents of dress and
jewellery for the women, handsome arms, especially pistols and Balas[1] (yataghans), silk tassels, amber pipe-
pieces, slippers, and embroidered purses.   They are
packed up in one or two large Sahharahs, and then com-
mences the labour of returning home gratis.   Besides the
Ikram, most of the Madani, when upon these begging
trips, are received as guests by great men at Constantinople,   The citizens whose turn it is not to travel, await
the Aukaf and Sadakat (bequests and alms),[2] forwarded
every year by the Damascus Caravan; besides which,
as has been before explained, the Harim supplies even
those not officially employed in it with many perquisites.

Without these advantages Al-Madinah would soon
be abandoned to cultivators and Badawin.   Though commerce is here honourable, as everywhere in the East,
business is "slack,[3]" because the higher classes prefer the
idleness of administering their landed estates, and being
servants to the Mosque.   I heard of only four respectable houses, Al-Isawi, Al-Sha'ab, Abd al-Jawwad, and a
family from Al-Shark (the Eastern Region).[4]   They all deal
in grain, cloth, and provisions, and perhaps the richest
have a capital of twenty thousand dollars.   Caravans in

---

1 The Turkish "yataghan." It is a long dagger, intended for
thrusting rather than cutting, and has a curve, which, methinks, has
been wisely copied by the Duke of Orleans, in the bayonet of the
Chasseurs de Vincennes.

2 See chapter xvii.

3 Omar Effendi's brothers, grandsons of the principal Mufti of
Al-Madinah, were both shopkeepers, and were always exhorting him
to do some useful work, rather than muddle his brains and waste his
time on books.

4 See chapter xiv.

the cold weather are constantly passing between Al-Madinah and Egypt, but they are rather bodies of visitors
to Constantinople than traders travelling for gain.   Corn
is brought from Jeddah by land, and imported into
Yambu' or *via* Al-Rais, a port on the Red Sea, one day
and a half's journey from Safra.   There is an active provision trade with the neighbouring Badawin, and the
Syrian Hajj supplies the citizens with apparel and articles
of luxury—tobacco, dried fruits, sweetmeats, knives, and
all that is included under the word "notions."   There are
few store-keepers, and their dealings are petty, because
articles of every kind are brought from Egypt, Syria, and
Constantinople.   As a general rule, labour is exceedingly
expensive,[1] and at the Visitation time a man will demand
fifteen or twenty piastres from a stranger for such a
trifling job as mending an umbrella.   Handicraftsmen
and artisans—carpenters, masons, locksmiths, potters,
and others—are either slaves or foreigners, mostly Egyptians.[2]   This proceeds partly from the pride of the people.
They are taught from their childhood that the Madani is
a favoured being, to be respected however vile or schis-
matic ; and that the vengeance of Allah will fall upon any
one who ventures to abuse, much more to strike him.[3]
They receive a stranger at the shop window with the
haughtiness of Pashas, and take pains to show him, by
words as well as by looks, that they consider themselves as

1 To a townsman, even during the dead season, the pay of a
gardener would be 2 piastres, a carpenter 8 piastres per diem, and a
common servant (a Bawwab or porter, for instance), 25 piastres per
mensem, or £3 per annum, besides board and dress.   Considering the
value of money in the country, these are very high rates.

2 Who alone sell milk, curds, or butter.   The reason of their
monopoly has been given in Chapter xiii.

3 History informs us that the sanctity of their birth-place has
not always preserved the people of Al-Madinah.   But the memory of
their misfortunes is soon washed away by the overwhelming pride of
the race.

" good gentlemen as the king, only not so rich." Added
to this pride are indolence, and the true Arab prejudice,
which, even in the present day, prevents a Badawi from
marrying the daughter of an artisan. Like Castilians,
they consider labour humiliating to any but a slave ; nor
is this, as a clever French author remarks, by any means
an unreasonable idea, since Heaven, to punish man for
disobedience, caused him to eat daily bread by the sweat
of his brow. Besides, there *is* degradation, moral and
physical, in handiwork compared with the freedom of the
Desert. The loom and the file do not conserve courtesy
and chivalry like the sword and spear ; man "extends
his tongue," to use an Arab phrase, when a cuff and not
a stab is to be the consequence of an injurious expression.
Even the ruffian becomes polite in California, where his
brother-ruffian carries his revolver, and those European
nations who were most polished when every gentleman
wore a rapier, have become the rudest since Civilisation
disarmed them.

By the tariff quoted below it will be evident that
Al-Madinah is not a cheap place.[1] Yet the citizens,

---

1 The market is under the charge of an Arab Muhtasib or
Bazar-master, who again is subject to the Muhafiz or Pasha
governing the place. The following was the current price of provisions
at Al-Madinah early in August, 1853: during the Visitation season
everything is doubled :—

1 lb. mutton, 2 piastres, (beef is half-price, but seldom eaten;
  there is no buffalo meat, and only Badawin will touch the camel).
A fowl, 5 piastres.
Eggs, in summer 8, in winter 4, for the piastre.
1 lb. clarified butter, 4 piastres, (when cheap it falls to 2½. Butter
  is made at home by those who eat it, and sometimes by the
  Egyptians for sale).
1 lb. milk, 1 piastre.
1 lb. cheese, 2 piastres, (when cheap it is 1, when dear 3 piastres
  per lb.)
Wheaten loaf weighing 12 dirhams, 10 parahs. (There are loaves
  of 24 dirhams, costing ½ piastre.)
1 lb. dry biscuits, (imported), 3 piastres.

despite their being generally in debt, manage to live well. Their cookery, like that of Meccah, has borrowed something from Egypt, Turkey, Syria, Persia, and India : as all Orientals, they are exceedingly fond of clarified butter.[1]

1 lb. of vegetables, ½ piastre.

1 Mudd dates, varies according to quality from 4 piastres to 100.

1 lb. grapes, 1½ piastre.

A lime, 1 parah.

A pomegranate, from 20 parahs to 1 piastre.

A water-melon, from 3 to 6 piastres each.

1 lb. peaches, 2 piastres.

1 lb. coffee, 4 piastres, (the Yamani is the only kind drunk here).

1 lb. tea, 15 piastres, (black tea, imported from India).

1 lb. European loaf-sugar, 6 piastres, (white Egyptian, 5 piastres brown Egyptian, 3 piastres; brown Indian, for cooking and conserves, 3 piastres).

1 lb. spermaceti candles, 7 piastres, (called wax, and imported from Egypt).

1 lb. tallow candles, 3 piastres.

1 Ardeb wheat, 295 piastres.

1 Ardeb onions, 33 piastres, (when cheap 20, when dear 40).

1 Ardeb barley, 120 piastres, (minimum 90, maximum 180).

1 Ardeb rice, Indian, 302 piastres, (it varies from 260 to 350 piastres, according to quality).

Durrah or maize is generally given to animals, and is very cheap.

Barsim (clover, a bundle of) 3 Wakkiyahs, (36 Dirhams), costs 1 parah.

Adas or Lentil is the same price as rice.

1 lb. Latakia tobacco, 16 piastres.

1 lb. Syrian tobacco, 8 piastres.

1 lb. Tumbak (Persian), 6 piastres.

1 lb. olive oil, 6 piastres, (when cheap it is 4).

A skin of water, ½ piastre.

Bag of charcoal, containing 100 Wukkah, 10 piastres. The best kind is made from an Acacia called "Samur."

The Parah (Turkish), Faddah (Egyptian), or Diwani (Hijazi word), is the 40th part of a piastre, or nearly the quarter of a farthing. The piastre is about 2 and two-fifths pence. Throughout Al-Hijaz there is no want of small change, as in Egypt, where the deficiency calls for the attention of the Government.

1 Physiologists have remarked that fat and greasy food, contain-

I have seen the boy Mohammed drink off nearly a
tumbler-full, although his friends warned him that it
would make him as fat as an elephant.   When a man
cannot enjoy clarified butter in these countries, it is considered a sign that his stomach is out of order, and all
my excuses of a melancholic temperament were required
to be in full play to prevent the infliction of fried meat
swimming in grease, or that guest-dish,[1] rice saturated
with melted—perhaps I should say—rancid butter.   The
"Samn" of Ai-Hijaz, however, is often fresh, being
brought in by the Badawin ; it has not therefore the foul
flavour derived from the old and impregnated skin-bag
which distinguishes the "ghi" of India.[2]   The house of
a Madani in good circumstances is comfortable, for the
building is substantial, and the attendance respectable.
Black slave-girls here perform the complicated duties of
servant-maids in England ; they are taught to sew, to
cook, and to wash, besides sweeping the house and drawing water for domestic use.   Hasinah (the "Charmer,"
a decided misnomer) costs from $40 to $50; if she be a
mother, her value is less ; but neat-handedness, propriety
of demeanour, and skill in feminine accomplishments,
raise her to $100 = £25.   A little black boy, perfect in
all his points, and tolerably intelligent, costs about a
thousand piastres ; girls are dearer, and eunuchs fetch
double that sum.   The older the children become, the

---

ing a quantity of carbon, is peculiar to cold countries; whereas the
inhabitants of the tropics delight in fruits, vegetables, and articles of
diet which do not increase caloric.   This must be taken *cum grano*.
In Italy, Spain, and Greece, the general use of olive oil begins.   In
Africa and Asia—especially in the hottest parts—the people habitually
eat enough clarified butter to satisfy an Esquimaux.

1 In Persia, you jocosely say to a man, when he is threatened
with a sudden inroad of guests, "Go and swamp the rice with
Raughan (clarified butter)."

2 Among the Indians, ghi, placed in pots carefully stopped up
and kept for years till a hard black mass only remains, is considered
a panacea for diseases and wounds.

more their value diminishes; and no one would purchase save under exceptional circumstances, an adult slave, because he is never parted with but for some incurable vice. The Abyssinian, mostly Galla, girls, so much prized because their skins are always cool in the hottest weather, are here rare; they seldom sell for less than £20, and they often fetch £60. I never heard of a Jariyah Bayza, a white slave girl, being in the market at Al-Madinah: in Circassia they fetch from £100 to £400 prime cost, and few men in Al-Hijaz could afford so expensive a luxury. The Bazar at Al-Madinah is poor, and as almost all the slaves are brought from Meccah by the Jallabs, or drivers, after exporting the best to Egypt, the town receives only the refuse.[1]

The personal appearance of the Madani makes the stranger wonder how this mongrel population of settlers has acquired a peculiar and almost an Arab physiognomy. They are remarkably fair, the effect of a cold climate; sometimes the cheeks are lighted up with red, and the hair is a dark chestnut—at Al-Madinah I was not stared at as a white man. The cheeks and different parts of the children's bodies are sometimes marked with Mashali or Tashrih, not the three long stripes of the Meccans,[2] but little scars generally in threes. In some points they approach very near the true Arab type, that is to say, the Badawi of ancient and noble family. The cheek-bones are high and *saillant*, the eye small, more round than long,

---

1 Some of these slaves come from Abyssinia: the greater part are driven from the Galla country, and exported at the harbours of the Somali coast, Berberah, Tajurrah, and Zayla. As many as 2000 slaves from the former place, and 4000 from the latter, are annually shipped off to Mocha, Jeddah, Suez, and Maskat. It is strange that the Imam of the latter place should voluntarily have made a treaty with us for the suppression of this vile trade, and yet should allow so extensive an importation to his dominions.

2 More will be said concerning the origin of this strange custom, when speaking of Meccah and the Meccans.

piercing, fiery, deep-set, and brown rather than black.
The head is small, the ears well-cut, the face long and
oval, though not unfrequently disfigured by what is popularly called the "lantern-jaw"; the forehead high, bony,
broad, and slightly retreating, and the beard and
mustachios scanty, consisting of two tufts upon the chin,
with, generally speaking, little or no whisker. These are
the points of resemblance between the city and the
country Arab. The difference is equally remarkable.
The temperament of the Madani is not purely nervous,
like that of the Badawi, but admits a large admixture of
the bilious, and, though rarely, the lymphatic. The
cheeks are fuller, the jaws project more than in the pure
race, the lips are more fleshy, more sensual and ill-fitting;
the features are broader, and the limbs are stouter and
more bony. The beard is a little thicker, and the young
Arabs of the towns are beginning to imitate the Turks in
that abomination to their ancestors—shaving. Personal
vanity, always a ruling passion among Orientals, and a
hopeless wish to emulate the flowing beards of the Turks
and the Persians—perhaps the only nations in the world
who ought not to shave the chin—have overruled even
the religious objections to such innovation. I was more
frequently appealed to at Al-Madinah than anywhere else,
for some means of removing the opprobrium "Kusah," or
scant-bearded man. They blacken the beard with gall-
nuts, henna, and other preparations, especially the
Egyptian mixture, composed of sulphate of iron
one part, ammoniure of iron one part, and gall-
nuts two parts, infused in eight parts of distilled
water. It is a very bad dye. Much refinement of dress
is now found at Al-Madinah,—Constantinople, the Paris
of the East, supplying it with the newest fashions.
Respectable men wear either a Benish or a Jubbah ; the
latter, as at Meccah, is generally of some light and flashy
colour, gamboge, yellow, tender green, or bright pink.

This is the sign of a " dressy" man. If you have a single coat, it should be of some modest colour, as a dark violet ; to appear always in the same tender green, or bright pink, would excite derision. But the Hijazis, poor and rich, always prefer these tulip tints. The proper Badan, or long coat without sleeves, still worn in truly Arab countries, is here confined to the lowest classes. That ugliest of head-dresses, the red Tunisian cap, called " Tarbush,¹" is much used, only the Arabs have too much regard for their eyes and faces to wear it, as the Turks do, without a turband. It is with regret that one sees the most graceful head-gear imaginable, the Kufiyah and the Aakal, proscribed except amongst the Sharifs and the Badawin. The women dress, like the men, handsomely. Indoors they wear, I am told, a Sudayriyah, or boddice of calico and other stuffs, like the Choli of India, which supports the bosom without the evils of European stays. Over this is a Saub, or white shirt, of the white stuff called Halaili or Burunjuk, with enormous sleeves, and flowing down to the feet ; the Sarwal or pantaloons are not wide, like the Egyptians', but rather tight, approaching to the Indian cut, without its exaggeration.² Abroad, they throw over the head a silk or a cotton Milayah, generally chequered white and blue. The Burka (face-veil), all over Al-Hijaz is white, a decided improvement in point of cleanliness upon that of Egypt. Women of all ranks die the soles of the feet and the palms of the hands black ; and trace thin lines down the inside of the

---

1 The word Tarbush is a corruption from the Persian Sarpush,— "head-covering," "head-dress." The Anglo-Saxon further debases it to " Tarbrush." The other name for the Tarbush, "Fez," denotes the place where the best were made. Some Egyptians distinguish between the two, calling the large high crimson cap " Fez," the small one " Tarbush."

2 In India, as in Sind, a lady of fashion will sometimes be occupied a quarter of an hour in persuading her "bloomers" to pass over the region of the ankle.

fingers, by first applying a plaster of henna and then a mixture, called "Shadar," of gall-nuts, alum, and lime. The hair parted in the centre, is plaited into about twenty little twists called Jadilah.[1] Of ornaments, as usual among Orientals, they have a vast variety, ranging from brass and spangles to gold and precious stones ; and they delight in strong perfumes,—musk, civet, ambergris, attar of rose, oil of jasmine, aloe-wood, and extract of cinnamon. Both sexes wear Constantinople slippers. The women draw on Khuff, inner slippers, of bright yellow leather, serving for socks, and covering the ankle, with Papush of the same material, sometimes lined with velvet and embroidered with a gold sprig under the hollow of the foot. In mourning the men show no difference of dress, like good Moslems, to whom such display of grief is forbidden. But the women, who cannot dissociate the heart and the toilette, evince their sorrow by wearing white clothes and by doffing their ornaments. This is a modern custom: the accurate Burckhardt informs us that in his day the women of Al-Madinah did not wear mourning.

The Madani generally appear abroad on foot. Few animals are kept here, on account, I suppose, of the expense of feeding them. The Cavalry are mounted on poor Egyptian nags. The horses generally ridden by rich men are generally Nijdi, costing from $200 to $300. Camels are numerous, but those bred in Al-Hijaz are small, weak, and consequently little prized. Dromedaries of good breed, called Ahrar[2] (the noble) and Namani, from the place of that name, are to be had for any sum between $10 and $400 ; they are diminutive, but exceedingly swift, surefooted, sagacious, thoroughbred, with eyes like the

---

1 In the plural called Jadail. It is a most becoming head-dress when the hair is thick, and when—which I regret to say is rare in Arabia—the twists are undone for ablution once a day.

2 Plural of "Hurrah," the free, the noble.

pleasures of marriage, lyings-in, circumcision feasts, holy
visitations, and funerals. At home, they employ themselves with domestic matters, and especially in scolding
"Hasinah" and "Za'afaran." In this occupation they
surpass even the notable English housekeeper of the
middle orders of society—the latter being confined to
"knagging" at her slavey, whereas the Arab lady is
allowed an unbounded extent of vocabulary. At Shaykh
Hamid's house, however, I cannot accuse the women of

> "Swearing into strong shudders
> The immortal gods who heard them."

They abused the black girls with unction, but without
any violent expletives. At Meccah, however, the old
lady in whose house I was living would, when excited by
the melancholy temperament of her eldest son and his
irregular hours of eating, scold him in the grossest
terms, not unfrequently ridiculous in the extreme. For
instance, one of her assertions was that he—the son—
was the offspring of an immoral mother; which assertion,
one might suppose, reflected not indirectly upon herself.
So in Egypt I have frequently heard a father, when
reproving his boy, address him by "O dog, son of a dog!"
and "O spawn of an Infidel—of a Jew—of a Christian!"
Amongst the men of Al-Madinah I remarked a considerable share of hypocrisy. Their mouths were as full of
religious salutations, exclamations, and hackneyed quota-
tions from the Koran, as of indecency and vile abuse—a
point in which they resemble the Persians. As before

---

plane discessit.) Virilis quoque circumcisio lentam venerem et
difficilem efficit. Glandis enim mollities frictione induratur, dehinc
coitus tristis, tardus parumque vehemens. Forsitan in quibusdam
populis localis quoque causa existit; caruncula immoderate crescente,
amputationis necessitas exurgit. Deinde apud Somalos, gentem
Africanam, excisio nympharum abscissioni clitoridis adjungitur.
"Feminina circumcisio in Kahira Egyptiana et El Hejazio mos est
universalis. Gens Bedouina uxorem salvam ducere nolit."—Shaykh
al-Nawawi "de Uxore ducenda," &c., &c.

antelope's, and muzzles that would almost enter a tumbler.
Mules are not found at Al-Madinah, although popular
prejudice does not now forbid the people to mount them.
Asses come from Egypt and Meccah: I am told that some
good animals are to be found in the town, and that certain ignoble Badawi clans have a fine breed, but I never
saw any. Of beasts intended for food, the sheep is the
only common one in this part of Al-Hijaz. There are
three distinct breeds. The larger animal comes from
Nijd and the Anizah Badawin, who drive a flourishing
trade; the smaller is a native of the country. Both are
the common Arab species, of a tawny colour, with a long
fat tail. Occasionally one meets with what at Aden is
called the Berberah sheep, a totally different beast,—white,
with a black broad face, a dew-lap, and a short fat tail,
that looks as if twisted up into a knot: it was doubtless
introduced by the Persians. Cows are rare at Al-Madinah.
Beef throughout the East is considered an unwholesome
food, and the Badawi will not drink cow's milk, preferring
that of the camel, the ewe, and the goat. The flesh of the
latter animal is scarcely ever eaten in the city, except by
the poorest classes.

The manners of the Madani are graver and somewhat
more pompous than those of any Arabs with whom I ever
mixed. This they appear to have borrowed from their
rulers, the Turks. But their austerity and ceremoniousness are skin-deep. In intimacy or in anger the garb of
politeness is thrown off, and the screaming Arab voice,
the voluble, copious, and emphatic abuse, and the mania
for gesticulation, return in all their deformity. They are
great talkers as the following little trait shows. When a
man is opposed to more than his match in disputing or
bargaining, instead of patiently saying to himself, *S'il
crache il est mort,* he interrupts the adversary with a *Sall'
ala Mohammed,*—Bless the Prophet. Every good Moslem
is obliged to obey such requisition by responding, *Allah-*

umma salli alayh,—O Allah bless him ! But the Madani curtails the phrase to "A'n,[1]" supposing it to be an equivalent, and proceeds in his loquacity. Then perhaps the baffled opponent will shout out *Wahhid,* i.e., " Attest the unity of the Deity " ; when, instead of employing the usual religious phrases to assert that dogma, he will briefly ejaculate " Al," and hurry on with the course of conversation. As it may be supposed, these wars of words frequently end in violent quarrels ; for, to do the Madani justice, they are always ready to fight. The desperate old feud between the " Juwwa," and the " Barra,"—the town and the suburbs—has been put down with the greatest difficulty. The boys, indeed, still keep it up, turning out in bodies and making determined onslaughts with sticks and stones.[2]

It is not to be believed that in a town garrisoned by Turkish troops, full of travelled traders, and which supports itself by plundering Hajis, the primitive virtues of the Arab could exist. The Meccans, a dark people, say of the Madani, that their hearts are black as their skins are white.[3] This is, of course, exaggerated ; but it is not too

---

1 See vol. i., p. 436, ante.

2 This appears to be, and to have been, a favourite weapon with the Arabs. At the battle of Ohod, we read that the combatants amused themselves with throwing stones. On our road to Meccah, the Badawi attacked a party of city Arabs, and the fight was determined with these harmless weapons. At Meccah, the men, as well as the boys, use them with as much skill as the Somalis at Aden. As regards these feuds between different quarters of the Arab towns, the reader will bear in mind that such things can co-exist with considerable amount of civilization. In my time, the different villages in the Sorrentine plain were always at war. The Irish still fight in bodies at Birkenhead. And in the days of our fathers, the *gamins* of London amused themselves every Sunday by pitched battles on Primrose Hill, and the fields about Marylebone and St. Pancras.

3 Alluding especially to their revengefulness, and their habit of storing up an injury, and of forgetting old friendships or benefits, when a trivial cause of quarrel arises.

much to assert that pride, pugnacity, a peculiar point honour and a vindictiveness of wonderful force and patien are the only characteristic traits of Arab character whi the citizens of Al-Madinah habitually display. Here y meet with scant remains of the chivalry of the Desert. man will abuse his guest, even though he will not din without him, and would protect him bravely against a enemy. And words often pass lightly between in dividuals which suffice to cause a blood feud amongst Badawin. The outward appearance of decorum is conspicuous amongst the Madani. There are no places where Corinthians dwell, as at Meccah, Cairo, and Jeddah. Adultery, if detected, would be punished by lapidation according to the rigour of the Koranic law[1]; and simple immorality by religious stripes, or, if of repeated occurrence, by expulsion from the city. But scandals seldom occur, and the women, I am told, behave with great decency.[2] Abroad, they have the usual Moslem

---

1 The sentence is passed by the Kazi: in cases of murder, he tries the criminal, and, after finding him guilty, sends him to the Pasha, who orders a Kawwas, or policeman, to strike off his head with a sword. Thieves are punished by mutilation of the hand. In fact, justice at Al-Madinah is administered in perfect conformity with the Shariat or Holy Law.

2 Circumcisio utriusque sexus apud Arabos mos est vetustissimus. Aiunt theologi mutilationis hujus religiosæ ínventricem esse Saram, Abrahami uxorem quæ, zelotypiâ incitata, Hagaris amorem minuendi gratiâ, somnientis puellæ clitoridem exstirpavit. Deinde, Allaho jubente, Sara et Abrahamus ambo pudendorum partem cultello abscissêre. Causa autem moris in viro mundities salusque, in puellâ impudicitiæ prophylactica esse videntur. Gentes Asiaticæ sinistrâ tantum manu abluentes utuntur; omnes quoque feminarem decies magis quam virorum libidinem æstimant. (*Clitoridem amputant, quia, ut monet Aristoteles, pars illa sedes est et scaturigo veneris—rem plane profanam cum Sonninio exclamemus!*) Nec excogitare potuit philosophus quanti et quam portentosi sunt talis mutilationis effectus. Mulierum minuuntur affectus, amor, voluptas. Crescunt tamen feminini doli, crudelitas, vitia et insatiabilis luxuria. (*Ita in Eunuchis nonnunquam, teste Abelardo, superstat cerebelli potestas, quum cupidinis satiandi facultas*

observed, they preserve their reputation as the sons of a
holy city by praying only in public. At Constantinople
they are by no means remarkable for sobriety. Intoxicating liquors, especially Araki, are made in Al-Madinah,
only by the Turks : the citizens seldom indulge in this
way at home, as detection by smell is imminent among a
people of water-bibbers. During the whole time of my
stay I had to content myself with a single bottle of Cog-
nac, coloured and scented to resemble medicine. The
Madani are, like the Meccans, a curious mixture of generosity and meanness, of profuseness and penuriousness.
But the former quality is the result of ostentation, the
latter is a characteristic of the Semitic race, long ago
made familiar to Europe by the Jew. The citizens will
run deeply in debt, expecting a good season of devotees to
pay off their liabilities, or relying upon the next begging
trip to Turkey; and such a proceeding, contrary to the
custom of the Moslem world, is not condemned by public
opinion. Above all their qualities, personal conceit is remarkable: they show it in their strut, in their looks, and
almost in every word. " I am such an one, the son of
such an one," is a common expletive, especially in times of
danger ; and this spirit is not wholly to be condemned, as
it certainly acts as an incentive to gallant actions. But
it often excites them to vie with one another in expensive
entertainments and similar vanities. The expression, so
offensive to English ears, *Inshallah Bukra*—Please God,
to-morrow—always said about what should be done to-day,
is here common as in Egypt or in India. This procras-
tination belongs more or less to all Orientals. But Arabia
especially abounds in the *Tawakkal al' Allah, ya Shaykh!*—
Place thy reliance upon Allah, O Shaykh!—enjoined when
a man should depend upon his own exertions. Upon the
whole, however, though alive to the infirmities of the
Madani character, I thought favourably of it, finding
among this people more of the redeeming point, manli-

ness, than in most Eastern nations with whom I am acquainted.

The Arabs, like the Egyptians, all marry. Yet, as usual, they are hard and facetious upon that ill-treated subject—matrimony. It has exercised the brain of their wits and sages, who have not failed to indite notable things concerning it. Saith "Harikar al-Hakim" Dominie Do-All) to his nephew Nadan (Sir Witless), whom he would dissuade from taking to himself a wife, " Marriage is joy for a month and sorrow for a life, and the paying of settlements and the breaking of back (*i.e.* under the load of misery), and the listening to a woman's tongue ! " And again we have in verse :—

> "They said 'marry!' I replied, 'far be it from me
> To take to my bosom a sackful of snakes.
> I am free—why then become a slave?
> May' Allah never bless womankind!' "

And the following lines are generally quoted, as affording a kind of bird's-eye view of female existence :—

> " From 10 (years of age) unto 20,
> A repose to the eyes of beholders.[1]
> From 20 unto 30,
> Still fair and full of flesh.
> From 30 unto 40,
> A mother of many boys and girls.
> From 40 unto 50,
> An old woman of the deceitful.
> From 50 unto 60,
> Slay her with a knife.
> From 60 unto 70,
> The curse of Allah upon them, one and all!"

Another popular couplet makes a most unsupported assertion :—

> "They declare womankind to be heaven to man,
> I say, 'Allah, give me Jahannam, and not this heaven.' "

Yet the fair sex has the laugh on its side, for these railers at Al-Madinah as at other places, invariably marry. The

---

[1] A phrase corresponding with our "*beauté du diable.*"

marriage ceremony is tedious and expensive. It begins with a Khitbah or betrothal : the father of the young man repairs to the parent or guardian of the girl, and at the end of his visit exclaims, " The Fatihah ! we beg of your kindness your daughter for our son." Should the other be favourable to the proposal, his reply is, " Welcome and congratulation to you : but we must perform Istik-harah[1] (religious lot casting) " ; and, when consent is given, both pledge themselves to the agreement by re-citing the Fatihah. Then commence negotiations about the Mahr or sum settled upon the bride[2]; and after the smoothing of this difficulty follow feastings of friends and relatives, male and female. The marriage itself is called Akd al-Nikah or Ziwaj. A Walimah or banquet is pre-pared by the father of the Aris (groom), at his own house, and the Kazi attends to perform the nuptial ceremony, the girl's consent being obtained through her Wakil, any male relation whom she commissions to act for her. Then, with great pomp and circumstance, the Aris visits his Arusah (bride) at her father's house ; and finally, with a Zuffah or procession and sundry ceremonies at the Harim, she is brought to her new home. Arab funerals are as simple as their marriages are complicated. Neither Naddabah (myriologist or hired keener), nor indeed any female, even a relation, is present at burials as in other parts of the Moslem world,[3] and it is esteemed disgraceful

---

1 This means consulting the will of the Deity, by praying for a dream in sleep, by the rosary, by opening the Koran, and other such devices, which bear blame if a negative be deemed necessary. It is a custom throughout the Moslem world, a relic, doubtless, of the Azlam or Kidah (seven divining-arrows) of the Pagan times. At Al-Madinah it is generally called Khirah.

2 Among respectable citizens 400 dollars would be considered a fair average sum; the expense of the ceremony would be about half. This amount of ready money (£150) not being always pro-curable, many of the Madani marry late in life.

3 Boys are allowed to be present, but they are not permitted

for a man to weep aloud. The Prophet, who doubtless had heard of those pagan mournings, where an effeminate and unlimited display of woe was often terminated by licentious excesses, like the Christian's half-heathen "wakes," forbad ought beyond a decent demonstration of grief. And his strong good sense enabled him to see through the vanity of professional mourners. At Al-Madinah the corpse is interred shortly after decease. The bier is carried though the streets at a moderate pace, by friends and relatives,[1] these bringing up the rear. Every man who passes lends his shoulder for a minute, a mark of respect to the dead, and also considered a pious and a prayerful act. Arrived at the Harim, they carry the corpse in visitation to the Prophet's window, and pray over it at Osman's niche. Finally, it is interred after the usual Moslem fashion in the cemetery Al-Bakia.

Al-Madinah, though pillaged by the Wahhabis, still abounds in books. Near the Harim are two Madrasah or colleges, the Mahmudiyah, so called from Sultan Mahmud, and that of Bashir Agha : both have large stores of theological and other works. I also heard of extensive private collections, particularly of one belonging to the Najíb al-Ashraf, or chief of the Sharifs, a certain Mohammed Jamal al-Layl, whose father is well-known in India. Besides which, there is a large Wakf or bequest of books, presented to the Mosque or entailed upon particular families.[2] The celebrated Mohammed Ibn Abdillah al-Sannusi[3] has re-

---

to cry. Of their so misdemeaning themselves there is little danger; the Arab in these matters is a man from his cradle.

1 They are called the Asdikah; in the singular, Sadik.

2 From what I saw at Al-Madinah, the people are not so unprejudiced on this point as the Cairenes, who think little of selling a book in Wakf. The subject of Wakf, however, is an extensive one, and does not wholly exclude the legality of sale.

3 This Shaykh is a Maliki Moslem from Algiers, celebrated as an Alim (sage), especially in the mystic study Al-Jafr. He is a Wali or saint; but opinions differ as regards his Kiramat (saint's miracles) :

moved his collection, amounting, it is said, to eight thousand volumes, from Al-Madinah to his house in Jabal Kubays at Meccah. The burial-place of the Prophet, therefore, no longer lies open to the charge of utter ignorance brought against it by my predecessor.[1] The people now praise their Olema for learning, and boast a superiority in respect of science over Meccah. Yet many students leave the place for Damascus and Cairo, where the Riwak al-Haramayn (College of the Two Shrines) in the Azhar Mosque University, is always crowded ; and though Omar Effendi boasted to me that his city was full of lore, he did not appear the less anxious to attend the lectures of Egyptian professors. But none of my informants claimed for Al-Madinah any facilities of studying other than the purely religious sciences.[2] Philosophy, medicine, arithmetic, mathematics, and algebra cannot be learnt here. I was careful to inquire about the occult sciences, remembering that Paracelsus had travelled in Arabia, and that the Count Cagliostro (Giuseppe Balsamo), who claimed the Meccan Sharif as his father, asserted that about A.D. 1765 he had studied alchemy at Al-Madinah. The only trace I could find was a superficial knowledge of the Magic Mirror. But after denying the Madani the praise of varied learning, it must be owned that their quick observation and retentive memories have stored up for

some disciples look upon him as the Mahdi (the forerunner of the Prophet), others consider him a clever impostor. His peculiar dogma is the superiority of live over dead saints, whose tombs are therefore not to be visited—a new doctrine in a Maliki! Abbas Pasha loved and respected him, and, as he refused all presents, built him a new Zawiyah (oratory) at Bulak ; and when the Egyptian ruler's mother was at Al-Madinah, she called upon him three times, it is said, before he would receive her. His followers and disciples are scattered in numbers about Tripoli and, amongst other oases of the Fezzan, at Siwah, where they saved the Abbé Hamilton's life in A.D, 1843.

1 Burckhardt's Travels in Arabia, vol. ii. p. 174.
2 Of which I have given an account in chapter xvi.

them an abundance of superficial knowledge, culled from conversations in the market and in the camp. I found it impossible here to display those feats which in Sind, Southern Persia, Eastern Arabia, and many parts of India, would be looked upon as miraculous. Most probably one of the company had witnessed the performance of some Italian conjuror at Constantinople or Alexandria, and retained a lively recollection of every manœuvre. As linguists they are not equal to the Meccans, who surpass all Orientals excepting only the Armenians; the Madani seldom know Turkish, and more rarely still Persian and Indian. Those only who have studied in Egypt chaunt the Koran well. The citizens speak and pronounce[1] their language purely; they are not equal to the people of the southern Hijaz, still their Arabic is refreshing after the horrors of Cairo and Maskat.

The classical Arabic, be it observed, in consequence of an extended empire, soon split up into various dialects, as the Latin under similar circumstances separated into the Neo-Roman *patois* of Italy, Sicily, Provence, and Languedoc. And though Niebuhr has been deservedly

---

1 The only abnormal sound amongst the consonants heard here and in Al-Hijaz generally is the pronouncing of *k* (ﻕ) a hard *g*—for instance, "Gur'án" for "Kur'an" (a Koran), and Haggi or Hakki (my right). This *g*, however, is pronounced deep in the throat, and does not resemble the corrupt Egyptian pronunciation of the jim (*j*, ﺝ), a letter which the Copts knew not, and which their modern descendants cannot articulate. In Al-Hijaz, the only abnormal sounds amongst the vowels are *o* for *ú*, as Khokh, a peach, and *ŏ* for *ŭ*, as Ohod for Uhud. The two short vowels *fath* and *kasr* are correctly pronounced, the former never becoming a short *e*, as in Egypt (El for Al and Yemen for Yaman), or a short *i*, as in Syria ("min" for "man" who? &c.) These vowels, however, are differently articulated in every part of the Arab world. So says St. Jerome of the Hebrew: "Nec refert atrum *Salem* aut *Salim* nominetur; cum vocalibus in medio literis perraro utantur Hebræi; et pro voluntate lectorum, ac varietate regionum, eadem verba diversis sonis atque accentibus proferantur."

censured for comparing the Koranic language to Latin and the vulgar tongue to Italian, still there is a great difference between them, almost every word having undergone some alteration in addition to the manifold changes and simplifications of grammar and syntax. The traveller will hear in every part of Arabia that some distant tribe preserves the linguistic purity of its ancestors, uses final vowels with the noun, and rejects the addition of the pronoun which apocope in the verb now renders necessary.[1] But I greatly doubt the existence of such a race of philologists. In Al-Hijaz, however, it is considered graceful in an old man, especially when conversing publicly, to lean towards classical Arabic. On the contrary, in a youth this would be treated as pedantic affectation, and condemned in some such satiric quotation as

" There are two things colder than ice,
A young old man, and an old young man."

---

1 *e. g.*, Ant Zarabt—thou struckedst—for Zarabta. The final vowel, suffering apocope, would leave "Zarabt" equally applicable to the first person singular and the second person singular masculine.

The Hibas.

CHAPTER XXII.

A VISIT TO THE SAINTS' CEMETERY.

A splendid comet, blazing in the western sky, had aroused the apprehensions of the Madani. They all fell to predicting the usual disasters—war, famine, and pestilence,—it being still an article of Moslem belief that the Dread Star foreshows all manner of calamities. Men discussed the probability of Abd al-Majid's immediate decease; for here as in Rome,

"When beggars die, there are no comets seen :
The heavens themselves blaze forth the death of princes:"

and in every strange atmospheric appearance about the time of the Hajj, the Hijazis are accustomed to read tidings of the dreaded Rih al-Asfar.[1]

Whether the event is attributable to the Zu Zuwabah —the " Lord of the Forelock,"—or whether it was a case of *post hoc, ergò, propter hoc*, I would not commit myself by deciding; but, influenced by some cause or other, the Hawazim and the Hawamid, sub-families of the Benu-Harb, began to fight about this time with prodigious fury. These tribes are generally at feud, and the least provocation fans their smouldering wrath into a flame. The Hawamid number, it is said, between three and four thousand fighting men, and the Hawazim not more than seven hundred: the latter however, are considered a race of desperadoes who pride themselves upon never retreating,

---

[1] The cholera. See chapter xviii.

and under their fiery Shaykhs, Abbas and Abu Ali, they are a thorn in the sides of their disproportionate foe. On the present occasion a Hamidah[1] happened to strike the camel of a Hazimi which had trespassed ; upon which the Hazimi smote the Hamidah, and called him a rough name. The Hamidah instantly shot the Hazimi, the tribes were called out, and they fought with asperity for some days. During the whole of the afternoon of Tuesday, the 30th of August, the sound of firing amongst the mountains was distinctly heard in the city. Through the streets parties of Badawin, sword and matchlock in hand, or merely carrying quarterstaves on their shoulders, might be seen hurrying along, frantic at the chance of missing the fray. The townspeople cursed them privily, expressing a hope that the whole race of vermin might consume itself. And the pilgrims were in no small trepidation, fearing the desertion of their camel-men, and knowing what a blaze is kindled in this inflammable land by an ounce of gunpowder. I afterwards heard that the Badawin fought till night, and separated after losing on both sides ten men.

This quarrel put an end to any lingering possibility of my prosecuting my journey to Maskat,[2] as originally intended. I had on the way from Yambu' to Al-Madinah privily made a friendship with one Mujrim of the Benu-Harb. The "Sinful," as his name, ancient and classical amongst the Arabs, means, understood that I had some motive of secret interest to undertake the perilous journey. He could not promise at first to guide me, as his beat lay between Yambu', Al-Madinah, Mecah, and Jeddah. But he offered to make all inquiries about the route, and to

1 The word Hawamid is plural of Hamidah, Hawazin of Hazimi.

2 Anciently there was a Caravan from Maskat to Al-Madinah. My friends could not tell me when the line had been given up, but all were agreed that for years they had not seen an Oman caravan, the pilgrims preferring to enter Al-Hijaz *viâ* Jeddah.

bring me the result at noonday, a time when the household
was asleep. He had almost consented at last to travel
with me about the end of August, in which case I should
have slipped out of Hamid's house and started like a
Badawi towards the Indian Ocean. But when the war
commenced, Mujrim, who doubtless wished to stand by
his brethren the Hawazim, began to show signs of recus-
ancy in putting off the day of departure to the end of
September. At last, when pressed, he frankly told me
that no traveller—nay, not a Badawi—could leave the
city in that direction, even as far as historic Khaybar,[1]
which information I afterwards ascertained to be correct.
It was impossible to start alone, and when in despair I
had recourse to Shaykh Hamid, he seemed to think me
mad for wishing to wend Northwards when all the world
was hurrying towards the South. My disappointment
was bitter at first, but consolation soon suggested itself.
Under the most favourable circumstances, a Badawi-trip
from Al-Madinah to Maskat, fifteen or sixteen hundred
miles, would require at least ten months ; whereas, under
pain of losing my commission,[2] I was ordered to be at
Bombay before the end of March. Moreover, entering
Arabia by Al-Hijaz, as has before been said, I was
obliged to leave behind all my instruments except a
watch and a pocket-compass, so the benefit rendered to
geography by my trip would have been scanty. Still re-

---

1 According to Abulfeda, Khaybar is six stations N.E. of Al-
Madinah; it is four according to Al-Idrisi; but my informants
assured me that camels go there easily, as the Tarikh al-Khamisy
says, in three days. I should place it 80 miles N.N.E. of Al-
Madinah. Al-Atwal locates it in 65° 20′ E. lon., and 25° 20′ N. lat;
Al-Kanun in lon. 67° 30′, and lat. 24° 20′; Ibn Sa'id in lon. 64° 56′,
and lat. 27°; and D'Anville in lon. 57°, and lat. 25°. In Burckhardt's map, and those copied from it, Khaybar is placed about 2°
distant from Al-Madinah, which I believe to be too far.

2 The Parliamentary limit of an officer's leave from India is five
years: if he overstay that period, he forfeits his commission.

mained to me the comfort of reflecting that possibly at
Meccah some opportunity of crossing the Peninsula
might present itself.   At any rate I had the certainty of
seeing the strange wild country of the Hijaz, and of being
present at the ceremonies of the Holy City.   I must request the reader to bear with a Visitation once more : we
shall conclude it with a ride to Al-Bakia.[1]   This venerable
spot is frequented by the pious every day after the prayer
at the Prophet's Tomb, and especially on Fridays.

Our party started one morning,—on donkeys, as
usual, for my foot was not yet strong,—along the Darb
al-Janazah round the Southern wall of the town.   The
locomotion was decidedly slow, principally in consequence
of the tent-ropes which the Hajis had pinned down literally all over the plain, and falls were by no means un-
frequent.   At last we arrived at the end of the Darb,
where I committed myself by mistaking the decaying
place of those miserable schismatics the Nakhawilah[2]
for Al-Bakia, the glorious cemetery of the Saints.   Hamid
corrected my blunder with tartness, to which I replied as
tartly, that in our country—Afghanistan—we burned the
body of every heretic upon whom we could lay our hands.
This truly Islamitic custom was heard with general
applause, and as the little dispute ended, we stood at the
open gate of Al-Bakia.   Then having dismounted I sat
down on a low Dakkah or stone bench within the walls,
to obtain a general view and to prepare for the most fatig-
uing of the Visitations.

There is a tradition that seventy thousand, or according to others a hundred thousand saints, all with faces like
full moons, shall cleave on the last day the yawning bosom

---

1 The name means "the place of many roots."   It is also called
Bakia Al-Gharkad—the place of many roots of the tree Rhamnus.
Gharkad is translated in different ways: some term it the lote, others
the tree of the Jews (Forskal, *sub voce*).

2 See chapter xxi., ante.

of Al-Bakia.[1] About ten thousand of the Ashab (Companions of the Prophet) and innumerable Sadat are here buried : their graves are forgotten, because, in the olden time, tombstones were not placed over the last resting-places of mankind. The first of flesh who shall arise is Mohammed, the second Abu Bakr, the third Omar, then the people of Al-Bakia (amongst whom is Osman, the fourth Caliph), and then the *incolæ* of the Jannat al-Ma'ala, the Meccan cemetery. The Hadis, "whoever dies at the two Harims shall rise with the Sure on the Day of Judgment," has made these spots priceless in value. And even upon earth they might be made a mine of wealth. Like the catacombs at Rome, Al-Bakia is literally full of the odour of sanctity, and a single item of the great aggregate here would render any other Moslem town famous. It is a pity that this people refuses to exhume its relics.

The first person buried in Al-Bakia was Osman bin Maz'un, the first of the Muhajirs, who died at Al-Madinah. In the month of Sha'aban, A.H. 3, the Prophet kissed the forehead of the corpse and ordered it to be interred within sight of his abode.[2] In those days the field was covered with the tree Gharkad; the vegetation was cut down, the ground was levelled, and Osman was placed in the centre of the new cemetery. With his own hands Mohammed planted two large upright stones at the head and the feet of his faithful follower[3]; and in process of time a dome covered the spot. Ibrahim, the Prophet's infant second

---

1 The same is said of the Makbarah Benu Salmah or Salim, a cemetery to the west of Al-Madinah, below rising ground called Jabal Sula. It has long ago been deserted. See chapter xiv.

2 In those days Al-Madinah had no walls, and was clear of houses on the East of the Harim.

3 These stones were removed by Al-Marwan, who determined that Osman's grave should not be distinguished from his fellows. For this act, the lieutenant of Mu'awiyah was reproved and blamed by pious Moslems.

son, was laid by Osman's side, after which Al-Bakia became a celebrated cemetery.

The Burial-place of the Saints is an irregular oblong
surrounded by walls which are connected with the suburb
at their south-west angle. The Darb al-Janazah separ-
ates it from the enceinte of the town, and the eastern
Desert Road beginning from the Bab al-Jumah bounds it
on the North. Around it palm plantations seem to
flourish. It is small, considering the extensive use made
of it: all that die at Al-Madinah, strangers as well as
natives, except only heretics and schismatics, expect to
be interred in it. It must be choked with corpses, which
it could never contain did not the Moslem style of burial
greatly favour rapid decomposition; and it has all the inconveniences of "intramural sepulture." The gate is
small and ignoble; a mere doorway in the wall. Inside
there are no flower-plots, no tall trees, in fact none of the
refinements which lightens the gloom of a Christian burial-
place: the buildings are simple, they might even be called
mean. Almost all are the common Arab Mosque, cleanly
whitewashed, and looking quite new. The ancient monuments were levelled to the ground by Sa'ad the Wahhabi
and his puritan followers, who waged pitiless warfare
against what must have appeared to them magnificent
mausolea, deeming as they did a loose heap of stones
sufficient for a grave. In Burckhardt's time the whole
place was a "confused accumulation of heaps of earth,
wide pits, and rubbish, without a singular regular tomb-
stone." The present erections owe their existence, I was
told, to the liberality of the Sultans Abd al-Hamid and
Mahmud.

A poor pilgrim has lately started on his last journey,
and his corpse, unattended by friends or mourners, is
carried upon the shoulders of hired buriers into the cemetery. Suddenly they stay their rapid steps, and throw
the body upon the ground. There is a life-like pliability

about it as it falls, and the tight cerements so define the outlines that the action makes me shudder.   It looks almost as if the dead were conscious of what is about to occur. They have forgotten their tools; one man starts to fetch them, and three sit down to smoke.   After a time a shallow grave is hastily scooped out.[1]   The corpse is packed in it with such unseemly haste that earth touches it in all directions,—cruel carelessness among Moslems, who believe this to torture the sentient frame.[2]   One comfort suggests itself.   The poor man being a pilgrim has has died "Shahid"—in martyrdom.   Ere long his spirit shall leave Al-Bakia,

> "And he on honey-dew shall feed,
> And drink the milk of Paradise."

I entered the holy cemetery right foot forwards, as if it were a Mosque, and barefooted, to avoid suspicion of being a heretic.   For though the citizens wear their shoes in the Bakia, they are much offended at seeing the Persians follow their example.   We began by the general benediction[3]: "Peace be upon Ye, O People of Al-Bakia! Peace be upon Ye, O Admitted to the Presence of the

---

1 It ought to be high enough for the tenant to sit upright when answering the interrogatory angels.

2 Because of this superstition, in every part of Al-Islam, some contrivance is made to prevent the earth pressing upon the body.

3 This blessing is in Mohammed's words, as the beauty of the Arabic shows.   Ayishah relates that in the month Safar, A.H. 11, one night the Prophet, who was beginning to suffer from the headache which caused his death, arose from his couch, and walked out into the darkness; whereupon she followed him in a fit of jealousy, thinking he might be about to visit some other wife.   He went to Al-Bakia, delivered the above benediction (which others give somewhat differently), raised his hands three times, and turned to go home. Ayishah hurried back, but she could not conceal her agitation from her husband, who asked her what she had done.   Upon her confessing her suspicions, he sternly informed her that he had gone forth, by order of the Archangel Gabriel, to bless and to intercede for the people of Al-Bakia.   Some authors relate a more facetious termination of the colloquy.—M. C. de Perceval (Essai, &c., vol. iii. p. 314.)

Most High ! Receive Ye what Ye have been promised! Peace be upon Ye, Martyrs of Al-Bakia, One and All! We verily, if Allah please, are about to join You! O Allah, pardon us and Them, and the Mercy of God, and His Blessings!" After which we recited the Chapter Al-Ikhlas and the Testification, then raised our hands, mumbled the Fatihah, passed our palms down our faces, and went on.

Walking down a rough narrow path, which leads from the western to the eastern extremity of Al-Bakia, we entered the humble mausoleum of the Caliph Osman —Osman "Al-Mazlum," or the "ill-treated," he is called by some Moslems. When he was slain,[1] his friends wished to bury him by the Prophet in the Hujrah, and Ayishah made no objection to the measure. But the people of Egypt became violent; swore that the corpse should neither be buried nor be prayed over, and only permitted it to be removed upon the threat of Habibah (one of the " Mothers of the Moslems," and daughter of Abu Sufiyan) to expose her countenance. During the night that followed his death, Osman was carried out by several of his friends to Al-Bakia, from which, however, they were driven away, and obliged to deposit their burden in a garden, eastward of and outside the saints' cemetery. It was called Hisn Kaukab, and was looked upon as an inauspicious place of sepulture, till Marwan included it in Al-Bakia. We stood before Osman's monument, repeating, " Peace be upon Thee, O our Lord Osman, Son of Affan![2] Peace be upon

---

1 "Limping Osman," as the Persians contemptuously call him, was slain by rebels, and therefore became a martyr according to the Sunnis. The Shi'ahs justify the murder, saying it was the act of an "Ijma al-Muslimin," or the general consensus of Al-Islam, which in their opinion ratifies an act of "lynch law."

2 This specifying the father Affan, proves him to have been a Moslem. Abu Bakr's father, "Kahafah," and Omar's "Al-Khattab," are not mentioned by name in the Ceremonies of Visitation.

Thee, O Caliph of Allah's Apostle! Peace be upon
Thee, O Writer of Allah's Book! Peace be upon Thee,
in whose Presence the Angels are ashamed![1] Peace be
upon Thee, O Collector of the Koran! Peace be upon
Thee, O Son-in-Law of the Prophet! Peace be upon
Thee, O Lord of the Two Lights (the two daughters of
Mohammed)![2] Peace be upon Thee, who fought the
Battle of the Faith! Allah be satisfied with Thee, and
cause Thee to be satisfied, and render Heaven thy Habitation! Peace be upon Thee, and the Mercy of Allah
and His Blessing, and Praise be to Allah, Lord of the
(three) Worlds!" This supplication concluded in the
usual manner. After which we gave alms, and settled
with ten piastres the demands of the Khadim[3] who takes
charge of the tomb: this double-disbursing process had
to be repeated at each station.

Then moving a few paces to the North, we faced
Eastwards, and performed the Visitation of Abu Sa'id al-
Khazari, a Sahib or Companion of the Prophet, whose
sepulchre lies outside Al-Bakia. The third place visited
was a dome containing the tomb of our lady Halimah,
the Badawi wet-nurse who took charge of Mohammed[4]:

1 The Christian reader must remember that the Moslems rank
angelic nature, under certain conditions, below human nature.

2 Osman married two daughters of the Prophet, a circumstance
which the Sunnis quote as honourable to him : the Shi'ahs, on the
contrary, declare that he killed them both by ill-treatment.

3 These men are generally descendants of the Saint whose tomb
they own: they receive pensions from the Mudir of the Mosque, and
retain all fees presented to them by visitors. Some families are
respectably supported in this way.

4 This woman, according to some accounts, also saved Mohammed's life, when an Arab Kahin or diviner, foreseeing that the child
was destined to subvert the national faith, urged the bystanders to
bury their swords in his bosom. The Sharifs of Mecca still entrust
their children to the Badawin, that they may be hardened by the
discipline of the Desert. And the late Pasha of Egypt gave one of
his sons in charge of the Anizah tribe, near Akabah. Burckhardt

she is addressed thus; "Peace be upon Thee, O Halimah the Auspicious![1] Peace be upon Thee, who performed thy Trust in suckling the Best of Mankind! Peace be upon Thee, O Wet-nurse of Al-Mustafa (the chosen)! Peace be upon Thee, O Wet-nurse of Al-Mujtaba (the (accepted)![2] May Allah be satisfied with Thee, and cause Thee to be satisfied, and render Heaven thy House and Habitation! and verily we have come visiting Thee, and by means of Thee drawing near to Allah's Prophet, and through Him to God, the Lord of the Heavens and the Earths.[3]"

After which, fronting the North, we stood before a low enclosure, containing ovals of loose stones, disposed side by side. These are the Martyrs of Al-Bakia, who received the crown of glory at the hands of Al-Muslim,[4] the general of the arch-heretic Yazid.[5] The prayer here recited differs so little from that addressed to the martyrs of Ohod, that I will not transcribe it. The fifth station is near the centre of the cemetery at the tomb of Ibrahim, who died, to the eternal regret of Al-Islam, some say six months old, others in his second year. He was the son

---

(Travels in Arabia, vol. i. p. 427) makes some sensible remarks about this custom, which cannot be too much praised.

1 Al- "Sadiyah," a *double entendre;* it means auspicious, and also alludes to Halimah's tribe, the Benu Sa'ad.

2 Both these words are titles of the Prophet. Al-Mustafa means the "Chosen"; Al-Mujtaba, the "Accepted."

3 There being, according to the Moslems, many heavens and many earths.

4 See chapter xx.

5 The Shafe'i school allows its disciples to curse Al-Yazid, the son of Mu'awiyah, whose cruelties to the descendants of the Prophet, and crimes and vices, have made him the Judas Iscariot of Al-Islam. I have heard Hanafi Moslems, especially Sayyids, revile him; but this is not, strictly speaking, correct. The Shi'ahs, of course, place no limits to their abuse of him. You first call a man "Omar," then "Shimr," (the slayer of Al-Hosayn), and lastly, "Yazid," beyond which insult does not extend.

of Mariyah, the Coptic girl, sent as a present to Mohammed by Jarih, the Mukaukas or governor of Alexandria. The Prophet with his own hand piled earth upon
the grave, and sprinkled it with water,—a ceremony then
first performed,—disposed small stones upon it, and pronounced the final salutation. For which reason many
holy men were buried in this part of the cemetery, every
one being ambitious to lie in ground which has been
honored by the Apostle's hands. Then we visited Al-Nafi
Maula, son of Omar, generally called Imam Nafi al-Kari,
or the Koran chaunter; and near him the great doctor
Imam Malik ibn Anas, a native of Al-Madinah, and one
of the most dutiful of her sons. The eighth station is at
the tomb of Ukayl bin Abi Talib, brother of Ali.[1] Then
we visited the spot where lie interred all the Prophet's
wives, Khadijah, who lies at Meccah, alone excepted.
Mohammed married fifteen wives of whom nine survived
him. After the "Mothers of the Moslems," we prayed at
the tombs of Mohammed's daughters, said to be ten in
number.

In compliment probably to the Hajj, the beggars
mustered strong that morning at Al-Bakia. Along the
walls and at the entrance of each building squatted ancient
dames, all engaged in anxious contemplation of every
approaching face, and in pointing to dirty cotton napkins
spread upon the ground before them, and studded with a
few coins, gold, silver, or copper, according to the expectations of the proprietress. They raised their voices to
demand largesse: some promised to recite Fatihahs, and
the most audacious seized visitors by the skirts of their

---

1 Ukayl or Akil, as many write the name, died at Damascus,
during the Caliphate of Al-Mu'awiyah. Some say he was buried
there, others that his corpse was transplanted to Al-Madinah, and
buried in a place where formerly his house, known as "Dar Ukayl,"
stood.

XXII.—A Visit to the Saints' Cemetery.

garments. Fakihs, ready to write "Y. S.," or anything else demanded of them, covered the little heaps and eminences of the cemetery, all begging lustily, and looking as though they would murder you, when told how beneficent is Allah—polite form of declining to be charitable. At the doors of the tombs old housewives, and some young ones also, struggled with you for your slippers as you doffed them, and not unfrequently the charge of the pair was divided between two. Inside, when the boys were not loud enough or importunate enough for presents, they were urged on by the adults and seniors, the relatives of the "Khadims" and hangers-on. Unfortunately for me, Shaykh Hamid was renowned for taking charge of wealthy pilgrims: the result was, that my purse was lightened of three dollars. I must add that although at least fifty female voices loudly promised that morning, for the sum of ten parahs each, to supplicate Allah in behalf of my lame foot, no perceptible good came of their efforts.

Before leaving Al-Bakia, we went to the eleventh station,[1] the Kubbat al-Abbasiyah, or Dome of Abbas. Originally built by the Abbaside Caliphs in A.H. 519, it is a larger and a handsomer building than its fellows, and it is situated on the right-hand side of the gate as you enter. The crowd of beggars at the door testified to its importance: they were attracted by the Persians who assemble here in force to weep and to pray. Crossing the threshold with some difficulty, I walked round a mass of tombs which occupies the centre of the building, leaving but a narrow passage between it and the walls. It is railed round, and covered over with several "Kiswahs" of green cloth worked with white letters: it looked like a confused

---

1 Some are of opinion that the ceremonies of Ziyarat formerly did, and still should begin here. But the order of visitation differs infinitely, and no two authors seem to agree. I was led by Shaykh Hamid, and indulged in no scruples.

heap, but it might have appeared irregular to me by the reason of the mob around. The Eastern portion contains the body of Al-Hasan, the son of Ali and grandson of the Prophet[1]; the Imam Zayn al-Abidin, son of Al-Hosayn, and great-grandson to the Prophet; the Imam Mohammed al-Bakir (fifth Imam), son to Zayn al-Abidin; and his son the Imam Ja'afar al-Sadik—all four descendants of the Prophet, and buried in the same grave with Abbas ibn Abd al-Muttalib, uncle to Mohammed. It is almost needless to say that these names are subjects of great controversy. Al-Musudi mentions that here was found an inscribed stone declaring it to be the tomb of the Lady Fatimah, of Hasan her brother, of Ali bin Hosayn, of Mohammed bin Ali, and of Ja'afar bin Mohammed. Ibn Jubayr, describing Al-Bakia, mentions only two in this tomb, Abbas and Hasan; the head of the latter, he says, in the direction of the former's feet. Other authors

---

1 Burckhardt makes a series of mistakes upon this subject. "*Hassan* ibn Aly, whose trunk only lies buried here (in El Bakia), his head having been sent to Cairo, where it is preserved in the fine Mosque called El-*Hassanya*." The Mosque Al-Hasanayn (the "two Hasans") is supposed to contain only the head of Al-*Hosayn*, which, when the Crusaders took Ascalon, was brought from thence by Sultan Salih or Beybars, and conveyed to Cairo. As I have said before, the Persians in Egypt openly show their contempt of this tradition. It must be remembered that Al-Hasan died poisoned at Al-Madinah by his wife Ja'adah. Al-Hosayn, on the other hand, was slain and decapitated at Kerbela. According to the Shi'ahs, Zayn al-Abidin obtained from Yazid, after a space of forty days, his father's head, and carried it back to Kerbela, for which reason the event is known to the Persians as "Chilleyeh sar o tan," the "forty days of (separation between) the head and trunk." They vehemently deny that the body lies at Kerbela, and the head at Cairo. Others, again, declare that Al-Hosayn's head was sent by Yazid to Amir bin al-As, the governor of Al-Madinah, and was by him buried near Fatimah's Tomb. Nor are they wanting who declare, that after Yazid's death the head was found in his treasury, and was shrouded and buried at Damascus. Such is the uncertainty which hangs over the early history of Al-Islam

relate that in it, about the ninth century of the Hijrah, was found a wooden box covered with fresh-looking red felt cloth, with bright brass nails, and they believe it to have contained the corpse of Ali, placed here by his own son Hasan.

Standing opposite this mysterious tomb, we repeated, with difficulty by reason of the Persians weeping, the following supplication:—"Peace be upon Ye, O Family of the Prophet! O Lord Abbas, the free from Impurity and Uncleanness, and Father's Brother to the Best of Men! And Thou too O Lord Hasan, Grandson of the Prophet! And thou also O Lord Zayn al-Abidin[1]! Peace be upon Ye, One and All, for verily God hath been pleased to deliver You from all Guile, and to purify You with all Purity. The Mercy of Allah and His Blessings be upon Ye, and verily He is the Praised, the Mighty!" After which, freeing ourselves from the hands of greedy boys, we turned round and faced the southern wall, close to which is a tomb attributed to the Lady Fatimah.[2] I will not repeat the prayer, it being the same as that recited in the Harim.

---

1 The names of the fifth and sixth Imams, Mohammed al-Bakia and Ja'afar al-Sadik, were omitted by Hamid, as doubtful whether they are really buried here or not.

2 Moslem historians seem to delight in the obscurity which hangs over the lady's last resting-place, as if it were an honour even for the receptacle of her ashes to be concealed from the eyes of men. Some place her in the Harim, relying upon this tradition: "Fatimah, feeling about to die, rose up joyfully, performed the greater ablution, dressed herself in pure garments, spread a mat upon the floor of her house near the Prophet's Tomb, lay down fronting the Kiblah, placed her hand under her cheek, and said to her attendant, "I am pure and in a pure dress; now let no one uncover my body, but bury me where I lie!" When Ali returned he found his wife dead, and complied with her last wishes. Omar bin Abd al-Aziz believed this tradition, when he included the room in the Mosque; and generally in Al-Islam Fatimah is supposed to be buried in the Harim. Those who suppose the Prophet's daughter to be buried in Al-Bakia rely

Issuing from the hot and crowded dome, we recovered our slippers after much trouble, and found that
our garments had suffered from the frantic gesticulations
of the Persians. We then walked to the gate of Al-
Bakia, stood facing the cemetery upon an elevated piece
of ground, and delivered the general benediction.

"O Allah! O Allah! O Allah! O full of Mercy! O
abounding in Beneficence! Lord of Length (of days), and
Prosperity, and Goodness! O Thou, who when asked,
grantest, and when prayed for aid, aidest! Have Mercy
upon the Companions of thy Prophet, of the Muhajirin,
and the Ansar! Have Mercy upon them, One and All!

---

upon a saying of the Imam Hasan, "If men will not allow me to
sleep beside my grandsire, place me in Al-Bakia, by my mother."
They give the following account of his death and burial. His body
was bathed and shrouded by Ali and Omar Salmah. Others say that
Asma Bint Umays, the wife of Abu Bakr, was present with Fatimah,
who at her last hour complained of being carried out, as was the
custom of those days, to burial like a man. Asma promised to make
her a covered bier, like a bride's litter, of palm sticks, in shape like
what she had seen in Abyssinia: whereupon Fatimah smiled for the
first time after her father's death, and exacted from her a promise to
allow no one entrance as long as her corpse was in the house.
Ayishah, shortly afterwards knocking at the door, was refused ad-
mittance by Asma; the former complained of this to her father, and
declared that her stepmother had been making a bride's litter to
carry out the corpse. Abu Bakr went to the door, and when informed
by his wife that all was the result of Fatimah's orders, he returned
home making no objection. The death of the Prophet's daughter
was concealed by her own desire from high and low; she was buried
at night, and none accompanied her bier, or prayed at her grave,
except Ali and a few relatives. The Shi'ahs found a charge of
irreverence and disrespect against Abu Bakr for absence on this
occasion. The third place which claims Fatimah's honoured
remains, is a small Mosque in Al-Bakia, South of the Sepulchre of
Abbas. It was called Bayt al-Huzn—House of Mourning—because
here the lady passed the end of her days, lamenting the loss of her
father. Her tomb appears to have formerly been shown there. Now
visitors pray, and pray only twice,—at the Harim, and in the Kubbat
al-Abbasiyah.

Have Mercy upon Abdullah bin Hantal" (and so on, specifying their names), "and make Paradise their Resting-
place, their Habitation, their Dwelling, and their Abode!
O Allah! accept our Ziyarat, and supply our Wants,
and lighten our Griefs, and restore us to our Homes, and
comfort our Fears, and disappoint not our Hopes, and
pardon us, for on no other do we rely; and let us depart
in Thy Faith, and after the Practice of Thy Prophet,
and be Thou satisfied with us! O Allah! forgive our
past Offences, and leave us not to our (evil) Natures
during the Glance of an Eye, or a lesser Time; and
pardon us, and pity us, and let us return to our Houses and
Homes safe," (*i.e.*, spiritually and physically) "fortunate,
abstaining from what is unlawful, re-established after our
Distresses, and belonging to the Good, thy Servants upon
whom is no Fear, nor do they know Distress. Repentance, O Lord! Repentance, O Merciful! Repentance, O
Pitiful! Repentance before Death, and Pardon after
Death! I beg pardon of Allah! Thanks be to Allah!
Praise be to Allah! Amen, O Lord of the (three)
Worlds!"

   After which, issuing from Al-Bakia,[1] we advanced

---

1 The other celebrities in Al-Bakia are:—
Fatimah bint As'ad, mother of Ali. She was buried with great
religious pomp. The Prophet shrouded her with his own garment (to
prevent hell from touching her), dug her grave, lay down in it (that it
might never squeeze or be narrow to her), assisted in carrying the
bier, prayed over her, and proclaimed her certain of future felicity.
Over her tomb was written, "The grave hath not closed upon one
like Fatimah, daughter of As'ad." Historians relate that Mohammed
lay down in only four graves: 1. Khadijah's, at Meccah. 2. Kasim's,
her son by him. 3. That of Umm Ruman, Ayishah's mother. 4.
That of Abdullah al-Mazni, a friend and companion.
   Abd al-Rahman bin Auf was interred near Osman bin Maz'un. Ayishah offered to bury him in her house near the Prophet, but he replied
that he did not wish to narrow her abode, and that he had promised
to sleep by the side of his friend Maz'un. I have already alluded to the
belief that none bas been able to occupy the spare place in the Hujrah.
   Ibn Hufazah al-Sahmi, who was one of the Ashab al-Hijratayn

northwards, leaving the city gate on the left hand, till we came to a small Kubbah (dome) close to the road. It is visited as containing the tomb of the Prophet's paternal aunts, especially of Safiyah, daughter of Abd al-Muttalib, sister of Hamzah, and one of the many heroines of early Al-Islam. Hurrying over our devotions here,—for we were tired indeed,—we applied to a Sakka for water, and entered a little coffee-house near the gate of the town : after which we rode home.

I have now described, at a wearying length I fear, the spots visited by every Zair at Al-Madinah. The guide-books mention altogether between fifty and fifty-five Mosques and other holy places, most of which are now unknown even by name to the citizens. The most celebrated of these are the few following, which I describe from hearsay. About three miles to the North-west of the town, close to the Wady al-Akik, lies the Mosque called Al-Kiblatayn—"The Two Directions of Prayer." Some give this title to the Masjid al-Takwa at Kuba.[1] Others assert that the Prophet, after visiting and eating

---

(who had accompanied both flights, the greater and the lesser), here died of a wound received at Ohod, and was buried in Shawwal, A.H. 3, one month after Osman bin Maz'un.

Abdullah bin Mas'ud, who, according to others, is buried at Kufah.

Sa'ad ibn Zararah, interred near Osman bin Maz'un.

Sa'ad bin Ma'az, who was buried by the Prophet. He died of a wound received during the battle of the Moat.

Abd al-Rahman al-Ausat, son of Omar, the Caliph. He was generally known as Abu Shahmah, the "Father of Fat" : he sickened and died, after receiving from his father the religious flogging— *impudicitiæ causâ.*

Abu Sufiyan bin al-Haris, grandson of Abd al-Muttalib. He was buried near Abdullah bin Ja'afar al-Tayyar, popularly known as the "most generous of the Arabs," and near Ukayl bin Abi Talib, the brother of Ali mentioned above.

These are the principal names mentioned by popular authors. The curious reader will find in old histories a multitude of others, whose graves are now utterly forgotten at Al-Madinah.

    1 See chapter xix.

at the house of an old woman named Umm Mabshar, went to pray the mid-day prayer in the Mosque of the Benu Salmah. He had performed the prostration with his face towards Jerusalem, when suddenly warned by revelation he turned Southwards and concluded his orisons in that direction.[1] I am told it is a mean dome without inner walls, outer enclosures, or minaret.

The Masjid Benu Zafar (some write the word Tifr) is also called Masjid al-Baghlah—of the She-mule,—because, according to Al-Matari, on the ridge of stone to the south of this Mosque are the marks where the Prophet leaned his arm, and where the she-mule, Duldul, sent by the Mukaukas as a present with Mariyah the Coptic girl and Yafur the donkey, placed its hoofs. At the Mosque was shown a slab upon which the Prophet sat hearing recitations from the Koran ; and historians declare that by following his example many women have been blessed with offspring.[2] This Mosque is to the East of Al-Bakia.

The Masjid al-Jumah—of Friday,—or Al-Anikah—of the Sand-heaps,—is in the valley near Kuba, where Mohammed prayed and preached on the first Friday after his flight from Meccah.[3]

The Masjid al-Fazikh—of Date-liquor—is so called because when Abu Ayyub and others of the Ansar were sitting with cups in their hands, they heard that intoxi-

---

1 The story is related in another way. Whilst Mohammed was praying the Asr or afternoon prayer at the Harim he turned his face towards Meccah. Some of the Companions ran instantly to all the Mosques, informing the people of the change. In many places they were not listened to, but the Benu Salmah who were at prayer instantly faced Southwards. To commemorate their obedience the Mosque was called Al-Kiblatayn.

2 I cannot say whether this valuable stone be still at the Mosque Benu Tifr. But I perfectly remember that my friend Larking had a mutilated sphynx in his garden at Alexandria, which was found equally efficacious.

3 See chapter xvii.

cating draughts were for the future forbidden, upon which they poured the liquor upon the ground. Here the Prophet prayed six days whilst he was engaged in warring down the Benu Nazir Jews. The Mosque derives its other name, Al-Shams—of the Sun—because, being erected on rising ground East of and near Kuba, it receives the first rays of morning light.

To the Eastward of the Masjid al-Fazikh lies the Masjid al-Kurayzah, erected on a spot where the Prophet descended to attack the Jewish tribe of that name. Returning from the battle of the Moat, wayworn and tired with fighting, he here sat down to wash and comb his hair, when suddenly appeared to him the Archangel Gabriel in the figure of a horseman dressed in a corslet and covered with dust. " The Angels of Allah," said the preternatural visitor, " are still in Arms, O Prophet, and it is Allah's Will that Thy foot return to the Stirrup. I go before Thee to prepare a Victory over the Infidels, the Sons of Kurayzah." The legend adds that the dust raised by the angelic host was seen in the streets of Al-Madinah, but that mortal eye fell not upon horseman's form. The Prophet ordered his followers to sound the battle-call, gave his flag to Ali,—the Arab token of appointing a commander-in-chief,—and for twenty-five days invested the habitations of the enemy. This hapless tribe was exterminated, sentence of death being passed upon them by Sa'ad ibn Ma'az, an Ausi whom they constituted their judge because he belonged to an allied tribe. Six hundred men were beheaded in the Market-place of Al-Madinah, their property was plundered, and their wives and children were reduced to slavery.

"Tantane relligio potuit suadere malorum!"

The Masjid Mashrabat Umm Ibrahim, or Mosque of the garden of Ibrahim's mother, is a place where Mariyah the Copt had a garden, and became the mother of

Ibrahim, the Prophet's second son.[1] It is a small building in what is called the Awali, or highest part of the Al-Madinah plain, to the North of the Masjid Benu Kuray-zah, and near the Eastern Harrah or ridge.[2]

Northwards of Al-Bakia is, or was, a small building called the Masjid al-Ijabah—of Granting,—from the following circumstance. One day the Prophet stopped to perform his devotions at this place, which then belonged to the Benu Mu'awiyah of the tribe of Aus. He made a long Dua or supplication, and then turning to his Companions, exclaimed, " I have asked of Allah three favours, two hath he vouchsafed to me, but the third was refused ! " Those granted were that the Moslems might never be destroyed by famine or by deluge. The third was that they might not perish by internecine strife.

The Masjid al-Fath (of Victory), vulgarly called the " Four Mosques," is situated in the Wady Al-Sayh,[3] which comes from the direction of Kuba, and about half a mile to the East of " Al-Kiblatayn." The largest is called the Masjid al-Fath, or Al-Ahzab—of the Troops,— and is alluded to in the Koran. Here it is said the Prophet prayed for three days during the Battle of the Moat, also called the affair " Al-Ahzab," the last fought with the Infidel Kuraysh under Abu Sufiyan. After three days of devotion, a cold and violent blast arose, with rain

---

1 Mohammed's eldest son was Kasim, who died in his infancy, and was buried at Meccah. Hence the Prophet's pædonymic, Abu Kasim, the sire of Kasim.

2 Ayishah used to relate that she was exceedingly jealous of the Coptic girl's beauty, and of the Prophet's love for her. Mohammed seeing this, removed Mariyah from the house of Harisat bin al-Numan, in which he had placed her, to the Awali of Al-Madinah, where the Mosque now is. Oriental authors use this term "Awali," high-grounds, to denote the plains to the Eastward and Southward of the City, opposed to Al-Safilah, the lower ground on the W. and N.W.

3 I am very doubtful about this location of the Masjid al-Fath.

and sleet, and discomfited the foe. The Prophet's prayer
having here been granted, it is supposed by ardent
Moslems that no petition put up at the Mosque Al-Ahzab
is ever neglected by Allah. The form of supplication is
differently quoted by different authors. When Al-Shafe'i
was in trouble and fear of Hárún al-Rashíd, by the virtue
of this formula he escaped all danger : I would willingly
offer so valuable a prophylactory to my readers, only it
is of an unmanageable length. The doctors of Al-Islam
also greatly differ about the spot where the Prophet stood
on this occasion ; most of them support the claims of the
Masjid al-Fath, the most elevated of the four, to that
distinction. Below, and to the South of the highest
ground, is the Masjid Salman al-Farsi, the Persian, from
whose brain emanated the bright idea of the Moat. At
the mature age of two hundred and fifty, some say three
hundred and fifty, after spending his life in search of
a religion, from a Magus (fire-worshipper)[1] becoming successively a Jew and a Nazarene, he ended with being a
Moslem, and a Companion of Mohammed. During his
eventful career he had been ten times sold into slavery.
Below Salman's Mosque is the Masjid Ali, and the
smallest building on the South of the hill is called Masjid
Abu Bakr. All these places owe their existence to Al-
Walid the Caliph : they were repaired at times by his
successors.

The Masjid al-Rayah—of the Banner—was originally built by Al-Walid upon a place where the Prophet
pitched his tent during the War of the Moat. Others
call it Al-Zubab, after a hill upon which it stands. Al-
Rayah is separated from the Masjid al-Fath by a rising
ground called Jabal Sula or Jabal Sawab[2]: the former

1 A magus, a magician, one supposed to worship fire. The other
rival sect of the time was the Sabœan who adored the heavenly
bodies.

2 The Mosque of "reward in heaven." It is so called because

being on the Eastern, whilst the latter lies upon .the Western declivity of the hill. The position of this place is greatly admired, as commanding the fairest view of the Harim.

About a mile and a half South-east of Al-Bakia is a dome called Kuwwat Islam, the "Strength of Al-Islam." Here the Apostle planted a dry palm-stick, which grew up, blossomed, and bore fruit at once. Moreover, on one occasion when the Moslems were unable to perform the pilgrimage, Mohammed here produced the appearance of a Ka'abah, an Arafat, and all the appurtenances of the Hajj. I must warn my readers not to condemn the founder of Al-Islam for these puerile inventions.

The Masjid Onayn lies South of Hamzah's tomb. It is on a hill called Jabal al-Rumat, the Shooters' Hill, and here during the battle of Ohod stood the archers of Al-Islam. According to some, the Prince of Martyrs here received his death-wound; others place that event at the Masjid al-Askar or the Masjid al-Wady.[1]

Besides these fourteen, I find the names, and nothing but the names, of forty Mosques. The reader loses little by my unwillingness to offer him a detailed list of such appellations as Masjid Benu Abd al-Ashhal, Masjid Benu Harisah, Masjid Benu Harim, Masjid al-Fash, Masjid al-Sukiya, Masjid Benu Bayazah, Masjid Benu Hatmah,

"Cum multis aliis quæ nunc perscribere longum est."

---

during the War of the Moat, the Prophet used to live in a cave there, and afterwards he made it a frequent resort for prayer.

1 Hamzah's fall is now placed at the Kubbat al-Masra. See chapter xx.

CHAPTER XXIII.

THE DAMASCUS CARAVAN.

The Damascus Caravan was to set out on the 27th
Zu'l Ka'adah (1st September). I had intended to stay at
Al-Madinah till the last moment, and to accompany the
Kafilat al-Tayyarah, or the " Flying Caravan," which
usually leaves on the 2nd Zu'l Hijjah, two days after
that of Damascus.

Suddenly arose the rumour that there would be no
Tayyarah,[1] and that all pilgrims must proceed with the
Damascus Caravan or await the Rakb. This is a
Dromedary Caravan, in which each person carries only
his saddle-bags. It usually descends by the road called
Al-Khabt, and makes Meccah on the fifth day. The
Sharif Zayd, Sa'ad the Robber's only friend, had paid
him an unsuccessful visit. Schinderhans demanded back
his Shaykh-ship, in return for a safe-conduct through his
country: "Otherwise," said he, "I will cut the throat of
every hen that ventures into the passes."

The Sharif Zayd returned to Al-Madinah on the
25th Zu'l Ka'adah (30th August). Early on the morning
of the next day, Shaykh Hamid returned hurriedly from
the bazar, exclaiming, "You must make ready at once,
Effendi!—there will be no Tayyarah—all Hajis start
to-morrow—Allah will make it easy to you!—have you

---

1 The "Tayyarah," or "Flying Caravan," is lightly laden, and
travels by forced marches.

your water-skins in order ?—you are to travel down the
Darb al-Sharki, where you will not see water for three
days !"

Poor Hamid looked horrorstruck as he concluded this
fearful announcement, which filled me with joy. Burckhardt had visited and had described the Darb al-Sultani,
the road along the coast. But no European had as yet
travelled down by Harun al-Rashid's and the Lady
Zubaydah's celebrated route through the Nijd Desert.

Not a moment, however, was to be lost : we expected
to start early the next morning. The boy Mohammed
went forth, and bought for eighty piastres a Shugduf,
which lasted us throughout the pilgrimage, and for fifteen
piastres a Shibriyah or cot to be occupied by Shaykh
Nur, who did not relish sleeping on boxes. The youth
was employed all day, with sleeves tucked up, and working like a porter, in covering the litter with matting and
rugs, in mending broken parts, and in providing it with
large pockets for provisions inside and outside, with
pouches to contain the gugglets of cooled water.

Meanwhile Shaykh Nur and I, having inspected the
water-skins, found that the rats had made considerable
rents in two of them. There being no workman procurable at this time for gold, I sat down to patch the
damaged articles ; whilst Nur was sent to lay in supplies
for fourteen days. The journey is calculated at eleven
days ; but provisions are apt to spoil, and the Badawi
camel-men expect to be fed. Besides which, pilferers
abound. By my companion's advice I took wheat-flour,
rice, turmeric, onions, dates, unleavened bread of two
kinds, cheese, limes, tobacco, sugar, tea and coffee.

Hamid himself started upon the most important part
of our business. Faithful camel-men are required upon
a road where robberies are frequent and stabbings occasional, and where there is no law to prevent desertion or
to limit new and exorbitant demands. After a time he

returned, accompanied by a boy and a Badawi, a short, thin, well-built old man with regular features, a white beard, and a cool clear eye; his limbs, as usual, were scarred with wounds. Mas'ud of the Rahlah, a sub-family of the Hamidah' family of the Benu-Harb, came in with a dignified demeanour, applied his dexter palm to ours,[1] sat down, declined a pipe, accepted coffee, and after drinking it, looked at us to show that he was ready for negociation. We opened the proceedings with " We want men, and not camels," and the conversation proceeded in the purest Hijazi.[2] After much discussion, we agreed, if compelled to travel by the Darb al-Sharki, to pay twenty dollars for two camels,[3] and to advance Arbun, or earnest-money, to half that amount.[4] The Shaykh bound himself to provide us with good animals, which, moreover, were to be changed in case of accidents : he was also to supply his beasts with water, and to accompany us to Arafat and back. But, absolutely refusing to carry my large chest, he declared that the tent under the Shugduf was burden enough for one camel; and that the green box of drugs, the saddle-bags, and the provision-sacks, surmounted by Nur's cot, were amply sufficient for the other. On our part, we bound ourselves to feed the

---

1 This " Musafahah," as it is called, is the Arab fashion of shaking hands. They apply the palms of the right hands flat to each other, without squeezing the fingers, and then raise the hand to the forehead.

2 On this occasion I heard three new words: "Kharitah," used to signify a single trip to Meccah (without return to Al-Madinah), " Ta'arifah," going out from Meccah to Mount Arafat, and " Tanzilah," return from Mount Arafat to Meccah.

3 And part of an extra animal which was to carry water for the party. Had we travelled by the Darb al-Sultani, we should have paid 6½ dollars, instead of 10, for each beast.

4 The system of advances, as well as earnest money, is common all over Arabia. In some places, Aden for instance, I have heard of two-thirds the price of a cargo of coffee being required from the purchaser before the seller would undertake to furnish a single bale.

Shaykh and his son, supplying them either with raw or with cooked provender, and, upon our return to Meccah from Mount Arafat, to pay the remaining hire with a discretionary present.

Hamid then addressed to me flowery praises of the old Badawi. After which, turning to the latter, he exclaimed, " Thou wilt treat these friends well, O Mas'ud the Harbi !" The ancient replied with a dignity that had no pomposity in it,—" Even as Abu Shawarib—the Father of Mustachios[1]—behaveth to us, so will we behave to him !" He then arose, bade us be prepared when the departure-gun sounded, saluted us, and stalked out of the room, followed by his son, who, under pretext of dozing, had mentally made an inventory of every article in the room, ourselves especially included.

When the Badawin disappeared, Shaykh Hamid shook his head, advising me to give them plenty to eat, and never to allow twenty-four hours to elapse without dipping hand in the same dish with them, in order that the party might always be " Málihín,"—on terms of salt.[2] He con-

---

[1] Most men of the Shafe'i school clip their mustachios exceedingly short ; some clean shave the upper lip, the imperial, and the parts of the beard about the corners of the mouth, and the forepart of the cheeks. I neglected so to do, which soon won for me the epithet recorded above. Arabs are vastly given to "nick-naming God's creatures " ; their habit is the effect of acute observation, and the want of variety in proper names. Sonnini appears not to like having been called the " Father of a nose." But there is nothing disrespectful in these personal allusions. In Arabia you must be "father" of something, and it is better to be father of a feature, than father of a cooking pot, or father of a strong smell ("Abu-Zirt.")

[2] Salt among the Hindus is considered the essence and preserver of the seas ; it was therefore used in their offerings to the gods. The old idea in Europe was, that salt is a body composed of various elements, into which it cannot be resolved by human means : hence, it became the type of an indissoluble tie between individuals. Homer calls salt sacred and divine, and whoever ate it with a stranger was supposed to become his friend. By the Greek authors, as by the Arabs, hospitality and salt are words expressing a kindred idea.

cluded with a copious lecture upon the villainy of Badawin, and on their habit of drinking travellers' water. I was to place the skins on a camel in front, and not behind; to hang them with their mouths carefully tied, and turned upwards, contrary to the general practice; always to keep a good store of liquid, and at night to place it under the safeguard of the tent.

In the afternoon, Omar Effendi and others dropped in to take leave. They found me in the midst of preparations, sewing sacks, fitting up a pipe, patching water-bags, and packing medicines. My fellow-traveller had brought me some pencils[1] and a penknife, as "forget-me-nots," for we were by no means sure of meeting again. He hinted, however, at another escape from the paternal abode, and proposed, if possible, to join the Dromedary-Caravan. Shaykh Hamid said the same, but I saw, by the expression of his face, that his mother and wife would not give him leave from home so soon after his return.

Towards evening-time the Barr al-Manakhah became a scene of exceeding confusion. The town of tents lay upon the ground. Camels were being laden, and were roaring under the weight of litters and cots, boxes and baggage. Horses and mules galloped about. Men were rushing wildly in all directions on worldly errands, or hurrying to pay a farewell visit to the Prophet's Tomb. Women and children sat screaming on the ground, or ran to and fro distracted, or called their vehicles to escape the danger of being crushed. Every now and then a random shot excited all into the belief that the departure-gun had sounded. At times we heard a volley from the robbers' hills, which elicited a general groan, for the pilgrims were still, to use their own phrase, "between fear

---

When describing the Badawin of Al-Hijaz, I shall have occasion to notice their peculiar notions of the Salt-law.

1 The import of such articles shows the march of progress in Al-Hijaz. During the last generation, schoolmasters used for pencils bits of bar lead beaten to a point.

and hope," and, consequently, still far from "one of the two comforts.[1]" Then would sound the loud "Jhin-Jhin" of the camels' bells, as the stately animals paced away with some grandee's gilt and emblazoned litter, the sharp plaint of the dromedary, and the loud neighing of excited steeds.

About an hour after sunset all our preparations were concluded, save only the Shugduf, at which the boy Mohammed still worked with untiring zeal; he wisely remembered that he had to spend in it the best portion of a week and a half. The evening was hot, we therefore dined outside the house. I was told to repair to the Harim for the Ziyarat al-Wida'a, or the "Farewell Visitation"; but my decided objection to this step was that we were all to part,—how soon!—and when to meet again we knew not. My companions smiled consent, assuring me that the ceremony could be performed as well at a distance as in the temple.

Then Shaykh Hamid made me pray a two-bow prayer, and afterwards, facing towards the Harim, to recite this supplication with raised hands:

"O Apostle of Allah, we beg Thee to entreat Almighty Allah, that He cut off no Portion of the Good resulting to us, from this Visit to Thee and to Thy Harim! May He cause us to return safe and prosperous to our Birthplaces; aid then us in the Progeny he hath given us, and continue to us his Benefits, and make us thankful for our daily Bread! O Allah, let not this be the last of our Visitations to Thy Apostle's Tomb! Yet if Thou summon us before such Blessing, verily in my Death I bear Witness, as in my Life," (here the forefinger of the right hand is extended, that the members of the body may take part with the tongue and the heart) "that there

---

1 The "two comforts" are success and despair; the latter, according to the Arabs, being a more enviable state of feeling than doubt or hope deferred.

is no god but Allah, One and without Partner, and verily
that our Lord Mohammed is His Servant and His Apostle!
O Allah, grant us in this World Weal, and in the future
Weal, and save us from the torments of Hell-fire!   Praise
to Thee, O Lord, Lord of Glory, greater than Man can
describe! and Peace be upon the Apostle, and Laud to
Allah, the Lord of the (three) Worlds."   This concludes,
as usual, with the Testification and the Fatihah.   Pious
men on such an occasion go to the Rauzah, where they
strive, if possible, to shed a tear,—a single drop being a
sign of acceptance,—give alms to the utmost of their
ability, vow piety, repentance, and obedience, and retire
overwhelmed with grief, at separating themselves from
their Prophet and Intercessor.   It is customary, too,
before leaving Al-Madinah, to pass at least one night in
vigils at the Harim, and for learned men to read through
the Koran once before the tomb.

Then began the uncomfortable process of paying off
little bills.   The Eastern creditor always, for divers
reasons, waits the last moment before he claims his debt.
Shaykh Hamid had frequently hinted at his difficulties;
the only means of escape from which, he said, was to rely
upon Allah.   He had treated me so hospitably, that I
could not take back any part of the £5 lent to him at
Suez.   His three brothers received a dollar or two each,
and one or two of his cousins hinted to some effect that
such a proceeding would meet with their approbation.

The luggage was then carried down, and disposed in
packs upon the ground before the house, so as to be ready
for loading at a moment's notice.   Many flying parties of
travellers had almost started on the high road, and late
in the evening came a new report that the body of the
Caravan would march about midnight.   We sat up till
about two A.M., when, having heard no gun, and having
seen no camels, we lay down to sleep through the sultry
remnant of the hours of darkness.

Thus, gentle reader, was spent my last night at Al-Madinah.

I had reason to congratulate myself upon having passed through the first danger. Meccah is so near the coast, that, in case of detection, the traveller might escape in a few hours to Jeddah, where he would find an English Vice-Consul, protection from the Turkish authorities, and possibly a British cruiser in the harbour. But at Al-Madinah discovery would entail more serious consequences. The next risk to be run was the journey between the two cities, where it would be easy for the local officials quietly to dispose of a suspected person by giving a dollar to a Badawi.

CHAPTER XXIV.

FROM AL-MADINAH TO AL-SUWAYRKIYAH.

FOUR roads lead from Al-Madinah to Meccah.   The
Darb al-Sultani," or " Sultan's Highway," follows the line
of coast : this general passage has been minutely described
by my exact predecessor.   The " Tarik al-Ghabir," a
mountain path, is avoided by the Mahmil and the great
Caravans on account of its rugged passes ; water abounds
along the whole line, but there is not a single village :
and the Sobh Badawin, who own the soil are inveterate
plunderers.   The route called " Wady al-Kura " is a
favourite with Dromedary Caravans ; on this road are
two or three small settlements, regular wells, and free
passage through the Benu Amr tribe.   The Darb al-
Sharki, or " Eastern road," down which I travelled, owes
its existence to the piety of the Lady Zubaydah, wife of
Harun al-Rashid.   That munificent princess dug wells
from Baghdad to Al-Madinah, and built, we are told, a
wall to direct pilgrims over the shifting sands.[1]   There is
a fifth road, or rather mountain path, concerning which I
can give no information.

At eight A.M. on Wednesday, the 26th Zu'l Ka'adah

[1] The distance from Baghdad to Al-Madinah is 180 parasangs,
according to 'Abd al-Karím : " *Voyage de l'Inde, à la Mecque;*" translated by M. Langlès, *Paris*, 1797.   This book is a disappointment, as
it describes everything except Al-Madinah and Meccah : these gaps
are filled up by the translator with the erroneous descriptions of other
authors, not eye-witnesses.

(31st August, 1853), as we were sitting at the window of
Hamid's house after our early meal, suddenly appeared,
in hottest haste, Mas'ud, our Camel-Shaykh. He was accompanied by his son, a bold boy about fourteen years of
age, who fought sturdily about the weight of each package
as it was thrown over the camel's back ; and his nephew,
an ugly pock-marked lad, too lazy even to quarrel. We
were ordered to lose no time in loading ; all started into
activity, and at nine A.M. I found myself standing opposite
the Egyptian Gate, surrounded by my friends, who had
accompanied me thus far on foot, to take leave with due
honour. After affectionate embraces and parting mementoes, we mounted, the boy Mohammed and I in the
litter, and Shaykh Nur in his cot. Then in company with
some Turks and Meccans, for Mas'ud owned a string of
nine camels, we passed through the little gate near the
castle, and shaped our course towards the North. On
our right lay the palm-groves, which conceal this part of
the city ; far to the left rose the domes of Hamzah's
Mosques at the foot of Mount Ohod ; and in front a band
of road, crowded with motley groups, stretched over a
barren stony plain.

After an hour's slow march, bending gradually from
North to North-East, we fell into the Nijd highway, and
came to a place of renown called Al-Ghadir, or the Basin.[1]
This is a depression conducting the drainage of the plain
towards the northern hills. The skirts of Ohod still
limited the prospect to the left. On the right was the
Bir Rashid (Well of Rashid), and the little whitewashed
dome of Ali al-Urays, a descendant from Zayn al-Abidin :
—the tomb is still a place of Visitation. There we halted
and turned to take farewell of the Holy City. All the

1 Here, it is believed, was fought the battle of Buas, celebrated
in the pagan days of Al-Madinah (A.D. 615). Our dictionaries translate "Ghadir" by "pool" or "stagnant water." Here it is applied
to places where water stands for a short time after rain.

pilgrims dismounted and gazed at the venerable minarets and the Green Dome,—spots upon which their memories would for ever dwell with a fond and yearning interest.

Remounting at noon, we crossed a Fiumara which runs, according to my Camel-Shaykh, from North to South; we were therefore emerging from the Madinah basin. The sky began to be clouded, and although the air was still full of Samun, cold draughts occasionally poured down from the hills.   Arabs fear this
"bitter change
Of fierce extremes, extremes by change more fierce,"
and call that a dangerous climate which is cold in the hot season and hot in the cold.   Travelling over a rough and stony path, dotted with thorny Acacias, we arrived about two P.M. at the bed of lava heard of by Burckhardt.[1]   The

1 Travels in Arabia, vol. 2, p, 217.   The Swiss traveller was prevented by sickness from visiting it.   The "Jazb al-Kulub" affords the following account of a celebrated eruption, beginning on the Salkh (last day) of Jamadi al-Awwal, and ending on the evening of the third of Jamadi al-Akhir, A.H. 654.   Terrible earthquakes, accompanied by a thundering noise, shook the town ; from fourteen to eighteen were observed each night.   On the third of Jamadi al-Akhir, after the Isha prayers, a fire burst out in the direction of Al-Hijaz (eastward) ; it resembled a vast city with a turreted and battlemental fort, in which men appeared drawing the flame about, as it were, whilst it roared, burned, and melted like a sea everything that came in its way.   Presently red and bluish streams, bursting from it, ran close to Al-Madinah; and, at the same time, the city was fanned by a cooling zephyr from the same direction.   Al-Kistlani, an eye-witness, asserts that " the brilliant light of the volcano made the face of the country as bright as day; and the interior of the Harim was as if the sun shone upon it, so that men worked and required nought of the sun and moon (the latter of which was also eclipsed ?)."   Several saw the light at Meccah, at Tayma (in Nijd, six days' journey from Al-Madinah), and at Busra, of Syria, reminding men of the Prophet's saying, " A fire shall burst forth from the direction of Al-Hijaz ; its light shall make visible the necks of the camels at Busra."   Historians relate that the length of the stream was four parasangs (from fourteen to sixteen miles), its breadth four miles (56⅔ to the degree), and its depth about

aspect of the country was volcanic, abounding in basalts
and scoriæ, more or less porous : sand veiled the black bed
whose present dimensions by no means equal the descriptions of Arabian historians. I made diligent enquiries
about the existence of active volcanoes in this part of Al-
Hijaz, and heard of none.

At five P.M., travelling towards the East, we entered
a Bughaz,[1] or Pass, which follows the course of a wide
Fiumara, walled in by steep and barren hills,—the portals
of a region too wild even for Badawin. The torrent-bed
narrowed where the turns were abrupt, and the drift of
heavy stones, with a water-mark from six to seven feet

---

nine feet. It flowed like a torrent with the waves of a sea;
the rocks, melted by its heat, stood up as a wall, and, for a time, it
prevented the passage of Badawin, who, coming from that direction,
used to annoy the citizens. Jamal Matari, one of the historians of Al-
Madinah, relates that the flames, which destroyed the stones, spared
the trees; and he asserts that some men, sent by the governor to
inspect the fire, felt no heat ; also that the feathers of an arrow shot
into it were burned whilst the shaft remained whole. This he attributes to the sanctity of the trees within the Harim. On the contrary, Al-Kistlani asserts the fire to have been so vehement that no
one could approach within two arrow-flights, and that it melted
the outer half of a rock beyond the limits of the sanctuary, leaving
the inner parts unscathed. The Kazi, the Governor, and the citizens
engaged in devotional exercises, and during the whole length of the
Thursday and the Friday nights, all, even the women and children,
with bare heads wept round the Prophet's tomb. Then the lava-
current turned northwards. (I remarked on the way to Ohod signs
of a lava-field.) This current ran, according to some, three entire
months. Al-Kistlani dates its beginning on Friday, 6 Jamadi al-Akhir,
and its cessation on Sunday, 27 Rajab: in this period of fifty-two
days he includes, it is supposed, the length of its extreme heat.
That same year (A.H. 654) is infamous in Al-Islam for other portents,
such as the inundation of Baghdad by the Tigris, and the burning of
the Prophet's Mosque. In the next year first appeared the Tartars,
who slew Al-Mu'tasim Bi'llah, the Caliph, massacred the Moslems
during more than a month, destroyed their books, monuments, and
tombs, and stabled their war-steeds in the Mustansariyah College.

1 In this part of Al-Hijaz they have many names for a pass:—
Nakb, Saghrah, and Mazik are those best known.

high, showed that after rains a violent stream runs from
East and South-East to West and North-West. The
fertilising fluid is close to the surface, evidenced by a
spare growth of Acacia, camel-grass, and at some angles
of the bed by the Daum, or Theban palm.[1] I remarked
what was technically called " Hufrah," holes dug for
water in the sand ; and the guide assured me that somewhere near there is a spring flowing from the rocks.

After the long and sultry afternoon, beasts of burden
began to sink in numbers. The fresh carcases of asses,
ponies, and camels dotted the wayside : those that had
been allowed to die were abandoned to the foul carrion-
birds, the Rakham (vulture), and the yellow Ukáb ; and
all whose throats had been properly cut, were surrounded
by troops of Takruri pilgrims. These half-starved
wretches cut steaks from the choice portions, and slung
them over their shoulders till an opportunity of cooking
might arrive. I never saw men more destitute. They
carried wooden bowls, which they filled with water by
begging ; their only weapon was a small knife, tied in a
leathern sheath above the elbow ; and their costume an
old skull-cap, strips of leather like sandals under the feet,
and a long dirty shirt, or sometimes a mere rag covering
the loins. Some were perfect savages, others had been
fine-looking men, broad-shouldered, thin-flanked, and
long-limbed ; many were lamed by fatigue and by thorns ;
and looking at most of them, I fancied death depicted in
their forms and features.

After two hours' slow marching up the Fiumara
eastwards, we saw in front of us a wall of rock ; and,
turning abruptly southwards, we left the bed, and
ascended rising ground. Already it was night ; an hour,
however, elapsed before we saw, at a distance, the twink-
ling fires, and heard the watch-cries of our camp. It was

---

1 This is the palm, capped with large fan-shaped leaves, described
by every traveller in Egypt and in the nearer East.

pitched in a hollow, under hills, in excellent order ; the Pasha's pavilion surrounded by his soldiers and guards disposed in tents, with sentinels, regularly posted, protecting the outskirts of the encampment. One of our men, whom we had sent forward, met us on the way, and led us to an open place, where we unloaded the camels, raised our canvas home, lighted fires, and prepared, with supper, for a good night's rest. Living is simple on such marches. The pouches inside and outside the Shugduf contain provisions and water, with which you supply yourself when inclined. At certain hours of the day, ambulant vendors offer sherbet, lemonade, hot coffee, and water-pipes admirably prepared.[1] Chibuks may be smoked in the litter ; but few care to do so during the Samun. The first thing, however, called for at the halting-place is the pipe, and its delightfully soothing influence, followed by a cup of coffee, and a "forty winks" upon the sand, will awaken an appetite not to be roused by other means. How could Waterton, the traveller, abuse a pipe ? During the night-halt, provisions are cooked : rice, or Kichri, a mixture of pulse and rice, is eaten with Chutnee and lime-pickle, varied, occasionally, by tough mutton and indigestible goat.

We arrived at Ja al-Sharifah at eight P.M., after a march of about twenty-two miles.[2] This halting-place is

---

1 The charge for a cup of coffee is one piastre and a half. A pipe-bearer will engage himself for about £1 per mensem : he is always a veteran smoker, and, in these regions, it is an axiom that the flavour of your pipe mainly depends upon the filler. For convenience the Persian Kaliun is generally used.

2 A day's journey in Arabia is generally reckoned at twenty-four or twenty-five Arab miles. Abulfeda leaves the distance of a Marhalah (or Manzil, a station) undetermined. Al-Idrisi reckons it at thirty miles, but speaks of short as well as long marches. The common literary measures of length are these:—3 Kadam (man's foot) = 1 Khatwah (pace): 1000 paces = 1 Mil (mile); 3 miles = 1 Farsakh (parasang); and 4 parasangs = 1 Barid or post. The "Burhan

the rendezvous of Caravans : it lies 50° south-east of Al-Madinah, and belongs rather to Nijd than to Al-Hijaz.

At three A.M., on Thursday (Sept. 1), we started up at the sound of the departure-gun, struck the tent, loaded the camels, mounted, and found ourselves hurrying through a gloomy pass, in the hills, to secure a good place in the Caravan. This is an object of some importance, as, during the whole journey, marching order must not be broken. We met with a host of minor accidents, camels falling, Shugdufs bumping against one another, and plentiful abuse. Pertinaciously we hurried on till six A.M., at which hour we emerged from the Black Pass. The large crimson sun rose upon us, disclosing, through purple mists, a hollow of coarse yellow gravel, based upon a hard whitish clay. About five miles broad by twelve long, it collects the waters of the high grounds after rain, and distributes the surplus through an exit towards the North-west, a gap in the low undulating hills around. Entering it, we dismounted, prayed, broke our fast, and after half an hour's halt proceeded to cross its breadth. The appearance of the Caravan was most striking, as it threaded its slow way over the smooth surface of the Khabt (low plain).[1] To judge by the eye, the host was composed of at fewest seven thousand souls, on foot, on horseback, in litters, or bestriding the splendid camels of Syria.[2] There were eight gradations of pilgrims.

---

i Katia " gives the table thus :—24 finger breadths (or 6 breadths of the clenched hand, from 20 to 24 inches !) = 1 Gaz or yard ; 1000 yards = 1 mile ; 3 miles = 1 parasang. Some call the four thousand yards measure a Kuroh (the Indian Cos), which, however, is sometimes less by 1000 Gaz. The only ideas of distance known to the Badawi of Al-Hijaz are the fanciful Sa'at or hour, and the uncertain Manzil or halt : the former varies from 2 to 3½ miles, the latter from 15 to 25.

1 " Khabt " is a low plain ; " Midan," " Fayhah," or " Sath," a plain generally ; and " Batha," a low, sandy flat.

2 In Burckhardt's day there were 5,000 souls and 15,000 camels.

The lowest hobbled with heavy staves. Then came the riders of asses, of camels, and of mules. Respectable men, especially Arabs, were mounted on dromedaries, and the soldiers had horses: a led animal was saddled for every grandee, ready whenever he might wish to leave his litter. Women, children, and invalids of the poorer classes sat upon a "Haml Musattah,"—rugs and cloths spread over the two large boxes which form the camel's load.[1] Many occupied Shibriyahs; a few, Shugdufs, and

only the wealthy and the noble rode in Takht-rawan (litters), carried by camels or mules.[2] The morning beams fell brightly upon the glancing arms which surrounded the stripped Mahmil,[3] and upon the scarlet and gilt conveyances of the grandees. Not the least beauty of the spectacle was its wondrous variety

The Shibriyah.

of detail: no man was dressed like his neighbour, no camel was caparisoned, no horse was

---

Capt. Sadlier, who travelled during the war (1819), found the number reduced to 500. The extent of this Caravan has been enormously exaggerated in Europe. I have heard of 15,000, and even of 20,000 men. I include in the 7,000 about 1,200 Persians. They are no longer placed, as Abd al-Karim relates, in the rear of the Caravan, or post of danger.

1 Lane has accurately described this article: in the Hijaz it is sometimes made to resemble a little tent.

2 The vehicle mainly regulates the expense, as it evidences a man's means. I have heard of a husband and wife leaving Alexandria with three months' provision and the sum of £5. They would mount a camel, lodge in public buildings when possible, probably be reduced to beggary, and possibly starve upon the road. On the other hand the minimum expenditure,—for necessaries, not donations and luxuries,—of a man who rides in a Takht-rawan from Damascus and back, would be about £1,200.

3 On the line of march the Mahmil, stripped of its embroidered cover, is carried on camel-back, a mere framewood. Even the gilt silver balls and crescent are exchanged for similar articles in brass.

clothed in uniform, as it were. And nothing stranger than
the contrasts; a band of half-naked Takruri marching with
the Pasha's equipage, and long-capped, bearded Persians
conversing with Tarbush'd and shaven Turks.

The plain even at an early hour reeked with vapours
distilled by the fires of the Samum: about noon, however,
the air became cloudy, and nothing of colour remained,
save that milky white haze, dull, but glaring withal,
which is the prevailing day-tint in these regions. At
mid-day we reached a narrowing of the basin, where,
from both sides, "Irk," or low hills, stretch their last
spurs into the plain. But after half a mile, it again
widened to upwards of two miles. At two P.M. (Friday,
Sept. 2), we turned towards the South-west, ascended
stony ground, and found ourselves one hour afterwards in
a desolate rocky flat, distant about twenty-four miles of
unusually winding road from our last station. "Mahattah
Ghurab,[1]" or the Raven's Station, lies 10° south-west from
Ja al-Sharifah, in the irregular masses of hill on the fron-
tier of Al-Hijaz, where the highlands of Nijd begin.

After pitching the tent, we prepared to recruit our
supply of water; for Mas'ud warned me that his camels
had not drunk for ninety hours, and that they would soon
sink under the privation. The boy Mohammed, mounting a dromedary, set off with the Shaykh and many
water-bags, giving me an opportunity of writing out my
journal. They did not return home until after nightfall,
a delay caused by many adventures. The wells are in a
Fiumara, as usual, about two miles distant from the
halting-place, and the soldiers, regular as well as irregular, occupied the water and exacted hard coin in
exchange for it. The men are not to blame; they would
die of starvation but for this resource. The boy Mohammed had been engaged in several quarrels; but after

---

1 Mahattah is a spot where luggage is taken down, *i.e.*, a station.
By some Hijazis it is used in the sense of a halting-place, where you
spend an hour or two.

snapping his pistol at a Persian pilgrim's head, he came
forth triumphant with two skins of sweetish water, for
which we paid ten piastres. He was in his glory. There
were many Meccans in the Caravan, among them his
elder brother and several friends: the Sharif Zayd had
sent, he said, to ask why he did not travel with his compatriots. That evening he drank so copiously of clarified
butter, and ate dates mashed with flour and other abomi-
nations to such an extent, that at night he prepared to
give up the ghost.

We passed a pleasant hour or two before sleeping. I
began to like the old Shaykh Mas'ud, who, seeing it,
entertained me with his genealogy, his battles, and his
family affairs. The rest of the party could not prevent
expressing contempt when they heard me putting frequent
questions about torrents, hills, Badawin, and the directions of places. "Let the Father of Moustachios ask
and learn," said the old man; "he is friendly with the
Badawin,[1] and knows better than you all." This reproof
was intended to be bitter as the poet's satire,—

> " All fools have still an itching to deride,
> And fain would be upon the laughing side."

It called forth, however. another burst of merriment, for
the jeerers remembered my nickname to have belonged to
that pestilent heretic, Sa'ud the Wahhabi.

On Saturday, the 3rd September, the hateful signal-
gun awoke us at one A.M. In Arab travel there is nothing
more disagreeable than the Sariyah or night-march, and
yet the people are inexorable about it. "Choose early
Darkness (daljah) for your Wayfarings," said the Prophet, "as the Calamities of the Earth (serpents and wild
beasts) appear not at Night." I can scarcely find words
to express the weary horrors of the long dark march, during which the hapless traveller, fuming, if a European,
with disappointment in his hopes of "seeing the country,"

---

1 "Khalik ma al-Badu" is a favourite complimentary saying,
among this people, and means that you are no greasy burgher.

is compelled to sit upon the back of a creeping camel. The day-sleep, too, is a kind of lethargy, and it is all but impossible to preserve an appetite during the hours of heat.

At half-past five A.M., after drowsily stumbling through hours of outer gloom, we entered a spacious basin at least six miles broad, and limited by a circlet of low hill. It was overgrown with camel-grass and Acacia (Shittim) trees, mere vegetable mummies; in many places the water had left a mark ; and here and there the ground was pitted with mud-flakes, the remains of recently dried pools. After an hour's rapid march we toiled over a rugged ridge, composed of broken and detached blocks of basalt and scoriæ, fantastically piled together, and dotted with thorny trees. Shaykh Mas'ud passed the time in walking to and fro along his line of camels, addressing us with a *Khallikum guddam*, "to the front (of the litter)!" as we ascended, and a *Khallikum wara*, "to the rear!" during the descent. It was wonderful to see the animals stepping from block to block with the sagacity of mountaineers; assuring themselves of their forefeet before trusting all their weight to advance. Not a camel fell, either here or on any other ridge : they moaned, however, piteously, for the sudden turns of the path puzzled them; the ascents were painful, the descents were still more so ; the rocks were sharp; deep holes yawned between the blocks, and occasionally an Acacia caught the Shugduf, almost overthrowing the hapless bearer by the suddenness and the tenacity of its clutch. This passage took place during daylight. But we had many at night, which I shall neither forget nor describe.

Descending the ridge, we entered another hill-encircled basin of gravel and clay. In many places basalt in piles and crumbling strata of hornblende schiste, disposed edgeways, green within, and without blackened by sun and rain, cropped out of the ground. At half-past ten we found ourselves in an "Acacia-barren," one of the things which pilgrims dread. Here Shugdufs are bodily pulled off the camel's back and broken upon the hard ground; the animals drop upon their knees, the whole line is deranged, and every one, losing temper, attacks his Moslem brother. The road was flanked on the left by an iron wall of black basalt. Noon brought us to another ridge, whence we descended into a second wooded basin surrounded by hills.

Here the air was filled with those pillars of sand so graphically described by Abyssinian Bruce. They scudded on the wings of the whirlwind over the plain,—huge yellow shafts, with lofty heads, horizontally bent backwards, in the form of clouds; and on more than one occasion camels were thrown down by them. It required little stretch of fancy to enter into the Arabs' superstition. These sand-columns are supposed to be Jinnis of the Waste, which cannot be caught, a notion arising from the fitful movements of the electrical wind-eddy that raises them, and as they advance, the pious Moslem stretches out his finger, exclaiming, "Iron! O thou ill-omened one[1]!"

During the forenoon we were troubled by the Samum, which, instead of promoting perspiration, chokes up and hardens the skin. The Arabs complain greatly of its violence on this line of road. Here I first remarked the difficulty with which the Badawin bear thirst. *Ya Latif,*— "O Merciful!" (Lord),—they exclaimed at times; and yet they behaved like men.[2] I had ordered them to place the

---

1 Even Europeans, in popular parlance, call them "devils."

2 The Eastern Arabs allay the torments of thirst by a spoonful of clarified butter, carried on journeys in a leathern bottle. Every European traveller has some recipe of his own. One chews a musket-bullet or a small stone. A second smears his legs with butter. Another eats a crust of dry bread, which exacerbates the torments, and afterwards brings relief. A fourth throws water over his face and hands or his legs and feet; a fifth smokes, and a sixth turns his dorsal region (raising his coat-tail) to the fire. I have always found

water-camel in front, so as to exercise due supervision.
Shaykh Mas'ud and his son made only an occasional reference to the skins. But his nephew, a short, thin, pock-
marked lad of eighteen, whose black skin and woolly head
suggested the idea of a semi-African and ignoble origin,
was always drinking; except when he climbed the camel's
back, and, dozing upon the damp load, forgot his thirst.
In vain we ordered, we taunted, and we abused him: he
would drink, he *would* sleep, but he would *not* work.

At one P.M. we crossed a Fiumara; and an hour
afterwards we pursued the course of a second. Mas'ud
called this the Wady al-Khunak, and assured me that it
runs from the East and the South-east in a North and
North-west direction, to the Madinah plain. Early
in the afternoon we reached a diminutive flat, on the
Fiumara bank. Beyond it lies a *Mahjar* or stony ground,
black as usual in Al-Hijaz, and over its length lay the
road, white with dust and with the sand deposited by the
camels' feet. Having arrived before the Pasha, we did
not know where to pitch; many opining that the Caravan
would traverse the *Mahjar* and halt beyond it. We soon
alighted, however, pitched the tent under a burning sun,
and were imitated by the rest of the party. Mas'ud
called the place Hijriyah. According to my computation,
it is twenty-five miles from Ghurab, and its direction is
South-East twenty-two degrees.

Late in the afternoon the boy Mohammed started
with a dromedary to procure water from the higher part
of the Fiumara. Here are some wells, still called Bir
Harun, after the great Caliph. The youth returned soon
with two bags filled at an expense of nine piastres. This
being the 28th Zu'l Ka'adah, many pilgrims busied them-

---

that the only remedy is to be patient and not to talk. The more you
drink, the more you require to drink—water or strong waters. But
after the first two hours' abstinence you have mastered the over-
powering feeling of thirst, and then to refrain is easy.

selves rather fruitlessly with endeavours to sight the
crescent moon. They failed; but we were consoled by
seeing through a gap in the Western hills a heavy cloud
discharge its blessed load, and a cool night was the
result.

We loitered on Sunday, the 4th September, at Al-
Hijriyah, although the Shaykh forewarned us of a long
march. But there is a kind of discipline in these great
Caravans. A gun[1] sounds the order to strike the tents,
and a second bids you move off with all speed. There
are short halts, of half an hour each, at dawn, noon, the
afternoon, and sunset, for devotional purposes, and these
are regulated by a cannon or a culverin. At such times
the Syrian and Persian servants, who are admirably
expert in their calling, pitch the large green tents, with
gilt crescents, for the dignitaries and their harims. The
last resting-place is known by the hurrying forward
of these "Farrash," or tent "Lascars," who are determined to be the first on the ground and at the well. A
discharge of three guns denotes the station, and when the
Caravan moves by night a single cannon sounds three or
four halts at irregular intervals. The principal officers
were the Emir Hajj, one Ashgar Ali Pasha, a veteran of
whom my companions spoke slightingly, because he had
been the slave of a slave, probably the pipe-bearer of
some grandee who in his youth had been pipe-bearer to
some other grandee. Under him was a Wakil, or lieutenant, who managed the executive. The Emir al-
Surrah—called simply Al-Surrah, or the Purse—had
charge of the Caravan-treasure, and of remittances to the
Holy Cities. And lastly there was a commander of the

1 We carried two small brass guns, which, on the line of march,
were dismounted and placed upon camels. At the halt they were
restored to their carriages. The Badawin think much of these harmless articles, to which I have seen a gunner apply a match thrice
before he could induce a discharge. In a "moral" point of view,
therefore, they are far more valuable than our twelve-pounders.

forces (Bashat al-Askar): his host consisted of about a
thousand Irregular horsemen, Bash-Buzuks, half bandits,
half soldiers, each habited and armed after his own
fashion, exceedingly dirty, picturesque-looking, brave, and
in such a country of no use whatever.

Leaving Al-Hijriyah at seven A.M., we passed over
the grim stone-field by a detestable footpath, and at nine
o'clock struck into a broad Fiumara, which runs from the
East towards the North-West. Its sandy bed is overgrown with Acacia, the Senna plant, different species of
Euphorbiæ, the wild Capparis, and the Daum Palm. Up
this line we travelled the whole day. About six P.M., we
came upon a basin at least twelve miles broad, which
absorbs the water of the adjacent hills. Accustomed as
I have been to mirage, a long thin line of salt efflorescence
appearing at some distance on the plain below us, when
the shades of evening invested the view, completely
deceived me. Even the Arabs were divided in opinion,
some thinking it was the effects of the rain which fell the
day before : others were more acute. It is said that
beasts are never deceived by the mirage, and this, as far
as my experience goes, is correct. May not the reason be
that most of them know the vicinity of water rather by
smell than by sight ? Upon the horizon beyond the plain
rose dark, fort-like masses of rock which I mistook for
buildings, the more readily as the Shaykh had warned me
that we were approaching a populous place. At last
descending a long steep hill, we entered upon the level
ground, and discovered our error by the crunching sound
of the camel's feet upon large curling flakes of nitrous
salt overlying caked mud.[1] Those civilised birds, the
kite and the crow, warned us that we were in the vicinity
of man. It was not, however, before eleven P.M. that we
entered the confines of Al-Suwayrkiyah. The fact was

---

1 Hereabouts the Arabs call these places "Bahr milh" or "Sea
of Salt"; in other regions "Bahr bila ma," or "Waterless Sea."

made patent to us by the stumbling and the falling of our
dromedaries over the little ridges of dried clay disposed
in squares upon the fields. There were other obstacles,
such as garden walls, wells, and hovels, so that midnight
had sped before our weary camels reached the resting-
place. A rumour that we were to halt here the next day,
made us think lightly of present troubles ; it proved,
however, to be false.

During the last four days I attentively observed the
general face of the country. This line is a succession of
low plains and basins, here quasi-circular, there irregularly oblong, surrounded by rolling hills and cut by
Fiumaras which pass through the higher ground. The
basins are divided by ridges and flats of basalt and greenstone averaging from one hundred to two hundred feet in
height. The general form is a huge prism ; sometimes
they are table-topped. From Al-Madinah to Al-Suwayrkiyah the low beds of sandy Fiumaras abound. From Al-
Suwayrkiyah to Al-Zaribah, their place is taken by
" Ghadir," or hollows in which water stagnates. And
beyond Al-Zaribah the traveller enters a region of watercourses tending West and South-West. The versant is
generally from the East and South-East towards the
West and North-West. Water obtained by digging is
good where rain is fresh in the Fiumaras ; saltish, so as
to taste at first unnaturally sweet, in the plains ; and bitter in
the basins and lowlands where nitre effloresces and rain
has had time to become tainted. The landward faces of
the hills are disposed at a sloping angle, contrasting
strongly with the perpendicularity of their seaward sides,
and I found no inner range corresponding with, and
parallel to, the maritime chain. Nowhere had I seen a
land in which Earth's anatomy lies so barren, or one
richer in volcanic and primary formations.[1] Especially

---

[1] Being but little read in geology, I submitted, after my return
to Bombay, a few specimens collected on the way, to a learned friend,

towards the South, the hills were abrupt and highly vertical, with black and barren flanks, ribbed with furrows and fissures, with wide and formidable precipices and castellated summits like the work of man. The predominant formation was basalt, called the Arabs' Hajar Jahannam, or Hell-stone ; here and there it is porous and cellular ; in some places compact and black ; and in others coarse and gritty, of a tarry colour, and when fractured shining with bright points. Hornblende is common at Al-Madinah and throughout this part of Al-Hijaz: it crops out of the ground edgeways, black and brittle. Greenstone, diorite, and actinolite are found, though not so abundantly as those above mentioned. The granites, called in Arabic Suwan,[1] abound. Some are large-grained, of a pink colour, and appear in blocks, which, flaking off under the influence of the atmosphere, form oöidal blocks and boulders piled in irregular heaps. Others are grey and compact enough to take a high polish when cut. The syenite is generally coarse, although there is occasionally found a rich red variety of that stone. I did not see eurite or euritic porphyry except in small pieces, and the same may be said of the petrosilex and the milky and waxy quartz.[2] In some parts, particularly between Yambu' and Al-Madinah, there is an abundance of tawny

Dr. Carter, Secretary to the Bombay branch of the Royal Asiatic Society. His name is a guarantee of accuracy.

1 The Arabic language has a copious terminology for the mineral as well as the botanical productions of the country: with little alteration it might be made to express all the requirements of our modern geology.

2 NOTE TO THIRD EDITION.—This country may have contained gold; but the superficial formation has long been exhausted. At Cairo I washed some sand brought from the eastern shore of the Red Sea, north of Al-Wijh, and found it worth my while. I had a plan for working the diggings, but H.B.M.'s Consul, Dr. Walne, opined that "gold was becoming too plentiful," and would not assist me. This wise saying has since then been repeated to me by men who ought to have known better than Dr. Walne.

yellow gneiss markedly stratified. The transition formations are represented by a fine calcareous sandstone of
a bright ochre colour : it is used at Meccah to adorn the
exteriors of houses, bands of this stone being here and
there inserted into the courses of masonry. There is also
a small admixture of the greenish sandstone which
abounds at Aden. The secondary formation is represented by a fine limestone, in some places almost fit for
the purposes of lithography, and a coarse gypsum often of
a tufaceous nature. For the superficial accumulations of
the country, I may refer the reader to any description of
the Desert between Cairo and Suez.

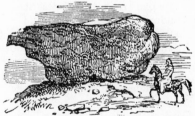

CHAPTER XXV.

THE BADAWIN OF AL-HIJAZ.

THE Arab may be divided into three races—a classification which agrees equally well with genesitic genealogy, the traditions of the country, and the observations of modern physiologists.[1]

[1] In Holy Writ, as the indigens are not alluded to—only the Noachian race being described—we find two divisions: 1 The children of Joktan (great grandson of Shem), Mesopotamians settled in Southern Arabia, "from Mesha (Musa or Meccah?) to Sephar" (Zafar), a "Mount of the East,"—Genesis, x. 30: that is to say, they occupied the lands from Al-Tahamah to Mahrah. 2. The children of Ishmael, and his Egyptian wife; they peopled only the Wilderness of Paran in the Sinaitic Peninsula and the parts adjacent. Dr. Aloys Sprenger (Life of Mohammed, p. 18), throws philosophic doubt upon the Ishmaelitish descent of Mohammed, who in personal appearance was a pure Caucasian, without any mingling of Egyptian blood. And the Ishmaelitish origin of the whole Arab race is an utterly untenable theory. Years ago, our great historian sensibly remarked that "the name (Saracens), used by Ptolemy and Pliny in a more confined, by Ammianus and Procopius in a larger sense, has been derived ridiculously from Sarah the wife of Abraham." In Gibbon's observation, the erudite Interpreter of the One Primæval Language,—the acute bibliologist who metamorphoses the quail of the wilderness into a "ruddy goose,"—detects "insidiousness" and "a spirit of restless and rancorous hostility" against revealed religion. He proceeds on these sound grounds to attack the accuracy, the honesty and the learning of the mighty dead. This may be Christian zeal; it is not Christian charity. Of late years it has been the fashion for every aspirant to ecclesiastical honours to deal a blow at the ghost of Gibbon. And, as has before been remarked, Mr.

The first race, indigens or autochthones, are those sub-Caucasian tribes which may still be met with in the province of Mahrah, and generally along the coast between Maskat and Hazramaut.[1] The Mahrah, the Janábah, and the Gara especially show a low development, for which hardship and privation alone will not satisfactorily account.[2] These are *Arab al-Aribah* for whose inferiority oriental fable accounts as usual by thaumaturgy.

The principal advenæ are the Noachians, a great Chaldæan or Mesopotamian tribe which entered Arabia about

Foster gratuitously attacked Burckhardt, whose manes had long rested in the good-will of man. This contrasts offensively with Lord Lindsay's happy compliment to the memory of the honest Swiss and the amiable eulogy quoted by Dr. Keith from the Quarterly (vol. xxiii.), and thus adopted as his own. It may seem folly to defend the historian of the Decline and Fall against the compiler of the Historical Geography of Arabia. But continental Orientalists have expressed their wonder at the appearance in this nineteenth century of the "Voice of Israel from Mount Sinai" and the "India in Greece"· they should be informed that all our Eastern students are not votaries of such obsolete vagaries.

1 This is said without any theory. According to all historians of long inhabited lands, the advenæ—whether migratory tribes or visitors—find indigens or αυθιγενεις.

2 They are described as having small heads, with low brows and ill-formed noses, (strongly contrasting with the Jewish feature), irregular lines, black skins, and frames for the most part frail and slender. For a physiological description of this race, I must refer my readers to the writings of Dr. Carter of Bombay, the medical officer of the Palinurus, when engaged on the Survey of Eastern Arabia. With ample means of observation he has not failed to remark the similarity between the lowest type of Badawi and the Indigens of India, as represented by the Bhils and other Jungle races. This, from a man of science who is not writing up to a theory, may be considered strong evidence in favour of variety in the Arabian family. The fact has long been suspected, but few travellers have given their attention to the subject since the downfall of Sir William Jones' Indian origin theory. I am convinced that there is not in Arabia "one Arab face, cast of features and expression," as was formerly supposed to be the case, and I venture to recommend the subject for consideration to future observers.

2200 A.C., and by slow and gradual encroachments drove before them the ancient owners and seized the happier lands of the Peninsula. The great Anzah and the Nijdi families are types of this race, which is purely Caucasian, and shows a highly nervous temperament, together with those signs of "blood" which distinguish even the lower animals, the horse and the camel, the greyhound and the goat of Arabia. These advenæ would correspond with the *Arab al-Mutarribah* or Arabicized Arabs of the eastern historians.[1]

The third family, an ancient and a noble race dating from A.C. 1900, and typified in history by Ishmael, still occupies the so-called Sinaitic Peninsula. These Arabs, however, do not, and never did, extend beyond the limits of the mountains, where, still dwelling in the presence of their brethren, they retain all the wild customs and the untamable spirit of their forefathers. They are distinguished from the pure stock by an admixture of Egyptian blood,[2]

---

1 Of this Mesopotamian race there are now many local varieties. The subjects of the four Abyssinian and Christian sovereigns who succeeded Yusuf, the Jewish "Lord of the Pit," produced, in Al-Yaman, the modern "Akhdam" or "Serviles." The "Hujur" of Al-Yaman and Oman are a mixed race whose origin is still unknown. And to quote no more cases, the "Ebna" mentioned by the Ibn Ishak were descended from the Persian soldiers of Anushirwan, who expelled the Abyssinian invader.

2 That the Copts, or ancient Egyptians, were "Half-caste Arabs," a mixed people like the Abyssinians, the Gallas, the Somal, and the Kafirs, an Arab graft upon an African stock, appears highly probable. Hence the old Nilotic race has been represented as woolly-headed and of negro feature. Thus Leo Africanus makes the Africans to be descendants of the Arabs. Hence the tradition that Egypt was peopled by Æthiopia, and has been gradually whitened by admixture of Persian and Median, Greek and Roman blood. Hence, too, the fancied connection of Æthiopia with Cush, Susiana, Khuzistan or the lands about the Tigris. Thus learned Virgil, confounding the Western with the Eastern Æthiopians, alludes to

"Usque coloratos Nilus devexus ad Indos."

And Strabo maintains the people of Mauritania to be Indians who and by preserving the ancient characteristics of the Nilotic family. The Ishmaelities are sub-Caucasian, and are denoted in history as the *Arab al-Mustarribah*, the insititious or half-caste Arab.

Oriental ethnography, which, like most Eastern sciences, luxuriates in nomenclative distinction, recognises a fourth race under the name of *Arab al-Mustajamah*. These " barbarized Arabs " are now represented by such a population as that of Meccah.

That Aus and Khazraj, the Himyaritic tribes which emigrated to Al-Hijaz, mixed with the Amalikah, the Jurham, and the Katirah, also races from Al-Yaman, and with the Hebrews, a northern branch of the Semitic family, we have ample historical evidence. And they who know how immutable is race in the Desert, will scarcely doubt that the Badawi of Al-Hijaz preserves in purity the blood transmitted to him by his ancestors.[1]

---

had come with Hercules. We cannot but remark in Southern Arabia the footprints of the Hindu, whose superstitions, like the Phœnix which flew from India to expire in Egypt, passed over to Arabia with Dwipa Sukhatra (Socotra) for a resting place on its way to the regions of the remotest West. As regards the difference between the Japhetic and Semitic tongues, it may be remarked that though nothing can be more distinct than Sanscrit and Arabic, yet that Pahlavi and Hebrew (Prof. Bohlen on Genesis) present some remarkable points of resemblance. I have attempted in a work on Sind to collect words common to both families. And further research convinces me that such vocables as the Arabic Taur ثور the Persian Tora تورا and the Latin "Taurus" denote an ancient *rapprochement*, whose mysteries still invite the elucidation of modern science.

1 The Sharif families affect marrying female slaves, thereby showing the intense pride which finds no Arab noble enough for them. Others take to wife Badawi girls: their blood, therefore, is by no means pure. The worst feature of their system is the forced celibacy of their daughters; they are never married into any but Sharif families; consequently they often die in spinsterhood. The effects of this custom are most pernicious, for though celibacy exists in the East it is by no means synonymous with chastity. Here it

I will not apologise for entering into details concerning the *personale* of the Badawin [1]; a precise physical portrait of race, it has justly been remarked, is the sole deficiency in the pages of Bruce and of Burckhardt.

The temperament of the Hijazi is not unfrequently the pure nervous, as the height of the forehead and the fine texture of the hair prove. Sometimes the bilious, and rarely the sanguine, elements predominate ; the lymphatic I never saw. He has large nervous centres, and well-formed spine and brain, a conformation favourable to longevity. Bartema well describes his colour as a " dark leonine "; it varies from the deepest Spanish to a chocolate hue, and its varieties are attributed by the people to blood. The skin is hard, dry, and soon wrinkled by exposure. The xanthous complexion is rare, though not unknown in cities, but the leucous does not exist. The crinal hair is frequently lightened by bleaching, and the pilar is browner than the crinal. The voice is strong and clear, but rather barytone than bass : in anger it becomes a shrill chattering like the cry of a wild animal. The look of a chief is dignified and grave even to pensiveness ; the "respectable man's " is self-sufficient and fierce ; the lower orders look ferocious, stupid, and inquisitive. Yet there is not much difference in this point between men of the same tribe, who have similar pursuits which engen-

---

springs from a morbid sense of honour, and arose, it is popularly said, from an affront taken by a Sharif against his daughter's husband. But all Arabs condemn the practice.

[1] I use this word as popular abuse has fixed it. Every Orientalist knows that Badawin (Bedouin) is the plural form of Badawi, an "ism al-nisbah," or adjective derived from Badu, a Desert. "Some words notoriously corrupt," says Gibbon, "are fixed, and as it were naturalised, in the vulgar tongue." The word "Badawi" is not insulting, like " Turk" applied to an Osmanli, or "Fellah" to the Egyptian. But you affront the wild man by mistaking his clan for a lower one. "Ya Hitaymi," for instance, addressed to a Harb Badawi, makes him finger his dagger.

BADAWI AND WAHHABI[1] HEADS AND HEAD-DRESSES.

To face vol. ii. page 81.

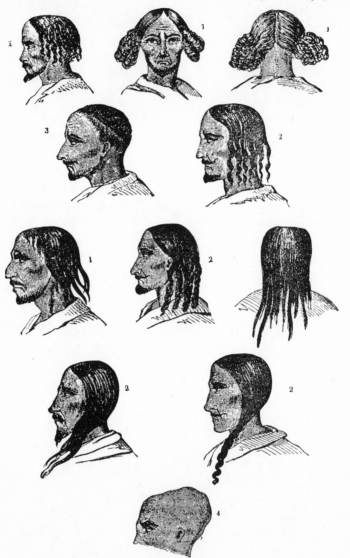

1. This is the typical face.

2. دليك Ringlets called " Dalik."

3. شوشه The hair on crown called "Shushah."

4. Shape of shaved head : firmness and self-esteem high.

---

1 The Wahhabi tribe generally shave the head, whilst some amongst them still wear the hair long, which is the ancient Badawi practice.

der similar passions. Expression is the grand diversifier
of appearance among civilised people: in the Desert it
knows few varieties.

The Badawi cranium is small, oöidal, long, high, narrow, and remarkable in the occiput for the development
of Gall's second propensity: the crown slopes upwards
towards the region of firmness, which is elevated; whilst
the sides are flat to a fault. The hair, exposed to sun,
wind, and rain, acquires a coarseness not natural to it[1]:
worn in *Kurun*[2]—ragged elf-locks,—hanging down to the
breast, or shaved in the form *Shushah*, a skull-cap of hair,
nothing can be wilder than its appearance. The face is
made to be a long oval, but want of flesh detracts from its
regularity. The forehead is high, broad, and retreating:
the upper portion is moderately developed; but nothing
can be finer than the lower brow, and the frontal sinuses
stand out, indicating bodily strength and activity of character. The temporal fossa are deep, the bones are salient,
and the elevated zygomata combined with the "lantern-
jaw," often give a "death's-head" appearance to the face.
The eyebrows are long, bushy, and crooked, broken, as it
were, at the angle where "Order" is supposed to be, and
bent in sign of thoughtfulness. Most popular writers,
following De Page,[3] describe the Arab eye as large, ardent,

---

1 This coarseness is not a little increased by a truly Badawi habit
of washing the locks with—بول الابل. It is not considered wholly
impure, and is also used for the eyes, upon which its ammonia would
act as a rude stimulant. The only cosmetic is clarified butter freely
applied to the body as well as to the hair.

2 "Kurun" (قرون) properly means "horns." The Sharifs generally wear their hair in "Haffah" (حفة), long locks hanging down both
sides of the neck and shaved away about a finger's breadth round
the forehead and behind the neck.

3 This traveller describes the modern Mesopotamian and Northern
race, which, as its bushy beard—unusual feature in pure Arab blood
—denotes, is mixed with central Asian. In the North, as might be
expected, the camels are hairy; whereas, in Al-Hijaz and in the
low parts of Al-Yaman, a whole animal does not give a handful fit

and black.   The Badawi of the Hijaz, and indeed the
race generally, has a small eye, round, restless, deep-set,
and fiery, denoting keen inspection with an ardent temperament and an impassioned character.   Its colour is dark
brown or green-brown, and the pupil is often speckled.
The habit of pursing up the skin below the orbits, and
half closing the lids to exclude glare, plants the outer
angles with premature crows'-feet.   Another peculiarity
is the sudden way in which the eye opens, especially under
excitement.   This, combined with its fixity of glance, forms
an expression now of lively fierceness, then of exceeding
sternness ; whilst the narrow space between the orbits im-
presses the countenance in repose with an intelligence
not destitute of cunning.   As a general rule, however, the
expression of the Badawi face is rather dignity than that
cunning for which the Semitic race is celebrated, and
there are lines about the mouth in variance with the stern
or the fierce look of the brow.   The ears are like those of
Arab horses, small, well-cut, " castey," and   elaborate,
with many elevations aud depressions.   The nose is pronounced, generally aquiline, but sometimes straight like
those Greek statues which have been treated as prodigious
exaggerations of the facial angle.   For the most part, it
is a well-made feature with delicate nostrils, below which
the septum appears : in anger they swell and open like a
blood mare's.   I have, however, seen, in not a few instances, pert and offensive " pugs."   Deep furrows
descend from the wings of the nose, showing an uncertain
temper, now too grave, then too gay.   The mouth is irregular.   The lips are either *bordés*, denoting rudeness and
want of taste, or they form a mere line.   In the latter case
there is an appearance of undue development in the upper
portion of the countenance, especially when the jaws are
ascetically thin, and the chin weakly retreats.   The latter

---

for weaving.   The Arabs attribute this, as we should, to heat, which
causes the longer hairs to drop off.

feature, however, is generally well and strongly made. The teeth, as usual among Orientals, are white, even, short and broad—indications of strength. Some tribes trim their mustaches according to the "Sunnat"; the Shafe'i often shave them, and many allow them to hang Persian-like over the lips. The beard is represented by two tangled tufts upon the chin; where whisker should be, the place is either bare or is thinly covered with straggling pile.

The Badawin of Al-Hijaz are short men, about the height of the Indians near Bombay, but weighing on an average a stone more. As usual in this stage of society, stature varies little; you rarely see a giant, and scarcely ever a dwarf. Deformity is checked by the Spartan restraint upon population, and no weakly infant can live through a Badawi life. The figure, though spare, is square and well knit; fulness of limb seldom appears but about spring, when milk abounds: I have seen two or three muscular figures, but never a fat man. The neck is sinewy, the chest broad, the flank thin, and the stomach in-drawn; the legs, though fleshless, are well made, especially when the knee and ankle are not bowed by too early riding. The shins do not bend cucumber-like to the front as in the African race.[1] The arms are thin, with muscles like whipcords, and the hands and feet are, in point of size and delicacy, a link between Europe and India. As in the Celt, the Arab thumb is remarkably long, extending almost to the first joint of the index,[2] which, with its easy rotation, makes it a perfect prehensile instrument: the palm also is fleshless, small-boned, and

---

1 " Magnum inter Arabes et Africanos discrimen efficit η ουρη. Arabum parvula membra sicut nobilis æqui. Africanum tamen flaccum, crassum longumque: ita quiescens, erectum tamen parum distenditur. Argumentum validissimum est ad indagandam Egyptorum originem: Nilotica enim gens membrum habet Africanum."

2 Whereas the Saxon thumb is thick, flat, and short, extending scarcely half way to the middle joint of the index.

elastic. With his small active figure, it is not strange
that the wildest Badawi gait should be pleasing; he
neither unfits himself for walking, nor distorts his ankles
by turning out his toes according to the farcical rule of
fashion, and his shoulders are not dressed like a drill-
sergeant's, to throw all the weight of the body upon the
heels. Yet there is no slouch in his walk; it is light and
springy, and errs only in one point, sometimes becoming
a strut.

Such is the Badawi, and such he has been for ages.
The national type has been preserved by systematic
intermarriage. The wild men do not refuse their
daughters to a stranger, but the son-in-law would be
forced to settle among them, and this life, which has its
charms for a while, ends in becoming wearisome. Here
no evil results are anticipated from the union of first
cousins, and the experience of ages and of a mighty
nation may be trusted. Every Badawi has a right to
marry his father's brother's daughter before she is given
to a stranger; hence "cousin" (*Bint Amm*) in polite
phrase signifies a " wife.[1] " Our physiologists[2] adduce the
Sangre Azul of Spain and the case of the lower animals to
prove that degeneracy inevitably follows " breeding-in.[3] "

1 A similar unwillingness to name the wife may be found in some
parts of southern Europe, where probably jealousy or possibly Asiatic
custom has given rise to it. Among the Maltese it appears in a truly
ridiculous way, *e.g.*, "dice la mia moglie, *con rispetto parlando*, &c.,"
says the husband, adding to the word spouse a " saving your presence," as if he were speaking of something offensive.

2 Dr. Howe (Report on Idiotcy in Massachussetts, 1848,) asserts
that "the law against the marriage of relations is made out as clearly
as though it were written on tables of stone." He proceeds to show
that in seventeen households where the parents were connected by
blood, of ninety-five children one was a dwarf, one deaf, twelve scrof-
ulous, and forty-four idiots—total fifty-eight diseased!

3 Yet the celebrated " Flying Childers " and all his race were
remarkably bred in. There is still, in my humble opinion, much
mystery about the subject, to be cleared up only by the studies of
physiologists.

Either they have theorised from insufficient facts, or civilisation and artificial living exercise some peculiar influence, or Arabia is a solitary exception to a general rule. The fact which I have mentioned is patent to every Eastern traveller.

After this long description, the reader will perceive with pleasure that we are approaching an interesting theme, the first question of mankind to the wanderer—" What are the women like ?" Truth compels me to state that the women of the Hijazi Badawin are by no means comely. Although the Benu Amur boast of some pretty girls, yet they are far inferior to the high-bosomed beauties of Nijd. And I warn all men that if they run to Al-Hijaz in search of the charming face which appears in my sketch-book as " a Badawi girl," they will be bitterly disappointed : the dress was Arab, but it was worn by a fairy of the West. The Hijazi woman's eyes are fierce, her features harsh, and her face haggard ; like all people of the South, she soon fades, and in old age her appearance is truly witch-like. Withered crones abound in the camps, where old men are seldom seen. The sword and the sun are fatal to

" A green old age, unconscious of decay."

The manners of the Badawin are free and simple : " vulgarity " and affectation, awkwardness and embarrassment, are weeds of civilised growth, unknown to the People of the Desert.[1] Yet their manners are sometimes dashed with a strange ceremoniousness. When two friends meet, they either embrace or both extend the right hands, clapping palm to palm ; their foreheads are either pressed together, or their heads are moved from side to side, whilst for minutes together mutual inquiries are made and answered. It is a breach of decorum, even when eating, to turn the back upon a person, and if a Badawi

---

1 This sounds in English like an "Irish bull." I translate "Badu," as the dictionaries do, "a Desert."

does it, he intends an insult. When a man prepares coffee, he drinks the first cup: the *Sharbat Kajari* of the Persians, and the *Sulaymani* of Egypt,[1] render this precaution necessary. As a friend approaches the camp,—it is not done to strangers for fear of start- ling them,—those who catch sight of him shout out his name, and gallop up saluting with lances or firing matchlocks in the air. This is the well-known *La'ab al- Barut*, or gunpowder play. Badawin are generally polite in language, but in anger temper is soon shown, and, although life be in peril, the foulest epithets—dog, drunk- ard, liar, and infidel—are discharged like pistol-shots by both disputants.

The best character of the Badawi is a truly noble compound of determination, gentleness, and generosity. Usually they are a mixture of worldly cunning and great simplicity, sensitive to touchiness, good-tempered souls, solemn and dignified withal, fond of a jest, yet of a grave turn of mind, easily managed by a laugh and a soft word, and placable after passion, though madly revengeful after injury. It has been sarcastically said of the Benu-Harb that there is not a man

> " Que s'il ne violoit, voloit, tuoit, brûloit
> Ne fût assez bonne personne."

The reader will inquire, like the critics of a certain modern humourist, how the fabric of society can be supported by such material. In the first place, it is a kind of *société léonine*, in which the fiercest, the strongest, and the craftiest obtains complete mastery over his fellows, and this gives a

---

1 The Sharbat Kajari is the "Acquetta" of Persia, and derives its name from the present royal family. It is said to be a mixture of verdigris with milk; if so, it is a very clumsy engine of state policy. In Egypt and Mosul, Sulaymani (the common name for an Afghan) is used to signify "poison"; but I know not whether it be merely euphuistic or confined to some species. The banks of the Nile are infamous for these arts, and Mohammed Ali Pasha imported, it is said, professional poisoners from Europe.

keystone to the arch. Secondly, there is the terrible
blood-feud, which even the most reckless fear for their
posterity. And, thirdly, though the revealed law of the
Koran, being insufficient for the Desert, is openly disre-
garded, the immemorial customs of the *Kazi al-Arab* (the
Judge of the Arabs)[1] form a system stringent in the
extreme.

The valour of the Badawi is fitful and uncertain.
Man is by nature an animal of prey, educated by the complicated relations of society, but readily relapsing into his
old habits. Ravenous and sanguinary propensities grow
apace in the Desert, but for the same reason the reckless-
ness of civilisation is unknown there. Savages and semi-
barbarians are always cautious, because they have nothing
valuable but their lives and limbs. The civilised man, on
the contrary, has a hundred wants or hopes or aims, without which existence has for him no charms. Arab ideas
of bravery do not prepossess us. Their romances, full of
foolhardy feats and impossible exploits, might charm for a
time, but would not become the standard works of a really
fighting people.[2] Nor would a truly valorous race admire

---

1 Throughout the world the strictness of the Lex Scripta is in
inverse ratio to that of custom: whenever the former is lax, the
latter is stringent, and *vice versâ*. Thus in England, where law leaves
men comparatively free, they are slaves to a grinding despotism of
conventionalities, unknown in the land of tyrannical rule. This
explains why many men, accustomed to live under despotic governments, feel fettered and enslaved in the so-called free countries.
Hence, also, the reason why notably in a republic there is less private
and practical liberty than under a despotism, The "Kazi al-Arab"
(Judge of the Arabs) is in distinction to the Kazi al-Shara, or the
Kazi of the Koran. The former is, almost always, some sharp-
witted greybeard, wtth a minute knowledge of genealogy and prece-
dents, a retentive memory and an eloquent tongue.

2 Thus the Arabs, being decidedly a parsimonious people, indulge
in exaggerated praises and instances of liberality. Hatim Tai, whose
generosity is unintelligible to Europeans, becomes the Arab model of
the "open hand." Generally a high *beau idéal* is no proof of a people's
practical pre-eminence, and when exaggeration enters into it and

the cautious freebooters who safely fire down upon Caravans from their eyries.   Arab wars, too, are a succession
of skirmishes, in which five hundred men will retreat after
losing a dozen of their number.   In this partisan-fighting
the first charge secures a victory, and the vanquished fly
till covered by the shades of night.   Then come cries and
taunts of women, deep oaths, wild poetry, excitement, and
reprisals, which will probably end in the flight of the
former victor.   When peace is to be made, both parties
count up their dead, and the usual blood-money is paid for
excess on either side.   Generally, however, the feud
endures till, all becoming weary of it, some great man, as
the Sharif of Meccah, is called upon to settle the terms of
a treaty, which is nothing but an armistice.   After a few
months' peace, a glance or a word will draw blood, for
these hates are old growths, and new dissensions easily
shoot up from them.

   But, contemptible though their battles be, the Badawin are not cowards.   The habit of danger in raids and
blood-feuds, the continual uncertainty of existence,
the desert, the chase, the hard life and exposure to the
air, blunting the nervous system ; the presence and the
practice of weapons, horsemanship, sharpshooting, and
martial exercises, habituate them to look death in the
face like men, and powerful motives will make them
heroes.   The English, it is said, fight willingly for liberty, our neighbours for glory ; the Spaniard fights,
or rather fought, for religion and the *Pundonor ;* and
the Irishman fights for the fun of fighting.   Gain and
revenge draw the Arab's sword ; yet then he uses
it fitfully enough, without the gay gallantry of the

suits the public taste, a low standard of actuality may be fairly
suspected.   But to convince the oriental mind you must dazzle it.
Hence, in part, the superhuman courage of Antar, the liberality of
Hatim, the justice of Omar, and the purity of Laila and Majnun
under circumstances more trying than aught chronicled in Mathilde,
or in the newest American novel.

French or the persistent stay of the Anglo-Saxon. To become desperate he must have the all-powerful stimulants of honour and of fanaticism. Frenzied by the insults of his women, or by the fear of being branded as a coward, he is capable of any mad deed.[1] And the obstinacy produced by strong religious impressions gives a steadfastness to his spirit unknown to mere enthusiasm. The history of the Badawi tells this plainly. Some unobserving travellers, indeed, have mistaken his exceeding cautiousness for stark cowardice. The incongruity is easily read by one who understands the principles of Badawi warfare ; with them, as amongst the Red Indians, one death dims a victory. And though reckless when their passions are thoroughly aroused, though heedless of danger when the voice of honour calls them, the Badawin will not sacrifice themselves for light motives. Besides, they have, as has been said, another and a potent incentive to cautiousness. Whenever peace is concluded, they must pay for victory.

There are two things which tend to soften the ferocity of Badawi life. These are, in the first place, intercourse with citizens, who frequently visit and entrust their children to the people of the Black tents ; and, secondly, the social position of the women.

The Rev. Charles Robertson, author of a certain

1 At the battle of Bissel, when Mohammed Ali of Egypt broke the 40,000 guerillas of Faisal son of Sa'ud the Wahhabi, whole lines of the Benu Asir tribe were found dead and tied by the legs with ropes. This system of colligation dates from old times in Arabia, as the " Affair of Chains " (Zat al-Salasil) proves. It is alluded to by the late Sir Henry Elliot in his " Appendix to the Arabs in Sind,"—a work of remarkable sagacity and research. According to the "Beglar-Nameh," it was a "custom of the people of Hind and Sind, whenever they devote themselves to death, to bind themselves to each other by their mantles and waistbands." It seems to have been an ancient practice in the West as in the East : the Cimbri, to quote no other instances, were tied together with cords when attacked by Marius. Tactic truly worthy of savages to prepare for victory by expecting a defeat !

" Lecture on Poetry, addressed to Working Men," asserts
that Passion became Love under the influence of Christianity, and that the idea of a Virgin Mother spread over
the sex a sanctity unknown to the poetry or to the philosophy of Greece and Rome.[1] Passing over the objections
of deified Eros and Immortal Psyche, and of the Virgin
Mother—symbol of moral purity—being common to every
old and material faith,[2] I believe that all the noble tribes of
savages display the principle. Thus we might expect to
find, wherever the fancy, the imagination, and the ideality
are strong, some traces of a sentiment innate in the human
organisation. It exists, says Mr. Catlin, amongst the
North American Indians, and even the Gallas and the
Somal of Africa are not wholly destitute of it. But when
the barbarian becomes a semi-barbarian, as are the most
polished Orientals, or as were the classical authors of
Greece and Rome, then women fall from their proper place
in society, become mere articles of luxury, and sink into
the lowest moral condition. In the next stage, " civilisation," they rise again to be " highly accomplished," and
not a little frivolous.

---

1 Though differing in opinion, upon one subject, from the Rev.
Mr. Robertson, the lamented author of this little work, I cannot refrain from expressing the highest admiration of those noble thoughts,
those exalted views, and those polished sentiments which, combining
the delicacy of the present with the chivalry of a past age, appear in
a style
          "As smooth as woman and as strong as man."
Would that it were in my power to pay a more adequate tribute to
his memory!

2 Even Juno, in the most meaningless of idolatries, became,
according to Pausanias (lib. ii. cap. 38), a virgin once every year.
And be it observed that Al-Islam (the faith, not the practice) popularly decided to debase the social state of womankind, exalts it by
holding up to view no fewer than two examples of perfection in the
Prophet's household. Khadijah, his first wife, was a minor saint,
and the Lady Fatimah is supposed to have been spiritually unspotted
by sin, and materially ever a virgin, even after giving birth to Hasan
and to Hosayn.

Miss Martineau, when travelling through Egypt, once visited a harim, and there found, among many things, especially in ignorance of books and of book-making, materials for a heart-broken wail over the degradation of her sex. The learned lady indulges, too, in sundry strong and unsavoury comparisons between the harim and certain haunts of vice in Europe.

On the other hand, male travellers generally speak lovingly of the harim. Sonnini, no admirer of Egypt, expatiates on " the generous virtues, the examples of magnanimity and affectionate attachment, the sentiments ardent, yet gentle, forming a delightful unison with personal charms in the harims of the Mamluks."

As usual, the truth lies somewhere between the two extremes. Human nature, all the world over, differs but in degree. Everywhere women may be " capricious, coy, and hard to please " in common conjunctures : in the hour of need they will display devoted heroism. Any chronicler of the Afghan war will bear witness that warm hearts, noble sentiments, and an overflowing kindness to the poor, the weak, and the unhappy are found even in a harim. Europe now knows that the Moslem husband provides separate apartments and a distinct establishment for each of his wives, unless, as sometimes happens, one be an old woman and the other a child. And, confessing that envy, hatred, and malice often flourish in polygamy, the Moslem asks, Is monogamy open to no objections ? As far as my limited observations go, polyandry is the only state of society in which jealousy and quarrels about the sex are the exception and not the rule of life.

In quality of doctor I have seen a little and heard much of the harim. It often resembles a European home composed of a man, his wife, and his mother. And I have seen in the West many a " happy fireside " fitter to make Miss Martineau's heart ache than any harim in Grand Cairo.

Were it not evident that the spiritualising of sexuality by sentiment, of propensity by imagination, is universal among the highest orders of mankind,—*c'est l'étoffe de la nature que l'imagination a brodée*, says Voltaire,— I should attribute the origin of "love" to the influence of the Arabs' poetry and chivalry upon European ideas rather than to mediæval Christianity.   Certain "Fathers of the Church," it must be remembered, did not believe that women have souls.   The Moslems never went so far.

In nomad life, tribes often meet for a time, live together whilst pasturage lasts, and then separate perhaps for a generation.   Under such circumstances, youths who hold with the Italian that

> "Perduto e tutto il tempo
> Che in amor non si spende,"

will lose heart to maidens, whom possibly, by the laws of the clan, they may not marry,[1] and the light o' love will fly her home.   The fugitives must brave every danger, for revenge, at all times the Badawi's idol, now becomes the lodestar of his existence.   But the Arab lover will dare all consequences.   "Men have died and the worms have eaten them, but not for love," may be true in the West: it is false in the East.   This is attested in every tale where love, and not ambition, is the groundwork of the narrative.[2]   And nothing can be more tender, more

---

1 There is no objection to intermarriage between equal clans, but the higher will not give their daughters to the lower in dignity.

2 For instance: "A certain religious man was so deeply affected with the love of a king's daughter, that he was brought to the brink of the grave," is a favourite inscriptive formula.   Usually the hero "sickens in consequence of the heroine's absence, and continues to the hour of his death in the utmost grief and anxiety."   He rarely kills himself, but sometimes, when in love with a pretty infidel, he drinks wine and he burns the Koran.   The "hated rival" is not a formidable person; but there are for good reasons great jealousy of female friends, and not a little fear of the beloved's kinsmen.   Such are the material sentiments; the spiritual part is a thread of mysticism, upon which all the pearls of adventure and incident are strung.

pathetic than the use made of these separations and long
absences by the old Arab poets. Whoever peruses the
Suspended Poem of Labid, will find thoughts at once so
plaintive and so noble, that even Dr. Carlyle's learned
verse cannot wholly deface their charm.

The warrior-bard returns from afar. He looks upon
the traces of hearth and home still furrowing the Desert
ground. In bitterness of spirit he checks himself from
calling aloud upon his lovers and his friends. He melts
at the remembrance of their departure, and long indulges
in the absorbing theme. Then he strengthens himself by
the thought of Nawara's inconstancy, how she left him
and never thought of him again. He impatiently dwells
upon the charms of the places which detain her, advocates
flight from the changing lover and the false friend, and,
in the exultation with which he feels his swift dromedary
start under him upon her rapid course, he seems to seek
and finds some consolation for women's perfidy and
forgetfulness. Yet he cannot abandon Nawara's name or
memory. Again he dwells with yearning upon scenes of
past felicity, and he boasts of his prowess—a fresh
reproach to her,—of his gentle birth, and of his hospitality.
He ends with an encomium upon his clan, to which he
attributes, as a noble Arab should, all the virtues of man.
This is Goldsmith's deserted village in Al-Hijaz. But
the Arab, with equal simplicity and pathos, has a fire, a
force of language, and a depth of feeling, which the
Irishman, admirable as his verse is, could never rival.

As the author of the Peninsular War well remarks,
women in troubled times, throwing off their accustomed
feebleness and frivolity, become helpmates meet for man.
The same is true of pastoral life.[1] Here, between the

---

1 It is curious that these pastoral races, which supply poetry
with namby-pamby Colinades, figure as the great tragedians of
history. The Scythians, the Huns, the Arabs, and the Tartars were
all shepherds. They first armed themselves with clubs to defend
their flocks from wild beasts. Then they learned warfare, and im

extremes of fierceness and sensibility, the weaker sex,
remedying its great want, power, raises itself by courage,
physical as well as moral.   In the early days of Al-
Islam, if history be credible, Arabia had a race of
heroines.   Within the last century, Ghaliyah, the wife of
a Wahhabi chief, opposed Mohammed Ali himself in many
a bloody field.   A few years ago, when Ibn Asm, popularly called Ibn Rumi, chief of the Zubayd clan about
Rabigh, was treacherously slain by the Turkish general,
Kurdi Osman, his sister, a fair young girl, determined to
revenge him.   She fixed upon the "Arafat-day" of
pilgrimage for the accomplishment of her designs, dis-
guised herself in male attire, drew her kerchief in the form
Lisam over the lower part of her face, and with lighted
match awaited her enemy.   The Turk, however, was not
present, and the girl was arrested to win for herself a
local reputation equal to the "maid" of Salamanca.
Thus it is that the Arab has learned to swear that great
oath " by the honour of my women."

The Badawin are not without a certain Platonic affection, which they call *Hawá* (or *Ishk*) *uzri*—pardonable love.[1]
They draw the fine line between *amant* and *amoureux :* this
is derided by the towspeople, little suspecting how much
such a custom says in favour of the wild men.   Arabs,
like other Orientals, hold that, in such matters, man is
saved, not by faith, but by want of faith.   They have
also a saying not unlike ours—

"She partly is to blame who has been tried;
He comes too near who comes to be denied."

proved means of destruction by petty quarrels about pastures; and,
finally, united by the commanding genius of some skin-clad Cæsar
or Napoleon, they fell like avalanches upon those valleys of the
world—Mesopotamia, India, and Egypt—whose enervate races
offered them at once temptations to attack, and certainty of success.

1 Even amongst the Indians, as a race the least chivalrous of
men, there is an oath which binds two persons of different sex in the
tie of *friendship*, by making them brother and sister to each other.

The evil of this system is that they, like certain Southerns—*pensano sempre al male*—always suspect, which may be worldly-wise, and also always show their suspicions, which is assuredly foolish. For thus they demoralise their women, who might be kept in the way of right by self-respect and by a sense of duty.

From ancient periods of the Arab's history we find him practising knight-errantry, the wildest form of chivalry.[1] "The Songs of Antar," says the author of the "Crescent and the Cross," "show little of the true chivalric spirit." What thinks the reader of sentiments like these[2]? "This valiant man," remarks Antar (who was "ever interested for the weaker sex,") "hath defended the honour of women." We read in another place, "Mercy, my lord, is the noblest quality of the noble." Again, "it is the most ignominious of deeds to take free-born women prisoners." "Bear not malice, O Shibub," quoth the hero, "for of malice good never came." Is there no true greatness in this sentiment ?—"Birth is the boast of the *fainéant;* noble is the youth who beareth every ill, who clotheth himself in mail during the noontide heat, and who wandereth through the outer darkness of night." And why does the "knight of knights" love Ibla ? Because "she is blooming as the sun at dawn, with hair black as the midnight shades, with Paradise in her eye, her bosom an enchantment, and a form waving like the tamarisk when the soft wind blows from the hills of Nijd"? Yes! but his chest expands also with the thoughts of her "faith, purity, and affection,"—it is her moral as well as her material excellence that makes her

---

1 Richardson derives our "knight" from *Nikht* (نخت), a tilter with spears, and "Caitiff" from Khattaf, (خطّاف), a snatcher or ravisher.

2 I am not ignorant that the greater part of "Antar" is of modern and disputed origin. Still it accurately expresses Arab sentiment.

the hero's "hope, and hearing, and sight." Briefly, in
Antar I discern

> "a love exalted high,
> By all the glow of chivalry;"

and I lament to see so many intelligent travellers mis-
judging the Arab after a superficial experience of a few
debased Syrians or Sinaites. The true children of Antar,
my Lord Lindsay, have *not* " ceased to be gentlemen."

In the days of ignorance, it was the custom for
Badawin, when tormented by the tender passion, which
seems to have attacked them in the form of "possession,"
for long years to sigh and wail and wander, doing the
most truculent deeds to melt the obdurate fair. When
Arabia Islamized, the practice changed its element for
proselytism.

The Fourth Caliph is fabled to have travelled far,
redressing the injured, punishing the injurer, preaching
to the infidel, and especially protecting women—the chief
end and aim of knighthood. The Caliph Al-Mu'tasim
heard in the assembly of his courtiers that a woman of
Sayyid family had been taken prisoner by a " Greek barbarian " of Ammoria. The man on one occasion struck
her: when she cried " Help me, O Mu'tasim !" and the
clown said derisively, " Wait till he cometh upon his pied
steed !" The chivalrous prince arose, sealed up the wine-
cup which he held in his hand, took oath to do his knightly
devoir, and on the morrow started for Ammoria with seventy
thousand men, each mounted on a piebald charger.
Having taken the place, he entered it, exclaiming, " Labbayki, Labbayki !" — " Here am I at thy call !" He
struck off the caitiff's head, released the lady with his own
hands, ordered the cupbearer to bring the sealed bowl, and
drank from it, exclaiming, " Now, indeed, wine is good !"

To conclude this part of the subject with another far-
famed instance. When Al-Mutanabbi, the poet, prophet,
and warrior of Hams (A.H. 354) started together with his

son on their last journey, the father proposed to seek a
place of safety for the night. " Art thou the Mutanabbi,"
exclaimed his slave, " who wrote these lines,—

> "'I am known to the night, the wild, and the steed,
> To the guest, and the sword, to the paper and reed[1]'?"

The poet, in reply, lay down to sleep on Tigris' bank, in a
place haunted by thieves, and, disdaining flight, lost his
life during the hours of darkness.

It is the existence of this chivalry among the " Children of Antar " which makes the society of Badawin
("damned saints," perchance, and "honourable villains,")
so delightful to the traveller who like the late Haji Wali
(Dr. Wallin), understands and is understood by them.
Nothing more *naïve* than his lamentations at finding himself in the "loathsome company of Persians," or among
Arab townspeople, whose " filthy and cowardly minds "
he contrasts with the " high and chivalrous spirit of the
true Sons of the Desert." Your guide will protect you
with blade and spear, even against his kindred, and he
expects you to do the same for him. You may give a man
the lie, but you must lose no time in baring your sword.
If involved in dispute with overwhelming numbers, you
address some elder, *Dakhîl-ak ya Shaykh !*—(I am) thy protected, O Sir,—and he will espouse your quarrel with
greater heat and energy, indeed, than if it were his own.[2]
But why multiply instances ?

The language of love and war and all excitement is
poetry, and here, again, the Badawi excels. Travellers
complain that the wild men have ceased to sing. This is
true if "poet" be limited to a few authors whose existence

---

1 I wish that the clever Orientalist who writes in the Saturday
Review would not translate " Al-Layl," by *lenes sub nocte susurri :* the
Arab bard alluded to no such effeminacies.

2 The subject of "Dakhl" has been thoroughly exhausted by
Burckhardt and Layard. It only remains to be said that the Turks,
through ignorance of the custom, have in some cases made themselves contemptible by claiming the protection of women.

everywhere depends upon the accidents of patronage or political occurrences. A far stronger evidence of poetic feeling is afforded by the phraseology of the Arab, and the highly imaginative turn of his commonest expressions. Destitute of the poetic taste, as we define it, he certainly is : as in the Milesian, wit and fancy, vivacity and passion, are too strong for reason and judgment, the reins which guide Apollo's car.[1] And although the Badawin no longer boast a Labid or a Maysunah, yet they are passionately fond of their ancient bards.[2] A man skilful in reading Al-Mutanabbi and the suspended Poems would be received by them with the honours paid by civilisation to the travelling millionaire.[3] And their elders have a goodly store of ancient and modern war songs, legends, and love ditties which all enjoy.

1 It is by no means intended to push this comparison of the Arab's with the Hibernian's poetry. The former has an intensity which prevents our feeling that "there are too many flowers for the fruit"; the latter is too often a mere blaze of words, which dazzle and startle, but which, decomposed by reflection, are found to mean nothing. Witness
"The diamond turrets of Shadukiam,
    And the fragrant bowers of Amberabad!"

2 I am informed that the Benu Kahtan still improvise, but I never heard them. The traveller in Arabia will always be told that some remote clan still produces mighty bards, and uses in conversation the terminal vowels of the classic tongue, but he will not believe these assertions till personally convinced of their truth. The Badawi dialect, however, though debased, is still, as of yore, purer than the language of the citizens. During the days when philology was a passion in the East, those Stephens and Johnsons of Semitic lore, Firuzabadi and Al-Zamakhshari, wandered from tribe to tribe and from tent to tent, collecting words and elucidating disputed significations. Their grammatical expeditions are still remembered, and are favourite stories with scholars.

3 I say "skilful in reading," because the Arabs, like the Spaniards, hate to hear their language mangled by mispronunciation. When Burckhardt, who spoke badly, began to read verse to the Badawin, they could not refrain from a movement of impatience, and used to snatch the book out of his hands.

I cannot well explain the effect of Arab poetry to one who has not visited the Desert.[1] Apart from the pomp of words, and the music of the sound,[2] there is a dreaminess of idea and a haze thrown over the object, infinitely attractive, but indescribable. Description,

1 The civilized poets of the Arab cities throw the charm of the Desert over their verse, by images borrowed from its scenery—the dromedary, the mirage, and the well—as naturally as certain of our songsters, confessedly haters of the country, babble of lowing kine, shady groves, spring showers, and purling rills.

2 Some will object to this expression; Arabic being a harsh and guttural tongue. But the sound of language, in the first place, depends chiefly upon the articulator. Who thinks German rough in the mouth of a woman, with a suspicion of a lisp, or that English is the dialect of birds, when spoken by an Italian? Secondly, there is a music far more spirit-stirring in harshness than in softness: the languages of Castile and of Tuscany are equally beautiful, yet who does not prefer the sound of the former? The gutturality of Arabia is less offensive than that of the highlands of Barbary. Professor Willis, of Cambridge, attributes the broad sounds and the guttural consonants of mountaineers and the people of elevated plains to the physical action of cold. Conceding this to be a partial cause, I would rather refer the phenomenon to the habit of loud speaking, acquired by the dwellers in tents, and by those who live much in the open air. The Todas of the Neilgherry Hills have given the soft Tamil all the harshness of Arabic, and he who hears them calling to each other from the neighbouring peaks, can remark the process of broadening vowel and gutturalising consonant. On the other hand, the Gallas and the Persians, also a mountain-people, but in-habiting houses, speak comparatively soft tongues. The Cairenes actually omit some of the harshest sounds of Arabia, turning Makass into Ma'as, and Sakká into Sa'á. It is impossible to help remarking the bellowing of the Badawi when he first enters a dwell-ing-place, and the softening of the sound when he has become accustomed to speak within walls. Moreover, it is to be observed there is a great difference of articulation, not pronunciation, among the several Badawi clans. The Benu Auf are recognised by their sharp, loud, and sudden speech, which the citizens compare to the barking of dogs. The Benu Amr, on the contrary, speak with a soft and drawling sound. The Hutaym, in addition to other peculiarities, add a pleonastic "ah," to soften the termination of words, as A'atiní hawájiy*ah*, (for hawáiji), "Give me my clothes."

indeed, would rob the song of indistinctness, its essence. To borrow a simile from a sister art ; the Arab poet sets before the mental eye, the dim grand outlines of picture,—which must be filled up by the reader, guided only by a few glorious touches, powerfully standing out, and by the sentiment which the scene is intended to express ; —whereas, we Europeans and moderns, by stippling and minute touches, produce a miniature on a large scale so objective as to exhaust rather than to arouse reflection. As the poet is a creator, the Arab's is poetry, the European's versical description.[1] The language, "like a faithful wife, following the mind and giving birth to its offspring," and free from that "luggage of particles" which clogs our modern tongues, leaves a mysterious vagueness between the relation of word to word, which materially assists the sentiment, not the sense, of the poem. When verbs and nouns have, each one, many different significations, only the radical or general idea suggests itself.[2] Rich and varied synonyms, illustrating the finest shades of meaning, are artfully used ; now scattered to startle us by distinctness, now to form as it were a star about which dimly seen satellites revolve. And, to cut short a disquisition

---

1 The Germans have returned for inspiration to the old Eastern source. Rückert was guided by Jalal al-Din to the fountains of Sufyism. And even the French have of late made an inroad into Teutonic mysticism successfully enough to have astonished Racine and horrified La Harpe.

2 This, however, does not prevent the language becoming optionally most precise in meaning; hence its high philosophical character. The word "farz," for instance, means, radically "cutting," secondarily "ordering," or "paying a debt," after which come numerous meanings foreign to the primal sense, such as a shield, part of a tinder-box, an unfeathered arrow, and a particular kind of date. In theology it is limited to a single signification, namely, a divine command revealed in the Koran. Under these circumstances the Arabic becomes, in grammar, logic, rhetoric, and mathematics, as perfect and precise as Greek. I have heard Europeans complain that it is unfit for mercantile transactions.—Perhaps!

which might be prolonged indefinitely, there is in the Semitic dialect a copiousness of rhyme which leaves the poet almost unfettered to choose the desired expression.[1] Hence it is that a stranger speaking Arabic becomes poetical as naturally as he would be witty in French and philosophic in German. Truly spake Mohammed al-Damiri, " Wisdom hath alighted upon three things—the brain of the Franks, the hands of the Chinese, and the tongues of the Arabs."

The name of *Harami*—brigand—is still honourable among the Hijazi Badawin. Slain in raid or foray, a man is said to die *Ghandúr*, or a brave. He, on the other hand, who is lucky enough, as we should express it, to die in his bed, is called *Fatis* (carrion, the *corps crévé* of the Klephts) ; his weeping mother will exclaim, " O that my son had perished of a cut throat! " and her attendant crones will suggest, with deference, that such evil came of the will of Allah. It is told of the Lahabah, a sept of the Auf near Rabigh, that a girl will refuse even her cousin unless, in the absence of other opportunities, he plunder some article from the Hajj Caravan in front of the Pasha's links. Detected twenty years ago, the delinquent would have been impaled ; now he escapes with a rib-roasting. Fear of the blood-feud, and the certainty of a shut road to future travellers, prevent the Turks proceeding to extremes. They conceal their weakness by pretending that

---

1 As a general rule there is a rhyme at the end of every second line, and the unison is a mere fringe—a long *a*, for instance, throughout the poem sufficing for the delicate ear of the Arab. In this they were imitated by the old Spaniards, who, neglecting the consonants, merely required the terminating vowels to be alike. We speak of the " sort of harmonious simple flow which atones for the imperfect nature of the rhyme." But the fine organs of some races would be hurt by that ponderous unison which a people of blunter senses find necessary to produce an impression. The reader will feel this after perusing in " Percy's Reliques " Rio Verde! Rio Verde! and its translation.

the Sultan hesitates to wage a war of extermination with the thieves of the Holy Land.

It is easy to understand this respect for brigands. Whoso revolts against society requires an iron mind in an iron body, and these mankind instinctively admires, however misdirected be their energies. Thus, in all imaginative countries, the brigand is a hero; even the assassin who shoots his victim from behind a hedge appeals to the fancy in Tipperary or on the Abruzzian hills. Romance invests his loneliness with grandeur; if he have a wife or a friend's wife, romance becomes doubly romantic, and a tithe of the superfluity robbed from the rich and bestowed upon the poor will win to Gasparoni the hearts of a people. The true Badawi style of plundering, with its numerous niceties of honour and gentlemanly manners, gives the robber a consciousness of moral rectitude. "Strip off that coat, O certain person! and that turband," exclaims the highwayman, "they are wanted by the daughter of my paternal uncle (wife)." You will (of course, if necessary) lend ready ear to an order thus politely attributed to the wants of the fair sex. If you will add a few obliging expressions to the bundle, and offer Latro a cup of coffee and a pipe, you will talk half your toilette back to your own person; and if you can quote a little poetry, you will part the best of friends, leaving perhaps only a pair of sandals behind you. But should you hesitate, Latro, lamenting the painful necessity, touches up your back with the heel of his spear. If this hint suffice not, he will make things plain by the lance's point, and when blood shows, the tiger-part of humanity appears. Between Badawin, to be tamely plundered, especially of the mare,[1] is a lasting disgrace; a man of

---

1 In our knightly ages the mare was ridden only by jugglers and charlatans. Did this custom arise from the hatred of, and contempt for, the habits of the Arabs, imported into Europe by the Crusaders?

family lays down his life rather than yield even to over-powering numbers. This desperation has raised the courage of the Badawin to high repute amongst the settled Arabs, who talk of single braves capable, like the Homeric heroes, of overpowering three hundred men.

I omit general details about the often-described Sar, or Vendetta. The price of blood is $800 = 200*l*., or rather that sum imperfectly expressed by live stock. All the Khamsah or A'amam, blood relations of the slayer, assist to make up the required amount, rating each animal at three or four times its proper value. On such occasions violent scenes arise from the conflict of the Arab's two pet passions, avarice and revenge. The "avenger of blood" longs to cut the foe's throat. On the other hand, how let slip an opportunity of enriching himself? His covetousness is intense, as are all his passions. He has always a project of buying a new dromedary, or of investing capital in some marvellous colt; the conse-quence is, that he is insatiable. Still he receives blood-money with a feeling of shame ; and if it be offered to an old woman,—the most revengeful variety of our species, be it remarked,—she will dash it to the ground and clutch her knife, and fiercely swear by Allah that she will not "eat" her son's blood.

The Badawi considers himself a man only when mounted on horseback, lance in hand, bound for a foray or a fray, and carolling some such gaiety as—

> "A steede! a steede of matchlesse speede!
> A sword of metal keene!
> All else to noble minds is drosse,
> All else on earth is meane."

Even in his sports he affects those that imitate war. Preserving the instinctive qualities which lie dormant in civilisation, he is an admirable sportsman. The children,

---

Certainly the popular Eastern idea of a Frank was formed in those days, and survives to these.

men in miniature, begin with a rude system of gymnastics when they can walk. " My young ones play upon the backs of camels," was the reply made to me by a Jahayni Badawi when offered some Egyptian plaything. The men pass their time principally in hawking, shooting, and riding. The " Sakr,[1]" I am told, is the only falcon in general use ; they train it to pursue the gazelle, which

---

[1] Baron Von Hammer-Purgstall, in the " Falkner-Klee," calls this bird the " Saker-falke." Hence the French and English names sacre and saker. The learned John Beckmann (History of Inventions, Discoveries, and Origins : *sub voce*) derives falconry from India, where, " as early as the time of Ctesias, hares and foxes were hunted by means of rapacious birds." I believe, however, that no trace of this sport is found in the writings of the Hindus. Beckmann agrees with Giraldus, against other literati, that the ancient Greeks knew the art of hawking, and proves from Aristotle, that in Thrace men trained falcons. But Aristotle alludes to the use of the bird, as an owl is employed in Italy: the falcon is described as frightening, not catching the birds. Œlian corroborates Aristotle's testimony. Pliny, however, distinctly asserts that the hawks strike their prey down. " In Italy it was very common," says the learned Beckmann, " for Martial and Apuleius speak of it as a thing everywhere known. Hence the science spread over Europe, and reached perfection at the principal courts in the twelfth century." The Emperor Frederic II. wrote " De Arte Venandi cum Avibus," and the royal author was followed by a host of imitators in the vulgar tongue. Though I am not aware that the Hindus ever cultivated the art, Œlian, it must be confessed, describes their style of training falcons exactly similar to that in use among the modern Persians, Sindians, and Arabs. The Emperor Frederic owes the " capella," or hood to the Badawi, and talks of the " most expert falconers " sent to him with various kinds of birds by some of the kings of Arabia. The origin of falconry is ascribed by Al-Mas'udi, on the authority of Adham bin Muhriz, to the king Al-Haris bin Mu'awiyah, and in Dr. Sprenger's admirable translation the reader will find (pp. 426, 428), much information upon the subject. The Persians claim the invention for their Just King, Anushirawan, contemporary with Mohammed. Thence the sport passed into Turkey, where it is said the Sultans maintained a body of 6000 falconers. And Frederic Barbarossa, in the twelfth century, brought falcons to Italy. We may fairly give the honour of the invention to Central Asia.

greyhounds pull down when fatigued. I have heard much
of their excellent marksmanship, but saw only moderate
practice with a long matchlock rested and fired at standing objects. Double-barreled guns are rare amongst them.[1]
Their principal weapons are matchlocks and firelocks,
pistols, javelins, spears, swords, and the dagger called
Jambiyah ; the sling and the bow have long been given
up. The guns come from Egypt, Syria, and Turkey ; for
the Badawi cannot make, although he can repair, this
arm. He particularly values a good old barrel seven
spans long, and would rather keep it than his coat ; consequently, a family often boasts of four or five guns, which
descend from generation to generation. Their price varies
from two to sixty dollars. The Badawin collect nitre in
the country, make excellent charcoal, and import sulphur
from Egypt and India ; their powder, however, is coarse
and weak. For hares and birds they cut up into slugs a
bar of lead hammered out to a convenient size, and they
cast bullets in moulds. They are fond of ball-practice,
firing, as every sensible man does, at short distances, and
striving at extreme precision. They are ever backing
themselves with wagers, and will shoot for a sheep, the
loser inviting his friends to a feast : on festivals they boil
the head, and use it as mark and prize. Those who affect
excellence are said to fire at a bullet hanging by a thread ;
curious, however, to relate, the Badawin of Al-Hijaz have
but just learned the art, general in Persia and Barbary, of
shooting from horseback at speed.

Pistols have been lately introduced into the Hijaz,
and are not common amongst the Badawin. The citizens
incline to this weapon, as it is derived from Constantinople.
In the Desert a tolerable pair with flint locks may be
worth thirty dollars, ten times their price in England.

---

1 Here called "bandukiyah bi ruhayn," or the two-mouthed gun.
The leathern cover is termed "gushat"; it is a bag with a long-
fringed tassel at the top of the barrel, and a strap by which it is
slung to the owner's back.

The spears[1] called *Kanat*, or reeds, are made of male
bamboos imported from India.   They are at least twelve
feet long, iron shod, with a tapering point, beneath which
are one or two tufts of black ostrich feathers.[2] Besides the
Mirzak, or javelin, they have a spear called *Shalfah*, a
bamboo or a palm stick garnished with a head about the
breadth of a man's hand.

No good swords are fabricated in Al-Hijaz.   The
Khalawiyah and other Desert clans have made some poor
attempts at blades.   They are brought from Persia, India,
and Egypt ; but I never saw anything of value.

The *Darakah*, or shield, also comes from India.   It is
the common Cutch article, supposed to be made of rhinoc-
eros hide, and displaying as much brass knob and gold
wash as possible.   The Badawin still use in the remoter
parts *Diraa*, or coats of mail, worn by horsemen over buff
jackets.

The dagger is made in Al-Yaman and other places : it
has a vast variety of shapes, each of which, as usual, has its
proper names.   Generally they are but little curved
(whereas the *Gadaymi* of Al-Yaman and Hazramaut is almost
a semicircle), with tapering blade, wooden handle, and
scabbard of the same material overlaid with brass.   At the
point of the scabbard is a round knob, and the weapon is
so long, that a man when walking cannot swing his right

1 I have described elsewhere the Mirzak, or javelin.

2 Ostriches are found in Al-Hijaz, where the Badawin shoot after
coursing them.   The young ones are caught and tamed, and the eggs
may be bought in the Madinah bazar.   Throughout Arabia there is
a belief that the ostrich throws stones at the hunter.   The superstition may have arisen from the pebbles being flung up behind by the
bird's large feet in his rapid flight, or it may be a mere "foolery of
fancy."   Even in lands which have long given up animal-worship,
wherever a beast is conspicuous or terrible, it becomes the subject of
some marvellous tale.   So the bear in Persia imitates a moolah's
dress; the wolf in France is a human being transformed, and the
beaver of North America, also a metamorphosis, belts trees so as to
fell them in the direction most suitable to his after purpose.

arm. In narrow places he must enter sideways. But it is the mode always to appear in dagger, and the weapon, like the French soldier's *coupe-choux*, is really useful for such bloodless purposes as cutting wood and gathering grass. In price they vary from one to thirty dollars.

The Badawin boast greatly of sword-play; but it is apparently confined to delivering a tremendous slash, and to jumping away from the return-cut instead of parrying either with sword or shield. The citizens have learned the Turkish scimitar-play, which, in grotesqueness and general absurdity, rivals the East Indian school. None of these Orientals knows the use of the point which characterises the highest school of swordsmanship.

The Hijazi Badawin have no game of chance, and dare not, I am told, ferment the juice of the Daum palm, as proximity to Aden has taught the wild men of Al-Yaman.[1] Their music is in a rude state. The principal instrument is the Tabl, or kettle-drum, which is of two kinds: one, the smaller, used at festivals; the other, a large copper "tom-tom," for martial purposes, covered with leather, and played upon, pulpit-like, with fist, and not with stick. Besides which, they have the one-stringed Rubabah, or guitar, that "monotonous but charming instrument of the Desert." In another place I have described their dancing, which is an ignoble spectacle.

The Badawin of Al-Hijaz have all the knowledge necessary for procuring and protecting the riches of savage life. They are perfect in the breeding, the training, and the selling of cattle. They know sufficient of astronomy to guide themselves by night, and are ac-

---

1 Not that the "Agrebi" of Bir Hamid and other parts have much to learn of us in vice. The land of Al-Yaman is, I believe, the most demoralised country, and Sana'a the most depraved city in Arabia. The fair sex distinguishes itself by a peculiar laxity of conduct, which is looked upon with an indulgent eye. And the men drink and gamble, to say nothing of other peccadilloes, with perfect impunity.

quainted with the names of the principal stars. Their local memory is wonderful. And such is their instinct in the art of Ásár, or tracking, that it is popularly said of the Zubayd clan, which lives between Meccah and Al-Madinah, a man will lose a she-camel and know her four-year-old colt by its foot. Always engaged in rough exercises and perilous journeys, they have learned a kind of farriery and a simple system of surgery. In cases of fracture they bind on splints with cloth bands, and the patient drinks camel's milk and clarified butter till he is cured. Cuts are carefully washed, sprinkled with meal gunpowder, and sewn up. They dress gunshot wounds with raw camel's flesh, and rely entirely upon nature and diet. When bitten by snakes or stung by scorpions, they scarify the wound with a razor, recite a charm, and apply to it a dressing of garlic.[1] The wealthy have *Fiss* or ring-stones, brought from India, and used with a formula of prayer to extract venom. Some few possess the *Tariyak* (Theriack) of Al-Irak—the great counter-poison, internal as well as external, of the East. The poorer classes all wear the *Za'al* or *Hibas* of Al-Yaman ; two yarns of black sheep's wool tied round the leg, under the knee and above the ankle. When bitten, the sufferer tightens these cords above the injured part, which he immediately scarifies ; thus they act as tourniquets. These ligatures also cure cramps—and there is no other remedy. The Badawi knowledge of medicine is unusually limited in this part of Arabia, where even simples are not required by a people who rise with dawn, eat little, always breathe Desert air, and " at night make the camels their curfew." The great tonic is clarified butter, and the *Kay*, or actual cautery, is used even for rheumatism. This counter-irritant, together with a curious and artful phlebotomy,

---

1 In Al-Yaman, it is believed, that if a man eat three heads of garlic in good mountain-samn (or clarified butter) for forty days, his blood will kill the snake that draws it.

blood being taken, as by the Italians, from the toes, the fingers, and other parts of the body, are the Arab panaceas. They treat scald-head with grease and sulphur. Ulcers, which here abound, without, however, assuming the fearful type of the " *Helcoma Yemenense,*" are cauterised and stimulated by verdigris. The evil of which Fracastorius sang is combated by sudorifics, by unguents of oil and sulphur, and especially by the sand-bath. The patient, buried up to the neck, remains in the sun fasting all day ; in the evening he is allowed a little food. This rude course of " packing " lasts for about a month. It suits some constitutions ; but others, especially Europeans, have tried the sand-bath and died of fever. Mules' teeth, roasted and imperfectly pounded, remove cataract. Teeth are extracted by the farrier's pincers, and the worm which throughout the East is supposed to produce toothache, falls by fumigation. And, finally, after great fatigue, or when suffering from cold, the body is copiously greased with clarified butter and exposed to a blazing fire.

Mohammed and his followers conquered only the more civilised Badawin ; and there is even to this day little or no religion amongst the wild people, except those on the coast or in the vicinity of cities. The faith of the Badawi comes from Al-Islam, whose hold is weak. But his customs and institutions, the growth of his climate, his nature, and his wants, are still those of his ancestors, cherished ere Meccah had sent forth a Prophet, and likely to survive the day when every vestige of the Ka'abah shall have disappeared. Of this nature are the Hijazi's pagan oaths, his heathenish names (few being Moslem except " Mohammed "), his ordeal of licking red-hot iron, his Salkh, or scarification,—proof of manliness,—his blood revenge, and his eating carrion (*i.e.*, the body of an animal killed without the usual formula), and his lending his wives to strangers. All these I hold to be remnants of some old creed ; nor should I despair of finding among the Badawin bordering upon the Great Desert some lingering system of idolatry.

The Badawin of Al-Hijaz call themselves Shafe'i ; but what is put into the mouths of their brethren in the West applies equally well here. " We pray not, because we must drink the water of ablution ; we give no alms, because we ask them ; we fast not the Ramazan month, because we starve throughout the year ; and we do no pilgrimage, because the world is the House of Allah." Their blunders in religious matters supply the citizens with many droll stories. And it is to be observed that they do not, like the Greek pirates or the Italian bandits, preserve a religious element in their plunderings ; they make no vows, and they carefully avoid offerings.

The ceremonies of Badawi life are few and simple— circumcisions, marriages, and funerals. Of the former rite there are two forms, *Taharah*, as usual in Al-Islam, and *Salkh*, an Arab invention, derived from the times of Paganism.[1] During Wahhabi rule it was forbidden under pain of death, but now the people have returned to it. The usual age for *Taharah* is between five and six ; among

---

[1] Circumcisionis causa apud Arabos manifestissima, ulceratio enim endemica, abrasionem glandis aut præputii, maximâ cum facilitate insequitur. Mos autem quem vocant Arabes Al-Salkh (ٱلْسَّلْخِ *i.e.* scarificatio) virilitatem animumque ostendendi modus esse videtur. Exeunt amici paterque, et juvenem sub dio sedentem circumstant. Capit tunc pugionem tonsor et præputio abscisso detrahit pellem τῶν αἰδοίων καὶ τῶν κοιλίων ab umbilico incipiens aut parum infra, ventremque usque ad femora nudat. Juvenis autem dextrâ pugionem super tergum tonsoris vibrans magnâ clamat voce ولاتخاف واقطع *i. e.* cæde sine timore. Væ si hæsitet tonsor aut si tremeat manus ! Pater etiam filium si dolore ululet statim occidit. Re confectâ surgit juvenis et اَللّٰهُ أَكْبَرُ "Gloria Deo" intonans, ad tentoria tendit, statim nefando oppressus dolore humi procumbit. Remedia Sal, et الهرد (tumerica) ; cibus lac cameli. Nonnullos occidit ingens suppuratio, decem autem excoriatis supersunt plerumque octo : hi pecten habent nullum, ventremque pallida tegit cutis.

some classes, however, it is performed ten years later. On such occasions feastings and merrymakings take place, as at our christenings.

Women being a marketable commodity in barbarism as in civilisation, the youth in Al-Hijaz is not married till his father can afford to buy him a bride. There is little pomp or ceremony save firing of guns, dancing, singing, and eating mutton. The " settlement " is usually about thirty sound Spanish dollars,[1] half paid down, and the other owed by the bridegroom to the father, the brothers, or the kindred of his spouse. Some tribes will take animals in lieu of ready money. A man of wrath not contented with his bride, puts her away at once. If peaceably inclined, by a short delay he avoids scandal. Divorces are very frequent among Badawin, and if the settlement money be duly paid, no evil comes of them.[2]

The funerals of the wild men resemble those of the citizens, only they are more simple, the dead being buried where they die. The corpse, after ablution, is shrouded in any rags procurable ; and, women and hired weepers

---

[1] The Spanish dollar is most prized in Al-Hijaz; in Al-Yaman the Maria Theresa. The Spanish Government has refused to perpetuate its Pillar-dollar, which at one time was so great a favourite in the East. The traveller wonders how " Maria Theresas" still supply both shores of the Red Sea. The marvel is easily explained: the Austrians receive silver at Milan, and stamp it for a certain percentage. This coin was doubtless preferred by the Badawin for its superiority to the currency of the day: they make from it ornaments for their women and decorations for their weapons. The generic term for dollars is " Riyal Fransah."

[2] Torale, sicut est mos Judaicus et Persicus, non inspiciunt. Novæ nuptæ tamen maritus mappam manu capit : manè autem puellæ mater virginitatis signa viris mulieribusque domi ostendit eosque jubilare jubet quod calamitas domestica, sc. filia, intacta abiit. Si non ostendeant mappam, mæret domus, " prima enim Venus " in Arabiâ "debet esse cruenta." Maritus autem humanior, etiamsi absit sanguis, cruore palumbino mappam tingit et gaudium fingens cognatis parentibusque ostendit; paululum postea puellæ nonnullâ causâ dat divortium. Hic urbis et ruris mos idem est.

not being permitted to attend, it is carried to the grave by men only. A hole is dug, according to Moslem custom ; dry wood, which everywhere abounds, is disposed to cover the corpse, and an oval of stones surrounding a mound of earth keeps out jackals and denotes the spot. These Badawin have not, like the wild Sindis and Baluchis, favourite cemeteries, to which they transport their dead from afar.

The traveller will find no difficulty in living amongst the Hijazi Badawin. " Trust to their honour, and you are safe," as was said of the Crow Indians ; "to their honesty and they will steal the hair off your head." But the wanderer must adopt the wild man's motto, *omnia mea mecum porto ;* he must have good nerves, be capable of fatigue and hardship, possess some knowledge of drugs, shoot and ride well, speak Arabic and Turkish, know the customs by reading, and avoid offending against local prejudices, by causing himself, for instance, to be called *Taggáa.* The payment of a small sum secures to him a *Rafík,*[1] and this "friend," after once engaging in the task, will be faithful. " We have eaten salt together" *(Nahnu Malihin)* is still a bond of friendship : there are, however, some tribes who require to renew the bond every twenty-four hours, as otherwise, to use their own phrase, " the salt is not in their stomachs." Caution must be exercised in choosing a companion who has not too many blood feuds. There is no objection to carrying a copper watch and a pocket compass, and a Koran could be fitted with secret pockets for notes and pencil. Strangers should especially avoid handsome weapons ; these tempt the Badawin's cupidity more than gold. The other extreme, defencelessness, is equally objectionable. It is needless to say that the traveller must never be seen writing anything but charms, and must on no account sketch in public. He should be careful in questioning, and rather lead up

---

1 An explanation of this term will be found below.

XXV.—*The Badawin of Al-Hijaz.* 113

to information than ask directly. It offends some
Badawin, besides denoting ignorance and curiosity, to be
asked their names or those of their clans : a man may be
living incognito, and the tribes distinguish themselves
when they desire to do so by dress, personal appearance,
voice, dialect, and accentuation, points of difference plain
to the initiated. A few dollars suffice for the road, and if
you would be " respectable," a taste which I will not
deprecate, some such presents as razors and Tarbushes
are required for the chiefs.

The government of the Arabs may be called almost
an autonomy. The tribes never obey their Shaykhs,
unless for personal considerations, and, as in a civilised
army, there generally is some sharp-witted and brazen-
faced individual whose voice is louder than the general's.
In their leonine society the sword is the greater adminis-
trator of law.

Relations between the Badawi tribes of Al-Hijaz are
of a threefold character : they are either *Ashab, Kiman,* or
Akhwan.

Ashab, or " comrades," are those who are bound by
oath to an alliance offensive and defensive : they inter-
marry, and are therefore closely connected.

Kiman,[1] or foes, are tribes between whom a blood feud,
the cause and the effect of deadly enmity, exists.

Akhawat, or " brotherhood," denotes the tie between
the stranger and the Badawi, who asserts an immemorial
and inalienable right to the soil upon which his forefathers
fed their flocks. Trespass by a neighbour instantly causes
war. Territorial increase is rarely attempted, for if of a
whole clan but a single boy escape he will one day assert
his claim to the land, and be assisted by all the *Ashab,* or

---

1 It is the plural of "Kaum," which means "rising up in rebel-
lion or enmity against," as well as the popular signification, a
"people." In some parts of Arabia it is used for a "plundering
party."

allies of the slain.   By paying· to man, woman, or child,
a small sum, varying, according to your means, from a
few pence worth of trinkets to a couple of dollars, you
share bread and salt with the tribe, you and your horse
become *Dakhil* (protected), and every one must afford you
brother-help.   If tiaveller or trader attempt to pass
through the land without paying *Al-Akhawah* or *Al-Rifkah*,
as it is termed, he must expect to be plundered, and, resist-
ing, to be slain : it is no dishonour to pay it, and he clearly
is in the wrong who refuses to conform to custom.   The
Rafik, under different names, exists throughout this part
of the world ; at Sinai he was called a *Ghafir*, a *Rabia* in
Eastern Arabia, amongst the Somal an *Abban*, and by the
Gallas a *Mogasa*.   I have called the tax " black-mail"; it
deserves a better name, being clearly the rudest form of
those transit-dues and octrois which are in nowise improved by " progress."   The Ahl Bayt,[1] or dwellers in the
Black Tents, levy the tax from the Ahl Hayt, or the
People of Walls; that is to say, townsmen and villagers
who have forfeited right to be held Badawin.   It is demanded from bastard Arabs, and from tribes who, like
the Hutaym and the Khalawiyah, have been born basely
or have become " nidering."   And these people are obliged
to pay it at home as well as abroad.   Then it becomes a
sign of disgrace, and the pure clans, like the Benu Harb,
will not give their damsels in marriage to " brothers."

Besides this Akhawat-tax and the pensions by the
Porte to chiefs of clans, the wealth of the Badawi consists in his flocks and herds, his mare, and his weapons.
Some clans are rich in horses; others are celebrated for
camels; and not a few for sheep, asses, or greyhounds.
The Ahamidah tribe, as has been mentioned, possesses
few animals ; it subsists by plunder and by presents from

---

1 Bayt (in the plural Buyut) is used in this sense to denote the
tents of the nomades. "Bayt" radically means a "nighting-place";
thence a tent, a house, a lair, &c., &c.

pilgrims.   The principal wants of the country are sulphur,
lead, cloths of all kinds, sugar, spices, coffee, corn, and
rice.   Arms are valued by the men, and it is advisable to
carry a stock of Birmingham jewellery for the purpose of
conciliating womankind.   In exchange the Badawin give
sheep,[1] cattle, clarified butter, milk, wool, and hides, which
they use for water-bags, as the Egyptians and other
Easterns do potteries.   But as there is now a fair store of
dollars in the country, it is rarely necessary to barter.

The Arab's dress marks his simplicity; it gives him
a nationality, as, according to John Evelyn, "prodigious
breeches" did to the Swiss.   It is remarkably picturesque,
and with sorrow we see it now confined to the wildest
Badawin and a few Sharifs.   To the practised eye, a
Hijazi in Tarbush and Caftan is ridiculous as a Basque
or a Catalonian girl in a cachemire and a little chip.
The necessary dress of a man is his *Saub* (Tobe), a blue
calico shirt, reaching from neck to ankles, tight or loose-
sleeved, opening at the chest in front, and rather narrow
below; so that the wearer, when running, must either
hold it up or tuck it into his belt.   The latter article,
called *Hakw*, is a plaited leathern thong, twisted round
the waist very tightly, so as to support the back.   The
trousers and the *Futah*, or loin-cloth of cities, are looked
upon as signs of effeminacy.   In cold weather the chiefs
wear over the shirt an *Abá*, or cloak.   These garments
are made in Nijd and the Eastern districts; they are of
four colours, white, black, red, and brown-striped.   The
best are of camels' hair, and may cost fifteen dollars; the
worst, of sheep's wool, are worth only three; both are
cheap, as they last for years.   The *Mahramah* (head-cloth)
comes from Syria; which, with Nijd, supplies also the
Kufiyah or headkerchief.   The *Ukal*,[2] fillets bound over

1 Some tribes will not sell their sheep, keeping them for guests
or feasts.

2 So the word is pronounced at Meccah.   The dictionaries give
"Aakál," which in Eastern Arabia is corrupted to "Igál."

the kerchief, are of many kinds; the Bishr tribe near Meccah make a kind of crown like the gloria round a saint's head, with bits of wood, in which are set pieces of mother-o'-pearl. Sandals, too, are of every description, from the simple sole of leather tied on with thongs, to the handsome and elaborate chaussure of Meccah ; the price varies from a piastre to a dollar, and the very poor walk barefooted. A leathern bandoleer, called *Majdal*, passed over the left shoulder, and reaching to the right hip, supports a line of brass cylinders for cartridges.[1] The other cross-belt (*Al-Masdar*), made of leather ornamented with brass rings, hangs down at the left side, and carries a *Kharizah*, or hide-case for bullets. And finally, the *Hizam*, or waist-belt, holds the dagger and extra cartridge cases. A Badawi never appears in public unarmed.

Women wear, like their masters, dark blue cotton Tobes, but larger and looser. When abroad they cover the head with a *Yashmak* of black stuff, or a poppy-coloured *Burká* (nose-gay) of the Egyptian shape. They wear no pantaloons, and they rarely affect slippers or sandals. The hair is twisted into *Majdul*, little pig-tails, and copiously anointed with clarified butter. The rich perfume the skin with rose and cinnamon-scented oils, and adorn the hair with Al-Shayh (*Absinthium*), sweetest herb of the Desert ; their ornaments are bracelets, collars, ear and nose-rings of gold, silver, or silver-gilt. The poorer classes have strings of silver coins hung round the neck.

The true Badawi is an abstemious man, capable of living for six months on ten ounces of food per diem ; the milk of a single camel, and a handful of dates, dry or fried in clarified butter, suffice for his wants. He despises the obese and all who require regular and plentiful meals, sleeps on a mat, and knows neither luxury nor comfort, freezing during one quarter and frying for three quarters of the year. But though he can endure hunger, like all

---

1 Called "Tatarif," plural of Tatrifah, a cartridge.

J Brandard.   C.F. Kell, Lith.

THE PRETTY BADAWI GIRL.

savages, he will gorge when an opportunity offers. I
never saw the man who could refrain from water upon
the line of march; and in this point they contrast disadvantageously with the hardy Wahhabis of the East,
and the rugged mountaineers of Jabal Shammar. They
are still " acridophagi," and even the citizens far prefer a
dish of locusts to the *Fasikh*, which act as anchovies, sar-
dines, and herrings in Egypt. They light a fire at night,
and as the insects fall dead they quote this couplet to
justify their being eaten—
> "We are allowed two carrions and two bloods,
> The fish and locust, the liver and the spleen.[1]"

Where they have no crops to lose, the people are
thankful for a fall of locusts. In Al-Hijaz the flights are
uncertain; during the last five years Al-Madinah has
seen but few. They are prepared for eating by boiling in
salt water and drying four or five days in the sun: a
"wet" locust to an Arab is as a snail to a Briton. The
head is plucked off, the stomach drawn, the wings and
the prickly part of the legs are plucked, and the insect is
ready for the table. Locusts are never eaten with sweet
things, which would be nauseous: the dish is always
" hot," with salt and pepper, or onions fried in clarified
butter, when it tastes nearly as well as a plate of stale
shrimps.

The favourite food on the line of march is meat cut
into strips and sun-dried. This, with a bag of milk-balls[2]

---

1 The liver and the spleen are both supposed to be "congealed
blood." Niebuhr has exhausted the names and the description of the
locust. In Al-Hijaz they have many local and fantastic terms: the
smallest kind, for instance, is called *Jarad Iblis*, Satan's locust.

2 This is the Kurut of Sind and the Kashk of Persia. The
butter-milk, separated from the butter by a little water, is simmered
over a slow fire, thickened with wheaten flour, about a handful to a
gallon, well-mixed, so that no knots remain in it, and allowed to cool.
The mixture is then put into a bag and strained, after which salt is
sprinkled over it. The mass begins to harden after a few hours,
when it is made up into balls and dried in the sun.

and a little coffee, must suffice for journey or campaign. The Badawin know neither fermented nor distilled liquors, although *Ikhs ya 'l Khammar!* (Fie upon thee, drunkard!) is a popular phrase, preserving the memory of another state of things. Some clans, though not all, smoke tobacco. It is generally the growth of the country called Hijazi or Kazimiyah ; a green weed, very strong, with a foul smell, and costing about one piastre per pound. The Badawin do not relish Persian tobacco, and cannot procure Latakia : it is probably the pungency of the native growth offending the delicate organs of the Desert-men, that caused nicotiana to be proscribed by the Wahhabis, who revived against its origin a senseless and obsolete calumny.

The almost absolute independence of the Arabs, and of that noble race the North American Indians of a former generation, has produced a similarity between them worthy of note, because it may warn the anthropologist not always to detect in coincidence of custom identity of origin. Both have the same wild chivalry, the same fiery sense of honour, and the same boundless hospitality : elopements from tribe to tribe, the blood feud, and the Vendetta are common to the two. Both are grave and cautious in demeanour, and formal in manner,—princes in rags or paint. The Arabs plunder pilgrims ; the Indians, bands of trappers ; both glory in forays, raids, and cattle-lifting ; and both rob according to certain rules. Both are alternately brave to desperation, and shy of danger. Both are remarkable for nervous and powerful eloquence ; dry humour, satire, whimsical tales, frequent tropes ; boasts, and ruffling style ; pithy proverbs, extempore songs, and languages wondrous in their complexity. Both, recognising no other occupation but war and the chase, despise artificers and the effeminate people of cities, as the game-cock spurns the vulgar roosters of the poultry-yard.[1] The

---

[1] The North American trappers adopted this natural prejudice :

chivalry of the Western wolds, like that of the Eastern wilds, salutes the visitor by a charge of cavalry, by discharging guns, and by wheeling around him with shouts and yells. The "brave" stamps a red hand upon his mouth to show that he has drunk the blood of a foe. Of the Utaybah "Harami" it is similarly related, that after mortal combat he tastes the dead man's gore.

Of these two chivalrous races of barbarians, the Badawi claims our preference on account of his treatment of women, his superior development of intellect, and the glorious page of history which he has filled.

The tribes of Al-Hijaz are tediously numerous : it will be sufficient to enumerate the principal branches of the Badawi tree, without detailing the hundred little offshoots which it has put forth in the course of ages.[1]

Those ancient clans the Abs and Adnan have almost died out. The latter, it is said, still exists in the neighbourhood of Taif ; and the Abs, I am informed, are to be found near Kusayr (Cosseir), on the African coast, but not in Al-Hijaz. Of the Aus, Khazraj, and Nazir details have been given in a previous chapter. The Benu Harb is now the ruling clan in the Holy Land. It is divided by genealogists into two great bodies, first, the Benu Salim, and, secondly, the Masruh,[2] or "roaming tribes."

the "free trapper" called his more civilized *confrère*, "mangeur de lard."

1 Burckhardt shrank from the intricate pedigree of the Meccan Sharifs. I have seen a work upon the subject in four folio volumes in point of matter equivalent to treble the number in Europe. The best known genealogical works are Al-Kalkashandi (originally in seventy-five books, extended to one hundred) ; the Umdat al-Tullab by Ibn Khaldun ; the "Tohfat al-Arab fi Ansar al-Arab," a well-known volume by Al-Siyuti ; and, lastly, the Sirat al-Halabi, in six volumes 8vo. Of the latter work there is an abridgment by Mohammed al-Banna al-Dimyati in two volumes 8vo. ; but both are rare, and consequently expensive.

2 I give the following details of the Harb upon the authority of my friend Omar Effendi, who is great in matters of genealogy.

The Benu Salim, again, have eight subdivisions, viz. :—

1. Ahamidah (Ahmadi)[1]: this clan owns for chief, Shaykh Sa'ad of the mountains. It is said to contain about 3500 men. Its principal sub-clan is the Hadari.
2. Hawazim (Hazimi), the rival tribe, 3000 in number : it is again divided into Muzayni and Zahiri.
3. Sobh (Sobhi), 3500, habitat near Al-Badr.
4. Salaymah (Salimi), also called Aulad Salim.
5. Sa'adin (Sa'adani).
6. Mahamid (Mahmadi), 8000.
7. Rahalah (Rihayli), 1000.
8. Timam (Tamimi).

The Masruh tree splits into two great branches, Benu Auf, and Benu Amur.[2]   The former is a large clan, extending from Wady Nakia وادى نقـيـﻊ near Njd, to Rabigh and Al-Madinah. They have few horses, but many dromedaries, camels, and sheep, and are much feared by the people, on account of their warlike and savage character. They separate into ten sub-divisions, viz. :—

1. Sihliyah (Sihli), about 2000 in number.
2. Sawaid (Sa'idi), 1000.
3. Rukhasah (Rakhis).
4. Kassanin (Kassan) : this sub-clan claims origin from the old " Gassan " stock, and is found in considerable numbers at Wady Nakia and other places near Al-Madinah.
5. Ruba'ah (Rabai).
6. Khazarah (Khuzayri).
7. Lahabah (Lahaybi), 1500 in number.
8. Faradah (Faradi).
9. Benu Ali (Alawi).
10. Zubayd (Zubaydi), near Meccah, a numerous clan of fighting thieves.

Also under the Benu Amur—as the word is popularly pronounced—are ten sub-families.

1. Marabitah (Murabti).   They principally inhabit the
2. Hussar (Hasir).   lands about Al-Fara الفرع a
3. Benu Jabir (Jabiri).   collection of settlements four

---

1 The first word is the plural, the second the singular form of the word.
2 In the singular Aufi and Amri.

4. Rabaykah (Rubayki).   marches South of Al-Madinah, number about 10,000 men, and have droves of sheep and camels but few horses.
5. Hisnan (Hasuni).
6. Bizan (Bayzani).
7. Badarin (Badrani).
8. Biladiyah (Biladi).
9. Jaham (the singular and plural forms are the same).
10. Shatarah (Shitayri).[1]

The great Anizah race now, I was told, inhabits Khaybar, and it must not visit Al-Madinah without a Rafik or protector. Properly speaking there are no outcasts in Al-Hijaz, as in Al-Yaman and the Somali country. But the Hitman (pl. of Hutaym or Hitaym), inhabiting the sea-board about Yambu', are taxed by other Badawin as low and vile of origin. The unchastity of the women is connived at by the men, who, however, are brave and celebrated as marksmen: they make, eat, and sell cheese, for which reason that food is despised by the Harb. And the Khalawiyah (pl. of Khalawi) are equally despised ; they are generally blacksmiths, have a fine breed of greyhounds, and give asses as a dowry, which secures for them the derision of their fellows.

Mr. C. Cole, H. B. M.'s Vice-Consul at Jeddah, was kind enough to collect for me notices of the different tribes in Central and Southern Hijaz. His informants divide the great clan Juhaynah living about Yambu' and Yambu' al-Nakhl into five branches, viz. :—

1. Benu Ibrahimah, in number about 5000.
2. Ishran, 700.
3. Benu Malik, 6000.

---

[1] To these Mr. Cole adds seven other sub-divisions, viz. :—
1. Ahali al-Kura (" the people of Kura ? "), 5000.
2. Radadah, 800.
3. Hijlah, 600.
4. Dubayah, 1500.
5. Benu Kalb, 2000.
6. Bayzanah, 800.
7. Benu Yahya, 800.

And he makes the total of the Benu Harb about Al-Jadaydah amount to 35,000 men. I had no means of personally ascertaining the correctness of this information.

4. Arwah, 5000.
5. Kaunah, 3000.

Thus giving a total of 19,700 men capable of carrying arms.[1]

The same gentleman, whose labours in Eastern Arabia during the coast survey of the "Palinurus" are well known to the Indian world, gives the following names of the tribes under allegiance to the Sharif of Meccah.

  1. Sakif (Thakif) al-Yaman, 2000.
  2. Sakif al-Sham,[2] 1000.
  3. Benu Malik, 6000.
  4. Nasirah, 3000.
  5. Benu Sa'ad, 4000.
  6. Huzayh (Hudhayh), 5000.
  7. Bakum (Begoum), 5000.
  8. Adudah, 500.
  9. Bashar, 1000.
  10. Sa'id, 1500.
  11. Zubayd, 4000.
  12. Aydah, 1000.

The following is a list of the Southern Hijazi tribes, kindly forwarded to me by the Abbé Hamilton, after his return from a visit to the Sharif at Taif.

  1. Ghamid al-Badawy ("of the nomades"), 30,000.
  2. Ghamid al-Hazar ("the settled"), 40,000.
  3. Zahran, 38,000.
  4. Benu Malik, 30,000.
  5. Nasirah, 15,000.
  6. Asir, 40,000.
  7. Tamum, } together, 80,000.
  8. Bilkarn, }
  9. Benu Ahmar, 10,000.
  10. Utaybah, living north of Meccah : no number given.
  11. Shu'abin.
  12. Daraysh, 2000.

1 The reader will remember that nothing like exactitude in numbers can be expected from an Arab. Some rate the Benu Harb at 6000; others, equally well informed, at 15,000; others again at 80,000. The reason of this is that, whilst one is speaking of the whole race, another may be limiting it to his own tribe and its immediate allies.

2 "Sham" which, properly speaking, means Damascus or Syria, in Southern Arabia and Eastern Africa is universally applied to Al-Hijaz.

13. Benu Sufyan, 15,000.
14. Al-Hullad, 3000.

It is evident that the numbers given by this traveller include the women, and probably the children of the tribes. Some exaggeration will also be suspected.

The principal clans which practise the pagan Salkh, or excoriation, are, in Al-Hijaz, the Huzayl and the Benu Sufyan, together with the following families in Al-Tahamah:

1. Juhadilah.
2. Kabakah.
3. Benu Fahm.
4. Benu Mahmud.
5. Saramu (?)
6. Majarish.
7. Benu Yazid.

I now take leave of a subject which cannot but be most uninteresting to English readers.

CHAPTER XXVI.

WE have now left the territory of Al-Madinah. Al-Suwayrkiyah, which belongs to the Sharif of Meccah, is about twenty-eight miles distant from Hijriyah, and by dead reckoning ninety-nine miles along the road from the Prophet's burial-place. Its bearing from the last station was S. W. 11°. The town, consisting of about one hundred houses, is built at the base and on the sides of a basaltic mass, which rises abruptly from the hard clayey plain. The summit is converted into a rude fortalice—without one, no settlement can exist in Al-Hijaz—by a bulwark of uncut stone, piled up so as to make a parapet. The lower part of the town is protected by a mud wall, with the usual semicircular towers. Inside there is a bazar, well supplied with meat (principally mutton) by the neighbouring Badawin; and wheat, barley, and dates are grown near the town. There is little to describe in the narrow streets and the mud houses, which are essentially Arab. The fields around are divided into little square plots by earthen ridges and stone walls; some of the palms are fine-grown trees, and the wells appear numerous. The water is near the surface and plentiful, but it has a brackish taste, highly disagreeable after a few days' use, and the effects are the reverse of chalybeate.

The town belongs to the Benu Hosayn, a race of

R. Burton. delt.

C.F. Kell. Lith.

THE VILLAGE AL-SUWAYRKIYAH.

schismatics mentioned in the foregoing pages. They claim the allegiance of the Badawi tribes around, principally Mutayr, and I was informed that their fealty to the Prince of Meccah is merely nominal.

The morning after our arrival at Al-Suwayrkiyah witnessed a commotion in our little party: hitherto they had kept together in fear of the road. Among the number was one Ali bin Ya Sin, a perfect " old man of the sea." By profession he was a " Zemzemi," or dispenser of water from the Holy Well,[1] and he had a handsome " palazzo " at the foot of Abu Kubays in Meccah, which he periodically converted into a boarding-house. Though past sixty, very decrepit, bent by age, white-bearded, and toothless, he still acted cicerone to pilgrims, and for that purpose travelled once every year to Al-Madinah. These trips had given him the cunning of a veteran voyageur. He lived well and cheaply; his home-made Shugduf, the model of comfort, was garnished with soft cushions and pillows, whilst from the pockets protruded select bottles of pickled limes and similar luxuries; he had his travelling Shishah (water-pipe),[2] and at the halting-place, disdaining the crowded, reeking tent, he had a contrivance for converting his vehicle into a habitation. He was a type of the Arab old man. He mumbled all day and three-quarters of the night, for he had *des insomnies.* His nerves were so fine, that if any

---

1 There are certain officers called Zemzemi, who distribute the holy water. In the case of a respectable pilgrim they have a large jar of the shape described in Chap. iv., marked with his names and titles, and sent every morning to his lodgings. If he be generous, one or more will be placed in the Harim, that men may drink in his honour. The Zemzemi expects a present varying from five to eleven dollars.

2 The shishah, smoked on the camel, is a tin canister divided into two compartments, the lower half for the water, the upper one for the tobacco. The cover is pierced with holes to feed the fire, and a short hookah-snake projects from one side.

one mounted his Shugduf, the unfortunate was condemned to lie like a statue. Fidgety and priggishly neat, nothing annoyed him so much as a moment's delay or an article out of place, a rag removed from his water-gugglet, or a cooking-pot imperfectly free from soot ; and I judged his avarice by observing that he made a point of picking up and eating the grains scattered from our pomegranates, exclaiming that the heavenly seed (located there by Arab superstition) might be one of those so wantonly wasted.

Ali bin Ya Sin, returning to his native city, had not been happy in his choice of a companion this time. The other occupant of the handsome Shugduf was an ignoble-faced Egyptian from Al-Madinah. This ill-suited pair clave together for awhile, but at Al-Suwayrkiyah some dispute about a copper coin made them permanent foes. With threats and abuse such as none but an Egyptian could tamely hear, Ali kicked his quondam friend out of the vehicle. But terrified, after reflection, by the possibility that the man, now his enemy, might combine with two or three Syrians of our party to do him a harm, and frightened by a few black looks, the senior determined to fortify himself by a friend. Connected with the boy Mohammed's family, he easily obtained an introduction to me; he kissed my hand with great servility, declared that his servant had behaved disgracefully; and begged my protection together with an occasional attendance of my "slave."

This was readily granted in pity for the old man, who became immensely grateful. He offered at once to take Shaykh Nur into his Shugduf. The Indian boy had already reduced to ruins the frail structure of his Shib-riyah by lying upon it lengthways, whereas prudent travellers sit in it cross-legged and facing the camel. Moreover, he had been laughed to scorn by the Badawin, who seeing him pull up his dromedary to mount and dis-mount, had questioned his sex, and determined him to be a woman of the "Miyan.¹" I could not rebuke them; the poor fellow's timidity was a ridiculous contrast to the Badawi's style of mounting; a pull at the camel's head, the left foot placed on the neck, an agile spring, and a scramble into the saddle. Shaykh Nur, elated by the sight of old Ali's luxuries, promised himself some joyous hours ; but next morning he owned with a sigh that he had purchased splendour at the extravagant price of happiness—the senior's tongue never rested throughout the livelong night.

During our half-halt at Al-Suwayrkiyah we determined to have a small feast ; we bought some fresh dates, and we paid a dollar and a half for a sheep. Hungry travellers consider "liver and fry" a dish to set before a Shaykh. On this occasion, however, our enjoyment was marred by the water ; even Soyer's dinners would scarcely charm if washed down with cups of a certain mineral-spring found at Epsom.

We started at ten A.M. (Monday, 5th September) in a South-Easterly direction, and travelled over a flat, thinly dotted with Desert vegetation. At one P.M we passed a basaltic ridge ; and then, entering a long depressed line of country, a kind of valley, paced down it five tedious hours. The Samum as usual was blowing hard, and it seemed to affect the travellers' tempers. In one place I saw a Turk, who could not speak a word of Arabic, violently disputing with an Arab who could not understand a word of Turkish. The pilgrim insisted upon adding to the camel's load a few dry sticks, such as are picked up for cooking. The camel-man as perseveringly threw off the extra burthen. They screamed with rage, hustled each other, and at last the Turk dealt the Arab a heavy blow. I afterwards heard that the pilgrim was mortally wounded that night, his stomach being ripped

---

1 The Hindustani "sir." Badawin address it slightingly to Indians, Chapter xii.

open with a dagger. On enquiring what had become of
him, I was assured that he had been comfortably wrapped
up in his shroud, and placed in a half-dug grave. This is
the general practice in the case of the poor and solitary,
whom illness or accident incapacitates from proceeding.
It is impossible to contemplate such a fate without horror:
the torturing thirst of a wound,[1] the burning sun heating
the brain to madness, and—worst of all, for they do not
wait till death—the attacks of the jackal, the vulture, and
the raven of the wild.

At six P.M., before the light of day had faded, we
traversed a rough and troublesome ridge. Descending
it our course lay in a southerly direction along a road
flanked on the left by low hills of red sandstone and bright
porphyry. About an hour afterwards we came to a
basalt field, through whose blocks we threaded our way
painfully and slowly, for it was then dark. At eight P.M.
the camels began to stumble over the dwarf dykes of the
wheat and barley fields, and presently we arrived at our
halting-place, a large village called Al-Sufayna. The
plain was already dotted with tents and lights. We found
the Baghdad Caravan, whose route here falls into the Darb
al-Sharki. It consists of a few Persians and Kurds, and
collects the people of North-Eastern Arabia, Wahhabis
and others. They are escorted by the Agayl tribe and by
the fierce mountaineers of Jabal Shammar. Scarcely was
our tent pitched, when the distant pattering of musketry
and an ominous tapping of the kettle-drum sent all my
companions in different directions to enquire what was
the cause of quarrel. The Baghdad Cafilah, though not
more than 2000 in number, men, women and children, had
been proving to the Damascus Caravan, that, being perfectly ready to fight, they were not going to yield any
point of precedence. From that time the two bodies

---

1 When Indians would say "he was killed upon the spot," they
use the picturesque phrase, "he asked not for water."

encamped in different places. I never saw a more pug-
nacious assembly : a look sufficed for a quarrel. Once a
Wahhabi stood in front of us, and by pointing with his
finger and other insulting gestures, showed his hatred
to the chibuk, in which I was peaceably indulging. It
was impossible to refrain from chastising his insolence by
a polite and smiling offer of the offending pipe. This
made him draw his dagger without a thought; but it was
sheathed again, for we all cocked our pistols, and these
gentry prefer steel to lead. We had travelled about
seventeen miles, and the direction of Al-Sufayna from our
last halting place was South-East five degrees. Though
it was night when we encamped, Shaykh Mas'ud set out
to water his moaning camels : they had not quenched
their thirst for three days. He returned in a depressed
state, having been bled by the soldiery at the well to the
extent of forty piastres, or about eight shillings.

After supper we spread our rugs and prepared to
rest. And here I first remarked the coolness of the
nights, proving, at this season of the year, a considerable altitude above the sea. As a general rule the atmosphere stagnated between sunrise and ten A.M., when
a light wind rose. During the forenoon the breeze
strengthened, and it gradually diminished through the
afternoon. Often about sunset there was a gale accompanied by dry storms of dust. At Al-Sufayna, though
there was no night-breeze and little dew, a blanket was
necessary, and the hours of darkness were invigorating
enough to mitigate the effect of the sand and Samum-
ridden day. Before sleeping I was introduced to a name-
sake, one Shaykh Abdullah, of Meccah. Having committed his Shugduf to his son, a lad of fourteen, he had
ridden forward on a dromedary, and had suddenly fallen
ill. His objects in meeting me were to ask for some
medicine, and for a temporary seat in my Shugduf; the
latter I offered with pleasure, as the boy Mohammed was

longing to mount a camel. The Shaykh's illness was
nothing but weakness brought on by the hardships of the
journey : he attributed it to the hot wind, and to the
weight of a bag of dollars which he had attached to his
waist-belt. He was a man about forty, long, thin, pale,
and of a purely nervous temperament ; and a few questions elicited the fact that he had lately and suddenly
given up his daily opium pill. I prepared one for him,
placed him in my litter, and persuaded him to stow away
his burden in some place where it would be less troublesome. He was my companion for two marches, at the end
of which he found his own Shugduf. I never met amongst
the Arab citizens a better bred or a better informed
man. At Constantinople he had learned a little French,
Italian, and Greek ; and from the properties of a shrub
to the varieties of honey,[1] he was full of " useful knowledge," and openable as a dictionary. We parted near
Meccah, where I met him only once, and then accidentally,
in the Valley of Muna.

At half-past five A.M. on Tuesday, the 6th of September, we arose refreshed by the cool, comfortable night,
and loaded the camels. I had an opportunity of inspect-
ing Al-Sufayna. It is a village of fifty or sixty mud-
walled, flat-roofed houses, defended by the usual rampart.
Around it lie ample date-grounds, and fields of wheat,
barley, and maize. Its bazar at this season of the year
is well supplied : even fowls can be procured.

We travelled towards the South-East, and entered a
country destitute of the low ranges of hill, which from
Al-Madinah southwards had bounded the horizon. After

---

1 The Arabs are curious in and fond of honey : Meccah alone
affords eight or nine different varieties. The best, and in Arab parlance the "coldest," is the green kind, produced by bees that feed
upon a thorny plant called "sihhah." The white and red honeys
rank next. The worst is the Asal Asmar (brown honey), which sells
for something under a piastre per pound. The Abyssinian mead is
unknown in Al-Hijaz, but honey enters into a variety of dishes.

a two miles' march our camels climbed up a precipitous ridge, and then descended into a broad gravel plain. From ten to eleven A.M. our course lay southerly over a high table-land, and we afterwards traversed, for five hours and a half, a plain which bore signs of standing water. This day's march was peculiarly Arabia. It was a desert peopled only with echoes,—a place of death for what little there is to die in it,—a wilderness where, to use my companion's phrase, there is nothing but He.[1] Nature scalped, flayed, discovered all her skeleton to the gazer's eye. The horizon was a sea of mirage; gigantic sand-columns whirled over the plain; and on both sides of our road were huge piles of bare rock, standing detached upon the surface of sand and clay. Here they appeared in oval lumps, heaped up with a semblance of symmetry; there a single boulder stood, with its narrow foundation based upon a pedestal of low, dome-shapen rock. All were of a pink coarse-grained granite, which flakes off in large crusts under the influence of the atmosphere. I remarked one block which could not measure fewer than thirty feet in height. Through these scenes we travelled till about half-past four P.M., when the guns suddenly roared a halt. There was not a trace of human habitation around us: a few parched shrubs and the granite heaps were the only objects diversifying the hard clayey plain. Shaykh Mas'ud correctly guessed the cause of our detention at the inhospitable "halting-place of the Mutayr" (Badawin). "Cook your bread and boil your coffee," said the old man; "the camels will rest for awhile, and the gun will sound at nightfall."

We had passed over about eighteen miles of ground; and our present direction was South-west twenty degrees of Al-Sufayna.

At half-past ten that evening we heard the signal for

---

1 " La Siwa Hu," *i.e.*, where there is none but Allah.

departure, and, as the moon was still young, we prepared for a hard night's work. We took a south-westerly course through what is called a Wa'ar—rough ground covered with thicket. Darkness fell upon us like a pall. The camels tripped and stumbled, tossing their litters like cockboats in a short sea ; at times the Shugdufs were well nigh torn off their backs. When we came to a ridge worse than usual, old Mas'ud would seize my camel's halter, and, accompanied by his son and nephew bearing lights, encourage the animals with gesture and voice. It was a strange, wild scene. The black basaltic field was dotted with the huge and doubtful forms of spongy-footed camels with silent tread, looming like phantoms in the midnight air ; the hot wind moaned, and whirled from the torches flakes and sheets of flame and fiery smoke, whilst ever and anon a swift-travelling Takht-rawan, drawn by mules, and surrounded by runners bearing gigantic mashals or cressets,[1] threw a passing glow of red light upon the dark road and the dusky multitude. On this occasion the rule was " every man for himself." Each pressed forward into the best path, thinking only of preceding his neighbour. The Syrians, amongst whom our little party had become entangled, proved most unpleasant companions : they often stopped the way, insisting upon their right to precedence. On one occasion a horseman had the audacity to untie the halter of my dromedary, and thus to cast us adrift, as it were, in order to make room for some excluded friend. I seized my sword ; but Shaykh Abdullah stayed my hand, and addressed the intruder in terms sufficiently violent to make him slink away. Nor was this the only occasion on which my

---

1 This article, an iron cylinder with bands, mounted on a long pole, corresponds with the European cresset of the fifteenth century. The Pasha's cressets are known by their smell, a little incense being mingled with the wood. By this means the Badawin discover the dignitary's place.

companion was successful with the Syrians. He would begin with a mild "Move a little, O my father!" followed, if fruitless, by "Out of the way, O Father of Syria[1]!" and if still ineffectual, advancing to a "Begone, O he!" This ranged between civility and sternness. If without effect, it was supported by revilings to the "Abusers of the Salt," the "Yazid," the "Offspring of Shimr." Another remark which I made about my companion's conduct well illustrates the difference between the Eastern and the Western man. When traversing a dangerous place, Shaykh Abdullah the European attended to his camel with loud cries of "Hai! Hai[2]!" and an occasional switching. Shaykh Abdullah the Asiatic commended himself to Allah by repeated ejaculations of *Yá Sátir ! Yá Sattár[3] !*

---

[1] "Abu Sham," a familiar address in Al-Hijaz to Syrians. They are called "abusers of the salt," from their treachery, and "offspring of Shimr" (the execrated murderer of the Imam Hosayn), because he was a native of that country. Such is the detestation in which the Shi'ah sect, especially the Persians, hold Syria and the Syrians, that I hardly ever met with a truly religious man who did not desire a general massacre of the polluted race. And history informs us that the plains of Syria have repeatedly been drenched with innocent blood shed by sectarian animosity. Yet Jalal al-Din (History of Jerusalem) says, " As to Damascus, all learned men fully agree that it is the most eminent of cities after Meccah and Al-Madinah." Hence its many titles, "the Smile of the Prophet," the "Great Gate of Pilgrimage," "Sham Sharif," the "Right Hand of the Cities of Syria," &c., &c. And many sayings of Mohammed in honour of Syria are recorded. He was fond of using such Syriac words as "Bakh[un]! Bakh[un]!" to Ali, and "Kakh[un]! Kakh[un]!" to Hosayn. I will not enter into the curious history of the latter word, which spread to Egypt, and, slightly altered, passed through Latin mythology into French, English, German, Italian, and other modern European tongues.

[2] There is a regular language to camels. "Ikh! ikh!" makes them kneel; "Yáhh! Yáhh!" urges them on; "Hai! Hai!" induces caution, and so on.

[3] Both these names of the Almighty are of kindred origin. The

The morning of Wednesday (September 7th) broke as we entered a wide plain. In many places were signs of water : lines of basalt here and there seamed the surface, and wide sheets of the tufaceous gypsum called by the Arabs *Sabkhah* shone like mirrors set in the russet framework of the flat. This substance is found in cakes, often a foot long by an inch in depth, curled by the sun's rays and overlying clay into which water had sunk. After our harassing night, day came on with a sad feeling of oppression, greatly increased by the unnatural glare :—

> "In vain the sight, dejected to the ground,
> Stoop'd for relief: thence hot ascending streams
> And keen reflection pain'd."

We were disappointed in our expectations of water, which usually abounds near this station, as its name, *Al-Ghadir*, denotes. At ten A.M. we pitched the tent in the first convenient spot, and we lost no time in stretching our cramped limbs upon the bosom of mother Earth. From the halting-place of the Mutayr to Al-Ghadir is a march of about twenty miles, and the direction southwest twenty-one degrees. Al-Ghadir is an extensive plain, which probably presents the appearance of a lake after heavy rains. It is overgrown in parts with Desert vegetation, and requires nothing but a regular supply of water to make it useful to man. On the East it is bounded by a wall of rock, at whose base are three wells, said to have been dug by the Caliph Harun. They are guarded by a Burj, or tower, which betrays symptoms of decay.

In our anxiety to rest we had strayed from the Damascus Caravan amongst the mountaineers of Shammar. Our Shaykh Mas'ud manifestly did not like the company ; for shortly after three P.M. he insisted upon our striking the tent and rejoining the Hajj, which lay encamped about two miles distant in the western part of the basin. We

---

former is generally used when a woman is in danger of exposing her face by accident, or an animal of falling.

loaded, therefore, and half an hour before sunset found ourselves in more congenial society. To my great disappointment, a stir was observable in the Caravan. I at once
understood that another night-march was in store for us.

At six P.M. we again mounted, and turned towards
the Eastern plain. A heavy shower was falling upon the
Western hills, whence came damp and dangerous blasts.
Between nine P.M. and the dawn of the next day we had
a repetition of the last night's scenes, over a road so
rugged and dangerous, that I wondered how men could
prefer to travel in the darkness. But the camels of Damascus were now worn out with fatigue; they could not
endure the sun, and our time was too precious for a halt.
My night was spent perched upon the front bar of my
Shugduf, encouraging the dromedary; and that we had
not one fall excited my extreme astonishment. At five
A.M. (Thursday, 8th September) we entered a wide plain
thickly clothed with the usual thorny trees, in whose
strong grasp many a Shugduf lost its covering, and not a
few were dragged with their screaming inmates to the
ground. About five hours afterwards we crossed a high
ridge, and saw below us the camp of the Caravan, not
more than two miles distant. As we approached it, a
figure came running out to meet us. It was the boy Mohammed, who, heartily tired of riding a dromedary with
his friend, and possibly hungry, hastened to inform my
companion Abdullah that he would lead him to his Shugduf and to his son. The Shaykh, a little offended by the
fact that for two days not a friend nor an acquaintance
had taken the trouble to see or to inquire about him, received Mohammed roughly; but the youth, guessing the
grievance, explained it away by swearing that he and all
the party had tried in vain to find us. This wore the
semblance of truth: it is almost impossible to come upon
any one who strays from his place in so large and motley
a body.

At eleven A.M. we had reached our station. It is about twenty-four miles from Al-Ghadir, and its direction is South-east ten degrees.   It is called Al-Birkat (the Tank), from a large and now ruinous cistern built of hewn stone by the Caliph Harun.¹ The land belongs to the Utaybah Badawin, the bravest and most ferocious tribe in Al-Hijaz ; and the citizens denote their dread of these banditti by asserting that to increase their courage they drink their enemy's blood.²   My companions shook their heads when questioned upon the subject, and prayed that we might not become too well acquainted with them—an ill-omened speech!

The Pasha allowed us a rest of five hours at Al-Birkat: we spent them in my tent, which was crowded with Shaykh Abdullah's friends.   To requite me for this inconvenience, he prepared for me an excellent water-pipe, a cup of coffee, which, untainted by cloves and by cinnamon, would have been delicious, and a dish of dry fruits. As we were now near the Holy City, all the Meccans were busy canvassing for lodgers and offering their services to pilgrims.   Quarrels, too, were of hourly occurrence.   In our party was an Arnaut, a white-bearded old man, so

1 A "birkat" in this part of Arabia may be an artificial cistern or a natural basin; in the latter case it is smaller than a " ghadir." This road was a favourite with Harun al-Rashid, the pious tyrant who boasted that every year he performed either a pilgrimage or a crusade.   The reader will find in d'Herbelot an account of the celebrated visit of Harun to the Holy Cities.   Nor less known in Oriental history is the pilgrimage of Zubaydah Khatun (wife of Harun and mother of Amin) by this route.

2 Some believe this literally, others consider it a phrase expressive of blood-thirstiness.   It is the only suspicion of cannibalism, if I may use the word, now attaching to Al-Hijaz.   Possibly the disgusting act may occasionally have taken place after a stern fight of more than usual rancour.   Who does not remember the account of the Turkish officer licking his blood after having sabred the corpse of a Russian spy?   It is said that the Mutayr and the Utaybah are not allowed to enter Meccah, even during the pilgrimage season.

decrepit that he could scarcely stand, and yet so violent
that no one could manage him but his African slave, a
brazen-faced little wretch about fourteen years of age.
Words were bandied between this angry senior and
Shaykh Mas'ud, when the latter insinuated sarcastically,
that if the former had teeth he would be more intelligible.
The Arnaut in his rage seized a pole, raised it, and delivered a blow which missed the camel-man, but, which
brought the striker headlong to the ground. Mas'ud exclaimed, with shrieks of rage, "Have we come to this,
that every old-woman Turk smites us?" Our party had
the greatest trouble to quiet the quarrelers. The Arab
listened to us when we threatened him with the Pasha.
But the Arnaut, whose rage was "like red-hot steel," would
hear nothing but our repeated declarations, that unless
he behaved more like a pilgrim, we should be compelled
to leave him and his slave behind.

At four P.M. we left Al-Birkat, and travelled Eastwards over rolling ground thickly wooded. There was a
network of footpaths through the thickets, and clouds
obscured the moon; the consequence was inevitable loss
of way. About 2 A.M. we began ascending hills in a
south-westerly direction, and presently we fell into the
bed of a large rock-girt Fiumara, which runs from east to
west. The sands were overgrown with saline and sal-
solaceous plants; the Coloquintida, which, having no
support, spreads along the ground[1]; the Senna, with its
small green leaf; the Rhazya stricta[2]; and a large luxuri-
ant variety of the Asclepias gigantea,[3] cottoned over with

1 Coloquintida is here used, as in most parts of the East, medi-
cinally. The pulp and the seeds of the ripe fruit are scooped out,
and the rind is filled with milk, which is exposed to the night air,
and drunk in the morning.

2 Used in Arabian medicine as a refrigerant and tonic. It
abounds in Sind and Afghanistan, where, according to that most
practical of botanists, the lamented Dr. Stocks, it is called "ishwarg.'

3 Here called Ashr. According to Seetzen it bears the long-

mist and dew.   At 6 A.M. (Sept. 9th) we left the Fiumara,
and, turning to the West, we arrived about an hour afterwards at the station.   Al-Zaribah, "the valley," is an
undulating plain amongst high granite hills.   In many
parts it was faintly green; water was close to the surface,
and rain stood upon the ground.   During the night we
had travelled about twenty-three miles, and our present
station was south-east 56° from our last.

Having pitched the tent and eaten and slept, we prepared to perform the ceremony of *Al-Ihram* (assuming the
pilgrim-garb), as Al-Zaribah is the Mikat, or the appointed place.[1]   Between the noonday and the afternoon
prayers a barber attended to shave our heads, cut our
nails, and trim our mustachios.   Then, having bathed
and perfumed ourselves,—the latter is a questionable

---

sought apple of Sodom.   Yet, if truth be told, the soft green bag is
as unlike an apple as can be imagined; nor is the hard and brittle
yellow rind of the ripe fruit a whit more resembling.   The Arabs
use the thick and acrid milk of the green bag with steel filings as a
tonic, and speak highly of its effects; they employ it also to intoxi-
cate or narcotise monkeys and other animals which they wish to
catch.   It is esteemed in Hindu medicine.   The Nubians and Indians
use the filaments of the fruit as tinder; they become white and shining as floss-silk.   The Badawin also have applied it to a similar purpose.   Our Egyptian travellers call it the "Silk-tree"; and in Northern
Africa, where it abounds, Europeans make of it stuffing for the
mattresses, which are expensive, and highly esteemed for their coolness and cleanliness.   In Bengal a kind of gutta percha is made by
boiling the juice.   This weed, so common in the East, may one day
become in the West an important article of commerce.

1 "Al-Ihram" literally meaning "prohibition" or "making
unlawful," equivalent to our "mortification," is applied to the
ceremony of the toilette, and also to the dress itself.   The vulgar
pronounce the word "heram," or "l'ehram."   It is opposed to
"ihlal," "making lawful" or "returning to laical life."   The further
from Meccah it is assumed, provided that it be during the three
months of Hajj, the greater is the religious merit of the pilgrim;
consequently some come from India and Egypt in the dangerous
attire.   Those coming from the North assume the pilgrim-garb at or
off the village of Rabigh.

J. Brandard.

C.F. Kell, Lith.

THE PILGRIM'S COSTUME.

point,—we donned the attire, which is nothing but two new cotton cloths, each six feet long by three and a half broad, white, with narrow red stripes and fringes: in fact, the costume called *Al-Eddeh*, in the baths at Cairo.[1] One of these sheets, technically termed the *Rida*, is thrown over the back, and, exposing the arm and shoulder, is knotted at the right side in the style *Wishah*. The *Izar* is wrapped round the loins from waist to knee,and, knotted or tucked in at the middle, supports itself. Our heads were bare, and nothing was allowed upon the instep.[2] It is said that some clans of Arabs still preserve this religious but most uncomfortable costume; it is doubtless of ancient date, and to this day, in the regions lying west of the Red Sea, it continues to be the common dress of the people.

After the toilette, we were placed with our faces in the direction of Meccah, and ordered to say aloud,[3] "I vow this Ihram of Hajj (the pilgrimage) and the Umrah (the Little pilgrimage) to Allah Almighty!" Having thus performed a two-bow prayer, we repeated, without rising from the sitting position, these words, "O Allah! verily I purpose the Hajj and the Umrah, then enable me to accomplish the two, and accept them both of me, and make both blessed to me!" Followed the *Talbiyat*, or exclaiming—

"Here I am! O Allah! here am I—
No partner hast Thou, here am I;
Verily the praise and the grace are Thine, and the empire—

1 These sheets are not positively necessary; any clean cotton cloth not sewn in any part will serve equally well. Servants and attendants expect the master to present them with an "ihram."

2 Sandals are made at Meccah expressly for the pilgrimage: the poorer classes cut off the upper leathers of an old pair of shoes.

3 This Niyat, as it is technically called, is preferably performed aloud. Some authorities, however, direct it to be meditated *sotto-voce.*

No partner hast Thou, here am I[1]!"
And we were warned to repeat these words as often as
possible, until the conclusion of the ceremonies. Then
Shaykh Abdullah, who acted as director of our con-
sciences, bade us be good pilgrims, avoiding quarrels,
immorality, bad language, and light conversation. We
must so reverence life that we should avoid killing game,
causing an animal to fly, and even pointing it out for destruction[2]; nor should we scratch ourselves, save with the
open palm, lest vermin be destroyed, or a hair uprooted by
the nail. We were to respect the sanctuary by sparing the
trees, and not to pluck a single blade of grass. As regards
personal considerations, we were to abstain from all oils,
perfumes, and unguents; from washing the head with
mallow or with lote leaves; from dyeing, shaving, cutting,
or vellicating a single pile or hair; and though we might
take advantage of shade, and even form it with upraised
hands, we must by no means cover our sconces. For
each infraction of these ordinances we must sacrifice a
sheep[3]; and it is commonly said by Moslems that none

---

1 "Talbiyat" is from the word Labbayka ("here I am") in
the cry—
    "Labbayk' Allahumma, Labbayk'!
(Labbayka)   Lá Sharíka laka, Labbayk'!
    Inna 'l-hamda wa 'l ni'amata laka wa 'l mulk!
    La Sharika laka, Labbayk'!"
Some add, "Here I am, and I honour thee, I the son of thy two
slaves: beneficence and good are all between thy hands." A single
Talbiyah is a "Shart" or positive condition, and its repetition is a
Sunnat or Custom of the Prophet. The "Talbiyat" is allowed in
any language, but is preferred in Arabic. It has a few varieties;
the form above given is the most common.

2 The object of these ordinances is clearly to inculcate the
strictest observance of the "truce of God." Pilgrims, however, are
allowed to slay, if necessary, "the five noxious," viz., a crow, a kite,
a scorpion, a rat, and a biting dog.

3 The victim is sacrificed as a confession that the offender deems
himself worthy of death: the offerer is not allowed to taste any
portion of his offering.

but the Prophet could be perfect in the intricacies of pilgrimage. Old Ali began with an irregularity: he declared that age prevented his assuming the garb, but that, arrived at Meccah, he would clear himself by an offering.

The wife and daughters of a Turkish pilgrim of our party assumed the Ihram at the same time as ourselves. They appeared dressed in white garments; and they had exchanged the Lisam, that coquettish fold of muslin which veils without concealing the lower part of the face, for a hideous mask, made of split, dried, and plaited palm-leaves, with two "bulls'-eyes" for light.[1] I could not help laughing when these strange figures met my sight, and, to judge from the shaking of their shoulders, they were not less susceptible to the merriment which they had caused.

At three P.M. we left Al-Zaribah, travelling towards the South-West, and a wondrously picturesque scene met the eye. Crowds hurried along, habited in the pilgrim-garb, whose whiteness contrasted strangely with their black skins; their newly shaven heads glistening in the sun, and their long black hair streaming in the wind. The rocks rang with shouts of *Labbayk! Labbayk!* At a pass we fell in with the Wahhabis, accompanying the Baghdad Caravan, screaming "Here am I"; and, guided by a large loud kettle-drum, they followed in double file the camel of a standard-bearer, whose green flag bore in huge white letters the formula of the Moslem creed. They were wild-looking mountaineers, dark and fierce, with hair twisted into thin Dalik or plaits: each was armed with a long spear, a matchlock, or a dagger. They were seated upon coarse wooden saddles, without cushions or stirrups, a fine saddle-cloth alone denoting a

---

1 The reason why this "ugly" must be worn, is, that a woman's veil during the pilgrimage ceremonies is not allowed to touch her face.

chief.   The women emulated the men; they either guided
their own dromedaries, or, sitting in pillion, they clung to
their husbands; veils they disdained, and their counten-
ances certainly belonged not to a "soft sex."   These
Wahhabis were by no means pleasant companions.   Most
of them were followed by spare dromedaries, either un-
laden or carrying water-skins, fodder, fuel, and other
necessaries for the march.   The beasts delighted in
dashing furiously through our file, which being lashed
together, head and tail, was thrown each time into the
greatest confusion.   And whenever we were observed
smoking, we were cursed aloud for Infidels and Idolaters.

Looking back at Al-Zaribah, soon after our departure, I saw a heavy nimbus settle upon the hill-tops,
a sheet of rain being stretched between it and the plain.
The low grumbling of thunder sounded joyfully in our
ears.   We hoped for a shower, but were disappointed by
a dust-storm, which ended with a few heavy drops.
There arose a report that the Badawin had attacked a
party of Meccans with stones, and the news caused men
to look exceeding grave.

At five P.M. we entered the wide bed of the Fiumara,
down which we were to travel all night.   Here the
country falls rapidly towards the sea, as the increasing
heat of the air, the direction of the watercourses, and
signs of violence in the torrent-bed show.   The Fiumara
varies in breadth from a hundred and fifty feet to three-
quarters of a mile; its course, I was told, is towards the
South-West, and it enters the sea near Jeddah.   The
channel is a coarse sand, with here and there masses of
sheet rock and patches of thin vegetation.

At about half-past five P.M. we entered a suspicious-
looking place.   On the right was a stony buttress, along
whose base the stream, when there is one, swings; and
to this depression was our road limited by the rocks and
thorn trees which filled the other half of the channel.

The left side was a precipice, grim and barren, but not so
abrupt as its brother. Opposite us the way seemed
barred by piles of hills, crest rising above crest into the
far blue distance. Day still smiled upon the upper peaks,
but the lower slopes and the Fiumara bed were already
curtained with grey sombre shade.

A damp seemed to fall upon our spirits as we
approached this Valley Perilous. I remarked that the
voices of the women and children sank into silence, and
the loud Labbayk of the pilgrims were gradually stilled.
Whilst still speculating upon the cause of this phenomenon,
it became apparent. A small curl of the smoke, like a
lady's ringlet, on the summit of the right-hand precipice,
caught my eye; and simultaneous with the echoing crack
of the matchlock, a high-trotting dromedary in front of
me rolled over upon the sands,—a bullet had split its
heart,—throwing the rider a goodly somersault of five or
six yards.

Ensued terrible confusion; women screamed, children
cried, and men vociferated, each one striving with might
and main to urge his animal out of the place of death.
But the road being narrow, they only managed to jam
the vehicles in a solid immovable mass. At every matchlock shot, a shudder ran through the huge body, as when
the surgeon's scalpel touches some more sensitive nerve.
The Irregular horsemen, perfectly useless, galloped up
and down over the stones, shouting to and ordering one
another. The Pasha of the army had his carpet spread
at the foot of the left-hand precipice, and debated over
his pipe with the officers what ought to be done. No
good genius whispered "Crown the heights."

Then it was that the conduct of the Wahhabis
found favour in my eyes. They came up, galloping their
camels,—

"Torrents less rapid, and less rash,—"
with their elf-locks tossing in the wind, and their flaring

matches casting a strange lurid light over their features.
Taking up a position, one body began to fire upon the
Utaybah robbers, whilst two or three hundred, dismounting, swarmed up the hill under the guidance of the
Sharif Zayd. I had remarked this nobleman at Al-
Madinah as a model specimen of the pure Arab. Like
all Sharifs, he is celebrated for bravery, and has killed
many with his own hand.[1] When urged at Al-Zaribah
to ride into Meccah, he swore that he would not leave
the Caravan till in sight of the walls; and, fortunately
for the pilgrims, he kept his word. Presently the firing
was heard far in our rear, the robbers having fled. The
head of the column advanced, and the dense body of
pilgrims opened out. Our forced halt was now exchanged
for a flight. It required much management to steer our
Desert-craft clear of danger; but Shaykh Mas'ud was
equal to the occasion. That many were not, was evident
by the boxes and baggage that strewed the shingles. I
had no means of ascertaining the number of men killed
and wounded: reports were contradictory, and exaggeration unanimous. The robbers were said to be a hundred
and fifty in number; their object was plunder, and they
would eat the shot camels. But their principal ambition
was the boast, "We, the Utaybah, on such and such a

---

1 The Sharifs are born and bred to fighting: the peculiar
privileges of their caste favour their development of pugnacity.
Thus, the modern diyah, or price of blood, being 800 dollars for a
common Moslem, the chiefs demand for one of their number double
that sum, with a sword, a camel, a female slave, and other items;
and, if one of their slaves or servants be slain, a fourfold price. The
rigorous way in which this custom is carried out gives the Sharif
and his retainer great power among the Arabs. As a general rule,
they are at the bottom of all mischief. It was a Sharif (Hosayn bin
Ali) who tore down and trampled upon the British flag at Mocha; a
Sharif (Abd al-Rahman of Waht) who murdered Captain Mylne
near Lahedge. A page might be filled with the names of the distinguished ruffians.

night, stopped the Sultan's Mahmil one whole hour in the Pass."

At the beginning of the skirmish I had primed my pistols, and sat with them ready for use. But soon seeing that there was nothing to be done, and wishing to make an impression,—nowhere does Bobadil now "go down" so well as in the East,—I called aloud for my supper. Shaykh Nur, exanimate with fear, could not move. The boy Mohammed ejaculated only an "Oh, sir!" and the people around exclaimed in disgust, "By Allah, he eats!" Shaykh Abdullah, the Meccan, being a man of spirit, was amused by the spectacle. "Are these Afghan manners, Effendim?" he enquired from the Shugduf behind me. "Yes," I replied aloud, "in my country we always dine before an attack of robbers, because that gentry is in the habit of sending men to bed supperless." The Shaykh laughed aloud, but those around him looked offended. I thought the bravado this time *mal placé;* but a little event which took place on my way to Jeddah proved that it was not quite a failure.

As we advanced, our escort took care to fire every large dry Asclepias, to disperse the shades which buried us. Again the scene became wondrous wild:—

" Full many a waste I've wander'd o'er,
   Clomb many a crag, cross'd many a shore,
      But, by my halidome,
   A scene so rude, so wild as this,
   Yet so sublime in barrenness,
   Ne'er did my wandering footsteps press,
      Where'er I chanced to roam."

On either side were ribbed precipices, dark, angry, and towering above, till their summits mingled with the glooms of night ; and between them formidable looked the chasm, down which our host hurried with shouts and discharges of matchlocks. The torch-smoke and the night-fires of flaming Asclepias formed a canopy, sable

above and livid red below; it hung over our heads like a
sheet, and divided the cliffs into two equal parts. Here
the fire flashed fiercely from a tall thorn, that crackled
and shot up showers of sparks into the air; there it died
away in lurid gleams, which lit up a truly Stygian scene.
As usual, however, the picturesque had its inconveniences.
There was no path. Rocks, stone-banks, and trees ob-
structed our passage. The camels, now blind in darkness,
then dazzled by a flood of light, stumbled frequently; in
some places slipping down a steep descent, in others slid-
ing over a sheet of mud. There were furious quarrels
and fierce language between camel-men and their hirers,
and threats to fellow-travellers; in fact, we were united
in discord. I passed that night crying, "Hai! Hai!"
switching the camel, and fruitlessly endeavouring to fusti-
gate Mas'ud's nephew, who resolutely slept upon the
water-bags. During the hours of darkness we made
four or five halts, when we boiled coffee and smoked pipes;
but man and beasts were beginning to suffer from a deadly
fatigue.

Dawn (Saturday, Sept. 10th) found us still travelling
down the Fiumara, which here is about a hundred yards
broad. The granite hills on both sides were less precipitous; and the borders of the torrent-bed became natural
quays of stiff clay, which showed a water-mark of from
twelve to fifteen feet in height. In many parts the bed
was muddy; and the moist places, as usual, caused accidents. I happened to be looking back at Shaykh Abdullah, who was then riding in old Ali bin Ya Sin's fine
Shugduf; suddenly the camel's four legs disappeared from
under him, his right side flattening the ground, and the
two riders were pitched severally out of the smashed
vehicle. Abdullah started up furious, and with great
zest abused the Badawin, who were absent. "Feed these
Arabs," he exclaimed, quoting a Turkish proverb, "and

they will fire at Heaven!" But I observed that, when Shaykh Mas'ud came up, the citizen was only gruff.

We then turned Northward, and sighted Al-Mazik, more generally known as Wady Laymun, the Valley of Limes. On the right bank of the Fiumara stood the Meccan Sharif's state pavilion, green and gold: it was surrounded by his attendants, and he had prepared to receive the Pasha of the Caravan. We advanced half a mile, and encamped temporarily in a hill-girt bulge of the Fiumara bed. At eight A.M. we had travelled about twenty-four miles from Al-Zaribah, and the direction of our present station was South-west 50°.

Shaykh Mas'ud allowed us only four hours' halt; he wished to precede the main body. After breaking our fast joyously upon limes, pomegranates, and fresh dates, we sallied forth to admire the beauties of the place. We are once more on classic ground—the ground of the ancient Arab poets,—

" Deserted is the village—waste the halting place and home
At Mina, o'er Rijam and Ghul wild beasts unheeded roam,
On Rayyan hill the channel lines have left their naked trace,
Time-worn, as *primal Writ that dints the mountain's flinty
    face;*[1]"—

and this Wady, celebrated for the purity of its air, has from remote ages been a favourite resort of the Meccans. Nothing can be more soothing to the brain than the dark-green foliage of the limes and pomegranates; and from

---

1 In these lines of Labid, the "Mina" alluded to must not, we are warned by the scholiast, be confounded with "Mina" (*vulg.* "Muna"), the Valley of Victims. Ghul and Rayyan are hills close to the Wady Laymum. The passage made me suspect that inscriptions would be found among the rocks, as the scholiast informs us that "men used to write upon rocks in order that their writing might remain." (De Sacy's Moallaka de Lebid, p. 289.) I neither saw nor heard of any. But some months afterwards I was delighted to hear from the Abbé Hamilton that he had discovered in one of the rock monuments a "lithographed proof" of the presence of Sesostris (Rhameses II.).

the base of the Southern hill bursts a bubbling stream, whose
"Chaire, fresche e dolci acque"
flow through the gardens, filling them with the most delicious of melodies, the gladdest sound which Nature in
these regions knows.

Exactly at noon Mas'ud seized the halter of the foremost camel, and we started down the Fiumara. Troops
of Badawi girls looked over the orchard walls laughingly,
and children came out to offer us fresh fruit and sweet
water. At two P.M., travelling South-west, we arrived at
a point where the torrent-bed turns to the right: and, quitting it, we climbed with difficulty over a steep ridge of
granite. Before three o'clock we entered a hill-girt plain,
which my companions called "Sola." In some places
were clumps of trees, and scattered villages warned us that
we were approaching a city. Far to the left rose the
blue peaks of Taif, and the mountain road, a white thread
upon the nearer heights, was pointed out to me. Here
I first saw the tree, or rather shrub, which bears the
balm of Gilead, erst so celebrated for its tonic and stom-
achic properties.[1] I told Shaykh Mas'ud to break off a

---

1 The "balsamon" of Theophrastus and Dioscorides, a corruption of the Arabic "balisan" or "basham," by which name the
Badawin know it. In the valley of the Jordan it was worth its
weight in silver, and kings warred for what is now a weed. Cleopatra
by a commission brought it to Egypt. It was grown at Heliopolis.
The last tree died there, we are told by Niebuhr, in the early part of
the seventeenth century (according to others, in A.D. 1502); a circumstance the more curious, as it was used by the Copts in chrisome,
and by Europe for anointing kings. From Egypt it was carried to
Al-Hijaz, where it now grows wild on sandy and stony grounds; but
I could not discover the date of its naturalisation. Moslems generally believe it to have been presented to Solomon by Bilkis, Queen
of Sheba. Bruce relates that it was produced at Mohammed's
prayer from the blood of the Badr-Martyr. In the Gospel of
Infancy (book i. ch. 8) we read,—"9. Hence they (Joseph and
Mary) went out to that sycamore, which is now called Matarea

twig, which he did heedlessly. The act was witnessed by our party with a roar of laughter ; and the astounded Shaykh was warned that he had become subject to an atoning sacrifice.[1] Of course he denounced me as the instigator, and I could not fairly refuse assistance. The tree has of late years been carefully described by many botanists ; I will only say that the bark resembled in colour a cherry-stick pipe, the inside was a light yellow, and the juice made my fingers stick together.

At four P.M. we came to a steep and rocky Pass, up which we toiled with difficulty. The face of the country was rising once more, and again presented the aspect of numerous small basins divided and surrounded by hills. As we

---

(the modern and Arabic name for Heliopolis). 10. And in Matarea the Lord Jesus caused a well to spring forth, in which St. Mary washed his coat ; 11. And a balsam is produced or grows in that country from the sweat which ran down there from the Lord Jesus." The sycamore is still shown, and the learned recognise in this ridiculous old legend the " hiero-sykaminon," of pagan Egypt, under which Isis and Horus sat. Hence Sir J. Maundeville and an old writer allude reverently to the sovereign virtues of "bawme." I believe its qualities to have been exaggerated, but have found it useful in dressing wounds. Burckhardt (vol. ii. p. 124) alludes to, but appears not to have seen it. The best balsam is produced upon stony hills like Arafat and Muna. In hot weather incisions are made in the bark, and the soft gum which exudes is collected in bottles. The best kind is of the consistence of honey, and yellowish-brown, like treacle. It is frequently adulterated with water, when, if my informant Shaykh Abdullah speak truth, it becomes much lighter in weight. I never heard of the vipers which Pliny mentions as abounding in these trees, and which Bruce declares were shown to him alive at Jeddah and at Yambu'. Dr. Carter found the balm, under the name of Luban Dukah, among the Gara tribe of Eastern Arabia, and botanists have seen it at Aden. We may fairly question its being originally from the banks of the Jordan.

1 This being one of the " Muharramát," or actions forbidden to a pilgrim At all times, say the Moslems, there are three vile trades, viz., those of the Hárik al-Hajar (stone-burner), the Káti' al-Shajar (tree-cutter, without reference to Hawarden, N.B.), and the Báyi' al-Bashar (man-seller, vulg. Jalláb).

jogged on we were passed by the cavalcade of no less a personage than the Sharif of Meccah. Abd al-Muttalib bin Ghalib is a dark, beardless old man with African features derived from his mother. He was plainly dressed in white garments and a white muslin turban,[1] which made him look jet black; he rode an ambling mule, and the only emblem of his dignity was the large green satin

The " Main Pass " of Meccah.

umbrella born by an attendant on foot.[2] Scattered around him were about forty matchlock men, mostly slaves. At long intervals, after their father, came his four sons, Riza Bey, Abdullah, Ali, and Ahmad, the latter still a child. The three elder brothers rode splendid drome-daries at speed; they were young men of light complexion, with the true Meccan cast of features, showily dressed in bright coloured silks, and armed, to denote their rank, with sword and gold-hilted dagger.[3]

---

1 This attire was customary even in Al-Idrisi's time.

2 From India to Abyssinia the umbrella is the sign of royalty: the Arabs of Meccah and Sena'a probably derived the custom from the Hindus.

3 I purposely omit long descriptions of the Sharif, my fellow-travellers, Messrs. Didier and Hamilton, being far more competent to lay the subject before the public. A few political remarks may not be deemed out of place. The present Sharif, despite his civilised training at Constantinople, is, and must be a fanatic, bigoted man. He applied for the expulsion of the British Vice-Consul at Jeddah, on the grounds that an infidel should not hold position in the Holy Land. His pride and reserve have made him few friends, although

We halted as evening approached, and strained our
eyes, but all in vain, to catch sight of Meccah, which lies
in a winding valley. By Shaykh Abdullah's direction I
recited, after the usual devotions, the following prayer.
The reader is forwarned that it is difficult to preserve the
flowers of Oriental rhetoric in a European tongue.

---

the Meccans, with their enthusiastic nationality, extol his bravery to
the skies, and praise him for conduct as well as for courage. His
position at present is anomalous. Ahmad Pasha of Al-Hijáz rules
politically as representative of the Sultan. The Sharif, who, like
the Pope, claims temporal as well as spiritual dominion, attempts to
command the authorities by force of bigotry. The Pasha heads
the Turkish, now the ruling party. The Sharif has in his interest
the Arabs and the Badawin. Both thwart each other on all possible
occasions; quarrels are bitter and endless; there is no government,
and the vessel of the State is in danger of being water-logged, in consequence of the squabbling between her two captains. When I was
at Meccah all were in a ferment, the Sharif having, it is said,
insisted upon the Pasha leaving Taif. The position of the Turks in
Al-Hijaz becomes every day more dangerous. Want of money
presses upon them, and reduces them to degrading measures In
February, 1853, the Pasha hired a forced loan from the merchants,
and but for Mr. Cole's spirit and firmness, the English *protégés*
would have been compelled to contribute their share. After a long
and animated discussion, the Pasha yielded the point by imprisoning
his recusant subjects, who insisted upon Indians paying, like themselves. He waited in person with an apology upon Mr. Cole.
Though established at Jeddah since 1838, the French and English
Consuls, contented with a proxy, never required a return of visit
from the Governor. If the Turks be frequently reduced to such expedients for the payment of their troops, they will soon be swept
from the land. On the other hand, the Sharif approaches a crisis.
His salary, paid by the Sultan, may be roughly estimated at £15,000
per annum. If the Turks maintain their footing in Arabia, it will
probably be found that an honourable retreat at Stambul is better
for the thirty-first descendant of the Prophet than the turbulent life
of Meccah; or that a reduced allowance of £500 per annum would
place him in a higher spiritual, though in a lower temporal position.
Since the above was written the Sharif Abd al-Muttalib has been deposed. The Arabs of Al-Hijaz united in revolt against the Sultan,
but after a few skirmishes they were reduced to subjection by their
old ruler the Sharif bin Aun.

O Allah! verily this is Thy Safeguard *(Amn)* and Thy *(Harim)!* Into it whoso entereth becometh safe *(Amin).* So deny *(Harrim)* my Flesh and Blood, my Bones and Skin, to Hell-fire. O Allah! save me from Thy Wrath on the Day when Thy Servants shall be raised from the Dead. I conjure Thee by this that Thou art Allah, besides whom is none (Thou only), the Merciful, the Compassionate. And have Mercy upon our Lord Mohammed, and upon the Progeny of our Lord Mohammed, and upon his Followers, One and All!" This was concluded with the " Talbiyat," and with an especial prayer for myself.

We again mounted, and night completed our disappointment. About one A.M. I was aroused by general excitement. " Meccah! Meccah!" cried some voices; "The Sanctuary! O the Sanctuary!" exclaimed others; and all burst into loud " Labbayk," not unfrequently broken by sobs. I looked out from my litter, and saw by the light of the Southern stars the dim outlines of a large city, a shade darker than the surrounding plain. We were passing over the last ridge by a cutting called the Saniyat Kuda'a, the winding-place of the cut.[1] The " winding path " is flanked on both sides by watch-towers, which command the *Darb al-Ma'ala* or road leading from the North into Meccah. Thence we passed into the Ma'abidah (Northern suburb), where the Sharif's Palace is built.[2] After this, on the left hand, came

---

1 Saniyat means a "winding path," and Kuda'a, "the cut." Formerly Meccah had three gates: 1. Bab al-Ma'ala, North-East; 2. Bab al-Umrah, or Bab al-Zahir, on the Jeddah road, West; and 3, Bab al-Masfal on the Yaman road. These were still standing in the twelfth century, but the walls were destroyed. It is better to enter Meccah by day and on foot; but this is not a matter of vital consequence in pilgrimage.

2 It is a large whitewashed building, with extensive wooden balconied windows, but no pretensions to architectural splendour. Around it trees grow, and amongst them I remarked a young cocoa.

the deserted abode of the Sharif bin Aun, now said to be a " haunted house.[1]" Opposite to it lies the Jannat al-Ma'ala, the holy cemetery of Meccah. Thence, turning to the right, we entered the Sulaymaniyah or Afghan quarter. Here the boy Mohammed, being an inhabitant of the Shamiyah or Syrian ward, thought proper to display some apprehension. The two are on bad terms; children never meet without exchanging volleys of stones, and men fight furiously with quarterstaves. Sometimes, despite the terrors of religion, the knife and sabre are drawn. But their hostilities have their code. If a citizen be killed, there is a subscription for blood-money. An inhabitant of one quarter, passing singly through another, becomes a guest; once beyond the walls, he is likely to be beaten to insensibility by his hospitable foes.

At the Sulaymaniyah we turned off the main road into a byway, and ascended by narrow lanes the rough heights of Jabal Hindi, upon which stands a small whitewashed and crenellated building called a fort. Thence descending, we threaded dark streets, in places crowded with rude cots and dusky figures, and finally at two A.M. we found ourselves at the door of the boy Mohammed's house.

Al-Idrisi (A.D. 1154) calls the palace Al-Marba'ah. This may be a clerical error, for to the present day all know it as Al-Ma'abidah (pronounced Al-Mab'da). The Nubian describes it as a "stone castle, three miles from the town, in a palm garden." The word "Ma'abidah," says Kutb al-Din, means a "body of servants," and is applied generally to this suburb because here was a body of Badawin in charge of the Masjid al-Ijabah, a Mosque not now existing.

1 I cannot conceive what made the accurate Niebuhr fall into the strange error that "apparitions are unknown in Arabia." Arabs fear to sleep alone, to enter the bath at night, to pass by cemeteries during dark, and to sit amongst ruins, simply for fear of apparitions. And Arabia, together with Persia, has supplied half the Western world with its ghost stories and tales of angels, demons, and fairies. To quote Milton, the land is struck "with superstition as with a planet."

From Wady Laymun to Meccah the distance, according to my calculation, was about twenty-three miles, the direction South-East forty-five degrees. We arrived on the morning of Sunday, the 7th Zu'l Hijjah (11th September, 1853), and had one day before the beginning of the pilgrimage to repose and visit the Harim.

I conclude this chapter with a few remarks upon the watershed of Al-Hijaz. The country, in my humble opinion, has a compound slope, Southwards and West-

wards. I have, however, little but the conviction of the modern Arabs to support the assertion that this part of Arabia declines from the North. All declare the course of water to be Southerly, and believe the fountain of Arafat to pass underground from Baghdad. The slope, as geographers know, is still a disputed point. Ritter, Jomard, and some old Arab authors, make the country rise towards the south, whilst Wallin and others express an opposite opinion. From the sea to Al-Musahhal is a gentle rise. The water-marks of the Fiumaras show that Al-Madinah is considerably above the coast, though geographers may not be correct in claiming for Jabal Radhwa a height of six thousand feet; yet that elevation is not perhaps too great for the plateau upon which stands the Apostle's burial-place. From Al-Madinah to Al-Suwayrkiyah is another gentle rise, and from the latter to Al-Zaribah stagnating water denotes a level. I believe the report of a perennial lake on the eastern boundary of Al-Hijaz, as little as the river placed by Ptolemy between Yambu' and Meccah. No Badawi could tell me of this feature, which, had it existed, would have changed the whole conditions and history of the

country; we know the Greek's river to be a Fiumara, and the lake probably owes its existence to a similar cause, a heavy fall of rain. Beginning at Al-Zaribah is a decided fall, which continues to the sea. The Arafat torrent sweeps

The Pass of Death.

from East to West with great force, sometimes carrying away the habitations, and even injuring the sanctuary.[1]

1 This is a synopsis of our marches, which, protracted on Burckhardt's map, gives an error of ten miles.

			Miles.
1. From Al-Madinah to Ja al-Sharifah,	S.E.	50°	22
2. From Ja al-Sharifah to Ghurab, -	- S.W.	10°	24
3. From Ghurab to Al-Hijriyah, -	- S.E.	22°	25
4. From Al-Hijriyah to Al-Suwayrkiyah,	- S.W.	11°	28
5. From Al-Suwayrkiyah to Al-Sufayna, -	S.E.	5°	17
6. From Al-Sufayna to the "Benu Mutayr,"	S.W.	20°	18
7. From the "Benu Mutayr" to Al-Ghadir,	S.W.	21°	20
8. From Al-Ghadir to Al-Birkat, -	- S.E.	10°	24
9. From Al-Birkat to Al-Zaribah, -	- S.E.	56°	23
10. From Al-Zaribah to Wady Laymun,	- S.W.	50°	24
11. From Wady Laymun to Meccah,	- S.E.	45°	23=149

Total English miles 248

PART III.

MECCAH.

CHAPTER XXVII.

THE FIRST VISIT TO THE HOUSE OF ALLAH.

THE boy Mohammed left me in the street, and having at last persuaded the sleepy and tired Indian porter, by violent kicks and testy answers to twenty cautious queries, to swing open the huge gate of his fortress, he rushed up stairs to embrace his mother. After a minute I heard the *Zaghritah*,[1] *Lululú*, or shrill cry which in these lands welcomes the wanderer home; the sound so gladdening to the returner sent a chill to the stranger's heart.

Presently the youth returned. His manner had changed from a boisterous and jaunty demeanour to one of grave and attentive courtesy—I had become his guest. He led me into the gloomy hall, seated me upon a large carpeted Mastabah, or platform, and told his *bara Miyan*[2] (great Sir), the Hindustani porter, to bring a light.

---

1 The Egyptian word is generally pronounced "Zaghrutah," the plural is Zagharit, corrupted to Ziraleet. The classical Arabic term is "Tahlil"; the Persians call the cry "Kil." It is peculiar to women, and is formed by raising the voice to its highest pitch, vibrating it at the same time by rolling the tongue, whose modulations express now joy, now grief. To my ear it always resembled the brain-piercing notes of a fife. Dr. Buchanan likens it to a serpent uttering human sounds. The "unsavoury comparison," however, may owe its origin to the circumstance that Dr. Buchanan heard it at the orgies of Jagannath.

2 As an Indian is called "Miyan," sir, an elderly Indian becomes "bara Miyan," great or ancient sir. I shall have occasion to speak at a future period of these Indians at Meccah.

Meanwhile a certain shuffling of slippered feet above informed my hungry ears that the *Kabirah*,[1] the mistress of the house, was intent on hospitable thoughts. When the camels were unloaded, appeared a dish of fine vermicelli, browned and powdered with loaf-sugar. The boy Mohammed, I, and Shaykh Nur, lost no time in exerting our right hands; and truly, after our hungry journey, we found the *Kunafah* delicious. After the meal we procured cots from a neighbouring coffee-house, and we lay down, weary, and anxious to snatch an hour or two of repose. At dawn we were expected to perform our *Tawaf al-Kudum*, or "Circumambulation of Arrival," at the Harim.

Scarcely had the first smile of morning beamed upon the rugged head of the eastern hill, Abu Kubays,[2] when we arose, bathed, and proceeded in our pilgrim-garb to the Sanctuary. We entered by the Bab al-Ziyadah, or principal northern door, descended two long flights of steps, traversed the cloister, and stood in sight of the Bayt Allah.

    *   *   *   *   *   *   *

There at last it lay, the bourn of my long and weary Pilgrimage, realising the plans and hopes of many and many a year. The mirage medium of Fancy invested the

1 " Sitt al-Kabirah," or simply " Al-Kabirah," the Great Lady, is the title given to the mistress of the house.

2 This hill bounds Meccah on the East. According to many Moslems, Adam, with his wife and his son Seth, lie buried in a cave here. Others place his tomb at Muna; the Majority at Najaf. The early Christians had a tradition that our first parents were interred under Mount Calvary; the Jews place their grave near Hebron. Habil (Abel), it is well known, is supposed to be entombed at Damascus; and Kabil (Cain) rests at last under Jabal Shamsan, the highest wall of the Aden crater, where he and his progeny, tempted by Iblis, erected the first fire-temple. It certainly deserves to be the sepulchre of the first murderer. The worship, however, was probably imported from India, where Agni (the fire god) was, as the Vedas prove, the object of man's earliest adoration.

huge catafalque and its gloomy pall with peculiar charms.
There were no giant fragments of hoar antiquity as in
Egypt, no remains of graceful and harmonious beauty as
in Greece and Italy, no barbarous gorgeousness as in the
buildings of India ; yet the view was strange, unique—and
how few have looked upon the celebrated shrine! I may
truly say that, of all the worshippers who clung weeping
to the curtain, or who pressed their beating hearts to the
stone, none felt for the moment a deeper emotion than did
the Haji from the far-north. It was as if the poetical
legends of the Arab spoke truth, and that the waving
wings of angels, not the sweet breeze of morning,
were agitating and swelling the black covering of the
shrine. But, to confess humbling truth, theirs was the
high feeling of religious enthusiasm, mine was the ecstasy
of gratified pride.

Few Moslems contemplate for the first time the
Ka'abah, without fear and awe : there is a popular jest
against new comers, that they generally inquire the
direction of prayer. This being the Kiblah, or fronting
place, Moslems pray all around it; a circumstance which
of course cannot take place in any spot of Al-Islam but
the Harim. The boy Mohammed, therefore, left me for
a few minutes to myself; but presently he warned me
that it was time to begin. Advancing, we entered
through the Bab Benu Shaybah, the "Gate of the Sons
of the Shaybah[1]" (old woman). There we raised our

---

1 The popular legend of this gate is, that when Abraham and his
son were ordered to rebuild the Ka'abah, they found the spot occupied by an old woman. She consented to remove her house on condition that the key of the new temple should be entrusted to her and
to her descendants for ever and ever. The origin of this is, that
Benu Shaybah means the "sons of an old woman" as well as
"descendants of Shaybah." And history tells us that the Benu Shaybah are derived from one Shaybah (bin Osman, bin Talhah, bin
Shaybah, bin Talhah, bin Abd al-Dar), who was sent by Mu'awiyah
to make some alterations in the Ka'abah. According to others, the

hands, repeated the Labbayk, the Takbir, and the Tahlil;
after which we uttered certain supplications, and drew
our hands down our faces.   Then we proceeded to the
Shafe'is' place of worship—the open pavement between
the Makam Ibrahim and the well Zemzem—where we
performed the usual two-bow prayer in honour of the
Mosque.   This was followed by a cup of holy water and
a present to the Sakkas, or carriers, who for the consideration distributed, in my name, a large earthen vaseful to
poor pilgrims.

The word Zemzem has a doubtful origin.   Some
derive it from the Zam Zam, or murmuring of its waters,
others from Zam! Zam! (fill! fill! *i.e.* the bottle), Hagar's
impatient exclamation when she saw the stream.   Sale
translates it stay! stay! and says that Hagar called out
in the Egyptian language, to prevent her son wandering.
The Hukama, or Rationalists of Al-Islam, who invariably
connect their faith with the worship of Venus, especially,
and the heavenly bodies generally, derive Zemzem from
the Persian, and make it signify the "great luminary."
Hence they say the Zemzem, as well as the Ka'abah,
denoting the Cuthite or Ammonian worship of sun and
fire, deserves man's reverence.   So the Persian poet
Khakani addresses these two buildings:—

"O Ka'abah, thou traveller of the heavens!"
"O Venus, thou fire of the world!"

Thus Wahid Mohammed, founder of the Wahidiyah sect,
identifies the Kiblah and the sun ; wherefore he says the
door fronts the East.   By the names Yaman ("right-
hand"), Sham ("left-hand"), Kubul, or the East wind
("fronting"), and Dubur, or the West wind ("from the
back"), it is evident that worshippers fronted the rising
sun.   According to the Hukama, the original Black
Stone represents Venus, "which in the border of the
heavens is a star of the planets," and symbolical of the

Ka'abah key was committed to the charge of Osman bin Talhah by
the Prophet.

generative power of nature, " by whose passive energy the universe was warmed into life and motion." The Hindus accuse the Moslems of adoring the Bayt Ullah.

" O Moslem, if thou worship the Ka'abah,
  Why reproach the worshippers of idols ? "

says Rai Manshar. And Musaylimah, who in his attempt to found a fresh faith, gained but the historic epithet of " Liar," allowed his followers to turn their faces in any direction, mentally ejaculating, " I address myself to thee, who hast neither side nor figure ; " a doctrine which might be sensible in the abstract, but certainly not material enough and pride-flattering to win him many converts in Arabia.

The produce of Zemzem is held in great esteem. It is used for drinking and religious ablution, but for no baser purposes ; and the Meccans advise pilgrims always to break their fast with it. It is apt to cause diarrhœa and boils, and I never saw a stranger drink it without a wry face. Sale is decidedly correct in his assertion : the flavour is a salt-bitter, much resembling an infusion of a teaspoonful of Epsom salts in a large tumbler of tepid water. Moreover, it is exceedingly "heavy" to the digestion. For this reason Turks and other strangers prefer rain-water, collected in cisterns and sold for five farthings a gugglet. It was a favourite amusement with me to watch them whilst they drank the holy water, and to taunt their scant and irreverent potations.

The strictures of the *Calcutta Review* (No. 41, art. 1), based upon the taste of Zemzem, are unfounded. In these days a critic cannot be excused for such hasty judgments; at Calcutta or Bombay he would easily find a jar of Zemzem water, which he might taste for himself. Upon this passage Mr. W. Muir (Life of Mahomet, vol. 1, p. cclviii.) remarks that " the flavour of stale water bottled up for months would not be a criterion of the same water freshly drawn." But it might easily be analysed.

The water is transmitted to distant regions in glazed

earthern jars covered with basket-work, and sealed by the Zemzemis. Religious men break their lenten fast with it, apply it to their eyes to brighten vision, and imbibe a few drops at the hour of death, when Satan stands by holding a bowl of purest water, the price of the departing soul. Of course modern superstition is not idle about the waters of Zemzem. The copious supply of the well is considered at Meccah miraculous ; in distant countries it facilitates the pronounciation of Arabic to the student ; and everywhere the nauseous draught is highly meritorious in a religious point of view.

We then advanced towards the eastern angle of the Ka'abah, in which is inserted the Black Stone ; and, standing about ten yards from it, repeated with upraised hands, " There is no god but Allah alone, Whose Covenant is Truth, and Whose Servant is Victorious. There is no god but Allah, without Sharer ; His is the Kingdom, to Him be Praise, and He over all Things is potent." After which we approached as close as we could to the stone. A crowd of pilgrims preventing our touching it that time, we raised our hands to our ears, in the first position of prayer, and then lowering them, exclaimed, " O Allah (I do this), in Thy Belief, and in verification of Thy Book, and in Pursuance of Thy Prophet's Example— may Allah bless Him and preserve ! O Allah, I extend my Hand to Thee, and great is my Desire to Thee ! O accept Thou my Supplication, and diminish my Obstacles, and pity my Humiliation, and graciously grant me Thy Pardon !" After which, as we were still unable to reach the stone, we raised our hands to our ears, the palms facing the stone, as if touching it, recited the various religious formulæ, the Takbir, the Tahlil, and the Hamdilah, blessed the Prophet, and kissed the finger-tips of the right hand. The Prophet used to weep when he touched the Black Stone, and said that it was the place for the pouring forth of tears. According to most authors, the

second Caliph also used to kiss it. For this reason most
Moslems, except the Shafe'i school, must touch the stone
with both hands and apply their lips to it, or touch it with
the fingers, which should be kissed, or rub the palms upon
it, and afterwards draw them down the face. Under circumstances of difficulty, it is sufficient to stand before the
stone, but the Prophet's Sunnat, or practice, was to touch
it. Lucian mentions adoration of the sun by kissing the
hand.

Then commenced the ceremony of *Tawáf*,[1] or circumambulation, our route being the *Mataf*—the low oval of
polished granite immediately surrounding the Ka'abah. I

---

1 The Moslem in circumambulation presents his left shoulder;
the Hindu's Pradakshina consists in walking round with the right
side towards the fane or idol. Possibly the former may be a
modification of the latter, which would appear to be the original
form of the rite. Its conjectural significance is an imitation of
the procession of the heavenly bodies, the motions of the spheres,
and the dances of the angels. These are also imitated in the circular whirlings of the Darwayshes. And Al-Shahristani informs us
that the Arab philosophers believed this sevenfold circumambulation
to be symbolical of the motion of the planets round the sun. It was
adopted by the Greeks and Romans, whose Ambarvalia and Ambur-
balia appear to be eastern superstitions, introduced by Numa, or by the
priestly line of princes, into their pantheism. And our processions
round the parish preserve the form of the ancient rites, whose life is
long since fled. Moslem moralists have not failed to draw spiritual
food from this mass of materialism. "To circuit the Bayt Ullah,"
said the Pir Raukhan (As. Soc. vol. xi. and Dabistan, vol. iii., "Miyan
Bayazid"), "and to be free from wickedness, and crime, and quarrels,
is the duty enjoined by religion. But to circuit the house of the
friend of Allah (*i.e.* the heart), to combat bodily propensities, and to
worship the Angels, is the business of the (mystic) path." Thus
Sa'adi, in his sermons,—which remind the Englishman of "poor
Yorick,"—" He who travels to the Ka'abah on foot makes a circuit of
the Ka'abah, but he who performs the pilgrimage of the Ka'abah in his
heart is encircled by the Ka'abah." And the greatest Moslem divines
sanction this visible representation of an invisible and heavenly shrine,
by declaring that, without a material medium, it is impossible for
man to worship the Eternal Spirit.

repeated, after my Mutawwif, or cicerone,[1] " In the Name of Allah, and Allah is omnipotent ! I purpose to circuit seven circuits unto Almighty Allah, glorified and exalted!" This is technically called the Niyat (intention) of Tawaf. Then we began the prayer, "O Allah (I do this), in Thy Belief, and in Verification of Thy Book, and in Faithfulness to Thy Covenant, and in Perseverance of the Example of the Apostle Mohammed—may Allah bless Him and preserve!" till we reached the place Al-Multazem, between the corner of the Black Stone and the Ka'abah door. Here we ejaculated, "O Allah, Thou hast Rights, so pardon my transgressing them." Opposite the door we repeated, "O Allah, verily the House is Thy House, and the Sanctuary Thy Sanctuary, and the Safeguard Thy Safeguard, and this is the Place of him who flies to Thee from (hell) Fire!" At the little building called Makam Ibrahim we said, "O Allah, verily this is the Place of Abraham, who took Refuge with and fled to Thee from the Fire!—O deny my Flesh and Blood, my Skin and Bones to the (eternal) Flames!" As we paced slowly round the north or Irak corner of the Ka'abah we exclaimed, "O Allah, verily I take Refuge with Thee from Polytheism, and Disobedience, and Hypocrisy, and evil Conversation, and evil Thoughts concerning Family, and Property, and Progeny!" When fronting the Mizab, or spout, we repeated the words, "O Allah, verily I beg of Thee Faith which shall not decline, and a Certainty which shall not perish, and the good Aid of Thy Prophet Mohammed—may Allah bless Him and preserve! O Allah, shadow me in Thy Shadow on that Day when there is no Shade but Thy Shadow, and cause me to drink from the Cup of Thine Apostle Mohammed—may Allah bless Him and preserve!— that pleasant Draught after which is no Thirst to all Eternity, O Lord of Honour and Glory!" Turning the

---

1 The Mutawwif, or Dalil, is the guide at Meccah.

west corner, or the Rukn al-Shami, we exclaimed, "O Allah, make it an acceptable Pilgrimage, and a Forgiveness of Sins, and a laudable Endeavour, and a pleasant Action (in Thy sight), and a store which perisheth not, O Thou Glorious! O Thou Pardoner!" This was repeated thrice, till we arrived at the Yamani, or south corner, where, the crowd being less importunate, we touched the wall with the right hand, after the example of the Prophet, and kissed the finger-tips. Finally, between the south angle and that of the Black Stone, where our circuit would be completed, we said, "O Allah, verily I take Refuge with Thee from Infidelity, and I take Refuge with Thee from Want, and from the Tortures of the Tomb, and from the Troubles of Life and Death. And I fly to Thee from Ignominy in this World and the next, and I implore Thy Pardon for the Present and for the Future. O Lord, grant to me in this Life Prosperity, and in the next Life Prosperity, and save me from the Punishment of Fire."

Thus finished a Shaut, or single course round the house. Of these we performed the first three at the pace called Harwalah, very similar to the French *pas gymnastique*, or Tarammul, that is to say, "moving the shoulders as if walking in sand." The four latter are performed in Ta'ammul, slowly and leisurely; the reverse of the Sai, or running. These seven Ashwat, or courses, are called collectively one Usbu (اسبوع). The Moslem origin of this custom is too well known to require mention. After each Taufah or circuit, we, being unable to kiss or even to touch the Black Stone, fronted towards it, raised our hands to our ears, exclaimed, "In the Name of Allah, and Allah is omnipotent!" kissed our fingers, and resumed the ceremony of circumambulation, as before, with "Allah, in Thy Belief," &c.

At the conclusion of the Tawaf it was deemed advisable to attempt to kiss the stone. For a time I stood

looking in despair at the swarming crowd of Badawi and
other pilgrims that besieged it.   But the boy Mohammed
was equal to the occasion.   During our circuit he had
displayed a fiery zeal against heresy and schism, by foully
abusing every Persian in his path[1]; and the inopportune
introduction of hard words into his prayers made the
latter a strange patchwork; as "Ave Maria purissima,—
arrah, don't ye be letting the pig at the pot,—sanctis-
sima," and so forth.   He might, for instance, be repeating "And I take Refuge with Thee from Ignominy in this
World," when "O thou rejected one, son of the rejected!"
would be the interpolation addressed to some long-
bearded Khorasani,—"And in that to come"—"O hog
and brother of a hoggess!"   And so he continued till I
wondered that none dared to turn and rend him.   After
vainly addressing the pilgrims, of whom nothing could be
seen but a mosaic of occiputs and shoulder-blades, the
boy Mohammed collected about half a dozen stalwart
Meccans, with whose assistance, by sheer strength, we
wedged our way into the thin and light-legged crowd.
The Badawin turned round upon us like wild-cats, but

---

1 In A.D. 1674 some wretch smeared the Black Stone with
impurity, and every one who kissed it retired with a sullied beard.
The Persians, says Burckhardt, were suspected of this sacrilege, and
now their ill-fame has spread far; at Alexandria they were described
to me as a people who defile the Ka'abah.   It is scarcely necessary to
say that a Shi'ah, as well as a Sunni, would look upon such an action
with lively horror.   The people of Meccah, however, like the Madani,
have turned the circumstance to their own advantage, and make an
occasional "avanie."   Thus, nine or ten years ago, on the testimony
of a boy who swore that he saw the inside of the Ka'abah defiled by
a Persian, they rose up, cruelly beat the schismatics, aud carried them
off to their peculiar quarter the Shamiyah, forbidding their ingress to
the Ka'abah.   Indeed, till Mohammed Ali's time, the Persians rarely
ventured upon a pilgrimage, and even now that man is happy who
gets over it without a beating.   The defilement of the Black Stone
was probably the work of some Jew or Greek, who risked his life to
gratify a furious bigotry.

they had no daggers. The season being autumn, they had not swelled themselves with milk for six months; and they had become such living mummies, that I could have managed single-handed half a dozen of them. After thus reaching the stone, despite popular indignation testified by impatient shouts, we monopolised the use of it for at least ten minutes. Whilst kissing it and rubbing hands and forehead upon it I narrowly observed it, and came away persuaded that it is an aërolite. It is curious that almost all travellers agree upon one point, namely, that the stone is volcanic. Ali Bey calls it "mineralogically" a "block of volcanic basalt, whose circumference is sprinkled with little crystals, pointed and straw-like, with rhombs of tile-red feldspath upon a dark background, like velvet or charcoal, except one of its protuberances, which is reddish." Burckhardt thought it was "a lava containing several small extraneous particles of a whitish and of a yellowish substance."

Having kissed the stone we fought our way through the crowd to the place called Al-Multazem. Here we pressed our stomachs, chests, and right cheeks to the Ka'abah, raising our arms high above our heads and exclaiming, "O Allah! O Lord of the Ancient House, free my Neck from Hell-fire, and preserve me from every ill Deed, and make me contented with that daily bread which Thou hast given to me, and bless me in all Thou hast granted!" Then came the Istighfar, or begging of pardon; "I beg Pardon of Allah the most high, who, there is no other God but He, the Living, the Eternal, and unto Him I repent myself!" After which we blessed the Prophet, and then asked for ourselves all that our souls most desired.[1]

---

1 Prayer is granted at fourteen places besides Al-Multazem, viz. :—

    1. At the place of circumambulation.

    2. Under the Mizab, or spout of the Ka'abah.

    3. Inside the Ka'abah.

After embracing the Multazem, we repaired to the Shafe'is' place of prayer near the Makam Ibrahim, and there recited two prostrations, technically called *Sunnat al-Tawaf,* or the (Apostle's) practice of circumambulation. The chapter repeated in the first was " Say thou, O Infidels": in the second, "Say thou He is the one God.[1]" We then went to the door of the building in which is Zemzem: there I was condemned to another nauseous draught, and was deluged with two or three skinfuls of water dashed over my head *en douche.* This ablution causes sins to fall from the spirit like dust.[2] During the potation we prayed, "O Allah, verily I beg of Thee plentiful daily Bread, and profitable Learning, and the healing of every Disease!" Then we returned towards the Black Stone, stood far away opposite, because unable to touch it, ejaculated the Takbir, the Tahlil, and the Hamdilah; and thoroughly worn out with scorched feet and a burning head,—both extremities, it must be remembered, were bare, and various delays had detained us till ten A.M.,—I left the Mosque.[3]

The boy Mohammed had miscalculated the amount of lodging in his mother's house. She, being a widow

4. At the well Zemzem.
5. Behind Abraham's place of prayer.
6 and 7. On Mounts Safa and Marwah.
8. During the ceremony called "Al-Sai."
9. Upon Mount Arafat.
10. At Muzdalifah.
11. In Muna.
12. During the devil-stoning.
13. On first seeing the Ka'abah.
14. At the Hatim or Hijr.

1 The former is the 109th, the latter the 112th chapter of the Koran (I have translated it in a previous volume).

2 These superstitions, I must remark, belong only to the vulgar.

3 Strictly speaking we ought, after this, to have performed the ceremony called Al-Sai, or the running seven times between Mounts Safa and Marwah. Fatigue put this fresh trial completely out of the question.

and a lone woman, had made over for the season all the apartments to her brother, a lean old Meccan, of true ancient type, vulture-faced, kite-clawed, with a laugh like a hyena, and a mere shell of body. He regarded me with no favouring eye when I insisted as a guest upon having some place of retirement ; but he promised that, after our return from Arafat, a little store-room should be cleared out for me. With that I was obliged to be content, and to pass that day in the common male drawing-room of the house, a vestibule on the

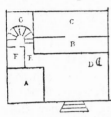

ground floor, called in Egypt a *Takhta-bush.*[1] Entering, to the left (A) was a large Mastabah, or platform, and at the bottom (B) a second, of smaller dimensions and foully dirty. Behind this was a dark and unclean store-room (c) containing the Hajis' baggage. Opposite the Mastabah was a firepan for pipes and coffee (D), superintended by a family of lean Indians; and by the side (E) a doorless passage led to a bathing-room (F) and staircase (G).

I had scarcely composed myself upon the carpeted Mastabah, when the remainder was suddenly invaded by the Turkish, or rather Slavo-Turk, pilgrims inhabiting the house, and a host of their visitors. They were large, hairy men, with gruff voices and square figures; they did not take the least notice of me, although feeling the intrusion, I stretched out my legs with a provoking *nonchalance.*[2] At last one of them addressed me in Turkish, to which I

---

1 I have been diffuse in my description of this vestibule, as it is the general way of laying out a ground-floor at Meccah. During the pilgrimage time the lower hall is usually converted into a shop for the display of goods, especially when situated in a populous quarter.

2 This is equivalent to throwing oneself upon the sofa in Europe. Only in the East it asserts a decided claim to superiority; the West would scarcely view it in that light.

replied by shaking my head. His question being interpreted to me in Arabic, I drawled out, " My native place
is the land of Khorasan." This provoked a stern and
stony stare from the Turks, and an " ugh !" which said
plainly enough, " Then you are a pestilent heretic." I
surveyed them with a self-satisfied simper, stretched my
legs a trifle farther, and conversed with my water-pipe.
Presently, when they all departed for a time, the boy
Mohammed raised, by request, my green box of medicines,
and deposited it upon the Mastabah ; thus defining, as it
were, a line of demarcation, and asserting my privilege to
it before the Turks. Most of these men were of one party,
headed by a colonel of Nizam, whom they called a Bey.
My acquaintance with them began roughly enough, but
afterwards, with some exceptions, who were gruff as an
English butcher when accosted by a lean foreigner, they
proved to be kind-hearted and not unsociable men. It
often happens to the traveller, as the charming Mrs. Mala-
prop observes, to find intercourse all the better by beginning with a little aversion.

In the evening, accompanied by the boy Mohammed,
and followed by Shaykh Nur, who carried a lantern and a
praying-rug, I again repaired to the " Navel of the World[1]";
this time æsthetically, to enjoy the delights of the hour
after the " gaudy, babbling, and remorseful day." The
moon, now approaching the full, tipped the brow of Abu
Kubays, and lit up the spectacle with a more solemn light.
In the midst stood the huge bier-like erection,—

> " Black as the wings
> Which some spirit of ill o'er a sepulchre flings,"—

---

1 Ibn Haukal begins his cosmography with Meccah "because
the temple of the Lord is situated there, and the holy Ka'abah is the
navel of the earth, and Meccah is styled in sacred writ the parent
city, or the mother of towns." Unfortunately, Ibn Haukal, like
most other Moslem travellers and geographers, says no more about
Meccah.

except where the moonbeams streaked it like jets of silver falling upon the darkest marble. It formed the point of rest for the eye ; the little pagoda-like buildings and domes around it, with all their gilding and fretwork, vanished. One object, unique in appearance, stood in view—the temple of the one Allah, the God of Abraham, of Ishmael, and of their posterity. Sublime it was, and expressing by all the eloquence of fancy the grandeur of the One Idea which vitalised Al-Islam, and the strength and steadfastness of its votaries.

The oval pavement round the Ka'abah was crowded with men, women, and children, mostly divided into parties, which followed a Mutawwif ; some walking staidly, and others running, whilst many stood in groups to prayer. What a scene of contrasts ! Here stalked the Badawi woman, in her long black robe like a nun's serge, and poppy-coloured face-veil, pierced to show two fiercely flashing orbs. There an Indian woman, with her semi-Tartar features, nakedly hideous, and her thin legs, encased in wrinkled tights, hurried round the fane. Every now and then a corpse, borne upon its wooden shell, circuited the shrine by means of four bearers, whom other Moslems, as is the custom, occasionally relieved. A few fair-skinned Turks lounged about, looking cold and repulsive, as their wont is. In one place a fast Calcutta *Khitmugar* stood, with turband awry and arms akimbo, contemplating the view jauntily, as those " gentlemen's gentlemen " will do. In another, some poor wretch, with arms thrown on high, so that every part of his person might touch the Ka'abah, was clinging to the curtain and sobbing as though his heart would break.

From this spectacle my eyes turned towards Abu Kubays. The city extends in that direction half-way up the grim hill : the site might be compared, at a humble distance, to Bath. Some writers liken it to Florence ; but conceive a Florence without beauty ! To the South lay Jabal Jiyad the Greater,[1] also partly built over and crowned with a fort, which at a distance looks less useful than romantic[2]: a flood of pale light was sparkling upon its stony surface. Below, the minarets became pillars of silver, and the cloisters, dimly streaked by oil lamps, bounded the views of the temple with horizontal lines of shade.

Before nightfall the boy Mohammed rose to feed the Mosque pigeons, for whom he had brought a pocketful of barley. He went to the place where these birds flock— the line of pavement leading from the isolated arch to the Eastern cloisters. During the day women and children are to be seen sitting here, with small piles of grain upon little plaited trays of basket-work. For each they demand a copper piece ; and religious pilgrims consider it their duty to provide the reverend blue-rocks with a plentiful meal.

The Hindu Pandits assert that Shiwa and his spouse, under the forms and names of Kapot-Eshwara (pigeon god) and Kapotesi, dwelt at Meccah. The dove was the device of the old Assyrian Empire, because it is supposed Semiramis was preserved by that bird. The Meccan pigeons, resembling those of Venice, are held sacred probably in consequence of the wild traditions of the Arabs about Noah's dove. Some authors declare that in Mohammed's time, among the idols of the Meccan Pantheon, was a pigeon carved in wood, and above it another, which Ali, mounting upon the Prophet's shoulder, pulled down. This might have been a Hindu, a Jewish, or a Christian symbol. The Moslems connect the pigeon

---

1 To distinguish it from the Jiyad (above the cemetery Al-Ma'ala) over which Khalid entered Meccah. Some topographers call the Jiyad upon which the fort is built "the lesser," and apply "greater" to Jiyad Amir, the hill north of Meccah.

2 The Meccans, however, do not fail to boast of its strength; and has stood some sieges.

on two occasions with their faith: first, when that bird appeared to whisper in Mohammed's ear; and, secondly, during the flight to Al-Madinah. Moreover, in many countries they are called "Allah's Proclaimers," because their movement when cooing resembles prostration.

Almost everywhere the pigeon has entered into the history of religion, which probably induced Mr. Lascelles to incur the derision of our grandfathers by pronouncing it a "holy bird." At Meccah they are called the doves of the Ka'abah, and they never appear at table. They are remarkable for propriety when sitting upon the holy building. This may be a minor miracle: I would rather believe that there is some contrivance on the roof. My friend Mr. Bicknell remarks: "This marvel, however, having of late years been suspended, many discern another omen of the approach of the long-predicted period when unbelievers shall desecrate the sacred soil."

Late in the evening I saw a negro in the state called Malbus—religious frenzy. To all appearance a Takruri, he was a fine and a powerful man, as the numbers required to hold him testified. He threw his arms wildly about him, uttering shrill cries, which sounded like *lé lé lé lé!* and when held, he swayed his body, and waved his head from side to side, like a chained and furious elephant, straining out the deepest groans. The Africans appear unusually subject to this nervous state which, seen by the ignorant and the imaginative, would at once suggest "demoniacal possession.[1]" Either their organisation is more impressionable, or more probably, the hardships, privations, and fatigues endured whilst wearily traversing inhospitable wilds, and perilous seas, have exalted their

---

[1] In the Mandal, or palm-divination, a black slave is considered the best subject. European travellers have frequently remarked their nervous sensibility. In Abyssinia the maladies called "bouda" and "tigritiya" appear to depend upon some obscure connection between a weak impressionable brain and the strong will of a feared and hated race—the blacksmiths.

imaginations to a pitch bordering upon frenzy. Often they are seen prostrate on the pavement, or clinging to the curtain, or rubbing their foreheads upon the stones, weeping bitterly, and pouring forth the wildest ejaculations.

That night I stayed in the Harim till two A.M., wishing to see if it would be empty. But the morrow was to witness the egress to Arafat; many, therefore, passed the hours of darkness in the Harim. Numerous parties of pilgrims sat upon their rugs, with lanterns in front of them, conversing, praying, and contemplating the Ka'abah. The cloisters were full of merchants, who resorted there to "talk shop," and to vend such holy goods as combs, tooth-sticks, and rosaries. Before ten P.M. I found no opportunity of praying the usual two prostrations over the grave of Ishmael. After waiting long and patiently, at last I was stepping into the vacant place, when another pilgrim rushed forward; the boy Mohammed, assisted by me, instantly seized him, and, despite his cries and struggles, taught him to wait. Till midnight we sat chatting with the different ciceroni who came up to offer their services. I could not help remarking their shabby and dirty clothes, and was informed that during pilgrimage, when splendour is liable to be spoiled, they wear out old dresses; and appear *endimanchés* for the Muharram fête, when most travellers have left the city. Presently my two companions, exhausted with fatigue, fell asleep; I went up to the Ka'abah, with the intention of "annexing" a bit of the torn old Kiswat or curtain, but too many eyes were looking on. At this season of the year the Kiswat is much tattered at the base, partly by pilgrims' fingers, and partly by the strain of the cord which confines it when the wind is blowing. It is considered a mere peccadillo to purloin a bit of the venerable stuff; but as the officers of the temple make money by selling it, they certainly would visit detection with an unmerciful application of the quarterstaff. The piece in my possession was given to me by the boy Mohammed before I left Meccah. Waistcoats cut out of the Kiswah still make the combatants invulnerable in battle, and are considered presents fit for princes. The Moslems generally try to secure a strip of this cloth as a mark for the Koran, or for some such purpose. The opportunity, however, was favourable for a survey, and with a piece of tape, and the simple processes of stepping and spanning, I managed to measure all the objects concerning which I was curious.

At last sleep began to weigh heavily upon my eyelids. I awoke my companions, and in the dizziness of slumber they walked with me through the tall narrow street from the Bab al-Ziyadah to our home in the Shamiyah. The brilliant moonshine prevented our complaining, as other travellers have had reason to do, of the darkness and the difficulty of Meccah's streets. The town, too, appeared safe; there were no watchmen, and yet people slept everywhere upon cots placed opposite their open doors. Arrived at the house, we made some brief preparations for snatching a few hours' sleep upon the Mastabah, a place so stifling, that nothing but utter exhaustion could induce lethargy there.

CHAPTER XXVIII.

THE CEREMONIES OF THE YAUM AL-TARWIYAH,
OR THE FIRST DAY.

AT ten A.M., on the 8th Zu'l Hijjah, A.H. 1269 (Monday, 12th Sept., 1853), habited in our Ihram, or pilgrim garbs, we mounted the litter. Shaykh Mas'ud had been standing at the door from dawn-time, impatient to start before the Damascus and the Egyptian caravans made the road dangerous. Our delay arose from the tyrannical conduct of the boy Mohammed, who insisted upon leaving his little nephew behind. It was long before he yielded. I then placed the poor child, who was crying bitterly, in the litter between us, and at last we started.

We followed the road by which the Caravans entered Meccah. It was covered with white-robed pilgrims, some few wending their way on foot[1]; others riding, and all men barefooted and bareheaded. Most of the wealthier classes mounted asses. The scene was, as usual, one of strange contrasts: Badawin bestriding swift dromedaries; Turkish dignitaries on fine horses; the most picturesque beggars, and the most uninteresting Nizam. Not a little wrangling mingled with the loud bursts of *Talbiyat*. Dead animals dotted the ground, and carcasses had been cast into a dry tank, the *Birkat al-Shami* which caused every Badawi to

---

[1] Pilgrims who would win the heavenly reward promised to those who walk, start at an early hour.

hold his nose.[1] Here, on the right of the road, the poorer
pilgrims, who could not find houses, had erected huts, and
pitched their ragged tents. Traversing the suburb Al-
Ma'b'dah (Ma'abadah), in a valley between the two
barren prolongations of Kayka'an and Khandamah, we
turned to the north-east, leaving on the left certain
barracks of Turkish soldiery, and the negro militia here
stationed, with the *Saniyat Kuda'a* in the background.
Then, advancing about 3000 paces over rising ground,
we passed by the conical head of Jabal Nur,[2] and entered the plain of many names.[3] It contained nothing
but a few whitewashed walls, surrounding places of
prayer, and a number of stone cisterns, some well preserved, others in ruins. All, however, were dry, and
water-vendors crowded the roadside. Gravel and lumps
of granite grew there like grass, and from under every
large stone, as Shaykh Mas'ud took a delight in showing,
a small scorpion, with tail curled over its back, fled,
Parthian-like, from the invaders of its home. At eleven
A.M., ascending a Mudarraj, or flight of stone steps, about
thirty yards broad, we passed without difficulty, for we
were in advance of the caravans, over the Akabah, or
Steeps,[4] and the narrow, hill-girt entrance, to the low
gravel basin in which Muna lies.

---

1 The true Badawi, when in the tainted atmosphere of towns, is
always known by bits of cotton in his nostrils, or by his kerchief tightly
drawn over his nose, a heavy frown marking extreme disgust.

2 Anciently called Hira. It is still visited as the place of the
Prophet's early lucubrations, and because here the first verse of the
Koran descended. As I did not ascend the hill, I must refer readers
for a description of it to Burckhardt, vol. i. p. 320.

3 Al-Abtah, "low ground"; Al Khayf, "the declivity"; Fina
Makkah, the "court of Meccah"; Al-Muhassib (from Hasba, a
shining white pebble), corrupted by our authors to Mihsab and
Mohsab.

4 The spot where Kusay fought and where Mohammed made his
covenant.

Muna, more classically called Mina,[1] is a place of considerable sanctity.   Its three standing miracles are these: The pebbles thrown at "the Devil" return by angelic agency to whence they came; during the three Days of Drying Meat rapacious beasts and birds cannot prey there; and, lastly, flies do not settle upon the articles of food exposed so abundantly in the bazars.[2] During pilgrimage, houses are let for an exorbitant sum, and it becomes a "World's Fair" of Moslem merchants.   At all other seasons it is almost deserted, in consequence, says popular superstition, of the *Rajm* or (diabolical) lapidation.[3] Distant about three miles from Meccah, it is a long, narrow, straggling village, composed of mud and stone houses of one or two stories, built in the common Arab style. Traversing a narrow street, we passed on the left the Great Devil, which shall be described at a future time. After a quarter of an hour's halt, spent over pipes and coffee, we came to an open space, where stands the Mosque "Al-Khayf."   Here, according to some Arabs, Adam lies, his head being at one end of one long wall, and his feet at another, whilst the dome covers his omphalic region.   Grand preparations for fireworks were being made in this square; I especially remarked a fire-

---

1 If Ptolemy's "Minœi" be rightly located in this valley, the present name and derivation "Muna" (desire), because Adam here desired Paradise of Allah, must be modern.   Sale, following Pococke, makes " Mina " (from Mana) allude to the flowing of victims' blood. Possibly it may be the plural of Minyat, which in many Arabic dialects means a village.   This basin was doubtless thickly populated in ancient times, and Moslem historians mention its seven idols, representing the seven planets.

2 According to Mohammed the pebbles of the accepted are removed by angels ; as, however, each man and woman must throw 49 or 70 stones, it is fair to suspect the intervention of something more material.   Animals are frightened away by the bustling crowd, and flies are found in myriads.

3 This demoniacal practice is still as firmly believed in Arabia as it formerly was in Europe.

ship, which savoured strongly of Stambul.   After passing
through the town, we came to *Batn al-Muhassir*, "The
Basin of the Troubler,[1]" (Satan) at the beginning of a
descent leading to *Muzdalifah* (the Approacher), where
the road falls into the valley of the Arafat torrent.

At noon we reached the Muzdalifah, also called
Mashar al-Harám, the "Place dedicated to religious
Ceremonies.[2]"   It is known in Al-Islam as "the Minaret
without the Mosque," opposed to Masjid Nimrah, which
is the "Mosque without the Minaret."   Half-way between
Muna and Arafat, it is about three miles from both.
There is something peculiarly striking in the distant appearance of the tall, solitary tower, rising abruptly from
the desolate valley of gravel, flanked with buttresses of
yellow rock.   No wonder that the ancient Arabs loved to
give the high-sounding name of this oratory to distant
places in their giant Caliph-empire.

Here as we halted to perform the mid-day prayer, we
were overtaken by the Damascus Caravan.   It was a
grand spectacle.   The Mahmil, no longer naked as upon
the line of march, flashed in the sun all green and gold.
Around the moving host of white-robed pilgrims hovered
a crowd of Badawin, male and female, all mounted on
swift dromedaries, and many of them armed to the teeth.
As their drapery floated in the wind, and their faces were
veiled with the "Lisam," it was frequently difficult to

1 Probably because here Satan appeared to tempt Adam, Abraham, and Ishmael.   The Qanoon e Islam erroneously calls it the
"Valley of Muhasurah," and corrupts Mashar al-Haram into "Muzar
al-Haram" (the holy shrine).

2 Many, even since Sale corrected the error, have confounded
this Mashar al-*Harám* with Masjid al-*Hărăm* of Meccah.   According
to Al-Fasi, quoted by Burckhardt, it is the name of a little eminence at
the end of the Muzdalifah valley, and anciently called Jabal Kuzah ;
it is also, he says, applied to "an elevated platform inclosing the
mosque of Muzdalifah."   Ibn Jubayr makes Mashar al-Haram synonymous with Muzdalifah, to which he gives a third name, "Jami."

distinguish the sex of the wild being, flogging its animal to speed. These people, as has been said, often resort to Arafat for blood-revenge, in hopes of finding the victim unprepared. Nothing can be more sinful in Al-Islam than such deed—it is murder, "made sicker" by sacrilege; yet the prevalence of the practice proves how feeble is the religion's hold upon the race. The women are as unscrupulous: I remarked many of them emulating the men in reckless riding, and striking with their sticks every animal in the way.

Travelling Eastward up the Arafat Fiumara, after about half an hour we came to a narrow pass called Al-Akhshabayn[1] or the " Two Rugged Hills." Here the spurs of the rock limited the road to about a hundred paces, and it is generally a scene of great confusion. After this we arrived at Al-Bazan (the Basin),[2] a widening of the plain ; and another half-hour brought us to the Alamayn (the " Two Signs "), whitewashed pillars, or rather thin, narrow walls, surmounted with pinnacles, which denote the precincts of the Arafat plain. Here, in full sight of the Holy Hill, standing boldly out from the deep blue sky, the host of pilgrims broke into loud Labbayks. A little beyond, and to our right, was the simple enclosure called the Masjid Nimrah.[3] We then

1 Buckhardt calls it "Mazoumeyn," or Al-Mazik, the pass. "Akeshab" may mean wooded or rugged ; in which latter sense it is frequently applied to hills. Kayka'an and Abu Kubays at Meccah are called Al-Akshshabayn in some books. The left hill, in Ibn Jubayr's time, was celebrated as a meeting-place for brigands.

2 Kutb al-Din makes another Bazan the Southern limit of Meccah.

3 Burckhardt calls this building, which he confounds with the "Jami Ibrahim," the Jami Nimre ; others Namirah, Nimrah, Namrah, and Namurah. It was erected, he says, by Kait Bey of Egypt, and had fallen into decay. It has now been repaired, and is generally considered neutral, and not Sanctuary ground, between the Harim of Meccah and the Holy Hill.

turned from our eastern course northwards, and began
threading our way down the main street of the town of
tents which clustered about the southern foot of Arafat.
At last, about three P.M., we found a vacant space near
the Matbakh, or kitchen, formerly belonging to a Sharif's
palace, but now a ruin with a few shells of arches.

Arafat is about six hours' very slow march, or twelve
miles,[1] on the Taif road, due east of Meccah. We arrived
there in a shorter time, but our weary camels, during the
last third of the way, frequently threw themselves upon
the ground. Human beings suffered more. Between
Muna and Arafat I saw no fewer than five men fall down
and die upon the highway : exhausted and moribund,
they had dragged themselves out to give up the ghost
where it departs to instant beatitude.[2] The spectacle
showed how easy it is to die in these latitudes[3]; each
man suddenly staggered, fell as if shot ; and, after a brief
convulsion, lay still as marble. The corpses were carefully taken up, and carelessly buried that same evening,
in a vacant space amongst the crowds encamped upon
the Arafat plain.[4]

The boy Mohammed, who had long chafed at my per-

1 Mr. W. Muir, in his valuable Life of Mahomet, vol. 1, p. ccv.,
remarks upon this passage that at p. 180 ante, I made Muna three miles
from Meccah, and Muzdalifah about three miles from Muna, and
Arafat three miles from Muzdalifah,—a total of nine. But the lesser
estimate does not include the outskirts of Meccah on the breadth
of the Arafat Plain. The Calcutta Review (art. 1, Sept. 1853) notably
errs in making Arafat *eighteen miles* east of Meccah. Ibn Jubayr
reckons five miles from Meccah to Muzdalifah, and five from this to
Arafat.

2 Those who die on a pilgrimage become martyrs.

3 I cannot help believing that some unknown cause renders death
easier to man in hot than in cold climates; certain it is that in
Europe rare are the quiet and painless deathbeds so common in the
East.

4 We bury our dead, to preserve them as it were; the Moslem
tries to secure rapid decomposition, and makes the graveyard a dangerous as well as a disagreeable place.

tinacious claim to Darwaysh-hood, resolved on this occasión to be grand. To swell the party he had invited Omar Effendi, whom we accidentally met in the streets of Meccah, to join us : but failing therein, he brought with him two cousins, fat youths of sixteen and seventeen, and his mother's ground-floor servants. These were four Indians : an old man ; his wife, a middle-aged woman of the most ordinary appearance ; their son, a sharp boy, who spoke excellent Arabic[1]; and a family friend, a stout fellow about thirty years old. They were Panjabis, and the bachelor's history was instructive. He was gaining an honest livelihood in his own country, when suddenly one night Hazrat Ali, dressed in green, and mounted upon his charger Duldul[2]—at least, so said the narrator—appeared, crying in a terrible voice, "How long wilt thou toil for this world, and be idle about the life to come?" From that moment, like an English murderer, he knew no peace ; Conscience and Hazrat Ali haunted him.[3] Find-

---

1 Arabs observe that Indians, unless brought young into the country, never learn its language well. They have a word to express the vicious pronunciation of a slave or an Indian, "Barbaret al-Hunud." This root Barbara (بربر), like the Greek "Barbaros," appears to be derived from the Sanscrit Varvvaraha, an outcast, a barbarian, a man with curly hair.

2 Ali's charger was named Maymun, or, according to others, Zu'l Janah (the winged). Indians generally confound it with "Duldul," Mohammed's mule.

3 These visions are common in history. Ali appeared to the Imam Shafe'i, saluted him,—an omen of eternal felicity,—placed a ring upon his finger, as a sign that his fame should extend wide as the donor's, and sent him to the Holy Land. Ibrahim bin Adham, the saint-poet hearing, when hunting, a voice exclaim, "Man! it is not for this that Allah made thee!" answered, "It is Allah who speaks, his servant will obey!" He changed clothes with an attendant, and wandered forth upon a pilgrimage, celebrated in Al-Islam. He performed it alone, and making 1100 genuflexions each mile, prolonged it to twelve years. The history of Colonel Gardiner, and of many others amongst ourselves, prove that these visions are not confined to the Arabs.

ing life unendurable at home, he sold everything; raised the sum of twenty pounds, and started for the Holy Land. He reached Jeddah with a few rupees in his pocket: and came to Meccah, where, everything being exorbitantly dear and charity all but unknown, he might have starved, had he not been received by his old friend. The married pair and their son had been taken as house-servants by the boy Mohammed's mother, who generously allowed them shelter and a pound of rice per diem to each, but not a farthing of pay. They were even expected to provide their own turmeric and onions. Yet these poor people were anxiously awaiting the opportunity to visit Al-Madinah, without which their pilgrimage would not, they believed, be complete. They would beg their way through the terrible Desert and its Badawin—an old man, a boy, and a woman! What were their chances of returning to their homes? Such, I believe, is too often the history of those wretches whom a fit of religious enthusiasm, likest to insanity, hurries away to the Holy Land. I strongly recommend the subject to the consideration of our Indian Government as one that calls loudly for their interference. No Eastern ruler parts, as we do, with his subjects; all object to lose productive power. To an " Empire of Opinion " this emigration is fraught with evils. It sends forth a horde of malcontents that ripen into bigots; it teaches foreign nations to despise our rule; and it unveils the present nakedness of once wealthy India. And we have both prevention and cure in our own hands.

As no Moslem, except the Maliki, is bound to pilgrimage without a sum sufficient to support himself and his family, all who embark at the different ports of India should be obliged to prove their solvency before being provided with a permit. Arrived at Jeddah, they should present the certificate at the British Vice-Consulate, where they would become entitled to assistance in case of necessity. The Vice-Consul at Jeddah ought also to be in-

structed to assist our Indian pilgrims. Mr. Cole, when
holding that appointment, informed me that, though men
die of starvation in the streets, he was unable to relieve
them. The highways of Meccah abound in pathetic Indian
beggars, who affect lank bodies, shrinking frames, whi-
ning voices, and all the circumstance of misery, because it
supports them in idleness.

There are no fewer than fifteen hundred Indians at
Meccah and Jeddah, besides seven or eight hundred in Al-
Yaman. Such a body requires a Consul.[1] By the representation of a Vice-Consul when other powers send an
officer of superior rank to Al-Hijaz, we voluntarily place
ourselves in an inferior position. And although the
Meccan Sharif might for a time object to establishing a
Moslem agent at the Holy City with orders to report to
the Consul at Jeddah, his opposition would soon fall to
the ground.

With the Indians' assistance the boy Mohammed
removed the handsome Persian rugs with which he had
covered the Shugduf, pitched the tent, carpeted the
ground, disposed a Diwan of silk and satin cushions
round the interior, and strewed the centre with new Chibuks, and highly polished Shishahs. At the doorway
was placed a large copper fire-pan, with coffee-pots singing a welcome to visitors. In front of us were the litters,
and by divers similar arrangements our establishment
was made to look fine. The youth also insisted upon my
removing the Rida, or upper cotton cloth, which had
become way-soiled, and he supplied its place by a rich
cashmere, left with him, some years before, by a son of
the King of Delhi. Little thought I that this bravery of
attire would lose me every word of the Arafat sermon
next day.

Arafat, anciently called Jabal Ilal (الآل), "the Mount

[1] There is a Consul for Jeddah now, 1879, but till lately he was
an unpaid.

C.F. Kell, Lith.

MOUNT ARAFAT DURING THE PILGRIMAGE.

of Wrestling in Prayer," and now Jabal al-Rahmah, the
" Mount of Mercy," is a mass of coarse granite split into

THE MOSQUE ON ARAFAT.

1. Dwarf wall enclosing the mountain.	3. The station of the Mahmils, side by side.
2. Flight of stone steps which the Mahmils ascend.	4. The place where the Khatib preaches.
	5. The fountain.

large blocks, with a thin coat of withered thorns.   About
one mile in circumference, it rises abruptly to the height
of a hundred and eighty or two hundred feet, from the
low gravelly plain—a dwarf wall at the Southern base
forming the line of demarcation.   It is separated by Batn
Arnah (عرنة), a sandy vale,[1] from the spurs of the Taif
hills.   Nothing can be more picturesque than the view it
affords of the azure peaks behind, and the vast encampment scattered over the barren yellow plain below.[2]   On
the North lay the regularly pitched camp of the guards
that defend the unarmed pilgrims.   To the Eastward was
the Sharif's encampment, with the bright Mahmils and

---

1 This vale is not considered "standing-ground," because Satan
once appeared to the Prophet as he was traversing it.

2 According to Kutb al-Din, the Arafat plain was once highly
cultivated.   Stone-lined cisterns abound, and ruins of buildings are
frequent.   At the Eastern foot of the mountain was a broad canal,
beginning at a spur of the Taif hills, and conveying water to Meccah;
it is now destroyed beyond Arafat.   The plain is cut with torrents,
which at times sweep with desolating violence into the Holy City,
and a thick desert vegetation shows that water is not deep below
the surface.

the gilt knobs of the grandees' pavilions; whilst on the Southern and Western sides the tents of the vulgar crowded the ground, disposed in *Dowar*, or circles. After many calculations, I estimated the number to be not fewer than 50,000 of all ages and sexes; a sad falling off, it is true, but still considerable.

Ali Bey (A.D. 1807) calculates 83,000 pilgrims; Burckhardt (1814), 70,000. I reduce it, in 1853, to 50,000; and in A.D. 1854, owing to political causes, it fell to about 25,000. Of these at fewest 10,000 are Meccans, as every one who can leave the city does so at pilgrimage-time. The Arabs have a superstition that the numbers at Arafat cannot be counted, and that if fewer than 600,000 mortals stand upon the hill to hear the sermon, the angels descend and complete the number. Even this year my Arab friends declared that 150,000 spirits were present in human shape. It may be observed that when the good old Bertrand de la Brocquière, esquire-carver to Philip of Burgundy, declares that the yearly Caravan from Damascus to Al-Madinah must always be composed of 700,000 persons, and that this number being incomplete, Allah sends some of his angels to make it up, he probably confounds the Caravan with the Arafat multitude.

The Holy Hill owes its name[1] and honours to a well-known legend. When our first parents forfeited Heaven by eating wheat, which deprived them of their primeval purity, they were cast down upon earth. The serpent descended at Ispahan, the peacock at Kabul, Satan at Bilbays (others say Semnan and Seistan), Eve upon Arafat, and Adam at Ceylon. The latter, determining to seek his wife, began a journey, to which earth owes its present mottled appearance. Wherever our first father

---

1 The word is explained in many ways. One derivation has already been mentioned. Others assert that when Gabriel taught Abraham the ceremonies, he ended by saying "A '*arafata* manásik'ak?"—hast thou learned thy pilgrim rites? To which the Friend of Allah replied, "*Araftu!*"—I have learned them.

placed his foot—which was large—a town afterwards arose; between the strides will always be "country." Wandering for many years, he came to the Mountain of Mercy, where our common mother was continually calling upon his name, and their *recognition* gave the place the name of Arafat. Upon its summit, Adam, instructed by the archangel Gabriel, erected a *Mada'a*, or place of prayer: and between this spot and the Nimrah Mosque the couple abode till death. Others declare that after recognition, the first pair returned to India, whence for 44 years in succession they visited the Sacred City at pilgrimage-time.

From the Holy Hill I walked down to look at the camp arrangements. The main street of tents and booths, huts and shops, was bright with lanterns, and the bazars were crowded with people and stocked with all manner of Eastern delicacies. Some anomalous spectacles met the eye. Many pilgrims, especially the soldiers, were in laical costume. In one place a half-drunken Arnaut stalked down the road, elbowing peaceful passengers and frowning fiercely in hopes of a quarrel. In another part, a huge dimly-lit tent, reeking hot, and garnished with cane seats, contained knots of Egyptians, as their red Tarbushes, white turbands, and black Za'abuts showed, noisily intoxicating themselves with forbidden hemp. There were frequent brawls and great confusion; many men had lost their parties, and, mixed with loud Labbayks, rose the shouted names of women as well as of men. I was surprised at the disproportion of female nomenclature—the missing number of fair ones seemed to double that of the other sex—and at a practice so opposed to the customs of the Moslem world. At length the boy Mohammed enlightened me. Egyptian and other bold women, when unable to join the pilgrimage, will pay or persuade a friend to shout their names

in hearing of the Holy Hill, with a view of ensuring a
real presence at the desired spot next year. So the
welkin rang with the indecent sounds of O Fatimah!
O Zaynab! O Khayz'ran!¹ Plunderers, too, were abroad.
As we returned to the tent we found a crowd assembled
near it; a woman had seized a thief as he was beginning
operations, and had the courage to hold his beard till men
ran to her assistance. And we were obliged to defend by
force our position against a knot of grave-diggers, who
would bury a little heap of bodies within a yard or two
of our tent.

One point struck me at once—the difference in point
of cleanliness between an encampment of citizens and of
Badawin. Poor Mas'ud sat holding his nose in ineffable
disgust, for which he was derided by the Meccans. I
consoled him with quoting the celebrated song of Maysunah, the beautiful Badawi wife of the Caliph Mu'a-
wiyah. Nothing can be more charming in its own Arabic
than this little song; the Badawin never hear it without
screams of joy.

> " O take these purple robes away,
>   Give back my cloak of camel's hair,
> And bear me from this tow'ring pile
>   To where the Black Tents flap i' the air.
> The camel's colt with falt'ring tread,
>   The dog that bays at all but me,
> Delight me more than ambling mules—
>   Than every art of minstrelsy;
> And any cousin, poor but free,
>   Might take me, fatted ass! from thee.² "

1 The latter name, "Ratan," is servile. Respectable women are
never publicly addressed by Moslems except as "daughter," "female
pilgrim," after some male relation, " O mother of Mohammed," " O
sister of Omar," or, *tout bonnement*, by a man's name. It would be
ill-omened and dangerous were the true name known. So most
women, when travelling, adopt an alias. Whoever knew an Afghan
fair who was not " Nur Jan," or "Sahib Jan"?

2 The British reader will be shocked to hear that by the term

The old man, delighted, clapped my shoulder, and exclaimed, "Verily, O Father of Mustachios, I will show thee the black tents of my tribe this year!"

At length night came, and we threw ourselves upon our rugs, but not to sleep.   Close by, to our bane, was a prayerful old gentleman, who began his devotions at a late hour and concluded them not before dawn.   He reminded me of the undergraduate my neighbour at Trinity College, Oxford, who would spout Æschylus at two A.M. Sometimes the chant would grow drowsy, and my ears would hear a dull retreating sound; presently, as if in self-reproach, it would rise to a sharp treble, and proceed at a rate perfectly appalling.   The coffee-houses, too, were by no means silent; deep into the night I heard the clapping of hands accompanying merry Arab songs, and the loud shouts of laughter of the Egyptian hemp-drinkers. And the guards and protectors of the camp were not "Charleys" or night-nurses.

"fatted ass" the intellectual lady alluded to her husband.   The story is that Mu'awiyah, overhearing the song, sent back the singer to her cousin and beloved wilds.   Maysunah departed with her son Yazid, and did not return to Damascus till the "fatted ass" had joined his forefathers.   Yazid inherited, with his mother's talents, all her contempt for his father; at least the following quatrain, addressed to Mu'awiyah, and generally known in Al-Islam, would appear to argue anything but reverence :—

"I drank the water of the vine : that draught had power to rouse
  Thy wrath, grim father! now, indeed, 'tis joyous to carouse!
  I'll drink!—Be wroth!—I reck not!—Ah! dear to this heart of mine
  It is to scoff a sire's command, to quaff forbidden wine."

CHAPTER XXIX.

THE CEREMONIES OF THE YAUM ARAFAT, OR THE SECOND DAY.

THE morning of the ninth Zu'l Hijjah (Tuesday, 13th Sept.) was ushered in by military sounds: a loud discharge of cannon warned us to arise and to prepare for the ceremonies of this eventful day.

After ablution and prayer, I proceeded with the boy Mohammed to inspect the numerous consecrated sites on the "Mountain of Mercy." In the first place, we repaired to a spot on rising ground to the south-east, and within a hundred yards of the hill. It is called "Jami al-Sakhrah[1]"—the Assembling Place of the Rock—from two granite boulders upon which the Prophet stood to perform "Talbiyat." There is nothing but a small enclosure of dwarf and whitewashed stone walls, divided into halves for men and women by a similar partition, and provided with a niche to direct prayer towards Meccah. Entering by steps, we found crowds of devotees and guardians, who for a consideration offered mats and carpets. After a two-bow prayer and a long supplication opposite the niche, we retired to the inner compartment, stood upon a boulder and shouted the "Labbayk."

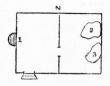

Thence, threading our way through many obstacles

---

1 Ali Bey calls it " Jami al-Rahmah "—of mercy.

of tent and stone, we ascended the broad flight of rugged steps which winds up the southern face of the rocky hill. Even at this early hour it was crowded with pilgrims, principally Badawin and Wahhabis, who had secured favourable positions for hearing the sermon. Already their green flag was planted upon the summit close to Adam's Place of Prayer. The wilder Arabs insist that "Wukuf" (standing) should take place upon the Hill. This is not done by the more civilised, who hold that all the plain within the Alamayn ranks as Arafat. According to Ali Bey, the Maliki school is not allowed to stand upon the mountain. About half way up I counted sixty-six steps, and remarked that they became narrower and steeper. Crowds of beggars instantly seized the pilgrims' robes, and strove to prevent our entering a second enclosure. This place, which resembles the former, except that it has but one compartment and no boulders, is that whence Mohammed used to address his followers; and here, to the present day, the Khatib, or preacher, in imitation of the "Last of the Prophets," sitting upon a dromedary, recites the Arafat sermon. Here, also, we prayed a two-bow prayer, and gave a small sum to the guardian.

Thence ascending with increased difficulty to the hill-top, we arrived at a large stuccoed platform,[1] with prayer-niche and a kind of obelisk, mean and badly built of lime and granite stone, whitewashed, and conspicuous from afar. It is called the Makam, or Mada'a Sayyidna Adam.[2] Here we performed the customary ceremonies amongst a crowd of pilgrims, and then we walked down the little hill.

---

1 Here was a small chapel, which the Wahhabis were demolishing when Ali Bey was at Meccah. It has not been rebuilt. Upon this spot the Prophet, according to Burckhardt, used to stand during the ceremonies.

2 Burckhardt gives this name to a place a little way on the left and about forty steps up the mountain.

Close to the plain we saw the place where the Egyptian and Damascus Mahmils stand during the sermon ; and, descending the wall that surrounds Arafat by a steep and narrow flight of coarse stone steps, we found on our right the fountain which supplies the place with water. It bubbles from the rock, and is exceedingly pure, as such water generally is in Al-Hijaz.

Our excursion employed us longer than the description requires—nine o'clock had struck before we reached the plain. All were in a state of excitement. Guns fired incessantly. Horsemen and camel-riders galloped about without apparent object. Even the women and the children stood and walked, too restless even to sleep. Arrived at the tent, I was unpleasantly surprised to find a new visitor in an old acquaintance, Ali ibn Ya Sin the Zemzemi. He had lost his mule, and, wandering in search of its keepers, he unfortunately fell in with our party. I had solid reasons to regret the mishap—he was far too curious and too observant to suit my tastes. On the present occasion, he, being uncomfortable, made us equally so. Accustomed to all the terrible "neatness" of an elderly damsel in Great Britain, a few specks of dirt upon the rugs, and half a dozen bits of cinder upon the ground, sufficed to give him attacks of "nerves."

That day we breakfasted late, for night must come before we could eat again. After mid-day prayer we performed ablutions ; some the greater, others the less, in preparation for the "Wukuf," or Standing. From noon onwards the hum and murmur of the multitude increased, and people were seen swarming about in all directions.

A second discharge of cannon (at about 3.15 P.M.) announced the approach of Al-Asr, the afternoon prayer, and almost immediately we heard the Naubat, or band preceding the Sharif's procession, as he wended his way towards the mountain. Fortunately my tent was pitched close to the road, so that without trouble I had a perfect view of the scene. First swept a cloud of mace-bearers, who, as usual on such occasions, cleared the path with scant ceremony. They were followed by the horsemen of the Desert, wielding long and tufted spears. Immediately behind them came the Sharif's led horses, upon which I fixed a curious eye. All were highly bred, and one, a brown Nijdi with black points, struck me as the perfection of an Arab. They were small, and all were apparently of the northern race.[1] Of their old crimson-velvet

---

1 In Solomon's time the Egyptian horse cost 150 silver shekels, which, if the greater shekel be meant, would still be about the average price, £18. Abbas, the late Pasha, did his best to buy first-rate Arab stallions: on one occasion he sent a mission to Al-Madinah for the sole purpose of fetching a rare work on farriery. Yet it is doubted whether he ever had a first-rate Nijdi. A Badawi sent to Cairo by one of the chiefs of Nijd, being shown by the viceroy's order over the stables, on being asked his opinion of the blood, replied bluntly, to the great man's disgust, that they did not contain a single thoroughbred, He added an apology on the part of his laird for the animals he had brought from Arabia, saying, that neither Sultan nor Shaykh could procure colts of the best strain. For none of these horses would a staunch admirer of the long-legged monster called in England a thoroughbred give twenty pounds. They are mere "rats," short and stunted, ragged and flesh-less, with rough coats and a slouching walk. But the experienced glance notes at once the fine snake-like head, ears like reeds, wide and projecting nostrils, large eyes, fiery and soft alternately, broad brow, deep base of skull, wide chest, crooked tail, limbs padded with muscle, and long elastic pasterns. And the animal put out to speed soon displays the wondrous force of blood. In fact, when buying Arabs, there are only three things to be considered,—blood, blood, and again blood. In Marco Polo's time, Aden supplied the Indian market. The state of the tribes round the "Eye of Yaman" has effectually closed the road against horse-caravans for many years past. It is said that the Zu Mohammed and the Zu Hosayn, sub-families of the Benu Yam, a large tribe living around and north of Sana'a, in Al-Yaman, have a fine large breed called Al-Jaufi, and the clan Al-Aulaki, (عولقي), rear animals celebrated for swiftness and endurance. The other races are stunted, and some Arabs declare that the air of Al-Yaman causes a degeneracy in the first generation. The Badawin, on the contrary, uphold their superiority, and talk

caparisons the less said the better; no little Indian Nawab would show aught so shabby on state occasions.

After the chargers paraded a band of black slaves on foot bearing huge matchlocks; and immediately preceded by three green and two red flags, came the Sharif, riding in front of his family and courtiers. The prince, habited in a simple white Ihram, and bare-headed, mounted a mule; the only sign of his rank was a large green and gold embroidered umbrella, held over him by a slave. The rear was brought up by another troop of Badawin on horses and camels. Behind this procession were the tents, whose doors and walls were scarcely visible for the crowd; and the picturesque background was the granite hill, covered, wherever standing-room was to be found, with white-robed pilgrims shouting "Labbayk," and waving the skirts of their glistening garments violently over their heads.

Slowly and solemnly the procession advanced towards the hill. Exactly at the hour Al-Asr, the two Mahmils had taken their station side by side on a platform in the lower slope. That of Damascus could be distinguished as the narrower and the more ornamented of the pair. The Sharif placed himself with his standard-bearers and his retinue a little above the Mahmils, within hearing of the preacher. The pilgrims crowded up to the foot of the mountain: the loud "Labbayk" of the Badawin and

with the utmost contempt of the African horse. In India we now depend for Arab blood upon the Persian Gulf, and the consequences of monopoly display themselves in an increased price for inferior animals. Our studs are generally believed to be sinks for rupees. The Governments of India now object, it is said, to rearing, at a great cost, animals distinguished by nothing but ferocity. It is evident that Al-Hijaz never can stock the Indian market. Whether Al-Nijd will supply us when the transit becomes safer, is a consideration which time only can decide. Meanwhile it would be highly advisable to take steps for restoring the Aden trade by entering into closer relations with the Imam of Sana'a and the Badawi chiefs in the North of Al-Yaman.

Wahhabis[1] fell to a solemn silence, and the waving of white robes ceased—a sign that the preacher had begun the Khutbat al-Wakfah, or Sermon of the Standing (upon Arafat). From my tent I could distinguish the form of the old man upon his camel, but the distance was too great for ear to reach.

But how came I to be at the tent?

A short confession will explain. They will shrive me who believe in inspired Spenser's lines—

> " And every spirit, as it is more pure,
>   And hath in it the more of heavenly light,
>   So it the fairer body doth procure
>   To habit in." ——

The evil came of a " fairer body." I had prepared *en cachette* a slip of paper, and had hid in my Ihram a pencil destined to put down the heads of this rarely heard discourse. But unhappily that red cashmere shawl was upon my shoulders. Close to us sat a party of fair Meccans, apparently belonging to the higher classes, and one of these I had already several times remarked. She was a tall girl, about eighteen years old, with regular features, a skin somewhat citrine-coloured, but soft and clear, symmetrical eyebrows, the most beautiful eyes, and a figure all grace. There was no head thrown back, no straightened neck, no flat shoulders, nor toes turned out— in fact, no " elegant " barbarisms : the shape was what the Arabs love, soft, bending, and relaxed, as a woman's

---

1 I obtained the following note upon the ceremonies of Wahhabi pilgrimage from one of their princes, Khalid Bey:—The Wahhabi (who, it must be borne in mind, calls himself a Muwahhid, or Unitarian, in opposition to Mushrik—Polytheist—any other sect but his own) at Meccah follows out his two principal tenets, public prayer for men daily, for women on Fridays, and rejection of the Prophet's mediation. Imitating Mohammed, he spends the first night of pilgrimage at Muna, stands upon the hill Arafat, and, returning to Muna, passes three whole days there. He derides other Moslems, abridges and simplifies the Ka'abah ceremonies, and, if possible, is guided in his devotions by one of his own sect.

figure ought to be. Unhappily she wore, instead of the usual veil, a " Yashmak " of transparent muslin, bound round the face ; and the chaperone, mother, or duenna, by whose side she stood, was apparently a very unsuspicious or complaisant old person. Flirtilla fixed a glance of admiration upon my cashmere. I directed a reply with interest at her eyes. She then by the usual coquettish gesture, threw back an inch or two of head-veil, disclosing broad bands of jetty hair, crowning a lovely oval. My palpable admiration of the new charm was rewarded by a partial removal of the Yashmak, when a dimpled mouth and a rounded chin stood out from the envious muslin. Seeing that my companions were safely employed, I entered upon the dangerous ground of raising hand to forehead. She smiled almost imperceptibly, and turned away. The pilgrim was in ecstasy.

The sermon was then half over. I was resolved to stay upon the plain and see what Flirtilla would do. *Grâce* to the cashmere, we came to a good understanding. The next page will record my disappointment—that evening the pilgrim resumed his soiled cotton cloth, and testily returned the red shawl to the boy Mohammed.

The sermon always lasts till near sunset, or about three hours. At first it was spoken amid profound silence. Then loud, scattered " Amins " (Amens) and volleys of " Labbayk " exploded at uncertain intervals At last the breeze brought to our ears a purgatorial chorus of cries, sobs, and shrieks. Even my party thought proper to be affected : old Ali rubbed his eyes, which in no case unconnected with dollars could by any amount of straining be made to shed even a crocodile's tear ; and the boy Mohammed wisely hid his face in the skirt of his Rida. Presently the people, exhausted by emotion, began to descend the hill in small parties ; and those below struck their tents and commenced loading their camels, although at least an hour's sermon remained. On this occassion,

however, all hurry to be foremost, as the " race from
Arafat " is enjoyed by none but the Badawin.

Although we worked with a will, our animals were not
ready to move before sunset, when the preacher gave the
signal of "Israf," or permission to depart. The pilgrims,

> "—— swaying to and fro,
> Like waves of a great sea, that in mid shock
> Confound each other, white with foam and fear,"

rushed down the hill with a " Labbayk" sounding like a
blast, and took the road to Muna. Then I saw the scene
which has given to this part of the ceremonies the name
of Al-Daf'a min Arafat, — the "Hurry from Arafat."
Every man urged his beast with might and main: it was
sunset; the plain bristled with tent-pegs, litters were
crushed, pedestrians were trampled, camels were overthrown: single combats with sticks and other weapons
took place; here a woman, there a child, and there an
animal were lost; briefly, it was a chaotic confusion.

To my disgust, old Ali insisted upon bestowing his
company upon me. He gave over his newly found mule
to the boy Mohammed, bidding him take care of the
beast, and mounted with me in the Shugduf. I had persuaded Shaykh Mas'ud, with a dollar, to keep close in
rear of the pretty Meccan; and I wanted to sketch the
Holy Hill. The senior began to give orders about the
camel—I, counter-orders. The camel was halted. I
urged it on: old Ali directed it to be stopped. Meanwhile
the charming face that smiled at me from the litter grew
dimmer and dimmer; the more I stormed, the less I was
listened to—a string of camels crossed our path—I lost
sight of the beauty. Then we began to advance. Again, my
determination to sketch seemed likely to fail before the
Zemzemi's little snake's eye. After a few minutes' angry
search for expedients, one suggested itself. "Effendi!"
said old Ali, "sit quiet; there is danger here." I tossed
about like one suffering from evil conscience or from the

colic. " Effendi!" shrieked the senior, "what art thou
doing? Thou wilt be the death of us." "Wallah!" I
replied with a violent plunge, "it is all thy fault ! There!"
(another plunge)—"put thy beard out of the other opening, and Allah will make it easy to us." In the ecstasy of
fear my tormentor turned his face, as he was bidden,
towards the camel's head. A second halt ensued, when
I looked out of the aperture in rear, and made a rough
drawing of the Mountain of Mercy.

At the Akhshabayn, double lines of camels, bristling
with litters, clashed with a shock more noisy than the
meeting of torrents. It was already dark : no man knew
what he was doing. The guns roared their brazen notes,
re-echoed far and wide by the harsh voices of the stony
hills. A shower of rockets bursting in the air threw into
still greater confusion the timorous mob of women and
children. At the same time martial music rose from the
masses of Nizam and the stouter-hearted pilgrims were
not sparing of their Labbayk[1] and " Íd kum Mubarak[2]"
—" May your Festival be happy ! "

After the pass of the Two Rugged Hills, the road
widened, and old Ali, who, during the bumping, had been
in a silent convulsion of terror, recovered speech and
spirits. This change he evidenced by beginning to be
troublesome once more. Again I resolved to be his
equal. Exclaiming, " My eyes are yellow with hunger! "
I seized a pot full of savoury meat which the old man had
previously stored for supper, and, without further preamble, began to eat it greedily, at the same time ready to
shout with laughter at the mumbling and grumbling
sounds that proceeded from the darkness of the litter.
We were at least three hours on the road before reach-

1 This cry is repeated till the pilgrim reaches Muna; not afterwards.

2 Another phrase is " Antum min al-áidin "—" May you be of the
keepers of festival!"

ing Muzdalifah, and being fatigued, we resolved to pass
the night there.[1] The Mosque was brilliantly illuminated,
but my hungry companions[2] apparently thought more of
supper and of sleep than of devotion.[3] Whilst the tent was
being raised, the Indians prepared our food, boiled our coffee,
filled our pipes, and spread our rugs. Before sleeping
each man collected for himself seven "Jamrah"—bits of
granite the size of a small bean.[4] Then, weary with
emotion and exertion, all lay down except the boy Mohammed, who preceded us to find encamping ground at
Muna. Old Ali, in lending his mule, made the most
stringent arrrangements with the youth about the exact
place and the exact hour of meeting—an act of simplicity
at which I could not but smile. The night was by no
means peaceful or silent. Lines of camels passed us
every ten minutes, and the shouting of travellers continued till near dawn. Pilgrims ought to have nighted at
the Mosque, but, as in Burckhardt's time, so in mine,
baggage was considered to be in danger thereabouts, and
consequently most of the devotees spent the sermon-hours
in brooding over their boxes.

---

1 Hanafis usually follow the Prophet's example in nighting at
Muzdalifah ; in the evening after prayers they attend at the Mosque,
listen to the discourse, and shed plentiful tears. Most Shafe'is spend
only a few hours at Muzdalifah.

2 We failed to buy meat at Arafat, after noon, although the bazar
was large and well stocked ; it is usual to eat flesh there, consequently
it is greedily bought up at an exorbitant price.

3 Some sects consider the prayer at Muzdalifah a matter of vital
importance.

4 Jamrah is a "small pebble ;" it is also called " Hasa," in the
plural, " Hasayat."

CHAPTER XXX.

THE CEREMONIES OF THE YAUM NAHR,
OR THE THIRD DAY.

At dawn on the Íd al-Kurban (10th Zu'l Hijjah, Wednesday, 14th September) a gun warned us to lose no time; we arose hurriedly, and started up the Batn Muhassir to Muna. By this means we lost at Muzdalifah the "Salat al-Íd," or "Festival Prayers," the great solemnity of the Moslem year, performed by all the community at daybreak. My companion was so anxious to reach Meccah, that he would not hear of devotions. About eight A.M. we entered the village, and looked for the boy Mohammed in vain. Old Ali was dreadfully perplexed; a host of high-born Turkish pilgrims were, he said, expecting him; his mule was missing—could never appear—he must be late—should probably never reach Meccah—what *would* become of him? I began by administering admonition to the mind diseased; but signally failing in a cure, I amused myself with contemplating the world from my Shugduf, leaving the office of directing it to the old Zemzemi. Now he stopped, then he pressed forward; here he thought he saw Mohammed, there he discovered our tent; at one time he would "nakh" the camel to await, in patience, his supreme hour; at another, half mad with nervousness, he would urge the excellent Mas'ud to hopeless inquiries. Finally, by good fortune, we found one of the boy Mohammed's cousins, who led us to an enclosure called Hosh al-Uzam, in the Southern portion of the Muna Basin, at the base of Mount Sabir.[1] There we pitched the tent, refreshed ourselves, and awaited the truant's return. Old Ali, failing to disturb my equanimity, attempted, as those who consort with philosophers often will do, to quarrel with me. But, finding no material wherewith to build a dispute in such fragments as "Ah!"— "Hem!"—"Wallah!" he hinted desperate intentions against the boy Mohammed. When, however, the youth appeared, with even more jauntiness of mien than usual, Ali bin Ya Sin lost heart, brushed by him, mounted his mule, and, doubtless cursing us "under the tongue," rode away, frowning viciously, with his heels playing upon the beast's ribs.

Mohammed had been delayed, he said, by the difficulty of finding asses. We were now to mount for "the Throwing,[2]" as a preliminary to which we washed "with seven waters" the seven pebbles brought from Muzdalifah, and bound them in our Ihrams. Our first destination was the entrance to the western end of the long line which composes the Muna village. We found a swarming crowd in the narrow road opposite the "Jamrat al-Akabah,[3]" or, as it is vulgarly called, the Shaytan al-Kabir—the "Great Devil." These names distinguish it from another pillar, the "Wusta," or "Central Place," (of stoning,) built in the middle of Muna, and a third at the eastern end, "Al-Aula," or the "First Place."[4]

The "Shaytan al-Kabir" is a dwarf buttress of rude

---

1 Even pitching ground here is charged to pilgrims.

2 Some authorities advise that this rite of "Ramy" be performed on foot.

3 The word "Jamrah" is applied to the place of stoning, as well as to the stones.

4 These numbers mark the successive spots where the Devil, in in the shape of an old Shaykh, appeared to Adam, Abraham, and Ishmael, and was driven back by the simple process taught by Gabriel, of throwing stones about the size of a bean.

masonry, about eight feet high by two and a half broad, placed against a rough wall of stones at the Meccan entrance to Muna. As the ceremony of "Ramy," or Lapidation, must be performed on the first day by all pilgrims between sunrise and sunset, and as the fiend was malicious enough to appear in a rugged Pass,[1] the crowd makes the place dangerous. On one side of the road, which is not forty feet broad, stood a row of shops belonging principally to barbers. On the other side is the rugged wall against which the pillar stands, with a *chevaux de frise* of Badawin and naked boys. The narrow space was crowded with pilgrims, all struggling like drowning men to approach as near as possible to the Devil; it would have been easy to run over the heads of the mass. Amongst them were horsemen with rearing chargers. Badawin on wild camels, and grandees on mules and asses, with out-runners, were breaking a way by assault and battery. I had read Ali Bey's self-felicitations upon escaping this place with "only two wounds in the left leg," and I had duly provided myself with a hidden dagger. The precaution was not useless. Scarcely had my donkey entered the crowd than he was overthrown by a drome-dary, and I found myself under the stamping and roaring beast's stomach. Avoiding being trampled upon by a judicious use of the knife, I lost no time in escaping from a place so ignobly dangerous. Some Moslem travellers assert, in proof of the sanctity of the spot, that no Moslem is ever killed here: Meccans assured me that accidents are by no means rare.

Presently the boy Mohammed fought his way out of the crowd with a bleeding nose. We both sat down upon a bench before a barber's booth, and, schooled by ad-

---

1 I borrow this phrase from Ali Bey, who, however, speaks more like an ignorant Catalonian than a learned Abbaside, when he calls the pillar "La Maison du Diable," and facetiously asserts that " le diable a eu la malice de placer sa maison dans un lieu fort étroit qui n'a peut-être pas 34 pieds de large."

R. Burton, delt.

C.F. Kell, Lith.

STONING THE "GREAT DEVIL".

versity, awaited with patience an opportunity. Finding an opening, we approached within about five cubits of the place, and holding each stone between the thumb and the forefinger[1] of the right hand, we cast it at the pillar, exclaiming, "In the name of Allah, and Allah is Almighty! (I do this) in Hatred of the Fiend and to his Shame." After which came the Tahlil and the "Sana," or praise to Allah. The seven stones being duly thrown, we retired, and entering the barber's booth, took our places upon one of the earthern benches around it. This was the time to remove the Ihram or pilgrim's garb, and to return to Ihlal, the normal state of Al-Islam. The barber shaved our heads,[2] and, after trimming our beards and cutting our nails, made us repeat these words: "I purpose loosening my Ihram according to the Practice of the Prophet, Whom may Allah bless and preserve! O Allah, make unto me in every Hair, a Light, a Purity, and a generous Reward! In the name of Allah, and Allah is Almighty!" At the conclusion of his labour, the barber politely addressed to us a "Na'íman—Pleasure to you!" To which we as ceremoniously replied, "Allah give thee pleasure!" We had no clothes with us, but we could use our cloths to cover our heads, and slippers to defend our feet from the fiery sun; and we now. could safely twirl our mustachios and stroke our beards— placid enjoyments of which we had been deprived by the

---

1 Some hold the pebble as a schoolboy does a marble, others between the thumb and forefinger extended, others shoot them from the thumb knuckle, and most men consult their own convenience.

2 The barber removed all my hair. Hanifis shave at least a quarter of the head, Shafe'is a few hairs on the right side. The prayer is, as usual, differently worded, some saying, " O Allah this my Forelock is in Thy Hand, then grant me for every Hair a Light on Resurrection-day, by Thy Mercy O most Merciful of the Merciful !" I remarked that the hair was allowed to lie upon the ground, whereas strict Moslems, with that reverence for man's body—the Temple of the Supreme—which characterizes their creed, carefully bury it in the earth.

Laws of Pilgrimage. After resting about an hour in the booth, which, though crowded with sitting customers, was delightfully cool compared with the burning glare of the road, we mounted our asses, and at eleven A.M. we started Meccah-wards.

This return from Muna to Meccah is called Al-Nafr, or the Flight[1]: we did not fail to keep our asses at speed, with a few halts to refresh ourselves with gugglets of water. There was nothing remarkable in the scene: our ride in was a repetition of our ride out. In about half an hour we entered the city, passing through that classical locality called "Batn Kuraysh," which was crowded with people, and then we repaired to the boy Mohammed's house for the purpose of bathing and preparing to visit the Ka'abah.

Shortly after our arrival, the youth returned home in a state of excitement, exclaiming, " Rise, Effendi! dress and follow me!" The Ka'abah, though open, would for a time be empty, so that we should escape the crowd. My pilgrim's garb, which had not been removed, was made to look neat and somewhat Indian, and we sallied forth together without loss of time.

A crowd had gathered round the Ka'abah, and I had no wish to stand bareheaded and barefooted in the midday September sun. At the cry of "Open a path for the Haji who would enter the House," the gazers made way. Two stout Meccans, who stood below the door, raised me in their arms, whilst a third drew me from above into the building. At the entrance I was accosted by several officials, dark-looking Meccans, of whom the blackest and plainest was a youth of the Benu Shaybah family,[2]

---

1 This word is confounded with "Dafa" by many Moslem authors. Some speak of the *Nafr* from Arafat to Muzdalifah and the *Dafa* from Muzdalifah to Muna. I have used the words as my Mutawwif used them.

2 They keep the keys of the House. In my day the head of the family was " Shaykh Ahmad."

the *sangre-azul* of Al-Hijaz. He held in his hand the
huge silver-gilt padlock of the Ka'abah,[1] and presently
taking his seat upon a kind of wooden press in the left
corner of the hall, he officially inquired my name, nation,
and other particulars. The replies were satisfactory, and
the boy Mohammed was authoritatively ordered to conduct me round the building, and to recite the prayers. I
will not deny that, looking at the windowless walls, the
officials at the door, and the crowd of excited fanatics
below—

"And the place death, considering who I was,"[2]
my feelings were of the trapped-rat description, acknow-
ledged by the immortal nephew of his uncle Perez. This
did not, however, prevent my carefully observing the
scene during our long prayers, and making a rough plan
with a pencil upon my white Ihram.

Nothing is more simple than the interior of this
celebrated building. The pavement, which is level with
the ground, is composed of slabs of fine and various coloured marbles, mostly, however, white, disposed chequer-
wise. The walls, as far as they can be seen, are of
the same material, but the pieces are irregularly shaped,
and many of them are engraved with long inscriptions in
the Suls and other modern characters. The upper part of
the walls, together with the ceiling, at which it is considered disrespectful to look,[3] are covered with handsome

1 In Ibn Jubayr's time this large padlock was of gold. It is said
popularly that none but the Benu Shaybah can open it; a minor
miracle, doubtless proceeding from the art of some Eastern Hobbs or
Bramah.

2 However safe a Christian might be at Meccah, nothing could
preserve him from the ready knives of enraged fanatics if detected in
the House. The very idea is pollution to a Moslem.

3 I do not known the origin of this superstition; but it would be
unsafe for a pilgrim to look fixedly at the Ka'abah ceiling. Under
the arras I was told is a strong planking of Saj, or Indian teak, and
above it a stuccoed Sath, or flat roof.

red damask, flowered over with gold,[1] and tucked up about six feet high, so as to be removed from pilgrims' hands. The flat roof is upheld by three cross-beams, whose shapes appear under the arras ; they rest upon the eastern and western walls, and are supported in the centre by three columns[2] about twenty inches in diameter, covered with carved and ornamented aloes wood.[3]   At the Iraki corner

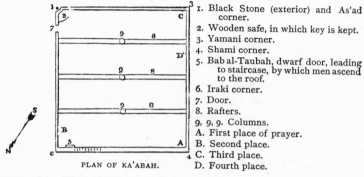

PLAN OF KA'ABAH.

1. Black Stone (exterior) and As'ad corner.
2. Wooden safe, in which key is kept.
3. Yamani corner.
4. Shami corner.
5. Bab al-Taubah, dwarf door, leading to staircase, by which men ascend to the roof.
6. Iraki corner.
7. Door.
8. Rafters.
9, 9, 9. Columns.
A. First place of prayer.
B. Second place.
C. Third place.
D. Fourth place.

there is a dwarf door, called Bab al-Taubah (of Repentance).[4]   It leads into a narrow passage and to the staircase by which the servants ascend to the roof : it is never opened except for working purposes.   The " Aswad " or

---

1 Exactly realising the description of our English bard:—

"Goodly arras of great majesty,
Woven with gold and silk so close and nere,
That the rich metal lurked privily,
As feigning to be hid from envious eye."

2 Ibn Jubayr mentions three columns of teak.   Burckhardt and Ali Bey, two.   In Al-Fasi's day there were four.   The Kuraysh erected six columns in double row.   Generally the pillars have been three in number.

3 This wood, which has been used of old to ornament sacred buildings in the East, is brought to Meccah in great quantities by Malay and Java pilgrims.   The best kind is known by its oily appearance and a "fizzing" sound in fire; the cunning vendors easily supply it with these desiderata.

4 Ibn Jubayr calls it Bab al-Rahmah.

" As'ad¹" corner is occupied by a flat-topped and quadrant-shaped press or safe,² in which at times is placed the key of the Ka'abah.³ Both door and safe are of aloes wood. Between the columns, and about nine feet from the ground, ran bars of a metal which I could not distinguish, and hanging to them were many lamps, said to be of gold.

Although there were in the Ka'abah but a few attendants engaged in preparing it for the entrance of pilgrims,⁴ the windowless stone walls and the choked-up door made it worse than the Piombi of Venice ; perspiration trickled in large drops, and I thought with horror what it must be when filled with a mass of furiously jostling and crushing fanatics. Our devotions consisted of a two-bow prayer,⁵ followed by long supplications at the Shami (West) corner, the Iraki (north) angle, the Yamani (south), and, lastly, opposite the southern third of the back wall.⁶ These concluded, I returned to the door, where payment is made. The boy Mohammed told me that the total expense would be seven dollars. At the same time he had been indulging aloud in his favourite rhodomontade, boasting of my greatness, and had declared me to be an Indian pilgrim, a race still supposed at

1 The Hajar al-Aswad is also called Al-As'ad, or the Propitious.

2 Here, in Ibn Jubayr's time, stood two boxes full of Korans.

3 The key is sometimes placed in the hands of a child of the house of Shaybah, who sits in state, with black slaves on both sides.

4 In Ibn Jubayr's day the Ka'abah was opened with more ceremony. The ladder was rolled up to the door, and the chief of the Benu Shaybah, ascending it, was covered by attendants with a black veil from head to foot, whilst he opened the padlock. Then, having kissed the threshold, he entered, shut the door behind him, and prayed two Rukats; after which, all the Benu Shaybah, and, lastly, the vulgar were admitted. In these day the veil is obsolete. The Shaykh enters the Ka'abah alone, perfumes it and prays; the pilgrims are then admitted *en masse;* and the style in which the eunuchs handle their quarter-staves forms a scene more animated than decorous.

5 Some pray four instead of two bows.

6 Burckhardt erroneously says, "in every corner."

Meccah to be made of gold.[1] When seven dollars were tendered, they were rejected with instance. Expecting something of the kind, I had been careful to bring no more than eight. Being pulled and interpellated by half a dozen attendants, my course was to look stupid, and to pretend ignorance of the language. Presently the Shaybah youth bethought him of a contrivance. Drawing forth from the press the key of the Ka'abah, he partly bared it of its green-silk gold-lettered *étui*,[2] and rubbed a golden knob quartrefoil-shaped upon my eyes, in order to brighten them. I submitted to the operation with a good grace, and added a dollar—my last—to the former offering. The Sharif received it with a hopeless glance, and, to my satisfaction, would not put forth his hand to be kissed. Then the attendants began to demand vails. I replied by opening my empty pouch. When let down from the door by the two brawny Meccans, I was expected to pay them, and accordingly appointed to meet them at the boy Mohammed's house; an arrangement to which they grumblingly assented. When delivered from these troubles, I was congratulated by my sharp companion thus: "Wallah, Effendi! thou hast escaped well! some men have left their skins behind.[3]"

---

1 These Indians are ever in extremes, paupers or millionaires, and, like all Moslems, the more they pay at Meccah the higher becomes their character and religious titles. A Turkish Pasha seldom squanders as much money as does a Moslem merchant from the far East. Khudabakhsh, the Lahore shawl-dealer, owned to having spent 800*l.* in feastings and presents. He appeared to consider that sum a trifle, although, had a debtor carried off one tithe of it, his health would have been seriously affected.

2 The cover of the key is made, like Abraham's veil, of three colours, red, black or green. It is of silk, embroidered with golden letters, and upon it are written the Bismillah, the name of the reigning Sultan, "Bag of the key of the holy Ka'abah," and a verselet from the "Family of Amran" (Koran, ch. 3). It is made, like the Kiswah, at Khurunfish, a place that will be noticed below.

3 "Ecorchés"—"pelati;" the idea is common to most imaginative nations.

All pilgrims do not enter the Ka'abah[1]; and many
refuse to do so for religious reasons. Omar Effendi, for
instance, who never missed a pilgrimage, had never seen
the interior.[2] Those who tread the hallowed floor are
bound, among many other things, never again to walk
barefooted, to take up fire with the fingers, or to tell lies.
Most really conscientious men cannot afford the luxuries
of slippers, tongs, and truth. So thought Thomas, when
offered the apple which would give him the tongue which
cannot lie:—

" ' My tongue is mine ain,' true Thomas said.
' A gudely gift ye wad gie to me !
I neither dought to buy nor sell
    At fair or tryst, where I may be,
I dought neither speak to prince or peer,
    Nor ask of grace from fair ladye ! ' "

Amongst the Hindus I have met with men who have
proceeded upon a pilgrimage to Dwarka, and yet who
would not receive the brand of the god, because lying
would then be forbidden to them. A confidential servant
of a friend in Bombay naïvely declared that he had not
been marked, as the act would have ruined him. There
is a sad truth in what he said : Lying to the Oriental is
meat and drink, and the roof that shelters him.

The Ka'abah had been dressed in her new attire when
we entered.[3] The covering, however, instead of being

1 The same is the case at Al-Madinah ; many religious men object
on conscientious grounds to enter the Prophet's mosque. The poet
quoted below made many visitations to Al-Madinah, but never could
persuade himself to approach the tomb. The Esquire Carver saw
two young Turks who had voluntarily had their eyes thrust out *at
Meccah* as soon as they had seen the glory and visible sanctity of *the
tomb of Mohammed.* I "doubt the fact," which thus appears ushered
in by a fiction.

2 I have not thought it necessary to go deep into the list of
" Muharramat," or actions forbidden to the pilgrim who has entered
the Ka'abah. They are numerous and meaningless.

3 The use of the feminine pronoun is explained below. When

secured at the bottom to the metal rings in the basement, was tucked up by ropes from the roof, and depended over each face in two long tongues.   It was of a brilliant black, and the Hizam—the zone or golden band running round the upper portion of the building—as well as the Burká (face-veil), were of dazzling brightness.[1]

The origin of this custom must be sought in the ancient practice of typifying the church visible by a virgin

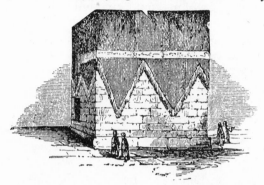

The Ka'abah in its new covering.

or bride.   The poet Abd al-Rahim al Bura'i, in one of his Gnostic effusions, has embodied the idea :—

وعروس ملكة بالكرامات تجلى

"And Meccah's bride (*i.e.* the Ka'abah) is displayed
with (miraculous) signs."

This idea doubtless led to the face-veil, the covering, and the guardianship of eunuchs.

The Meccan temple was first dressed as a mark of

unclothed, the Ka'abah is called Uryanah (naked), in opposition to its normal state, "Muhramah," or clad in Ihram. In Burckhardt's time the house remained naked for fifteen days ; now the investiture is effected in a few hours.

1 The gold-embroidered curtain covering the Ka'abah door is called by the learned " Burka al-Ka'abah " (the Ka'abah's face-veil), by the vulgar Burka Fatimah ; they connect it in idea with the Prophet's daughter.

honour by Tobba the Himyarite when he Judaized.[1] If
we accept this fact, which is vouched for by Oriental
history, we are led to the conclusion that the children of
Israel settled at Meccah had connected the temple with
their own faith, and, as a corollary, that the prophet of Al-
Islam introduced their apocryphal traditions into his
creed. The pagan Arabs did not remove the coverings :
the old and torn Kiswah was covered with a new cloth,
and the weight threatened to crush the building.[2] From
the time of Kusay, the Ka'abah was veiled by subscription,
till Abu Rabi'at al-Mughayrah bin Abdullah, who, having
acquired great wealth by commerce, offered to provide the
Kiswah on alternate years, and thereby gained the name
of Al-Ádil. The Prophet preferred a covering of fine
Yaman cloth, and directed the expense to be defrayed by
the Bayt al-Mal, or public treasury. Omar chose Egyptian linen, ordering the Kiswah to be renewed every year,
and the old covering to be distributed among the pilgrims.
In the reign of Osman, the Ka'abah was twice clothed, in
winter and summer. For the former season, it received a
Kamis, or Tobe (shirt) of brocade ; with an Izar, or veil :
for the latter a suit of fine linen. Mu'awiyah at first supplied linen and brocade ; he afterwards exchanged the
former for striped Yaman stuff, and ordered Shaybah bin
Osman to strip the Ka'abah and to perfume the walls with
Khaluk. Shaybah divided the old Kiswah among the
pilgrims, and Abdullah bin Abbas did not object to this
distribution.[3] The Caliph Ma'amun (9th century) ordered

---

1 The pyramids, it is said, were covered from base to summit with
yellow silk or satin.

2 At present the Kiswah, it need scarcely be said, does not cover
the flat roof.

3 Ayishah also, when Shaybah proposed to bury the old Kiswah,
that it might not be worn by the impure, directed him to sell it, and
to distribute the proceeds to the poor. The Meccans still follow the
first half, but neglect the other part of the order given by the " Mother
of the Moslems." Kazi Khan advises the proceeds of the sale being

the dress to be changed three times a year. In his day it
was red brocade on the 10th Muharram ; fine linen on
the 1st Rajab ; and white brocade on the 1st Shawwal.
At last he was informed that the veil applied on the 10th
of Muharram was too closely followed by the red brocade
in the next month, and that it required renewing on the
1st of Shawwal. This he ordered to be done. Al-
Mutawakkil (ninth century), when informed that the dress
was spoiled by pilgrims, at first ordered two to be given
and the brocade shirt to be let down as far as the pavement : at last he sent a new veil every two months.
During the Caliphat of the Abbasides this investiture
came to signify sovereignty in Al-Hijaz, which passed
alternately from Baghdad to Egypt and Al-Yaman. In
Al-Idrisi's time (twelth century A.D.) the Kiswah was composed of black silk, and renewed every year by the Caliph
of Baghdad. Ibn Jubayr writes that it was green and
gold. The Kiswah remained with Egypt when Sultan
Kalaun[1] (thirteenth century A.D.) conveyed the rents of two
villages, "Baysus" and "Sindbus,[2]" to the expense of
providing an outer black and an inner red curtain for the
Ka'abah, with hangings for the Prophet's tomb at Al-
Madinah. When the Holy Land fell under the power of
Osmanli, Sultan Salim ordered the Kiswah to be black ;
and his son Sultan Sulayman the Magnificent (sixteenth

---

devoted to the repairs of the temple. The "Siraj al-Wahhaj" positively forbids, as sinful, the cutting, transporting, selling, buying, and
placing it between the leaves of the Koran. Kutb al-Din (from whom
I borrow these particulars) introduces some fine and casuistic distinc-
tions. In his day, however, the Benu Shaybah claimed the old, after
the arrival of the new Kiswah ; and their right to it was admitted.
To the present day they continue to sell it.

1 Some authors also mention a green Kiswah, applied by this
monarch. Embroidered on it were certain verselets of the Koran, the
formula of the Moslem faith, and the names of the Prophet's Companions.

2 Burckhardt says "Bysous" and "Sandabeir."

century A.D.), devoted considerable sums to the purpose. The Kiswah was afterwards renewed at the accession of each Sultan. And the Wahhabis, during the first year of their conquest, covered the Ka'abah with a red Kiswah of the same stuff as the fine Arabian Aba or cloak, and made at Al-Hasa.

The Kiswah is now worked at a cotton manufactory called Al-Khurunfish, of the Tumn Bab al-Sha'ariyah, Cairo. It is made by a hereditary family, called the Bayt al-Sadi, and, as the specimen in my possession proves, it is a coarse tissue of silk and cotton mixed. The Kiswah is composed of eight pieces—two for each face of the Ka'abah—the seams being concealed by the Hizam, a broad band, which at a distance looks like gold; it is lined with white calico, and is supplied with cotton ropes. Anciently it is said all the Koran was interwoven into it. Now, it is inscribed "Verily, the First of Houses founded for Mankind (to worship in) is that at Bekkah[1]; blessed and a Direction to all Creatures"; together with seven chapters, namely, the Cave, Mariam, the Family of Amran, Repentance, T.H. with Y.S. and Tabarak. The character is that called Tumar, the largest style of Eastern calligraphy, legible from a considerable distance.[2] The Hizam is a band about two feet broad, and surrounding the Ka'abah at two-thirds of its height. It is divided into four pieces, which are sewn together. On the first and second is inscribed the "Throne verslet," and on the third and fourth the titles of the reigning Sultan. These inscriptions are, like the Burka, or door curtain, gold worked into red silk, by the Bayt al-Sadi. When the Kiswah is ready at Khurunfish, it is carried in

1 From the "Family of Amran" (chap. 3). "Bekkah" is "a place of crowding"; hence applied to Meccah generally. Some writers, however, limit it to the part of the city round the Harim.

2 It is larger than the suls. Admirers of Eastern calligraphy may see a "Bismillah," beautifully written in Tumar, on the wall of Sultan Mu'ayyad's Mosque at Cairo.

procession to the Mosque Al-Hasanayn, where it is lined, sewn, and prepared for the journey.[1]

After quitting the Ka'abah, I returned home exhausted, and washed with henna and warm water, to mitigate the pain of the sun-scalds upon my arms, shoulders, and breast. The house was empty, all the Turkish pilgrims being still at Muna; and the *Kabirah*—the old lady—received me with peculiar attention. I was ushered into an upper room, whose teak wainscotings, covered with Cufic and other inscriptions, large carpets, and ample Diwans, still showed a sort of ragged splendour. The family had "seen better days," the Sharif Ghalib having confiscated three of its houses; but it is still proud, and cannot merge the past into the present. In the "drawing-room," which the Turkish colonel occupied when at Meccah, the Kabirah supplied me with a pipe, coffee, cold water, and breakfast. I won her heart by praising the graceless boy Mohammed; like all mothers, she dearly loved the scamp of the family. When he entered, and saw his maternal parent standing near me, with only the end of her veil drawn over her mouth, he began to scold her with divers insinuations. "Soon thou wilt sit amongst the men in the hall!" he exclaimed. "O, my son," rejoined the Kabirah, "fear Allah: thy mother is in years!" —and truly she was so, being at least fifty. "A-a-h!" sneered the youth, who had formed, as boys of the world must do, or appear to do, a very low estimate of the sex. The old lady understood the drift of the exclamation, and departed with a half-laughing "May Allah disappoint thee!" She soon, however, returned, bringing me water for ablution; and having heard that I had not yet sacrificed a sheep at Muna, enjoined me to return and perform without delay that important rite.

---

[1] Mr. Lane (Mod. Egypt. vol. iii. chap. 25) has given an ample and accurate description of the Kiswah. I have added a few details, derived from " Khalil Effendi " of Cairo, a professor of Arabic, and an excellent French scholar.

After resuming our laical toilette, and dressing gaily for the great festival, we mounted our asses about the cool of the afternoon, and, returning to Muna, we found the tent full of visitors. Ali ibn Ya Sin, the Zemzemi, had sent me an amphora of holy water, and the carrier was awaiting the customary dollar. With him were several Meccans, one of whom spoke excellent Persian. We sat down, and chatted together for an hour; and I afterwards learned from the boy Mohammed, that all had pronounced me to be an 'Ajami.

After their departure we debated about the victim, which is only a Sunnat, or practice of the Prophet.[1] It is generally sacrificed immediately after the first lapidation, and we had already been guilty of delay. Under these circumstances, and considering the meagre condition of my purse, I would not buy a sheep, but contented myself with watching my neighbours. They gave themselves great trouble, especially a large party of Indians pitched near us, to buy the victim cheap; but the Badawin were not less acute, and he was happy who paid less than a dollar and a quarter. Some preferred contributing to buy a lean ox. None but the Sharif and the principal dignitaries slaughtered camels. The pilgrims dragged their victims to a smooth rock near the Akabah, above which stands a small open pavilion, whose sides, red with fresh blood, showed that the prince and his attendants had been busy at sacrifice.[2] Others stood before their tents, and, directing the victim's face towards the Ka'abah, cut its throat, ejaculating, " Bismillah! Alláho Akbar[3]"

---

1 Those who omit the rite fast ten days; three during the pilgrimage season, and the remaining seven at some other time.

2 The camel is sacrificed by thrusting a pointed instrument into the interval between the sternum and the neck. This anomaly may be accounted for by the thickness and hardness of the muscles of the throat.

3 It is strange that the accurate Burckhardt should make the Moslem say, when slaughtering or sacrificing, "In the name of the

The boy Mohammed sneeringly directed my attention to the Indians, who, being a mild race, had hired an Arab butcher to do the deed of blood; and he aroused all Shaykh Nur's ire by his taunting comments upon the chicken-heartedness of the men of Hind.   It is considered a meritorious act to give away the victim without eating any portion of its flesh.   Parties of Takruri might be seen sitting vulture-like, contemplating the sheep and goats; and no sooner was the signal given, than they fell upon the bodies, and cut them up without removing them.   The surface of the valley soon came to resemble the dirtiest slaughter-house, and my prescient soul drew bad auguries for the future.

We had spent a sultry afternoon in the basin of Muna, which is not unlike a volcanic crater, an Aden closed up at the seaside.   Towards night the occasional puffs of Samum ceased, and through the air of deadly stillness a mass of purple nimbus, bisected by a thin grey line of mist-cloud, rolled down upon us from the Taif hills.   When darkness gave the signal, most of the pilgrims pressed towards the square in front of the Muna Mosque, to enjoy the pyrotechnics and the discharge of cannon.   But during the spectacle came on a windy storm, whose light-nings, flashing their fire from pole to pole paled the rockets; and whose thunderings, re-echoed by the rocky hills, dumbed the puny artillery of man.   We were disappointed in our hopes of rain.   A few huge drops pattered upon the plain and sank into its thirsty entrails; all the rest was thunder and lightning, dust-clouds and whirlwind.

---

most Merciful God!"   As Mr. Lane justly observes, the attribute of mercy is omitted on these occasions.

CHAPTER XXXI.

THE THREE DAYS OF DRYING FLESH.

ALL was dull after the excitement of the Great Festival. The heat of the succeeding night rendered every effort to sleep abortive; and as our little camp required a guard in a place so celebrated for plunderers, I spent the greater part of the time sitting in the clear pure moonlight.[1]

After midnight we again repaired to the Devils, and, beginning with the Ula, or first pillar, at the Eastern extremity of Muna, threw at each. seven stones (making a total of twenty-one), with the ceremonies before described.

On Thursday (Sept. 15th, 1853), we arose before dawn, and prepared with a light breakfast for the fatigues of a climbing walk. After half an hour spent in hopping from boulder to boulder, we arrived at a place situated on the lower declivity of the Jabal Sabir, the northern wall of the Muna basin. Here is the *Majarr al-Kabsh*, "the Dragging-place of the Ram," a small, whitewashed square, divided

[1] It is not safe to perform this ceremony at an early hour, although the ritual forbids it being deferred after sunset. A crowd of women, however, assembled at the Devils in the earlier part of the 11th night (our 10th); and these dames, despite the oriental modesty of face-veils, attack a stranger with hands and stones as heartily as English hop-gatherers hasten to duck the Acteon who falls in their way. Hence, popular usage allows stones to be thrown by men until the morning prayers of the 11th Zu'l Hijjah.

into two compartments. The first is entered by a few ragged steps in the south-east angle, which lead to an enclosure thirty feet by fifteen. In the north-east corner is a block of granite (A), in which a huge gash, several inches broad, some feet deep, and completely splitting the stone in knife-shape, notes the spot where Ibrahim's blade fell when the archangel Gabriel forbade him to slay Ismail 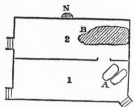 his son. The second compartment contains a diminutive hypogæum (B). In this cave the patriarch sacrificed the victim, which gives the place a name. We descended by a flight of steps, and under the stifling ledge of rock found mats and praying-rugs, which, at this early hour, were not overcrowded. We followed the example of the patriarchs, and prayed a two-bow prayer in each of the enclosures. After distributing the usual gratification, we left the place, and proceeded to mount the hill, in hope of seeing some of the apes said still to haunt the heights. These animals are supposed by the Meccans to have been Jews, thus transformed for having broken the Sabbath by hunting.[1] They abound in the elevated regions about Arafat and Taif, where they are caught by mixing the juice of the Asclepias and narcotics with dates and other sweet bait.[2] The Hijazi ape is a hideous cynocephalus, with small eyes placed close together, and almost hidden by a disproportionate snout; a greenish-brown coat, long arms, and a stern of lively pink, like fresh meat. They

---

[1] Traditions about these animals vary in the different parts of Arabia. At Aden, for instance, they are supposed to be a remnant of the rebellious tribe of 'Ád. It is curious that the popular Arabic, like the Persian names, Sa'adan, Maymun, Shadi, &c., &c., are all expressive of (a probably euphuistic) "propitiousness."

[2] The Egyptians generally catch, train, and take them to the banks of the Nile, where the "Kurayeati" (ape-leader) is a popular character.

are docile, and are said to be fond of spirituous liquors, and to display an inordinate affection for women. Al-Mas'udi tells about them a variety of anecdotes. According to him their principal use in Hind and Chin was to protect kings from poison, by eating suspected dishes. The Badawin have many tales concerning them. It is universally believed that they catch and kill kites, by exposing the rosy portion of their persons and concealing the rest ; the bird pounces upon what appears to be raw meat, and presently finds himself viciously plucked alive. Throughout Arabia an old story is told of them. A merchant was once plundered during his absence by a troop of these apes ; they tore open his bales, and, charmed with the scarlet hue of the Tarbushes, began applying those articles of dress to uses quite opposite to their normal purpose. The merchant was in despair, when his slave offered for a consideration to recover the goods. Placing himself in the front, like a fugleman to the ape-company, he went through a variety of manœuvres with a Tarbush, and concluded with throwing it far away. The recruits carefully imitated him, and the drill concluded with his firing a shot ; the plunderers decamped and the caps were recovered.

Failing to see any apes, we retired to the tent ere the sun waxed hot, in anticipation of a terrible day. Nor were we far wrong. In addition to the heat, we had swarms of flies, and the blood-stained earth began to reek with noisome vapours. Nought moved in the air except kites and vultures, speckling the deep blue sky : the denizens of earth seemed paralysed by the fire from above. I spent the time between breakfast and nightfall lying half-dressed upon a mat, moving round the tent-pole to escape the glare, and watching my numerous neighbours, male and female. The Indians were particularly kind, filling my pipe, offering cooled water, and performing similar little offices. I repaid them with a supply of provisions, which, at the Muna market-prices, these unfortunates could ill afford.

When the moon arose the boy Mohammed and I walked out into the town, performed our second lapidation,[1] and visited the coffee-houses. The shops were closed early, but business was transacted in places of public resort till midnight. We entered the houses of numerous acquaintances, who accosted my companion, and were hospitably welcomed with pipes and coffee. The first question always was, " Who is this pilgrim ? " and more than once the reply, " An Afghan," elicited the language of my own country, which I could no longer speak. Of this phenomenon, however, nothing was thought : many Afghans settled in India know not a word of Pushtu, and even above the Passes many of the townspeople are imperfectly

"The Great Devil."

---

1 This ceremony, as the reader will have perceived, is performed by the Shafe'is on the 10th, the 11th, and the 12th of Zu'l Hijjah. The Hanafis conclude their stoning on the 13th. The times vary with each day, and differ considerably in religious efficacy. On the night of the 10th (our 9th), for instance, lapidation, according to some authorities, cannot take place; others permit it, with a sufficient reason. Between the dawn and sunrise it is Makruh, or disapproved of. Between sunrise and the declination is the Sunnat-time, and therefore the best. From noon to sunset it is Mubah, or permissible : the same is the case with the night, if a cause exist. On the 11th and 12th of Zu'l Hijjah lapidation is disapproved of from sunset to sunrise. The Sunnat is from noon to sunset, and it is permissible at all other hours. The number of stones thrown by the Shafe'is, is 49, viz., 7 on the 10th day, 7 at each pillar (total 21) on the 11th day, and the same on the 12th Zu'l Hijjah. The Hanafis also throw 21 stones on the 13th, which raises their number to 70. The first 7 bits of granite must be collected at Muzdalifah; the rest may be taken from the Muna valley; and all must be washed 7 times before being thrown. In throwing, the Hanafis attempt to approach the pillar, if possible, standing within reach of it. Shafe'is may stand at a greater distance, which should not, however, pass the limits of 5 cubits.

acquainted with it. The Meccans in consequence of their extensive intercourse with strangers and habits of travelling, are admirable conversational linguists. They speak Arabic remarkably well, and with a volubility surpassing the most lively of our continental nations. Persian, Turkish, and Hindustani are generally known : and the Mutawwifs, who devote themselves to various races of pilgrims, soon become masters of many languages.

Returning homewards, we were called to a spot by the clapping of hands[1] and the loud sound of song. We found a crowd of Badawin surrounding a group engaged in their favourite occupation of dancing. The performance is wild in the extreme, resembling rather the hopping of bears than the inspirations of Terpischore. The bystanders joined in the song; an interminable recitative, as usual, in the minor key, and—Orientals are admirable timists—it sounded like one voice. The refrain appeared to be—

"Lá Yayhá!   Lá Yayhá!"

to which no one could assign a meaning. At other times they sang something intelligible. For instance:—

نهار العيد فى منا شفت سيدى
غريب الدار عند كم وارحمو زن[1]

That is to say,—

> "On the Great Festival-day at Muna I saw my lord.
> I am a stranger amongst you, therefore pity me!"

This couplet may have, like the puerilities of certain modern and European poets, an abstruse and mystical

---

1 Here called Safk. It is mentioned by Herodotus, and known to almost every oriental people. The Badawin sometimes, though rarely, use a table or kettledrum. Yet, amongst the "Pardah," or musical modes of the East, we find the Hijazi ranking with the Isfahani and the Iraki. Southern Arabia has never been celebrated for producing musicians, like the banks of the Tigris to which we owe, besides castanets and cymbals, the guitar, the drum, and the lute, father of the modern harp. The name of this instrument is a corruption of the Arabic "Al-'Úd" (العود), through liuto and luth, into lute.

meaning, to be discovered when the Arabs learn to write erudite essays upon nursery rhymes. The style of salta- tion, called Rufayah, rivalled the song. The dancers raised both arms above their heads, brandishing a dagger, pistol, or some other small weapon. They followed each other by hops, on one or both feet, sometimes indulging in the most demented leaps; whilst the bystanders clapped with their palms a more enlivening measure. This I was told is especially their war-dance. They have other forms, which my eyes were not fated to see. Amongst the Bada- win of Al-Hijaz, unlike the Somali and other African races, the sexes never mingle: the girls may dance to- gether, but it would be disgraceful to perform in the com- pany of men.

After so much excitement we retired to rest, and slept soundly.

On Friday, the 12th Zu'l Hijjah, the camels appeared, according to order, at early dawn, and they were loaded with little delay. We were anxious to enter Meccah in time for the sermon, and I for one was eager to escape the now pestilential air of Muna.

Literally, the land stank. Five or six thousand animals had been slain and cut up in this Devil's Punch- bowl. I leave the reader to imagine the rest. The evil might be avoided by building *abattoirs*, or, more easily still, by digging long trenches, and by ordering all pilgrims, under pain of mulct, to sacrifice in the same place. Un- happily, the spirit of Al-Islam is opposed to these pre- cautions of common sense,—" Inshallah" and "Kismat" must take the place of prevention and of cure. And at Meccah, the head-quarters of the faith, a desolating attack of cholera is preferred to the impiety of "flying in the face of Providence," and the folly of endeavouring to avert inevitable decrees.[1]

---

1 NOTE TO THIRD EDITION.—Since this was written there have been two deadly epidemics, which began, it is reported, at Muna.

Mounting our camels, and led by Mas'ud, we entered Muna by the eastern end, and from the litter threw the remaining twenty-one stones. I could now see the principal lines of shops, and, having been led to expect a grand display of merchandise, was surprised to find only mat-booths and sheds, stocked chiefly with provisions. The exit from Muna was crowded, for many, like ourselves, were flying from the revolting scene. I could not think without pity of those whom religious scruples detained another day and a half in this foul spot.

After entering Meccah we bathed, and when the noon drew nigh we repaired to the Harim for the purpose of hearing the sermon. Descending to the cloisters below the Bab al-Ziyadah, I stood wonder-struck by the scene before me. The vast quadrangle was crowded with worshippers sitting in long rows, and everywhere facing the central black tower : the showy colours of their dresses were not to be surpassed by a garden of the most brilliant flowers, and such diversity of detail would probably not to be seen massed together in any other building upon earth. The women, a dull and sombre-looking group, sat apart in their peculiar place. The Pasha stood on the roof of Zemzem, surrounded by guards in Nizam uniform. Where the principal Olema stationed themselves, the crowd was thicker ; and in the more auspicious spots nought was to be seen but a pavement of heads and shoulders. Nothing seemed to move but a few Darwayshes, who, censer in hand, sidled through the rows and received the unsolicited alms of the Faithful. Apparently in the midst, and raised above the crowd by the tall, pointed pulpit, whose gilt spire flamed in the sun, sat the preacher, an old man with snowy beard. The style of head-dress

---

The victims, however, have never numbered 700,000, nor is " each pilgrim required to sacrifice one animal at the *shrine of Mohammed*," (!) as we find it in "Cholera Prospects," by Tilbury Fox, M.D. (Hardwicke).

called *Taylasan*[1] covered his turband, which was white as his
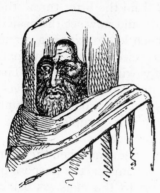
robes,[2] and a short staff sup-
ported his left hand.[3] Presently
he arose, took the staff in his
right hand, pronounced a few
inaudible words,[4] and sat down
again on one of the lower steps,
whilst a Mu'ezzin, at the foot of
the pulpit, recited the call to
sermon. Then the old man
stood up and began to preach.
As the majestic figure began to
exert itself there was a deep

"The Taylasan."

silence. Presently a general
"Amin" was intoned by the crowd at the conclusion
of some long sentence. And at last, towards the end of
the sermon, every third or fourth word was followed by
the simultaneous rise and fall of thousands of voices.

I have seen the religious ceremonies of many lands, but
never—nowhere—aught so solemn, so impressive as this.

1 A scarf thrown over the head, with one end brought round
under the chin and passed over the left shoulder composes the
"Taylasan."

2 As late as Ibn Jubayr's time the preacher was habited from
head to foot in black; and two Mu'ezzins held black flags fixed in
rings on both sides of the pulpit, with the staves propped upon the
first step.

3 Mr. Lane remarks, that the wooden sword is never held by the
preacher but in a country that has been won from infidels by Moslems.
Burckhardt more correctly traces the origin of the custom to the
early days of Al-Islam, when the preachers found it necessary to be
prepared for surprises. And all authors who, like Ibn Jubayr, described the Meccan ceremonies, mention the sword or staff. The
curious reader will consult this most accurate of Moslem travellers;
and a perusal of the pages will show that anciently the sermon dif-
fered considerably from, and was far more ceremonious than, the
present Khutbah.

4 The words were "Peace be upon ye! and the Mercy of Allah
and His Blessings!"

CHAPTER XXXII.

LIFE AT MECCAH, AND UMRAH, OR THE LITTLE PILGRIMAGE.

MY few remaining days at Meccah sped pleasantly enough. Omar Effendi visited me regularly, and arranged to accompany me furtively to Cairo. I had already consulted Mohammed Shiklibha—who suddenly appeared at Muna, having dropped down from Suez to Jeddah, and having reached Meccah in time for pilgrimage—about the possibility of proceeding Eastward. The honest fellow's eyebrows rose till they almost touched his turband, and he exclaimed in a roaring voice, "Wallah! Effendi! thou art surely mad." Every day he brought me news of the different Caravans. The Badawin of Al-Hijaz were, he said, in a ferment caused by the reports of the Holy War, want of money, and rumours of quarrels between the Sharif and the Pasha: already they spoke of an attack upon Jeddah. Shaykh Mas'ud, the camel man, from whom I parted on the best of terms, seriously advised my remaining at Meccah for some months even before proceeding to Sana'a. Others gave the same counsel. Briefly I saw that my star was not then in the ascendant, and resolved to reserve myself for a more propitious conjuncture by returning to Egypt.

The Turkish colonel and I had become as friendly as two men ignoring each other's speech could be. He had derived benefit from some prescription; but, like all his countrymen, he was pining to leave Meccah.[1] Whilst the

---

[1] Not more than one-quarter of the pilgrims who appear at Arafat go on to Al-Madinah : the expense, the hardships, and the dangers of

pilgrimage lasted, said they, no *mal de pays* came to
trouble them; but, its excitement over, they could think
of nothing but their wives and children.   Long-drawn
faces and continual sighs evidenced nostalgia.   At last
the house became a scene of preparation.   Blue china-
ware and basketed bottles of Zemzem water appeared
standing in solid columns, and pilgrims occupied themselves in hunting for mementoes of Meccah ; ground-plans;
combs, balm, henna, tooth-sticks; aloes-wood, turquoises,
coral, and mother-o'-pearl rosaries; shreds of Kiswah-
cloth and fine Abas, or cloaks of camels'-wool.   It was
not safe to mount the stairs without shouting "Tarik"
(Out of the way!) at every step, on peril of meeting face
to face some excited fair.[1]   The lower floor was crowded
with provision-vendors; and the staple article of conversation seemed to be the chance of a steamer from Jeddah
to Suez.

Weary of the wrangling and chaffering of the hall
below, I had persuaded my kind hostess, in spite of the
surly skeleton her brother, partially to clear out a small
store-room in the first floor, and to abandon it to me
between the hours of ten and four.   During the heat of
the day clothing is unendurable at Meccah.   The city is
so "compacted together" by hills, that even the Samum
can scarcely sweep it; the heat reverberated by the
bare rocks is intense, and the normal atmosphere of an
Eastern town communicates a faint lassitude to the
body and irritability to the mind.   The houses being unusually strong and well-built, might by some art of therm-
antidote be rendered cool enough in the hottest weather:

the journey account for the smallness of the number.   In theology it
is "Jaiz," or admissible, to begin with the Prophet's place of burial.
But those performing the "Hajjat al-Islam" are enjoined to commence
at Meccah.

1 When respectable married men live together in the same house,
a rare occurrence, except on journeys, this most ungallant practice of
clearing the way is and must be kept up in the East.

they are now ovens.[1] It was my habit to retire immediately after the late breakfast to the little room upstairs, to sprinkle it with water, and to lie down on a mat. In the few precious moments of privacy notes were committed to paper, but one eye was ever fixed on the door. Sometimes a patient would interrupt me, but a doctor is far less popular in Al-Hijaz than in Egypt. The people, being more healthy, have less faith in physic: Shaykh Mas'ud and his son had never tasted in their lives aught more medicinal than green dates and camel's milk. Occasionally the black slave-girls came into the room, asking if the pilgrim wanted a pipe or a cup of coffee : they generally retired in a state of delight, attempting vainly to conceal with a corner of tattered veil a grand display of ivory consequent upon some small and innocent facetiousness. The most frequent of my visitors was Abdullah, the Kabirah's eldest son. This melancholy Jacques had joined our caravan at Al-Hamra, on the

---

1 I offer no lengthened description of the town of Meccah : Ali Bey and Burckhardt have already said all that requires saying. Although the origin of the Bayt Ullah be lost in the glooms of past time, the city is a comparatively modern place, built about A.D. 450, by Kusay and the Kuraysh. It contains about 30,000 to 45,000 inhabitants, with lodging room for at least treble that number ; and the material of the houses is brick, granite, and sandstone from the neighbouring hills. The site is a winding valley, on a small plateau, half-way " below the Ghauts." Its utmost length is two miles and a half from the Mab'dah (North) to the Southern mount Jiyad ; and three-quarters of a mile would be the extreme breadth between Abu Kubays Eastward,—upon whose Western slope the most solid mass of the town clusters,—and Jabal Hindi Westward of the city. In the centre of this line stands the Ka'abah. I regret being unable to offer the reader a sketch of Meccah, or of the Great Temple. The stranger who would do this should visit the city out of the pilgrimage season, and hire a room looking into the quadrangle of the Harim. This addition to our knowledge is the more required, as our popular sketches (generally taken from D'Ohsson) are utterly incorrect. The Ka'abah is always a recognisable building ; but the "View of Meccah" known to Europe is not more like Meccah than like Cairo or Bombay.

Yambu' road, accompanied us to Al-Madinah, lived there, and journeyed to Meccah with the Syrian pilgrimage ; yet he had not once come to visit me or to see his brother, the boy Mohammed. When gently reproached for this omission, he declared it to be his way—that he never called upon strangers until sent for. He was a perfect *Saudawi* (melancholist) in mind, manners, and personal appearance, and this class of humanity in the East is almost as uncomfortable to the household as the idiot of Europe. I was frequently obliged to share my meals with him, as his mother—though most filially and reverentially entreated—would not supply him with breakfast two hours after the proper time, or with a dinner served up forty minutes before the rest of the household. Often, too, I had to curb, by polite deprecation, the impetuosity of the fiery old Kabirah's tongue. Thus Abdullah and I became friends, after a fashion. He purchased several little articles required, and never failed to pass hours in my closet, giving me much information about the country ; deploring the laxity of Meccan morals, and lamenting that in these evil days his countrymen had forfeited their name at Cairo and at Constantinople. His curiosity about the English in India was great, and I satisfied it by praising, as a Moslem would, their *politiké*, their even-handed justice, and their good star. Then he would in-quire into the truth of a fable extensively known on the shores of the Mediterranean and of the Red Sea. The English, it is said, sent a mission to Mohammed, inquiring into his doctrines, and begging that the heroic Khalid bin Walid[1] might be sent to proselytise them. Unfortunately,

---

1 It is curious that the Afghans should claim this Kuraysh noble as their compatriot. "On one occasion, when Khalid bin Walid was saying something in his native tongue (the Pushtu or Afghani), Mohammed remarked that assuredly that language was the peculiar dialect of the damned. As Khalid appeared to suffer from the observation, and to betray certain symptoms of insubordination, the Prophet condescended to comfort him by graciously pronouncing the

the envoys arrived too late—the Prophet's soul had winged its way to Paradise. An abstract of the Moslem scheme was, however, sent to the "Ingreez," who declined, as the Founder of the New Faith was no more, to abandon their own religion; but the refusal was accompanied with expressions of regard. For this reason many Moslems in Barbary and other countries hold the English to be of all "People of the Books" the best inclined towards them. As regards the Prophet's tradition concerning the fall of his birthplace, "and the thin-calved from the Habash (Abyssinians) shall destroy the Ka'abah," I was informed that towards the end of time a host will pass from Africa in such multitudes that a stone shall be conveyed from hand to hand between Jeddah and Meccah. This latter condition might easily be accomplished by sixty thousand men, the distance being only forty-four miles, but the citizens consider it to express a countless horde. Some pious Moslems have hoped that in Abdullah bin Zubayr's re-erection of the Ka'abah the prophecy was fulfilled[1]: the popular belief, however, remains that the fatal event is still in the womb of time. In a previous part of this volume I have alluded to similar evil presentiments which haunt the mind of Al-Islam; and the Christian, zealous for the propagation of his faith, may see in them an earnest of its still wider diffusion in future ages.[2]

Late in the afternoon I used to rise, perform ablution, and repair to the Harim, or wander about the bazars till sunset. After this it was necessary to return home and prepare for supper—dinner it would be called in the West.

---

words "Ghashe lindá ráorá," *i.e.*, bring me my bow and arrows. (Remarks on Dr. Dorn's Chrestomathy of the Pushtu or Afghan Language. Trans. Bombay As. Society, 1848.)

1 See the ninth building of the Ka'abah, described in chap. iv.

2 It requires not the ken of a prophet to foresee the day when political necessity—sternest of 'Ανάγκη!—will compel us to occupy in force the fountain-head of Al-Islam.

The meal concluded, I used to sit for a time outside the street-door in great dignity, upon a broken-backed black-wood chair, traditionally said to have been been left in the house by one of the princes of Delhi, smoking a Shishah, and drinking sundry cups of strong green tea with a slice of lime, a fair substitute for milk. At this hour the seat was as in a theatre, but the words of the actors were of a nature somewhat too Fescennine for a respectable public. After nightfall we either returned to the Harim or retired to rest. Our common dormitory was the flat roof of the house; under each cot stood a water-gugglet ; and all slept, as must be done in the torrid lands, *on* and not *in* bed.

I sojourned at Meccah but a short time, and, as usual with travellers, did not see the best specimens of the population. The citizens appeared to me more civilised and more vicious than those of Al-Madinah. They often leave

"Home, where small experience grows,"

and—*qui multum peregrinatur, rarò sanctificatur*—become a worldly-wise, God-forgetting, and Mammonish sort of folk. *Tuf w' asaa, w' aamil al-saba*—"Circumambulate and run (*i.e.* between Safa and Marwah) and commit the Seven (deadly sins)"—is a satire popularly levelled against them. Hence, too, the proverb *Al-harám f' il Haramayn* —"Evil (dwelleth) in the two Holy Cities"; and no wonder, since plenary indulgence is so easily secured.[1] The pilgrim is forbidden, or rather dissuaded, from abiding at Meccah after the rites, and wisely. Great emotions must be followed by a re-action. And he who stands struck by the first aspect of Allah's house, after a few months, the marvel waxing stale, sweeps past with indifference or something worse.

---

1 Good acts done at Meccah are rewarded a hundred-thousand-fold in heaven; yet it is not auspicious to dwell there. Omar informs us that an evil deed receives the punishment of seventy.

There is, however, little at Meccah to offend the eye. As among certain nations further West, a layer of ashes overspreads the fire: the mine is concealed by a green turf fair to look upon.   It is only when wandering by starlight through the northern outskirts of the town that citizens may be seen with light complexions and delicate limbs, coarse turbands, and Egyptian woollen robes, speaking disguise and the purpose of disguise.   No one within the memory of man has suffered the penalty of immorality.   Spirituous liquors are no longer sold, as in Burckhardt's day,[1] in shops; and some Arnaut officers assured me that they found considerable difficulty in smuggling flasks of Araki from Jeddah.

The Meccan is a darker man than the Madinite. The people explain this by the heat of the climate.   I rather believe it to be caused by the number of female slaves that find their way into the market.   Gallas, Sawa- hilis, a few Somalis, and Abyssinians are embarked at Suakin, Zayla, Tajurrah, and Berberah, carried in thou- sands to Jeddah, and the Holy City has the pick of every batch.   Thence the stream sets Northwards, a small cur- rent towards Al-Madinah, and the main line to Egypt and Turkey.[2]

Most Meccans have black concubines, and, as has been said, the appearance of the Sharif is almost that of a negro.   I did not see one handsome man in the Holy City, although some of the women appeared to me beauti- ful.   The male profile is high and bony, the forehead recedes, and the head rises unpleasantly towards the region of firm- ness.   In most families male children, when forty days old, are taken to the Ka'abah, prayed over, and carried home, where the barber draws with a razor three parallel gashes

1 It must be remembered that my predecessor visited Meccah when the Egyptian army, commanded by Mohammed Ali, held the town.

2 In another place I have ventured a few observations concern- ing the easy suppression of this traffic.

down the fleshy portion of each cheek, from the exterior angles of the eyes almost to the corners of the mouth. These *Mashali*, as they are called,[1] may be of modern date: the citizens declare that the custom was unknown to their ancestors. I am tempted to assign to it a high antiquity, and cannot but attribute a pagan origin to a custom still prevailing, despite all the interdictions of the Olema. In point of figure the Meccan is somewhat coarse and lymphatic. The ludicrous leanness of the outward man, as described by Ali Bey, survives only in the remnants of themselves belonging to a bygone century. The young men are rather stout and athletic, but in middle age—when man " swills and swells"—they are apt to degenerate into corpulence.

The Meccan is a covetous spendthrift. His wealth, lightly won, is lightly prized. Pay, pension, stipends, presents, and the *Ikram*, here, as at Al-Madinah, supply the citizen with the means of idleness. With him everything is on the most expensive scale, his marriage, his religious ceremonies, and his household expenses. His

---

1 The act is called "Tashrit," or gashing. The body is also marked, but with smaller cuts, so that the child is covered with blood. Ali Bey was told by some Meccans that the face-gashes served for the purpose of phlebotomy, by others that they were signs that the scarred was the servant of Allah's house. He attributes this male-gashing, like female-tatooing, to coquetry. The citizens told me that the custom arose from the necessity of preserving children from the kidnapping Persians, and that it is preserved as a mark of the Holy City. But its wide diffusion denotes an earlier origin. Mohammed expressly forbad his followers to mark the skin with scars. These " beauty marks " are common to the nations in the regions to the West of the Red Sea. The Barabarah of Upper Egypt adorn their faces with scars exactly like the Meccans. The Abyssinians moxa themselves in hetacombs for fashion's sake. I have seen cheeks gashed, as in the Holy City, among the Gallas. Certain races of the Sawahil trace around the head a corona of little cuts, like those of a cupping instrument. And, to quote no other instances, some Somalis raise ghastly seams upon their chocolate-coloured skins.

house is luxuriously furnished; entertainments are frequent, and the junketings of his women make up a heavy bill at the end of the year. It is a common practice for the citizen to anticipate the pilgrimage season by falling into the hands of the usurer. If he be in luck, he catches and "skins" one or more of the richest Hajis. On the other hand, should fortune fail him, he will feel for life the effect of interest running on at the rate of at least fifty per cent., the simple and the compound forms of which are equally familiar to the wily Sarraf.[1]

The most unpleasant peculiarities of the Meccans[2] are their pride and coarseness of language. Looking upon themselves as the cream of earth's sons, they resent with extreme asperity the least slighting word concerning the Holy City and its denizens. They plume themselves upon their holy descent, their exclusion of Infidels,[3] their strict fastings, their learned men, and their purity of language.[4] In fact, their pride shows itself at every moment;

1 Sayrafi, money-changer; Sarráf, banker; the Indian "Shroff," banker, money-changer, and usurer.

2 When speaking of the Meccans I allude only to the section of society which fell under my observation, and that more extensive division concerning which I obtained notices that could be depended upon.

3 The editor of Burckhardt's "Travels in Arabia" supposes that his author's "sect of light extinguishers" were probably Parsees from Surat or Bombay. The mistake is truly ludicrous, for no pious Parsee will extinguish a light. Moreover, infidels are not allowed by law to pass the frontiers of the Sanctuary. The sect alluded to is an obscure heresy in Central Asia; and concerning it the most improbable scandals have been propagated by the orthodox.

4 It is strange how travellers and linguists differ upon the subject of Arabic and its dialects. Niebuhr compares their relation to that of Provençal, Spanish, and Italian, whereas Lane declares the dialects to resemble each other more than those of some different counties in England. Herbin (Grammar) draws a broad line between ancient and modern Arabic; but Höchst (Nachrichten von Marokos und Fez) asserts that the difference is not so great as is imagined. Perhaps the soundest opinion is that proposed by Clodius, in his

but it is not the pride which makes a man too proud to do
"dirty work." My predecessor did not remark their
scurrility: he seems, on the contrary, rather to commend
them for respectability in this point. If he be correct, the
present generation has degenerated. The Meccans appeared to me distinguished, even in this foul-mouthed
East, by the superior licentiousness of their language.
Abuse was bad enough in the streets, but in the house it
became intolerable. The Turkish pilgrims remarked, but
they were too proud to notice it. The boy Mohammed
and one of his tall cousins at last transgressed the limits
of my endurance. They had been reviling each other
vilely one day at the house-door about dawn, when I administered the most open reprimand: "In my country
(Afghanistan) we hold this to be the hour of prayer, the
season of good thoughts, when men remember Allah;
even the Kafir doth not begin the day with curses and
abuse." The people around approved, and the offenders
could not refrain from saying, "Thou hast spoken truth,
O Effendi!" Then the bystanders began, as usual, to
"improve the occasion." "See," they exclaimed, "this
Sulaymani gentleman, he is not the Son of of a Holy City,
and yet he teacheth you—ye, the children of the Prophet!
—repent and fear Allah!" They replied, "Verily we do
repent, and Allah is a Pardoner and the Merciful!"—
were silent for an hour, and then abused each other more
foully than before. Yet it is a good point in the Meccan
character, that it is open to reason, it can confess itself

"Arabic Grammar": "dialectus Arabum vulgaris tantum differt
ab eruditâ, quantum Isocrates dictio ab hodiernâ linguâ Græcâ."
But it must be remembered that the Arabs divide their spoken and
even written language into two orders, the "Kálam Wáti," or vulgar
tongue, sometimes employed in epistolary correspondence, and the
"Nahwi," or grammatical and classical language. Every man of
education uses the former, and can use the latter. And the Koran
is no more a model of Arabic (as it is often assumed to be) than
"Paradise Lost" is of English. Inimitable, no man imitates them.

in error, and it displays none of that doggedness of vice which distinguishes the sinner of a more stolid race. Like the people of Southern Europe, the Semite is easily managed by a jest: though grave and thoughtful, he is by no means deficient in the sly wit which we call humour, and the solemn gravity of his words contrasts amusingly with his ideas. He particularly excels in the Cervantic art, the spirit of which, says Sterne, is to clothe low subjects in sublime language. In Mohammed's life we find that he by no means disdained a joke, sometimes a little *hasardé*, as in the case of the Paradise-coveting old woman. The redeeming qualities of the Meccan are his courage, his *bonhommie*, his manly suavity of manners, his fiery sense of honour, his strong family affections, his near approach to what we call patriotism, and his general knowledge: the reproach of extreme ignorance which Burckhardt directs against the Holy City has long ago sped to the Limbo of things that were. The dark half of the picture is formed by pride, bigotry, irreligion, greed of gain, immorality, and prodigal ostentation. Of the pilgrimage ceremonies I cannot speak harshly. It may be true that "the rites of the Ka'abah, emasculated of every idolatrous tendency, still hang a strange unmeaning shroud around the living theism of Islam." But what nation, either in the West or in the East, has been able to cast out from its ceremonies every suspicion of its old idolatry? What are the English mistletoe, the Irish wake, the Pardon of Brittany, the Carnival, and the Worship at Iserna ? Better far to consider the Meccan pilgrimage rites in the light of Evil-worship turned into lessons of Good than to philosophize about their strangeness, and to blunder in asserting them to be insignificant. Even the Badawi circumambulating the Ka'abah fortifies his wild belief by the fond thought that he treads the path of "Allah's friend."

At Arafat the good Moslem worships in imitation of

the " Pure of Allah[1]"; and when hurling stones and curses at three senseless little buttresses which commemorate the appearance of the fiend, the materialism of the action gives to its sentiment all the strength and endurance of reality. The supernatural agencies of pilgrimage are carefully and sparingly distributed. The angels who restore the stones from Muna to Muzdalifah ; the heavenly host whose pinions cause the Ka'abah's veil to rise and to wave, and the mysterious complement of the pilgrim's total at the Arafat sermon, all belong to the category of spiritual creatures walking earth unseen,—a poetical tenet, not condemned by Christianity. The Meccans are, it is true, to be reproached with their open Mammon-worship, at times and at places the most sacred and venerable ; but this has no other effect upon the pilgrims than to excite disgust and open reprehension. Here, however, we see no such silly frauds as heavenly fire drawn from a phosphor-match ; nor do two rival churches fight in the flesh with teeth and nails, requiring the contemptuous interference of an infidel power to keep around order. Here we see no fair dames staring with their glasses, *braqués* at the Head of the Church ; or supporting exhausted nature with the furtive sandwich; or carrying pampered curs who, too often, will not be silent; or scrambling and squeezing to hear theatrical music, reckless of the fate of the old lady who—on such occasions there is always one—has been "thrown down and cruelly trampled upon by the crowd." If the Meccan citizens are disposed to scoff at the wild Takruri, they do it not so publicly or shamelessly as the Roman jeering with ribald jest at the fanaticism of strangers from the bogs of Ireland. Finally, at Meccah there is nothing theatrical, nothing that suggests the opera ; but all is simple and impressive, filling the mind with

> " A weight of awe not easy to be borne,"

and tending, I believe, after its fashion, to good.

---

1 Safi Ullah—Adam.

As regards the Meccan and Moslem belief that
Abraham and his son built the Ka'abah, it may be
observed the Genesitic account of the Great Patriarch has
suggested to learned men the idea of two Abrahams, one
the son of Terah, another the son of Azar (fire), a
Prometheus who imported civilisation and knowledge into
Arabia from Harran, the sacred centre of Sabæan learning.[1] Moslem historians all agree in representing Abraham as a star-worshipper in youth, and Eusebius calls
the patriarch son of Athar; his father's name, therefore, is no Arab invention. Whether Ishmael or his
sire ever visited Meccah to build the Ka'abah is, in my
humble opinion, an open question. The Jewish Scripture
informs us only that the patriarch dwelt at Beersheba and
Gerar, in the south-west of Palestine, without any allusion
to the annual visit which Moslems declare he paid to
their Holy City. At the same time Arab tradition speaks
clearly and consistently upon the subject, and generally
omits those miraculous and superstitious adjuncts which
cast shadows of sore doubt upon the philosophic mind.

The amount of risk which a stranger must encounter
at the pilgrimage rites is still considerable. A learned
Orientalist and divine intimated his intention, in a work

[1] The legend that Abraham was the "Son of Fire" might have
arisen from his birthplace, Ur of the Chaldees. This Ur (whence
the Latin *uro*) becomes in Persian Hír; in Arabic Irr or Arr. It
explains the origin of "Orotalt" better than by means of "Allahu
Ta'ala." This word, variously spelt Ourotalt, Orotalt, and Orotal
(the latter would be the masculine form in Arabic), is Urrat-ilat, or
the goddess of fire, most probably the Sun (Al-Shams) which the
Semites make a feminine. Forbiggen translates it Sonnen-gott, an
error of gender, as the final consonant proves. The other deity of
pagan Arabia, Alilat, is clearly Al-Lat. May not the Phœnicians have
supplied the word "Irr," which still survives in Erin and in Ireland?
even so they gave to the world the name of Britain, Brettainke,
Barrat et Tanuki (ٮرّ الٮٮاك), the land of tin. And I should more
readily believe that Eeran is the land of fire, than accept its
derivation from Eer (*vir*) a man.

published but a few years ago, of visiting Meccah without
disguise. He was assured that the Turkish governor
would now offer no obstacle to a European traveller. I
would strongly dissuade a friend from making the attempt.
It is true that the Frank is no longer, as in Captain
Head's day,[1] insulted when he ventures out of the Meccan
Gate of Jeddah; and that our Vice-Consuls and travellers
are allowed, on condition that their glance do not pollute
the shrine, to visit Taif and the regions lying Eastward of
the Holy City. Neither the Pasha nor the Sharif would,
in these days, dare to enforce, in the case of an Englishman, the old law, a choice thrice offered between circumcision and death. But the first Badawi who caught
sight of the Frank's hat would not deem himself a man
if he did not drive a bullet through the wearer's head.
At the pilgrimage season disguise is easy on account
of the vast and varied multitudes which visit Meccah
exposing the traveller only to " stand the buffet with
knaves who smell of sweat." But woe to the unfortunate who happens to be recognised in public as an
Infidel—unless at least he could throw himself at once
upon the protection of the government.[2] Amidst, however,
a crowd of pilgrims, whose fanaticism is worked up to the
highest pitch, detection would probably ensure his dismissal
at once *al numero de' più*. Those who find danger the salt
of pleasure may visit Meccah ; but if asked whether the
results justify the risk, I should reply in the negative.
And the Vice-Consul at Jeddah would only do his duty in
peremptorily forbidding European travellers to attempt
Meccah without disguise, until the day comes when such
steps can be taken in the certainty of not causing a mishap ;

---

1 Captain C. F. Head, author of " Eastern and Egyptian
Scenery," was, as late as A.D. 1829, pelted by the Badawin, because
he passed the Eastern gate of Jeddah in a Frankish dress.

2 The best way would be to rush, if possible, into a house ; and
the owner would then, for his own interest, as well as honour, defend
a stranger till assistance could be procured.

an accident would not redound to our reputation, as we could not in justice revenge it.[1]

On the 14th Zu'l Hijjah we started to perform the rite of Umrah, or Little Pilgrimage. After performing ablution, and resuming the Ihram with the usual ceremonies, I set out, accompanied by the boy Mohammed and his brother Abdullah. Mounting asses which resembled mules in size and speed,[2] we rode to the Harim, and prayed there. Again remounting, we issued through the Bab al-Safa towards the open country north-east of the city. The way was crowded with pilgrims, on foot as well as mounted, and their loud *Labbayk* distinguished those engaged in the Umrah rite from the many whose business was with the camp of the Damascus Caravan. At about half a mile from the city we passed on the left a huge heap of stones, where my companions stood and cursed. This grim-looking cairn is popularly believed to note the place of the well where Abu Lahab laid an ambuscade for the Prophet. This wicked uncle stationed there a slave, with orders to throw headlong into the pit the first person who

---

1 Future pilgrims must also remember that the season is gradually receding towards the heart of the hot weather. For the next fifteen years, therefore, an additional risk will attend the traveller.

2 Pliny is certainly right about this useful quadruped and its congeners, the zebra and the wild ass, in describing it as "animal frigoris maxime impatiens." It degenerates in cold regions, unless, as in Afghanistan and Barbary, there be a long, hot, and dry summer. Aden, Cutch, and Baghdad have fine breeds, whereas those of India and South-Eastern Africa are poor and weak. The best and the highest-priced come from the Maghrib, and second to them ranks the Egyptian race. At Meccah careful feeding and kind usage transform the dull slave into an active and symmetrical friend of man : he knows his owner's kind voice, and if one of the two fast, it is generally the biped. The asses of the Holy City are tall and plump, with sleek coats, generally ash or grey-coloured, the eyes of deer, heads gracefully carried, an ambling gait, and extremely sure-footed. They are equal to great fatigue, and the stallions have been known, in their ferocity, to kill the groom. The price varies from 25 to 150 dollars.

approached him, and privily persuaded his nephew to visit
the spot at night : after a time, anxiously hoping to hear
that the deed had been done, Abu Lahab incautiously
drew nigh, and was precipitated by his own bravo into the
place of destruction.[1] Hence the well-known saying in
Islam, " Whoso diggeth a well for his brother shall fall
into it himself." We added our quota of stones,[2] and proceeding, saw the Jeddah road spanning the plain like a
white ribbon.   In front of us the highway was now lined
with coffee-tents, before which effeminate dancing-boys
performed to admiring Syrians ; a small whitewashed
" Bungalow," the palace of the Emir al-Hajj, lay on the
left, and all around it clustered the motley encampment
of his pilgrims. After cantering about three miles from
the city, we reached the Alamayn, or two pillars that limit
the Sanctuary ; and a little beyond it is the small settlement popularly called Al-Umrah.[3] Dismounting here, we

1 Such is the popular version of the tale, which differs in some
points from that recorded in books. Others declare that here, in
days gone by, stood the house of another notorious malignant, Abu
Jahl. Some, again, suppose that in this place a tyrannical governor
of Meccah was summarily " lynched " by the indignant populace.
The first two traditions, however, are the favourites, the vulgar—
citizens, as well as pilgrims—loving to connect such places with the
events of their early sacred history. Even in the twelfth century we
read that pilgrims used to cast stones at two cairns, covering the
remains of Abu Lahab, and the beautiful termagant, his wife.

2 Certain credulous authors have contrasted these heaps with
the clear ground at Muna, for the purpose of a minor miracle.
According to them this cairn steadily grows, as we may believe it
would ; and that, were it not for the guardian angels, the millions of
little stones annually thrown at the devils would soon form a mass
of equal magnitude. This custom of lapidation, in token of hate, is
an ancient practice, still common in the East. Yet, in some parts of
Arabia, stones are thrown at tombs as a compliment to the tenant.
And in the Somali country, the places where it is said holy men sat,
receive the same doubtful homage.

3 It is called in books Al-Tanim (bestowing plenty) ; a word
which readers must not confound with the district of the same name

sat down on rugs outside a coffee-tent to enjoy the beauty of the moonlit night, and an hour of *Kayf*, in the sweet air of the Desert.

Presently the coffee-tent keeper, after receiving payment, brought us water for ablution. This preamble over, we entered the principal chapel ; an unpretending building, badly lighted, spread with dirty rugs, full of pilgrims, and offensively close. Here we prayed the Isha, or night devotions, and then a two-bow prayer in honour of the Ihram,[1] after which we distributed gratuities to the guardians, and alms to the importunate beggars. And now I perceived the object of Abdullah's companionship. The melancholy man assured me that he had ridden out for love of me, and in order to perform as Wakil (substitute) a vicarious pilgrimage for my parents. Vainly I assured him that they had been strict in the exercises of their faith. He would take no denial, and I perceived that love of me meant love of my dollars. With a surly assent, he was at last permitted to act for the "pious pilgrim Yusuf (Joseph) bin Ahmad and Fatimah bint Yunus,"—my progenitors. It was impossible to prevent smiling at contrasts, as Abdullah, gravely raising his hands, and directing his face to the Ka'abah, intoned, " I do vow this Ihram of Umrah in the name of Yusuf Son of Ahmad, and Fatimah Daughter of Yunus ; then render it attainable unto them, and accept it of them ! Bismillah ! Allaho Akbar ! "

---

in the province Khaulan (made by Niebuhr the "Thumna," "Thomna," or "Tamna," capital of the Catabanites). Other authors apply Al-Tanim to the spot where Abu Lahab is supposed to lie. There are two places called Al-Umrah near Meccah. The Kabir, or greater, is, I am told, in the Wady Fatimah, and the Prophet ordered Ayishah and her sister to begin the ceremonies at that place. It is now visited by picnic parties and those who would pray at the tomb of Maimunah, one of the Prophet's wives. Modern pilgrims commence always, I am told, at the Umrah Saghir (the Lesser), which is about half-way nearer the city.

1 Some assume the Ihram garb at this place.

Remounting, we galloped towards Meccah, shouting *Labbayk*, and halting at every half-mile to smoke and drink coffee. In a short time we entered the city, and repairing to the Harim by the Safa Gate, performed the Tawaf, or circumambulation of Umrah. After this dull round and necessary repose we left the temple by the same exit, and mounting once more, turned towards Al-Safa, which stands about a hundred yards South-East of the Mosque, and as little deserves its name of " Mountain " as do those that undulate the face of modern Rome. The Safa end is closed by a mean-looking building, composed of three round arches, with a dwarf flight of stairs leading up to them out of a narrow road. Without dismounting, we wheeled our donkeys[1] round, " left shoulders forward," no easy task in the crowd, and, vainly striving to sight the Ka'abah through the Bab al-Safa, performed the Niyat, or vow of the rite Al-Sai, or the running.[2] After Tahlil, Takbir, and Talbiyat, we raised our hands in the supplicatory position, and twice repeated,[3] " There is no god but Allah, Alone, without Partner ; His is the Kingdom, unto Him be Praise ; He giveth Life and Death, He is alive and perisheth not ; in His Hand is Good, and He over all Things is Omnipotent." Then, with the donkey-boys leading our animals and a stout fellow preceding us with lantern and a quarter-staff to keep off the running Badawin, camel-men, and riders of asses, we descended Safa, and walked slowly down the street Al-Massa, towards Marwah.[4]

---

1 We had still the pretext of my injured foot. When the Sai rite is performed, as it should be, by a pedestrian, he mounts the steps to about the height of a man, and then. turns towards the temple.

2 I will not trouble the reader with this Niyat, which is the same as that used in the Tawaf rite.

3 Almost every Mutawwif, it must be remembered, has his own set of prayers.

4 " Safa " means a large, hard rock ; " Marwah," hard, white flints, full of fire.

During our descent we recited aloud, " O Allah, cause me
to act according to the Sunnat of Thy Prophet, and to die
in His faith, and defend me from errors and disobedience
by Thy Mercy, O most Merciful of the Merciful ! "
Arrived at what is called the Batn al-Wady (Belly of the
Vale), a place now denoted by the Milayn al-Akhzarayn
(the two green pillars[1]), one fixed in the Eastern course of
the Harim, the other in a house on the right side,[2] we
began the running by urging on our beasts. Here the
prayer was, " O Lord, pardon and pity, and pass over
what Thou knowest, for Thou art the most dear and the
most generous ! Save us from Hell-fire safely, and cause
us safely to enter Paradise ! O Lord, give us Happiness
here and Happiness hereafter, and spare us the Torture
of the Flames ! " At the end of this supplication we had
passed the Batn, or lowest ground, whose farthest limits
were marked by two other pillars.[3] Again we began to
ascend, repeating, as we went, " Verily, Safa and Marwah
are two of the Monuments of Allah. Whoso, therefore,
pilgrimeth to the Temple of Meccah, or performeth
Umrah, it shall be no Crime in him (to run between them
both). And as for him who voluntarily doeth a good Deed,
verily Allah is Grateful and Omniscient[4] ! " At length we
reached Marwah, a little rise like Safa in the lower slope
of Abu Kubays. The houses cluster in amphitheatre
shape above it, and from the Masa'a, or street below, a
short flight of steps to a platform, bounded on three sides
like a tennis-court, by tall walls without arches. The

1 In former times a devastating torrent used to sweep this place
after rains. The Fiumara bed has now disappeared, and the pillars
are used as landmarks. Galland observes that these columns are
planted upon the place which supported Eve's knees, when, after
300 years' separation, she was found by Adam.

2 This house is called in books Rubat al-Abbas.

3 Here once stood " As'af " and " Naylah," two idols, some say
a man and a woman metamorphosed for stupration in the Temple.

4 Koran, chap. ii.

street, seen from above, has a bowstring curve : it is between eight and nine hundred feet long,[1] with high houses on both sides, and small lanes branching off from it. At the foot of the platform we brought "right shoulders forward," so as to face the Ka'abah, and raising hands to ears, thrice exclaimed, "Allaho Akbar." This concluded the first course, and, of these, seven compose the ceremony Al-Sai, or the running. There was a startling contrast with the origin of this ceremony,—

"When the poor outcast on the cheerless wild,
Arabia's parent, clasped her fainting child,"—

as the Turkish infantry marched, in European dress, with sloped arms, down the Masa'a to relieve guard. By the side of the half-naked, running Badawin, they look as if Epochs, disconnected by long centuries, had met. A laxity, too, there was in the frequent appearance of dogs upon this holy and most memorial ground, which said little in favour of the religious strictness of the administration.[2]

Our Sai ended at Mount Marwah. There we dismounted, and sat outside a barber's shop, on the right-hand of the street. He operated upon our heads, causing us to repeat, "O Allah, this my Forelock is in Thy Hand, then grant me for every Hair a light on the Resurrection-day, O Most Merciful of the Merciful!" This, and the paying for it, constituted the fourth portion of the Umrah, or Little Pilgrimage.

Throwing the skirts of our garments over our heads, to show that our "Ihram" was now exchanged for the normal state, "Ihlal," we cantered to the Harim, prayed there a two-bow prayer, and returned home not a little fatigued.

1 Ibn Jubayr gives 893 steps: other authorities make the distance 780 short cubits, the size of an average man's forearm.

2 The ceremony of running between Safa and Marwah is supposed to represent Hagar seeking water for her son. Usually pilgrims perform this rite on the morning of visiting the Ka'abah.

CHAPTER XXXIII.

PLACES OF PIOUS VISITATION AT MECCAH.

THE traveller has little work at the Holy City. With exceptions of Jabal Nur and Jabal Saur,[1] all the places of pious visitation lie inside or close outside the city. It is well worth the while to ascend Abu Kubays; not so much to inspect the Makan al-Hajar and the Shakk al-Kamar,[2] as to obtain an excellent bird's-eye view of the Harim and the parts adjacent.[3]

The boy Mohammed had applied himself sedulously to commerce after his return home; and had actually been seen by Shaykh Nur sitting in a shop and selling small curiosities. With my plenary consent I was made

1 Jabal Nur, or Hira, has been mentioned before. Jabal Saur rises at some distance to the South of Meccah, and contains the celebrated cave in which Mohammed and Abu Bakr took refuge during the flight.

2 The tradition of these places is related by every historian. The former is the repository of the Black Stone during the Deluge. The latter, "splitting of the moon," is the spot where the Prophet stood when, to convert the idolatrous Kuraysh, he caused half the orb of night to rise from behind Abu Kubays, and the other from Jabal Kayka'an, on the Western horizon. This silly legend appears unknown to Mohammed's day.

3 The pilgrimage season, strictly speaking, concluded this year on the 17th September (13th Zu'l Hijjah); at which time travellers began to move towards Jeddah. Those who purposed visiting Al-Madinah would start about three weeks afterwards, and many who had leisure intended witnessing the Muharram ceremonies at Meccah.

over to Abdullah, his brother. On the morning of the 15th Zu'l Hijjah (19th Sept.) he hired two asses, and accompanied me as guide to the holy places.

Mounting our animals, we followed the road before described to the Jannat al-Ma'ala, the sacred cemetery of Meccah. A rough wall, with a poor gateway, encloses a patch of barren and grim-looking ground, at the foot of the chain which bounds the city's western suburb, and below Al-Akabah, the gap through which Khalid bin Walid entered Meccah with the triumphant Prophet.[1] Inside are a few ignoble, whitewashed domes: all are of modern construction, for here, as at Al-Bakia, further north, the Wahhabis indulged their levelling propensities.[2] The rest of the ground shows some small enclosures belonging to particular houses,—equivalent to our family vaults,— and the ruins of humble tombs, lying in confusion, whilst a few parched aloes spring from between the bricks and stones.[3]

1 This is the local tradition; it does not agree with authentic history. Muir (Life of Mahomet, vol. iv. p. 126) reminds me that Khalid and his Badawin attacked the citizens of Meccah without the Prophet's leave. But after the attack he may have followed in his leader's train.

2 The reason of their Vandalism has been noticed in a previous volume.

3 The Aloe here, as in Egypt, is hung, like the dried crocodile, over houses as a talisman against evil spirits. Burckhardt assigns, as a motive for it being planted in graveyards, that its name *Saber* denotes the patience with which the believer awaits the Last Day. And Lane remarks, "The Aloe thus hung (over the door), without earth and water, will live for several years, and even blossom: hence it is called *Saber*, which signifies patience." In India it is hung up to prevent Mosquitoes entering a room. I believe the superstition to be a fragment of African fetichism. The Gallas, to the present day, plant Aloes on graves, and suppose that when the plant sprouts the deceased has been admitted into the gardens of "Wak"—the Creator. Ideas breed vocables; but seldom, except among rhymesters, does a vocable give birth to a popular idea: and in Arabic "Sibr," as well as "Sabr," is the name of the Aloe.

The cemetery is celebrated in local history : here the body of Abdullah bin Zubayr was exposed by order of Hajjaj bin Yusuf ; and the number of saints buried in it has been so numerous, that even in the twelfth century many had fallen into oblivion. It is visited by the citizens on Fridays, and by women on Thursdays, to prevent that meeting of sexes which in the East is so detrimental to public decorum. I shall be sparing in my description of the Ma'ala ceremonies, as the prayers, prostrations, and supplications are almost identical with those performed at Al-Bakia.

After a long supplication, pronounced standing at the doorway, we entered, and sauntered about the burial-ground. On the left of the road stood an enclosure, which, according to Abdullah, belonged to his family. The door and stone slabs, being valuable to the poor, had been removed, and the graves of his forefathers appeared to have been invaded by the jackal. He sighed, recited a Fatihah with tears in his eyes, and hurried me away from the spot.

The first dome which we visited covered the remains of Abd al-Rahman, the son of Abu Bakr, one of the Worthies of Al-Islam, equally respected by Sunni and by Shi'ah. The tomb was a simple catafalque, spread with the usual cloth. After performing our devotions at this grave, and distributing a few piastres to guardians and beggars, we crossed the main path, and found ourselves at the door of the cupola, beneath which sleeps the venerable Khadijah, Mohammed's first wife. The tomb was covered with a green cloth, and the walls of the little building were decorated with written specimens of religious poetry. A little beyond it, we were shown into another dome, the resting-place of Sitt Aminah, the Prophet's mother.[1] Burckhardt chronicles its ill-usage by

1 Burckhardt mentions the "Tomb of Umna, the mother of Mohammed," in the Ma'ala at Meccah ; and all the ciceroni agree

the fanatic Wahhabis : it has now been rebuilt in that
frugal style that characterizes the architecture of Al-Hijaz.
An exceedingly garrulous old woman came to the door,
invited us in, and superintended our devotions ; at the
end of which she sprinkled rosewater upon my face.
When asked for a cool draught, she handed me a metal
saucer, whose contents smelt strongly of mastic, earnestly
directing me to drink it in a sitting posture. This tomb
she informed us is the property of a single woman, who
visits it every evening, receives the contributions of the
Faithful, prays, sweeps the pavement, and dusts the furniture. We left five piastres for this respectable maiden,
and gratified the officious crone with another shilling.
She repaid us by signalling to some score of beggars that
a rich pilgrim had entered the Ma'ala, and their impor-
tunities fairly drove me out of the hallowed walls.

Leaving the Jannat al-Ma'ala, we returned towards
the town, and halted on the left side of the road, at a
mean building called the Masjid al-Jinn (of the Genii).
Here was revealed the seventy-second chapter of the
Koran, called after the name of the mysterious fire-drakes
who paid fealty to the Prophet. Descending a flight of
steps,—for this Mosque, like all ancient localities at
Meccah, is as much below as above ground,—we entered
a small apartment containing water-pots for drinking and
all the appurtenances of ablution. In it is shown the
Mauza al-Khatt (place of the writing), where Mohammed
wrote a letter to Abu Mas'ud after the homage of the
Jinnis. A second and interior flight of stone steps led to
another diminutive oratory, where the Prophet used to
pray and receive the archangel Gabriel. Having performed a pair of bows, which caused the perspiration

---

about the locality.   Yet historians place it at Abwa, where she gave
up the ghost, after visiting Al-Madinah to introduce her son to his
relations.   And the learned believe that the Prophet refused to pray
over or to intercede for his mother, she having died before Al-Islam
was revealed.

to burst forth as if in a Russian bath, I paid a few piastres, and issued from the building with much satisfaction.

We had some difficulty in urging our donkeys through the crowded street, called the Zukak al-Hajar. Presently we arrived at the Bayt al-Nabi, the Prophet's old house, in which he lived with the Sitt Khadijah. Here, says Burckhardt, the Lady Fatimah first saw the light[1]; and here, according to Ibn Jubayr, Hasan and Hosayn were born. Dismounting at the entrance, we descended a deep flight of steps, and found ourselves in a spacious hall, vaulted, and of better appearance than most of the sacred edifices at Meccah. In the centre, and well railed round, stood a closet of rich green and gold stuffs, in shape not unlike an umbrella-tent. A surly porter guarded the closed door, which some respectable people vainly attempted to open by honeyed words: a whisper from Abdullah solved the difficulty. I was directed to lie at full length upon my stomach, and to kiss a black-looking stone—said to be the lower half of the Lady Fatimah's quern[2]—fixed at the bottom of a basin of the same material. Thence we repaired to a corner, and recited a two-bow at the place where the Prophet used to pray the Sunnat and the Nafilah, or supererogatory devotions.[3]

Again remounting, we proceeded at a leisurely pace homewards, and on the way passed through the principal

---

1 Burckhardt calls it " Maulid Sittna Fatimah " : but the name "Kubbat el Wahy," applied by my predecessor to this locality, is generally made synonymous with Al-Mukhtaba, the " hiding-place " where the Prophet and his followers used in dangerous times to meet for prayer.

2 So loose is local tradition, that some have confounded this quern with the Natak al-Nabi, the stone which gave God-speed to the Prophet.

3 He would of course pray the Farz, or obligatory devotions, at the shrine.

slave-market.   It is a large street roofed with matting, and full of coffee-houses.   The merchandise sat in rows, parallel with the walls.   The prettiest girls occupied the highest benches, below were the plainer sort, and lowest of all the boys.   They were all gaily dressed in pink and other light-coloured muslins, with transparent veils over their heads ;   and, whether from the effect of such unusual splendour, or from the re-action succeeding to their terrible land-journey and sea-voyage, they appeared perfectly happy, laughing loudly, talking unknown tongues, and quizzing purchasers, even during the delicate operation of purchasing.   There were some pretty Gallas, douce-looking Abyssinians, and Africans of various degrees of hideousness, from the half-Arab Somal to the baboon-like Sawahili.   The highest price of which I could hear was £60.   And here I matured a resolve to strike, if favoured by fortune, a death-blow at a trade which is eating into the vitals of industry in Eastern Africa.   The reflection was pleasant,—the idea that the humble Haji, contemplating the scene from his donkey, might become the instrument of the total abolition of this pernicious traffic.[1]   What would have become of that pilgrim had the crowd in the slave-market guessed his intentions ?

Passing through the large bazar, called the Suk al-Layl, I saw the palace of Mohammed bin Aun, quondam Prince of Meccah.   It has a certain look of rude magni-

---

1 About a year since writing the above a firman was issued by the Porte suppressing the traffic from Central Africa.   Hitherto we have respected slavery in the Red Sea, because the Turk thence drew his supplies ; we are now destitute of an excuse.   A single steamer would destroy the trade, and if we delay to take active measures, the people of England, who have spent millions in keeping up a West African squadron, will not hold us guiltless of negligence.

NOTE TO SECOND EDITION.—The slave trade has, since these remarks were penned, been suppressed with a high hand ; the Arabs of Al-Hijaz resented the measure by disowning the supremacy of the Porte, but they were soon reduced to submission.

ficence, the effect of huge hanging balconies scattered in
profusion over lofty walls, *claire-voies* of brickwork, and
courses of various-coloured stone. The owner is highly
popular among the Badawin, and feared by the citizens
on account of his fierce looks, courage, aud treachery.
They described him to me as *vir bonus, bene strangulando
peritus;* but Mr. Cole, who knew him personally, gave
him a high character for generosity and freedom from
fanaticism. He seems to have some idea of the state
which should " hedge in " a ruler. His palaces at Meccah,
and that now turned into a Wakalah at Jeddah, are the
only places in the country that can be called princely.
He is now a state prisoner at Constantinople, and the
Badawin pray in vain for his return.[1]

The other places of pious visitation at Meccah are
briefly these :—

1. Natak al-Nabi, a small oratory in the Zukak al-
Hajar. It derives its name from the following circum-

---

1. The Prince was first invested with the Sharifat by Mohammed
Ali of Egypt in A.D. 1827, when Yahya fled, after stabbing his nephew
in the Ka'abah, to the Benu Harb Badawin. He was supported by
Ahmad Pasha of Meccah, with a large army ; but after the battle of
Tarabah, in which Ibrahim Pasha was worsted by the Badawin,
Mohammed Bin Aun, accused of acting as Sylla, was sent in honourable bondage to Cairo. He again returned to Meccah, where the
rapacity of his eldest son, Abdullah, who would rob pilgrims, caused
fresh misfortunes. In A.D. 1851, when Abd al-Muttalib was appointed
Sharif, the Pasha was ordered to send Bin Aun to Stambul—no easy
task. The Turk succeeded by a manœuvre. Mohammed's two sons,
happening to be at Jeddah, were invited to inspect a man-of-war, and
were there made prisoners. Upon this the father yielded himself up ;
although, it is said, the flashing of the Badawi's sabre during his em-
barkation made the Turks rejoice that they had won the day by
state-craft. The wild men of Al-Hijaz still sing songs in honour of
this Sharif.

NOTE TO SECOND EDITION.—Early in 1856, when the Sharif Abd
al-Muttalib was deposed, Mohammed bin Aun was sent from Constantinople to quiet the insurrection caused by the new slave laws in
Al-Hijaz. In a short space of time he completely succeeded.

stance. As the Prophet was knocking at the door of
Abu Bakr's shop, a stone gave him God-speed, and told
him that the master was not at home. The wonderful
mineral is of a reddish-black colour, about a foot in dimen-
sion, and fixed in the wall somewhat higher than a man's
head. There are servants attached to it, and the street
sides are spread, as usual, with the napkins of importunate beggars.

2. *Maulid al-Nabi*, or the Prophet's birthplace.[1] It is
a little chapel in the Suk al-Layl, not far from Mohammed
bin Aun's palace. It is below the present level of the
ground, and in the centre is a kind of tent, concealing, it
is said, a hole in the floor upon which Aminah sat to be
delivered.

3. In the quarter "Sha'ab Ali," near the Maulid al-
Nabi, is the birthplace of Ali, another oratory below the
ground. Here, as in the former place, a *Maulid* and a
Ziyarah are held on the anniversary of the Lion's birth.

4. Near Khadijah's house and the Natak al-Nabi is
a place called *Al-Muttaka*, from a stone against which the
Prophet leaned when worn out with fatigue. It is much
visited by devotees ; and some declare that on one occasion, when the Father of Lies appeared to the Prophet in
the form of an elderly man, and tempted him to sin by
asserting that the Mosque-prayers were over, this stone,
disclosing the fraud, caused the Fiend to flee.

5. Maulid Hamzah, a little building at the old Bab
Umrah, near the Shabayki cemetery. Here was the
Bazan, or channel down which the Ayn Hunayn ran into
the Birkat Majid. Many authorities doubt that Hamzah
was born at this place.[2]

---

1 The 12th of Rabia al-Awwal, Mohammed's birthday, is here
celebrated with great festivities, feasts, prayers, and perusals of the
Koran. These " Maulid " (ceremonies of nativity) are by no means
limited to a single day in the year.

2 The reader is warned that I did not see the five places above

The reader must now be as tired of "Pious Visitations" as I was.

Before leaving Meccah I was urgently invited to dine by old Ali bin Ya Sin, the Zemzemi; a proof that he entertained inordinate expectations, excited, it appeared, by the boy Mohammed, for the simple purpose of exalting his own dignity. One day we were hurriedly summoned about three P.M. to the senior's house, a large building in the Zukak al-Hajar. We found it full of pilgrims, amongst whom we had no trouble to recognise our fellow-travellers, the quarrelsome old Arnaut and his impudent slave-boy. Ali met us upon the staircase, and conducted us into an upper room, where we sat upon diwans, and with pipes and coffee prepared for dinner. Presently the semicircle arose to receive a eunuch, who lodged somewhere in the house. He was a person of importance, being the guardian of some dames of high degree at Cairo and Constantinople: the highest place and

---

enumerated. The ciceroni and books mention twelve other visitations, several of which are known only by name.

1. Al-Mukhtaba, the " hiding-place " alluded to in the preceding pages. Its locality is the subject of debate.

2. Dar al-Khayzaran, where the Prophet prayed secretly till the conversion of Omar enabled him to dispense with concealment.

3. Maulid Omar, or Omar's birthplace, mentioned in books as being visited by devotees in the 14th Rabia al-Awwal of every year.

4. Abu Bakr's house near the Natak al-Nabi. It is supposed to have been destroyed in the twelfth century.

5. Maulid Ja'afar al-Tayyar, near the Shabayki cemetery.

6. Al-Mada'a, an oratory, also called Naf al-Arz, because creation here began.

7. Dar al-Hijrah, where Mohammed and Abu Bakr mounted for the flight.

8. Masjid al-Rayah, where the Prophet planted his flag when Meccah surrendered.

9. Masjid al-Shajarah, a spot at which Mohammed caused a tree to advance and to retire.

10. Masjid al-Ja'aranah, where Mohammed clad himself in the pilgrim garb. It is still visited by some Persians.

11. Majid Ibrahim, or Abu Kubays.

12. Masjid Zu Tawa.

the best pipe were unhesitatingly offered to and accepted by him. He sat down with dignity, answered diplomatically certain mysterious questions about the dames, and applied his blubber lips to a handsome mouthpiece of lemon-coloured amber. It was a fair lesson of humility for a man to find himself ranked beneath this high-shouldered, spindle-shanked, beardless bit of neutrality ; and as such I took it duly to heart.

The dinner was served up in a *Sini*, a plated copper tray about six feet in circumference, and handsomely ornamented with arabesques and inscriptions. Under this was the usual *Kursi*, or stool, composed of mother-o'-pearl facets set in sandal-wood ; and upon it a well-tinned and clean-looking service of the same material as the *Sini*. We began with a variety of stews—stews with spinach, stews with *Bamiyah* (hibiscus), and rich vegetable stews. These being removed, we dipped hands in *Biryani*, a meat pillaw, abounding in clarified butter; *Kimah*, finely chopped meat; *Warak Mahshi*, vine leaves filled with chopped and spiced mutton, and folded into small triangles ; *Kabab*, or bits of rôti spitted in mouthfuls upon a splinter of wood ; together with a *Salatah* of the crispest cucumber, and various dishes of water-melon cut up into squares.

Bread was represented by the Eastern scone, but it was of superior flavour, and far better than the ill-famed Chapati of India. Our drink was water perfumed with mastic. After the meat came a *Kunafah*, fine vermicelli sweetened with honey, and sprinkled with powdered white sugar ; several stews of apples and quinces ; *Muhallibah*, a thin jelly made of rice, flour, milk, starch, and a little perfume ; together with squares of *Rahah*,[1] a confiture

---

1 Familiar for " Rahat al-Hulkum,"—the pleasure of the throat, —a name which has sorely puzzled our tourists. This sweetmeat would be pleasant did it not smell so strongly of the perruquier's shop. Rosewater tempts to many culinary sins in the East ; and Europeans cannot dissociate it from the idea of a lotion. However,

highly prized in these regions, because it comes from Constantinople. Fruits were then placed upon the table; plates full of pomegranate grains and dates of the finest flavour.[1] The dinner concluded with a pillaw of rice and butter, for the easier discussion of which we were provided with carved wooden spoons.

Arabs ignore the delightful French art of prolonging a dinner. After washing your hands, you sit down, throw an embroidered napkin over your knees, and with a "Bismillah," by way of grace, plunge your hand into the attractive dish, changing *ad libitum*, occasionally sucking your finger-tips as boys do lollipops, and varying that diversion by cramming a chosen morsel into a friend's mouth. When your hunger is satisfied, you do not sit for your companions; you exclaim "Al Hamd!" edge away from the tray, wash your hands and mouth with soap, display signs of repletion, otherwise you will be pressed to eat more, seize your pipe, sip your coffee, and take your "Kayf." Nor is it customary, in these lands, to sit together after dinner—the evening prayer cuts short the *séance*. Before we rose to take leave of Ali bin Ya Sin, a boy ran into the room, and displayed those infantine civilities which in the East are equivalent to begging a present. I slipped a dollar into his hand; at the sight of which he, veritable little Meccan, could not contain his joy. " The Riyal ! " he exclaimed ; "the Riyal ! look, grandpa', the good Effendi has given me a Riyal!" The old gentleman's eyes twinkled with emotion : he saw how easily the coin had slipped from my fingers, and he fondly hoped that he had not seen the last piece. " Verily thou art a good

---

if a guest is to be honoured, rosewater must often take the place of the pure element, even in tea.

1 Meccah is amply supplied with water-melons, dates, limes, grapes, cucumbers, and other vegetables from Taif and Wady Fatimah. During the pilgrimage season the former place sends at least 100 camels every day to the capital.

young man ! " he ejaculated, adding fervently, as prayers cost nothing, " May Allah further all thy desires." A gentle patting of the back evidenced his high approval.

I never saw old Ali after that evening, but entrusted to the boy Mohammed what was considered a just equivalent for his services.

CHAPTER XXXIV.

A GENERAL plunge into worldly pursuits and pleasures announced the end of the pilgrimage ceremonies. All the devotees were now " whitewashed "—the book of their sins was a *tabula rasa* : too many of them lost no time in making a new departure "down south," and in opening a fresh account. The faith must not bear the blame of the irregularities. They may be equally observed in the Calvinist, after a Sunday of prayer, sinning through Monday with a zest, and the Romanist falling back with new fervour upon the causes of his confession and penance, as in the Moslem who washes his soul clean by running and circumambulation ; and, in fairness, it must be observed that, as amongst Christians, so in the Moslem persuasion, there are many notable exceptions to this rule of extremes. Several of my friends and acquaintances date their reformation from their first sight of the Ka'abah.

The Moslem's " Holy Week" over, nothing detained me at Meccah. For reasons before stated, I resolved upon returning to Cairo, resting there for awhile, and starting a second time for the interior, *viâ* Muwaylah.[1]

The Meccans are as fond of little presents as are nuns : the Kabirah took an affectionate leave of me, begged me to be careful of her boy, who was to accom-

---

[1] This second plan was defeated by bad health, which detained me in Egypt till a return to India became imperative.

pany me to Jeddah, and laid friendly but firm hands upon a brass pestle and mortar, upon which she had long cast the eye of concupiscence.

Having hired two camels for thirty-five piastres, and paid half the sum in advance, I sent on my heavy boxes with Shaykh, now Haji Nur, to Jeddah.[1] Omar Effendi was to wait at Meccah till his father had started, in command of the Dromedary Caravan, when he would privily take ass, join me at the port, and return to his beloved Cairo. I bade a long farewell to all my friends, embraced the Turkish pilgrims, and mounting our donkeys, the boy Mohammed and I left the house. Abdullah the Melancholy followed us on foot through the city, and took leave of me, though without embracing, at the Shabayki quarter.

Issuing into the open plain, I felt a thrill of pleasure —such joy as only the captive delivered from his dungeon can experience. The sunbeams warmed me into renewed life and vigour, the air of the Desert was a perfume, and the homely face of Nature was as the smile of a dear old friend. I contemplated the Syrian Caravan, lying on the right of our road, without any of the sadness usually suggested by a parting look.

It is not my intention minutely to describe the line down which we travelled that night : the pages of Burckhardt give full information about the country. Leaving Meccah, we fell into the direct road running south of Wady Fatimah, and traversed for about an hour a flat surrounded by hills. Then we entered a valley by a flight of rough stone steps, dangerously slippery and zigzag, intended to facilitate the descent for camels and for laden beasts. About midnight we passed into a hill-girt Wady, here covered with deep sands, there hard with

---

1 The usual hire is thirty piastres, but in the pilgrimage season a dollar is often paid. The hire of an ass varies from one to three riyals.

gravelly clay : and, finally, about dawn, we sighted the maritime plain of Jeddah.

Shortly after leaving the city, our party was joined by other travellers, and towards evening we found ourselves in force, the effect of an order that pilgrims must not proceed singly upon this road.   Coffee-houses and places of refreshment abounding, we halted every five miles to refresh ourselves and the donkeys.[1]   At sunset we prayed near a Turkish guard-house, where one of the soldiers kindly supplied me with water for ablution.

Before nightfall I was accosted, in Turkish, by a one-eyed old fellow, who,

" with faded brow,
Entrenched with many a frown, and conic beard,"

and habited in unclean garments, was bestriding a donkey as faded as himself.   When I shook my head, he addressed me in Persian.   The same manœuvre made him try Arabic ; still he obtained no answer.   Then he grumbled out good Hindustani.   That also failing, he tried successively Pushtu, Armenian, English, French, and Italian.   At last I could "keep a stiff lip" no longer ; at every change of dialect his emphasis beginning with " Then who the d—— are you ?" became more emphatic. I turned upon him in Persian, and found that he had been a pilot, a courier, and a servant to Eastern tourists, and that he had visited England, France, and Italy, the Cape, India, Central Asia, and China.   We then chatted in English, which Haji Akif spoke well, but with all manner of courier's phrases ; Haji Abdullah so badly, that he was counselled a course of study.   It was not a little strange to hear such phrases as " Come 'p, Neddy," and " *Cré nom d'un baudet,*" almost within earshot of the tomb of Ishmael, the birthplace of Mohammed, and the Sanctuary of Al-Islam.

1 Besides the remains of those in ruins, there are on this road eight coffee-houses and stations for travellers, private buildings, belonging to men who supply water and other necessaries.

About eight P.M. we passed the Alamayn, which
define the Sanctuary in this direction.   They stand
about nine miles from Meccah, and near them are a coffee-
house and a little oratory, popularly known as the Sabil
Agha Almas.   On the road, as night advanced, we met
long strings of camels, some carrying litters, others huge
beams, and others bales of coffee, grain, and merchandise.
Sleep began to weigh heavily upon my companions' eyelids, and the boy Mohammed hung over the flank of his
donkey in a most ludicrous position.

About midnight we reached a mass of huts, called Al-
Haddah.   Ali Bey places it eight leagues from Jeddah.
At "the Boundary" which is considered to be the half-
way halting-place, Pilgrims must assume the religious
garb,[1] and Infidels travelling to Taif are taken off the
Meccan road into one leading Northward to Arafat.   The
settlement is a collection of huts and hovels, built with
sticks and reeds, supporting brushwood and burned and
blackened palm leaves.   It is maintained for supplying
pilgrims with coffee and water.   Travellers speak with
horror of its heat during the day ; Ali Bey, who visited it
twice, compares it to a furnace.   Here the country slopes
gradually towards the sea, the hills draw off, and every
object denotes departure from the Meccan plateau.   At
Al-Haddah we dismounted for an hour's halt.   A coffee-
house supplied us with mats, water-pipes, and other
necessaries ; we then produced a basket of provisions,
the parting gift of the kind Kabirah, and, this late supper
concluded, we lay down to doze.

After half an hour's halt had expired, and the
donkeys were saddled, I shook up with difficulty the boy
Mohammed, and induced him to mount.   He was, to use
his own expression, " dead from sleep " ; and we had

[1] In Ibn Jubayr's time the Ihram was assumed at Al-Furayn,
now a decayed station, about two hours' journey from Al-Haddah,
towards Jeddah.

scarcely advanced an hour, when, arriving at another
little coffee-house, he threw himself upon the ground, and
declared it impossible to proceed. This act caused some
confusion. The donkey-boy was a pert little Badawi,
offensively republican in manner. He had several times
addressed me impudently, ordering me not to flog his
animal, or to hammer its sides with my heels. On these
occasions he received a contemptuous snub, which had
the effect of silencing him. But now, thinking we were
in his power, he swore that he would lead away the
beasts, and leave us behind to be robbed and murdered.
A pinch of the windpipe, and a spin over the ground,
altered his plans at the outset of execution. He gnawed
his hand with impotent rage, and went away, threatening
us with the Governor of Jeddah next morning. Then an
Egyptian of the party took up the thread of remonstrance;
and, aided by the old linguist, who said, in English " by
G——! you must budge, you'll catch it here!" he
assumed a brisk and energetic style, exclaiming, "Yallah!
rise and mount; thou art only losing our time; thou
dost not intend to sleep in the Desert!" I replied, " O
my Uncle, do not exceed in talk!"—*Fuzul* (excess) in
Arabic is equivalent to telling a man in English not to be
impertinent—rolled over on the other side heavily, as
doth Encelades, and pretended to snore, whilst the cowed
Egyptian urged the others to make us move. The
question was thus settled by the boy Mohammed who
had been aroused by the dispute: " Do you know," he
whispered, in awful accents, " what *that* person is?" and
he pointed to me. " Why, no," replied the others.
" Well," said the youth, " the other day the Utaybah
showed us death in the Zaribah Pass, and what do you
think he did?" "Wallah! what do we know!" exclaimed the Egyptian, " What *did* he do?" " He called
for—his dinner," replied the youth, with a slow and

sarcastic emphasis. That trait was enough. The others
mounted, and left us quietly to sleep.

I have been diffuse in relating this little adventure,
which is characteristic, showing what bravado can do in
Arabia. It also suggests a lesson, which every traveller
in these regions should take well to heart. The people
are always ready to terrify him with frightful stories,
which are the merest phantoms of cowardice. The
reason why the Egyptian displayed so much philanthropy
was that, had one of the party been lost, the survivors
might have fallen into trouble. But in this place, we
were, I believe,—despite the declarations of our companions that it was infested with Turpins and Fra
Diavolos,—as safe as in Meccah. Every night, during
the pilgrimage season, a troop of about fifty horsemen
patrol the roads ; we were all armed to the teeth, and
our party looked too formidable to be " cruelly beaten by
a single footpad." Our nap concluded, we remounted,
and resumed the weary way down a sandy valley, in
which the poor donkeys sank fetlock-deep. At dawn we
found our companions halted, and praying at the Kahwat
Turki, another little coffee-house. Here an exchange of
what is popularly called " chaff " took place. " Well,"
cried the Egyptian, " what have ye gained by halting ?
We have been quiet here, praying and smoking for the
last hour ! " " Go, eat thy buried beans,[1] " we replied.
" What does an Egyptian boor know of manliness ! "
The surly donkey-boy was worked up into a paroxysm of
passion by such small jokes as telling him to convey our
salams to the Governor of Jeddah, and by calling the
asses after the name of his tribe. He replied by " foul,
unmannered, scurril taunts," which only drew forth fresh
derision, and the coffee-house keeper laughed consumedly,

[1] The favourite Egyptian " kitchen " ; held to be contemptible
food by the Arabs.

having probably seldom entertained such "funny gentle-men."

Shortly after leaving the Kahwat Turki we found the last spur of the highlands that sink into the Jeddah Plain. This view would for some time be my last of

"Infamous hills, and sandy, perilous wilds;"

and I contemplated it with the pleasure of one escaping from it. Before us lay the usual iron flat of these regions, whitish with salt, and tawny with stones and gravel; but relieved and beautified by the distant white walls, whose canopy was the lovely blue sea. Not a tree, not a patch of verdure was in sight; nothing distracted our attention from the sheet of turquoises in the distance. Merrily the little donkeys hobbled on, in spite of their fatigue. Soon we distinguished the features of the town, the minarets, the fortifications—so celebrated since their honeycombed guns beat off in 1817 the thousands of Abdullah bin Sa'ud, the Wahhabi,[1] and a small dome outside the walls.

The sun began to glow fiercely, and we were not sorry when, at about eight A.M., after passing through the mass of hovels and coffee-houses, cemeteries and sand-hills, which forms the eastern approach to Jeddah, we entered the fortified Bab Makkah. Allowing eleven hours for our actual march,—we halted about three,—those wonderful donkeys had accomplished between forty-

---

1 In 1817 Abdullah bin Sa'ud attacked Jeddah with 50,000 men, determining to overthrow its " Kafir-works "; namely, its walls and towers. The assault is described as ludicrous. All the inhabitants aided to garrison : they waited till the wild men flocked about the place, crying, " Come, and let us look at the labours of the infidel," they then let fly, and raked them with matchlock balls and old nails acting grape. The Wahhabi host at last departed, unable to take a place which a single battery of our smallest siege-guns would breach in an hour. And since that day the Meccans have never ceased to boast of their Gibraltar, and to taunt the Madinites with their wall-less port, Yambu'.

four and forty-six miles,[1] generally in deep sand, in one night. And they passed the archway of Jeddah cantering almost as nimbly as when they left Meccah.

Shaykh Nur had been ordered to take rooms for me in a vast pile of madrepore—unfossilized coral, a recent formation,—once the palace of Mohammed bin Aun, and now converted into a Wakalah. Instead of so doing, Indian-like, he had made a gipsy encampment in the square opening upon the harbour. After administering the requisite correction, I found a room that would suit me. In less than an hour it was swept, sprinkled with water, spread with mats, and made as comfortable as its capability admitted. At Jeddah I felt once more at home. The sight of the sea acted as a tonic. The Maharattas were not far wrong when they kept their English captives out of reach of the ocean, declaring that we were an amphibious race, to whom the wave is a home.

After a day's repose at the Caravanserai, the camel-man and donkey-boy clamouring for money, and I not having more than tenpence of borrowed coin, it was necessary to cash at the British Vice-Consulate a draft given to me by the Royal Geographical Society. With some trouble I saw Mr. Cole, who, suffering from fever, was declared to be " not at home." His dragoman did by no means admire my looks ; in fact, the general voice of the household was against me. After some fruitless messages, I sent up a scrawl to Mr. Cole, who decided upon admitting the importunate Afghan. An exclamation of astonishment and a hospitable welcome followed my self-introduction as an officer of the Indian army. Amongst other things, the Vice-Consul informed me that, in divers discussions with the Turks about the possibility of an Englishman finding his way *en cachette* to Meccah,

---

1 Al-Idrisi places Meccah forty (Arab) miles from Jeddah. Burckhardt gives fifty-five miles, and Ali Bey has not computed the total distance.

he had asserted that his compatriots could do everything, even pilgrim to the Holy City. The Moslems politely assented to the first, but denied the second part of the proposition. Mr. Cole promised himself a laugh at the Turks' beards; but since my departure, he wrote to me that the subject made the owners look so serious, that he did not like recurring to it.

Truly gratifying to the pride of an Englishman was our high official position assumed and maintained at Jeddah. Mr. Cole had never, like his colleague at Cairo, lowered himself in the estimation of the proud race with which he has to deal, by private or mercantile transactions with the authorities. He has steadily withstood the wrath of the Meccan Sharif, and taught him to respect the British name. The Abbé Hamilton ascribed the attentions of the Prince to " the infinite respect which the Arabs entertain for Mr. Cole's straightforward way of doing business,—it was a delicate flattery addressed to him." And the writer was right; honesty of purpose is never thrown away amongst these people. The general contrast between our Consular proceedings at Cairo and Jeddah is another proof of the advisability of selecting Indian officials to fill offices of trust at Oriental courts. They have lived amongst Easterns, and they know one Asiatic language, with many Asiatic customs ; and, chief merit of all, they have learned to assume a tone of command, without which, whatever may be thought of it in England, it is impossible to take the lead in the East. The " home-bred " diplomate is not only unconscious of the thousand traps everywhere laid for him, he even plays into the hands of his crafty antagonists by a ceremonious politeness, which they interpret—taking ample care that the interpretation should spread—to be the effect of fear or of fraud.

Jeddah[1] has been often described by modern pens.

1 Abulfeda writes the word " Juddah," and Mr. Lane, as well as

Burckhardt (in A.D. 1841) devoted a hundred pages of his
two volumes to the unhappy capital of the Tihamat al-
Hijaz, the lowlands of the mountain region.   Later still,
MM. Mari and Chedufau wrote upon the subject; and two
other French travellers, MM. Galinier and Ferret, published tables of the commerce in its present state, quoting
as authority the celebrated Arabicist M. Fresnel.[1]   These

MM. Mari and Chedufau, adopt this form, which signifies a " plain
wanting water."   The water of Jeddah is still very scarce and bad ;
all who can afford it drink the produce of hill springs brought in
skins by the Badawin.   Ibn Jubayr mentions that outside the town
were 360 old wells (?), dug, it is supposed by the Persians.   "Jeddah,"
or "Jiddah," is the vulgar pronounciation ; and not a few of the
learned call it " Jaddah " (the grandmother), in allusion to the legend
of Eve's tomb.

        1 In Chapters iii. and vi. of this work I have ventured some
remarks upon the advisability of our being represented in Al-Hijaz
by a Consul, and at Meccah by a native agent, till the day shall
come when the tide of events forces us to occupy the mother-city of
Al-Islam.   My apology for reverting to these points must be the
nature of an Englishman, who would everywhere see his nation
" second to none," even at Jeddah.   Yet, when we consider that
from twenty-five to thirty vessels here arrive annually from India,
and that the value of the trade is about twenty-five lacs of rupees,
the matter may be thought worth attending to.   The following ex-
tracts from a letter written to me by Mr. Cole shall conclude this
part of my task :—
        " You must know, that in 1838 a commercial treaty was concluded be-
tween Great Britain and the Porte, specifying (amongst many other clauses
here omitted),—
        " 1. That all merchandise imported from English ports to Al-Hijaz
should pay 4 per cent. duty.
        " 2. That all merchandise imported by British subjects from countries
not under the dominion of the Porte should likewise pay but 5 per cent.
        " 3. That all goods exported from countries under the dominion of the
Porte should pay 12 per cent., after a deduction of 16 per cent. from the
market-value of the articles.
        " 4. That all monopolies be abolished."
        *   *   *   *   *   *
        " Now, when I arrived at Jeddah, the state of affairs was this.   A
monopoly had been established upon salt, and this weighed only upon our
Anglo-Indian subjects, they being the sole purchasers.   Five per cent. was

R. Burton, delt.

C.F. Kell Lith.

A SQUARE IN JEDDAH.

have been translated by the author of "Life in Abyssinia." Abd al-Karim, writing in 1742, informs us that the French had a factory at Jeddah; and in 1760, when Bruce revisited the port, he found the East India Company in possession of a post whence they dispersed their merchandise over the adjoining regions. But though the English were at an early epoch of their appearance in the East received here with especial favour, I failed to procure a single ancient document.

Jeddah, when I visited it, was in a state of commotion, owing to the perpetual passage of pilgrims, and provisions were for the same reason scarce and dear. The two large Wakalahs, of which the place boasts, were crowded with travellers, and many were reduced to encamping upon the squares. Another subject of confusion was the state of the soldiery. The Nizam, or Regulars, had not been paid for seven months, and the Arnauts could scarcely sum up what was owing to them. Easterns are wonderfully amenable to discipline; a European army, under the circumstances, would probably have helped itself. But the Pasha knew that there is a limit to a man's endurance, and he was anxiously casting about for some contrivance that would replenish the empty pouches of his troops. The worried dignitary must have sighed for those *beaux jours* when privily firing the town and allowing the soldiers to plunder, was the Oriental style of settling arrears of pay.[1]

levied upon full value of goods, no deduction of the 20 per cent. being allowed; the same was the case with exports; and most vexatious of all, various charges had been established by the local authorities, under the names of boat-hire, weighing, brokerage, &c., &c. The duties had thus been raised from 4 to at least 8 per cent. * * * This being represented at Constantinople, brought a peremptory Firman, ordering the governor to act up to the treaty letter by letter. * * * I have had the satisfaction to rectify the abuses of sixteen years' standing during my first few months of office, but I expect all manner of difficulties in claiming reimbursement for the over-exactions."

1 M. Rochet (*soi-disant* d'Héricourt) amusingly describes this manœuvre of the governor of Al-Hodaydah.

Jeddah displays all the license of a seaport and garrison town. Fair Corinthians establish themselves even within earshot of the Karakun, or guard-post; a symptom of excessive laxity in the authorities, for it is the duty of the watch to visit all such irregularities with a bastinado preparatory to confinement. My guardians and attendants at the Wakalah used to fetch *Araki* in a clear glass bottle, without even the decency of a cloth, and the messenger twice returned from these errands decidedly drunk. More extraordinary still, the people seemed to take no notice of the scandal.

The little "Dwarka" had been sent by the Bombay Steam Navigation Company to convey pilgrims from Al-Hijaz to India. I was still hesitating about my next voyage, not wishing to coast the Red Sea in this season without a companion, when one morning Omar Effendi appeared at the door, weary, and dragging after him an ass more weary than himself. We supplied him with a pipe and a cup of hot tea, and, as he was fearful of pursuit, we showed him a dark hole full of grass under which he might sleep concealed.

The student's fears were realised; his father appeared early the next morning, and having ascertained from the porter that the fugitive was in the house, politely called upon me. Whilst he plied all manner of questions, his black slave furtively stared at everything in and about the room. But we had found time to cover the runaway with grass, and the old gentleman departed, after a fruitless search. There was, however, a grim smile about his mouth which boded no good.

That evening, returning home from the Hammam, I found the house in an uproar. The boy Mohammed, who had been miserably mauled, was furious with rage; and Shaykh Nur was equally unmanageable, by reason of his fear. In my absence the father had returned with a *posse comitatus* of friends and relatives. They questioned the youth, who delivered himself of many circumstantial and emphatic mis-statements. Then they proceeded to open the boxes ; upon which the boy Mohammed cast himself sprawling, with a vow to die rather than to endure such a disgrace. This procured for him some scattered slaps, which presently became a storm of blows, when a prying little boy discovered Omar Effendi's leg in the hiding-place. The student was led away unresisting, but mildly swearing that he would allow no opportunity of escape to pass. I examined the boy Mohammed, and was pleased to find that he was not seriously hurt. To pacify his mind, I offered to sally out with him, and to rescue Omar Effendi by main force. This, which would only have brought us all into a brunt with quarterstaves, and similar servile weapons, was declined, as had been foreseen. But the youth recovered complacency, and a few well-merited encomiums upon his " pluck " restored him to high spirits.

The reader must not fancy such escapade to be a serious thing in Arabia. The father did not punish his son ; he merely bargained with him to return home for a few days before starting to Egypt. This the young man did, and shortly afterwards I met him unexpectedly in the streets of Cairo.

Deprived of my companion, I resolved to waste no time in the Red Sea, but to return to Egypt with the utmost expedition. The boy Mohammed having laid in a large store of grain, purchased with my money, having secured all my disposable articles, and having hinted that, after my return to India, a present of twenty dollars would find him at Meccah, asked leave, and departed with a coolness for which I could not account. Some days afterwards Shaykh Nur explained the cause. I had taken the youth with me on board the steamer, where a bad suspicion crossed his mind. " Now, I understand," said the boy Mohammed to his fellow-servant, " your master is a Sahib from India ; he hath laughed at our beards."

He parted as coolly from Shaykh Nur. These worthy
youths had been drinking together, when Mohammed,
having learned at Stambul the fashionable practice of
Bad-masti, or "liquor-vice," dug his "fives" into Nur's
eye. Nur erroneously considering such exercise likely to
induce blindness, complained to me ; but my sympathy
was all with the other side. I asked the Hindi why he
had not returned the compliment, and the Meccan once
more overwhelmed the *Miyan* with taunt and jibe.

It is not easy to pass the time at Jeddah. In the
square opposite to us was an unhappy idiot, who afforded
us a melancholy spectacle. He delighted to wander about
in a primitive state of toilette, as all such wretches do ;
but the people of Jeddah, far too civilised to retain Moslem
respect for madness, forced him, despite shrieks and
struggles, into a shirt, and when he tore it off they beat
him. At other times the open space before us was diversi-
fied by the arrival and the departure of pilgrims, but it
was a mere *réchauffé* of the feast, and had lost all power to
please. Whilst the boy Mohammed remained, he used to
pass the time in wrangling with some Indians, who were
living next door to us, men, women, and children, in a
promiscuous way. After his departure I used to spend
my days at the Vice-Consulate ; the proceeding was not
perhaps of the safest, but the temptation of meeting a
fellow-countryman, and of chatting "shop" about the
service was too great to be resisted. I met there the principal merchants of Jeddah ; Khwajah Sower, a Greek ;
M. Anton, a Christian from Baghdad, and others.[1] And I
was introduced to Khalid Bey, brother of Abdullah bin
Sa'ud, *the* Wahhabi. This noble Arab once held the

[1] Many of them were afterwards victims to the "Jeddah massacre" on June 30, 1858. I must refer the reader to my "Lake Regions
of Central Africa" (Appendix, vol. ii.) for an account of this event,
for the proposals which I made to ward it off, and for the miserable
folly of the "Bombay Government," who rewarded me by an official
reprimand.

official position of Mukayyid al-Jawabat, or Secretary, at
Cairo, where he was brought up by Mohammed Ali. He
is brave, frank, and unprejudiced, fond of Europeans, and
a lover of pleasure. Should it be his fate to become chief
of the tribe, a journey to Riyaz, and a visit to Central
Arabia, will offer no difficulties to our travellers.

I now proceed to the last of my visitations. Outside the
town of Jeddah lies no less a personage than Sittna Haw-
wa, the Mother of mankind. The boy Mohammed and I,
mounting asses one evening, issued through the Meccan
gate, and turned towards the North-East over a sandy
plain. After half an hour's ride, amongst dirty huts and
tattered coffee-hovels, we reached the enciente, and found
the door closed. Presently a man came running with
might from the town ; he was followed by two others ;
and it struck me at the time they applied the key with
peculiar *empressement*, and made inordinately low *congés* as
we entered the enclosure of whitewashed walls.

" The Mother " is supposed to lie, like a Moslemah,
fronting the Ka'abah, with her feet northwards, her head
southwards, and her right cheek propped by her right
hand. Whitewashed, and conspicuous to the voyager
and traveller from afar, is a diminutive dome with an
opening to the West; it is furnished as
such places usually are in Al-Hijaz. Under
it and in the centre is a square stone,
planted upright and fancifully carved, to
represent the omphalic region of the human frame. This, as well as the dome, is
called Al-Surrah, or the navel. The cicerone directed me to kiss this manner

The Surrah.

of hieroglyph, which I did, thinking the while, that, under
the circumstances, the salutation was quite uncalled-for.
Having prayed here, and at the head, where a few young
trees grow, we walked along the side of the two parallel
dwarf walls which define the outlines of the body : they are
about six paces apart, and between them, upon Eve's

neck, are two tombs, occupied, I was told, by Osman
Pasha and his son, who repaired the Mother's sepulchre.
I could not help remarking to the boy Mohammed, that if
our first parent measured a hundred and twenty paces
from head to waist, and eighty from waist to heel, she
must have presented much the appearance of a duck.
To this the youth replied, flippantly, that he thanked his
stars the Mother was underground, otherwise that men
would lose their senses with fright.

Ibn Jubayr (twelfth century) mentions only an old
dome, "built upon the place where Eve stopped on the
way to Meccah." Yet Al-Idrisi (A.D. 1154) declares Eve's

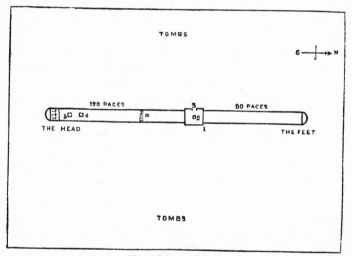

Plan of Eve's Tomb.

grave to be at Jeddah. Abd al-Karim (1742) compares it
to a parterre, with a little dome in the centre, and the
extremities ending in barriers of palisades; the circumference was a hundred and ninety of his steps. In
Rooke's Travels we are told that the tomb is twenty feet
long. Ali Bey, who twice visited Jeddah, makes no allusion to it; we may therefore conclude that it had been
destroyed by the Wahhabis. Burckhardt, who, I need

scarcely say, has been carefully copied by our popular authors, was informed that it was a "rude structure of stone, about four feet in length, two or three feet in height, and as many in breadth"; thus resembling the tomb of Noah, seen in the valley of Al-Buka'a in Syria. Bruce writes: "Two days' journey from this place (? Meccah or Jeddah) Eve's grave, of *green sods*, about fifty yards in length, is shown to this day"; but the great traveller probably never issued from the town-gates. And Sir W. Harris, who could not have visited the Holy Place, repeats, in 1840, that Eve's grave of *green sod* is still shown on the barren shore of the Red Sea." The present structure is clearly modern; anciently, I was told at Jeddah, the sepulchre consisted of a stone at the head, a second at the feet, and the navel-dome.

The idol of Jeddah, in the days of Arab litholatry, was called *Sakhrah Tawilah*, the Long Stone. May not this stone of Eve be the Moslemized revival of the old idolatry? It is to be observed that the Arabs, if the tombs be admitted as evidence, are inconsistent in their dimensions of the patriarchal stature. The sepulchre of Adam at the Masjid al-Khayf is, like that of Eve, gigantic. That of Noah at Al-Buka'a is a bit of Aqueduct thirty-eight paces long by one and a half wide. Job's tomb near Hulah (seven parasangs from Kerbela) is small. I have not seen the grave of Moses (south-east of the Red Sea), which is becoming known by the bitumen cups there sold to pilgrims. But Aaron's sepulchre in the Sinaitic peninsula is of moderate dimensions.

On leaving the graveyard I offered the guardian a dollar, which he received with a remonstrance that a man of my dignity should give so paltry a fee. Nor was he at all contented with the assurance that nothing more could be expected from an Afghan Darwaysh, however pious. Next day the boy Mohammed explained the man's *empressement* and disappointment,—I had been mistaken for the Pasha of Al-Madinah.

   *   *   *   *   *   *   *   *

For a time my peregrinations ended.   Worn out with fatigue, and the fatal fiery heat, I embarked (Sept. 26) on board the "Dwarka"; experienced the greatest kindness from the commander and chief officer (Messrs. Wolley and Taylor); and, wondering the while how the Turkish pilgrims who crowded the vessel did not take the trouble to throw me overboard, in due time I arrived at Suez.

And here, reader, we part.   Bear with me while I conclude, in the words of a brother traveller, long gone, but not forgotten—Fa-hian—this Personal Narrative of my Journey to Al-Hijaz: "I have been exposed to perils, and I have escaped from them; I have traversed the sea, and have not succumbed under the severest fatigues; and my heart is moved with emotions of gratitude, that I have been permitted to effect the objects I had in view."[1]

---

1 The curious reader will find details concerning Patriarchal and Prophetical Tombs in "Unexplored Syria," i. 33—35.

APPENDICES.

APPENDIX I.

OF HAJJ, OR PILGRIMAGE.

The word Hajj is explained by Moslem divines to mean " Kasd," or aspiration, and to express man's sentiment that he is but a wayfarer on earth wending towards another and a nobler world. This explains the origin and the belief that the greater the hardships the higher will be the reward of the pious wanderer. He is urged by the voice of his soul: " O thou who toilest so hard for worldly pleasures and perishable profit, wilt thou endure nothing to win a more lasting reward ? " Hence it is that pilgrimage is common to all old faiths. The Hindus still wander to Egypt, to Tibet, and to the inhospitable Caucasus; the classic philosophers visited Egypt ; the Jews annually flocked to Jerusalem; and the Tartars and Mongols— Buddhists—journey to distant Lamaserais. The spirit of pilgrimage was predominant in mediæval Europe, and the processions of the Roman Catholic Church are, according to her votaries,[1] modern memorials of the effete rite.

Every Moslem is bound, under certain conditions,[2]

---

1 M. Huc's "Travels in Tartary."

2 The two extremes, between which lie many gradations, are these. Abu Hanifah directs every Moslem and Moslemah to perform the pilgrimage if they have health and money for the road and for the support of their families ; moreover, he allows a deputy-pilgrim, whose expenses must be paid by the principal. Ibn Malik, on the contrary, enjoins every follower to visit Meccah, if able to walk, and to earn his bread on the way. As a general rule, in Al-Islam there are four Shurut al-Wujub, or necessary conditions, viz. :—

to pay at least one visit to the Holy City. This consti-
tutes the Hajjat al-Farz (the one obligatory pilgrimage),
or Hajjat al-Islam, of the Mohammedan faith. Repetitions become mere Sunnats, or practices of the Prophet,
and are therefore supererogatory. Some European writers
have of late years laboured to represent the Meccan pilgrimage as a fair, a pretext to collect merchants and to
afford Arabia the benefits of purchase and barter. It
would be vain to speculate whether the secular or the
spiritual element originally prevailed ; but most probably
each had its portion. But those who peruse this volume
will see that, despite the comparatively lukewarm piety of
the age, the Meccan pilgrimage is religious essentially,
accidentally an affair of commerce.

Moslem pilgrimage is of three kinds.

1. Al-Mukarinah (the uniting) is when the votary
performs the Hajj and the Umrah[1] together, as was done
by the Prophet in his last visit to Meccah.

2. Al-Ifrad (singulation) is when either the Hajj or
the Umrah is performed singularly, the former preceding
the latter. The pilgrim may be either Al-Mufrid b'il Hajj

---

1. Islam, the being a Moslem.
2. Bulugh, adolescence.
3. Hurriyat, the being a free man.
4. Akl, or mental sanity.

Other authorities increase the conditions to eight, viz.:—

5. Wujud al-Zad, sufficiency of provision.
6. Al-Rahlah, having a beast of burthen, if living two days' journey
from Meccah.
7. Takhliyat al-Tarik, the road being open; and
8. Imkan al-Masir, the being able to walk two stages, if the pilgrim
hath no beast.

Others, again, include all conditions under two heads :—

1. Sihhat, health.
2. Istita'at, ability.

These subjects have exercised not a little the casuistic talents of the
Arab doctors : a folio volume might be filled with differences of
opinion on the subject, "Is a blind man sound ?"

1 The technical meaning of these words will be explained below.

(one who is performing only the Hajj), or *vice versâ*, Al-Mufrid b'il Umrah.   According to Abu Hanifah, this form is more efficacious than the following.

3. Al-Tamattu (" possession ") is when the pilgrim assumes the Ihram, and preserves it throughout the months of Shawwal, Zu'l Ka'adah, and nine days (ten nights) in Zu'l Hijjah,[1] performing Hajj and Umrah the while.

There is another threefold division of pilgrimage:—

1. Umrah (the little pilgrimage), performed at any time except the pilgrimage season.   It differs in some of its forms from Hajj, as will afterwards appear.

2. Hajj (or simple pilgrimage), performed at the proper season.

3. Hajj al-Akbar (the great pilgrimage) is when the "day of Arafat" happens to fall upon a Friday.   This is a most auspicious occasion.   M. Caussin de Perceval and other writers, departing from the practice of (modern?) Islam, make " Hajj al-Akbar " to mean the simple pilgrimage, in opposition to the Umrah, which they call "Hajj al-Asghar."

The following compendium of the Shafe'i pilgrim-rites is translated from a little treatise by Mohammed of Shirbin, surnamed Al-Khatib, a learned doctor, whose work is generally read in Egypt and in the countries adjoining.

CHAPTER I.—OF PILGRIMAGE.[2]

" Know," says the theologist, with scant preamble, "that the acts of Al-Hajj, or pilgrimage, are of three kinds:—

---

1 At any other time of the year Ihram is considered Makruh, or objectionable, without being absolutely sinful.

2 In other books the following directions are given to the intended pilgrim:—Before leaving home he must pray two prostrations, concluding the orisons with a long supplication and blessings upon relatives, friends, and neighbours, and he must distribute not fewer than seven silver pieces to the poor.   The day should be either a Thursday or a Saturday; some, however, say

" Allah hath honoured the Monday and the Thursday."

"1. Al-Arkan or Farayz; those made obligatory by Koranic precepts, and therefore essentially necessary, and not admitting expiatory or vicarious atonement, either in Hajj or Umrah.

"2. Al-Wajibat (requisites); the omission of which may, according to some schools,[1] be compensated for by the Fidyat, or atoning sacrifice: and—

"3. Al-Sunan (pl. of Sunnat), the practice of the Prophet, which may be departed from without positive sin.

"Now, the Arkan, the 'pillars' upon which the rite stands, are six in number,[2] viz.:—

"1. Al-Ihram ('rendering unlawful'), or the wearing pilgrim garb and avoiding certain actions.

"2. Al-Wukuf, the 'standing' upon Mount Arafat.

"3. The Tawaf al-Ifazah, or circumambulation of impetuosity.[3]

If possible, the first of the month should be chosen, and the hour early dawn. Moreover, the pilgrim should not start without a Rafik, or companion, who should be a pious as well as a travelled man. The other Mukaddamat al-Safar, or preambles to journeying, are the following. Istikharah, consulting the rosary and friends. Khulus al-Niyat, vowing pilgrimage to the Lord (not for lucre or revenge). Settling worldly affairs, paying debts, drawing up a will, and making arrangements for the support of one's family. Hiring animals from a pious person. The best *monture* is a camel, because preferred by the Prophet; an ass is not commendable; a man should not walk if he can afford to ride; and the palanquin or litter is, according to some doctors, limited to invalids. Reciting long prayers when mounting, halting, dismounting, and at nightfall. On hills the Takbir should be used: the Tasbih is properest for vales and plains; and Meccah should be blessed when first sighted. Avoiding abuse, curses, or quarrels. Sleeping like the Prophet, namely, in early night (when prayer-hour is distant), with "Iftirash," or lying at length with the right cheek on the palm of the dexter hand; and near dawn with "Ittaka," *i. e.* propping the head upon the hand, with the arm resting upon the elbow. And, lastly, travelling with collyrium-pot, looking-glass and comb, needle and thread for sewing, scissors and tooth-stick, staff and razor.

1 In the Shafe'i school there is little difference between Al-Farz and Al-Wajib. In the Hanafi the former is a superior obligation to the latter.

2 The Hanafi, Maliki, and even some Shafe'i doctors, reduce the number from six to four, viz.:—

1. Ihram, with "Niyat."	3. Wukuf.
2. Tawaf.	4. Sai.

3 The Ifazah is the impetuous descent from Mount Arafat. Its Tawaf, generally called Tawaf al-Ziyarat, less commonly Tawaf al-Sadr or Tawaf

"4. The Sai, or course between Mounts Safa and Marwah.

"5. Al-Halk; tonsure (of the whole or part) of the head for men; or taksir, cutting the hair (for men or women).[1]

"6. Al-Tartib, or the due order of the ceremonies, as above enumerated.

"But Al-Sai (4), may either precede or follow Al-Wukuf (2), provided that the Tawaf al-Kudum, or the circumambulation of arrival, has previously been performed. And Halk (5) may be done before as well as after the Tawaf al-Ifazah (3).

"Now, the Wajibat (requisites of pilgrimage, also called 'Nusuk') are five in number, viz.:—

"1. Al-Ihram, or assuming pilgrim garb, from the Mikat, or fixed limit.[2]

"2. The Mabit, or nighting at Muzdalifah: for this a short portion, generally in the latter watch, preceding the Yaum al-Nahr, or victim-day, suffices.

"3. The spending at Muna the three nights of the 'Ayyam al-Tashrik,' or days of drying flesh: of these, the first is the most important.

"4. The Rami al-Jimar, or casting stones at the devil: and—

"5. The avoiding of all things forbidden to the pilgrim when in a state of Ihram.

"Some writers reduce these requisites by omitting the second and third. The Tawaf al-Wida'a, or the circumambulation of farewell, is a 'Wajib Mustakill,' or particular requisite, which may, however, be omitted without prejudice to pilgrimage.

"Finally, the Sunnat of pilgrimage are many in number. Of these I enumerate but a few. 'Hajj' should precede 'Umrah.' The 'Talbiyat' should be frequently ejaculated. The 'Tawaf al-Kudum' must be performed on arrival at Meccah, before proceeding to Mount Arafat.[3] The two-bow prayer should follow

---

al-Nuzul, is that performed immediately after throwing the stones and resuming the laical dress on the victim-day at Mount Muna.

1 Shaving is better for men, cutting for women. A razor must be passed over the bald head; but it is sufficient to burn, pluck, shave, or clip three hairs when the *chevelure* is long.

2 The known Mikat are: North, Zu'l Halifah; North-East, Karn al-Manazil; North-West, Al-Juhfah (الجحفة) South, Yalamlam ; East, Zat Irk.

3 This Tawaf is described in chapter v.

Tawaf. A whole night should be passed at Muzdalifah and Muna.[1] The circumambulation of farewell must not be forgotten,[2] and the pilgrim should avoid all sewn clothes, even slippers."

<h2 style="text-align:center">Section I.—*Of Ihram.*</h2>

"Before doffing his laical garment, the pilgrim performs a total ablution, shaves, and perfumes himself. He then puts on a 'Rida' and an 'Izar,'[3] both new, clean, and of a white colour: after which he performs a two-bow prayer (the 'Sunnat' of Al-Ihram), with a *sotto-voce* Niyat, specifying which rite he intends.[4]

"When Muhrim (*i.e.* in Ihram), the Moslem is forbidden (unless in case of sickness, necessity, over-heat, or unendurable cold, when a victim must expiate the transgression),—

"1. To cover his head with aught which may be deemed a covering, as a cap or turband; but he may carry an umbrella, dive under water, stand in the shade, and even place his hands upon his head. A woman may wear sewn clothes, white or light blue (not black), but her face-veil should be kept at a distance from her face.

"2. To wear anything sewn or with seams, as shirt, trowsers, or slippers; anything knotted or woven, as chain-armour; but the pilgrim may use, for instance, a torn-up shirt or trowsers bound round his loins or thrown over his shoulders, he may knot his 'Izar,' and tie it with a cord, and he may gird his waist.

"3. To knot the Rida, or shoulder-cloth.[5]

---

1 Generally speaking, as will afterwards be shown, the pilgrims pass straight through Muzdalifah, and spend the night at Muna.

2 The "Tawaf al-Wida'a" is considered a solemn occasion. The pilgrim first performs circumambulation. He drinks the waters of Zemzem, kisses the Ka'abah threshold, and stands for some time with his face and body pressed against the Multazem. There, on clinging to the curtain of the Ka'abah, he performs Takbir, Tahlil, Tahmid, and blesses the Prophet, weeping, if possible, but certainly groaning. He then leaves the Mosque, backing out of it with tears and lamentations, till he reaches the "Bab al-Wida'a," whence, with a parting glance at the Bayt Ullah, he wends his way home.

3 See chapter v.

4 Many pronounce this Niyat. If intending to perform pilgrimage, the devotee, standing, before prayer says, "I vow this intention of Hajj to Allah the most High."

5 In spite of this interdiction, pilgrims generally, for convenience, knot their shoulder-clothes under the right arm.

"4. To deviate from absolute chastity, even kissing being forbidden to the Muhrim. Marriage cannot be contracted during the pilgrimage season.

"5. To use perfumes, oil, curling the locks, or removing the nails and hair by paring, cutting, plucking, or burning. The nails may be employed to remove pediculi from the hair and clothes, but with care, that no pile fall off.

"6. To hunt wild animals, or to kill those which were such originally. But he may destroy the 'five noxious,'—a kite, a crow, a rat, a scorpion, and a dog given to biting. He must not cut down a tree,[1] or pluck up a self-growing plant; but he is permitted to reap and to cut grass.

"It is meritorious for the pilgrim often to raise the 'Talbiyat' cry (for which see p. 140 ante).

> " 'Labbayk' Allahumma Labbayk'!
> Lá Sharika laka Labbayk'!
> Inna 'l hamda wa 'l ni'amata laka w'al mulk!
> La Sharika laka, Labbayk.'[2]

"When assuming the pilgrim-garb, and before entering Meccah, 'Ghusl,' or total ablution, should be performed; but if water be not procurable, the Tayammum, or sand ablution, suffices. The pilgrim should enter the Holy City by day and on foot. When his glance falls upon the Ka'abah he should say, 'O Allah, increase this (Thy) house in degree, and greatness, and honour, and awfulness, and increase all those who have honoured it and glorified it, the Hajis and the Mutamirs (Umrah-performers), with degree, and greatness, and honour, and dignity!' Entering the outer Bab al-Salam, he must exclaim, 'O Allah, Thou art the Safety, and from Thee is the Safety!' And then passing into the Mosque, he should repair to the 'Black Stone,' touch it with his right hand, kiss it, and commence his circumambulation.[3]

---

1 Hunting, killing, or maiming beasts in Sanctuary land and cutting down trees, are acts equally forbidden to the Muhrim and the Muhill (the Moslem in his normal state). For a large tree a camel, for a small one a sheep, must be sacrificed.

2 See chapter v. After the "Talbiyat" the pilgrim should bless the Prophet, and beg from Allah paradise and protection from hell, saying, "O Allah, by thy mercy spare us from the pains of hell-fire!"

3 Most of these injunctions are "meritorious," and may therefore omitted without prejudice to the ceremony.

"Now, the victims of Al-Ihram are five in number, viz.:—

"1. The 'Victim of Requisites,' when a pilgrim accidentally or willingly omits to perform a requisite, such as the assumption of the pilgrim garb at the proper place. This victim is a sheep, sacrificed at the Íd al-Kurban (in addition to the usual offering),[1] or, in lieu of it, ten days' fast—three of them in the Hajj season (viz. on the 6th, 7th, and 8th days of Zu'l Hijjah) and seven after returning home.

"2. The 'Victim of Luxuries,' (Turfah), such as shaving the head or using perfumes. This is a sheep, or a three days' fast, or alms, consisting of three sá'a measures of grain, distributed among six paupers.

"3. The 'Victim of suddenly returning to Laical Life'; that is to say, before the proper time. It is also a sheep, after the sacrifice of which the pilgrim shaves his head.

"4. The 'Victim of killing Game.' If the animal slain be one for which the tame equivalents be procurable (a camel for an ostrich, a cow for a wild ass or cow, and a goat for a gazelle), the pilgrim should sacrifice it, or distribute its value, or purchase with it grain for the poor, or fast one day for each 'Mudd' measure. If the equivalent be not procurable, the offender must buy its value of grain for alms-deeds, or fast a day for every measure.

"5. The 'Victim of Incontinence.' This offering is either a male or a female camel[2]; these failing, a cow or seven sheep, or the value of a camel in grain distributed to the poor, or a day's fast for each measure."

Section II.—*Of Tawaf, or Circumambulation.*

"Of this ceremony there are five Wajibat, or requisites, viz.:—Concealing 'the shame,[3]' as in prayer. Ceremonial purity of body, garments, and place. Circumambulation inside the Mosque. Seven circuits of the house. Commencement of circuit from the Black Stone. Circumambulating the house with the left shoulder presented to it. Circuiting the house outside its Shazarwan, or marble basement.[4] And, lastly, the

1 Namely, the victim sacrificed on the great festival day at Muna.
2 So the commentators explain "Badanah."
3 A man's "Aurat" is from the navel to the knee; in the case of a free woman the whole of her face and person are "shame."
4 If the pilgrim place but his hand upon the Shazarwan, or on the Hijr, the Tawaf is nullified.

Niyat, or intention of Tawaf, specifying whether it be for Hajj or for Umrah.

"Of the same ceremony the principal Sunnat, or practices, are to walk on foot; to touch, kiss, and place his forehead upon the Black Stone, if possible after each circuit to place the hand upon the Rukn al-Yamani (South corner), but not to kiss it; to pray during each circuit for what is best for man (pardon of sins); to quote lengthily from the Koran,[1] and to often say, 'Subhan Allah!' and to mention none but Allah; to walk slowly, during the first three circuits, and trotting the last four,[2] all the while maintaining a humble and contrite demeanour, with downcast eyes.

"The following are the prayers which have descended to us by tradition:—

"When touching the Black Stone the pilgrim says,[3] after Niyat, 'In the name of Allah, and Allah is omnipotent! O Allah (I do this) in Thy belief and in verification of Thy book, and in faithfulness to Thy covenant, and in pursuance of the example of Thy Prophet Mohammed—may Allah bless Him and preserve!'

"Opposite the door of the house: 'O Allah, verily the House is Thy House, and the Sanctuary thy Sanctuary, and the Safeguard Thy Safeguard, and this is the place of the Fugitive to flee from Hell-fire!'

"Arrived at the Rukn al-Iraki (North corner): 'O Allah, verily I take refuge with Thee from Polytheism (Shirk), and Disobedience, and Hypocrisy, and Evil Conversation, and Evil Thoughts concerning Family (Ahl, 'a wife'), and Property, and Progeny!'

"Parallel with the Mizab, or rain-spout: 'O Allah, shadow me in Thy Shadow that day when there is no shade but Thy Shadow, and cause me to drink from the Cup of Thy Prophet Mohammed—may Allah bless Him and preserve!—that pleasant Draught after which is no thirst to all eternity, O Lord of Honour and Glory!'

---

1 This is a purely Shafe'i practice; the Hanafi school rejects it on the grounds that the Word of God should not be repeated when walking or running.

2 The reader will observe (chapter v.), that the Mutawwif made me reverse this order of things.

3 It is better to recite these prayers mentally; but as few pilgrims know them by heart, they are obliged to repeat the words of the cicerone.

"At the corners Al-Shami and Al-Yamani (West and South angles): 'O Allah, make it an Acceptable Pilgrimage, and the Forgiveness of Sins, and a Laudable Endeavour, and a Pleasant Action in Thy Sight, and a Store that perisheth not, O Thou Glorious! O Thou Pardoner!'[1]

"And between the Southern and Eastern corners: 'O Lord, grant to us in this World Prosperity, and in the next World Prosperity, and save us from the Punishment of Fire!'

"After the sevenfold circumambulation the pilgrim should recite a two-bow prayer, the 'Sunnat of Tawaf,' behind the Makam Ibrahim. If unable to pray there, he may take any other part of the Mosque. These devotions are performed silently by day and aloud by night. And after prayer the pilgrim should return to the Black Stone, and kiss it."

Section III.—*Of Sai, or Course between Mounts Safa and Marwah.*

"After performing Tawaf, the pilgrim should issue from the gate 'Al-Safa' (or another, if necessary), and ascend the steps of Mount Safa, about a man's height from the street.[2] There he raises the cry Takbir, and implores pardon for his sins. He then descends, and turns towards Mount Marwah at a slow pace. Arrived within six cubits of the Mil al-Akhzar (the 'green pillar,' planted in the corner of the temple on the left hand), he runs swiftly till he reaches the 'two green pillars,' the left one of which is fixed in the corner of the temple, and the other close to the Dar al-Abbas.[3] Thence he again walks slowly up to Marwah, and ascends it as he did Safa. This concludes a single course. The pilgrim then starts from Marwah, and walks, runs, and walks again through the same limits, till the seventh course is concluded.

"There are four requisites of Sai. The pilgrim must pass over all the space between Safa and Marwah; he must begin with Safa, and end with Marwah; he must traverse the distance seven times; and he must perform the rite after some important Tawaf, as that of arrival, or that of return from Arafat.

"The practices of Sai are, briefly, to walk, if possible, to

---

1 This portion is to be recited twice.

2 A woman, or a hermaphrodite, is enjoined to stand below the steps and in the street.

3 Women and hermaphrodites should not run here, but walk the whole way. I have frequently, however, seen the former imitating the men.

be in a state of ceremonial purity, to quote lengthily from the Koran, and to be abundant in praise of Allah.

"The prayer of Sai is, 'O my Lord, Pardon and Pity, and pass over that (Sin) which Thou knowest. Verily Thou knowest what is not known, and verily Thou art the most Glorious, the most Generous! O, our Lord, grant us in this World Prosperity, and in the Future Prosperity, and save us from the Punishment of Fire!

"When Sai is concluded, the pilgrim, if performing only Umrah, shaves his head, or clips his hair, and becomes 'Muhill,' returning to the Moslem's normal state. If he purpose Hajj, or pilgrimage after Umrah, he re-assumes the Ihram. And if he be engaged in pilgrimage, he continues 'Muhrim,' *i. e.*, in Ihram, as before."

Section IV.—*Of Wukuf, or standing upon Mount Arafat.*

"The days of pilgrimage are three in number: namely, the 8th, the 9th, and the 10th of the month Zu'l Hijjah.[1]

"On the first day (8th), called Yaum al-Tarwiyah, the pilgrim should start from Meccah after the dawn-prayer and sunrise, perform his noontide, afternoon, and evening devotions at Muna, where it is a Sunnat that he should sleep.[2]

---

[1] The Arab legend is, that the angels asking the Almighty why Ibrahim was called Al-Khalil (or God's friend); they were told that all his thoughts were fixed on heaven; and when they called to mind that he had a wife and child, Allah convinced them of the Patriarch's sanctity by a trial. One night Ibrahim saw, in a vision, a speaker, who said to him, "Allah orders thee to draw near him with a victim!" He awoke, and not comprehending the scope of the dream, took especial notice of it (روّى); hence the first day of pilgrimage is called Yaum al-Tarwiyah. The same speaker visited him on the next night, saying, "Sacrifice what is dearest to thee!" From the Patriarch's knowing (عرّف) what the first vision meant, the second day is called Yaum Arafat. On the third night he was ordered to sacrifice Ismail; hence that day is called Yaum Nahr (of "throat-cutting"). The English reader will bear in mind that the Moslem day begins at sunset. I believe that the origin of "Tarwiyat" (which may mean "carrying water") dates from the time of pagan Arabs, who spent that day in providing themselves with the necessary. Yaum Arafat derives its name from the hill, and Yaum al-Nahr from the victims offered to the idols in the Muna valley.

[2] The present generation of pilgrims, finding the delay inconvenient, always pass on to Arafat without halting, and generally arrive at the mountain late in the afternoon of the 8th, that is to say, the first day of

"On the second day (9th), the 'Yaum Arafat,' after performing the early prayer at 'Ghalas' (*i. e.* when a man cannot see his neighbour's face) on Mount Sabir, near Muna, the pilgrim should start when the sun is risen, proceed to the 'Mountain of Mercy,' encamp there, and after performing the noontide and afternoon devotions at Masjid Ibrahim,[1] joining and shortening them,[2] he should take his station upon the mountain, which is all standing ground.   But the best position is that preferred by the Prophet, near the great rocks lying at the lower slope of Arafat.   He must be present at the sermon,[3] and be abundant in Talbiyat (supplication), Tahlil (recitations of the chapter 'Say he is the one God!'[4]), and weeping, for that is the place for the outpouring of tears.   There he should stay till sunset, and then decamp and return hastily to Muzdalifah, where he should pass a portion of the night.[5]   After a visit to the Mosque 'Mashr al-Harim,' he should collect seven pebbles and proceed to Muna.[6]

"Yaum al-Nahr, the third day of the pilgrimage (10th Zu'l Hijjah), is the great festival of the Moslem year.   Amongst

pilgrimage.   Consequently, they pray the morning prayer of the 9th at Arafat.

1 This place will be described afterwards.

2 The Shafe'i when engaged on a journey which takes up a night and day, is allowed to shorten his prayers, and to "join" the noon with the afternoon, and the evening with the night devotions; thus reducing the number of times from five to three per diem.   The Hanafi school allows this on one day and on one occasion only, namely, on the ninth of Zu'l Hijjah (arriving at Muzdalifah), when at the "Isha" hour it prays the Maghib and the Isha prayers together.

3 If the pilgrim be too late for the sermon, his labour is irretrievably lost.—M. Caussin de Perceval (vol. iii. pp. 301-305) makes the Prophet to have preached from his camel Al-Kaswa on a platform at Mount Arafat before noon, and to have again addressed the people after the post-meridian prayers at the station Al-Sakharat.   Mohammed's last pilgrimage, called by Moslems Hajjat al-Bilagh ("of perfection," as completing the faith), Hajjat al-Islam, or Hajjat al-Wida'a ("of farewell"), is minutely described by historians as the type and pattern of pilgrimage to all generations.

4 Ibn Abbas relates a tradition, that whoever recites this short chapter 11,000 times on the Arafat day, shall obtain from Allah all he desires.

5 Most schools prefer to sleep, as the Prophet did, at Muzdalifah, pray the night devotions there, and when the yellowness of the next dawn appears, collect the seven pebbles and proceed to Muna.   The Shafe'i, however, generally leave Muzdalifah about midnight.

6 These places will be minutely described in a future chapter.

its many names,[1] 'Íd al-Kurban' is the best known, as expressive of Ibrahim's sacrifice in lieu of Ismail. Most pilgrims, after casting stones at the Akabah, or 'Great Devil,' hurry to Meccah. Some enter the Ka'abah, whilst others content themselves with performing the Tawaf al-Ifazah, or circumambulation of impetuosity, round the house.[2] The pilgrim should then return to Muna, sacrifice a sheep, and sleep there. Strictly speaking, this day concludes the pilgrimage.

"The second set of 'trois jours,' namely, the 11th,[3] the 12th, and the 13th of Zu'l Hijjah, are called Ayyam al-Tashrik, or the 'days of drying flesh in the sun.' The pilgrim should spend that time at Muna,[4] and each day throw seven pebbles at each of the three pillars.[5]

"When throwing the stones, it is desirable that the pilgrim should cast them far from himself, although he is allowed to place them upon the pillar. The act also should be performed after the Zawal, or declension of the sun. The pilgrim should begin with the pillar near the Masjid al-Khayf, proceed to the Wusta, or central column, and end with the Akabah. If unable to cast the stones during the daytime, he is allowed to do it at night.

"The 'throwing' over:—The pilgrim returns to Meccah, and when his journey is fixed, performs the Tawaf al-Wida'a ('of farewell'). On this occasion it is a Sunnat to drink the waters of Zemzem, to enter the temple with more than usual

---

1 Íd al-Kurban, or the Festival of Victims (known to the Turks as Kurban Bayram, to the Indians as Bakar-íd, the Kine Fête), Íd al-Zuha, "of forenoon," or Íd al-Azha, "of serene night." The day is called Yaum al-Nahr, "of throat-cutting."

2 If the ceremony of "Sai" has not been performed by the pilgrim after the circuit of arrival, he generally proceeds to it on this occasion.

3 This day is known in books as "Yaum al-Karr," because the pilgrims pass it in *repose* at Muna.

4 "The days of drying flesh," because at this period pilgrims prepare provisions for their return, by cutting up their victims, and exposing to the sun large slices slung upon long lines of cord. The schools have introduced many modifications into the ceremonies of these three days. Some spend the whole time at Muna, and return to Meccah on the morning of the 13th. Others return on the 12th, especially when that day happens to fall upon a Friday.

5 As will afterwards appear, the number of stones and the way of throwing them vary greatly in the various schools.

respect and reverence, and bidding it adieu, to depart from the Holy City.

"The Moslem is especially forbidden to take with him cakes made of the earth or dust of the Harim, and similar mementoes, as they savour of idolatry."

CHAPTER II.—OF UMRAH, OR THE LITTLE PILGRIMAGE.

"The word 'Umrah,' denotes a pilgrimage performed at any time except the pilgrim season (the 8th, 9th, and 10th of Zu'l Hijjah).

"The Arkan or pillars upon which the Umrah rite rests, are five in number, viz.:—

" 1. Al-Ihram.

" 2. Al-Tawaf.

" 3. Al-Sai (between Safa and Marwah).

" 4. Al-Halk (tonsure), or Al-Taksir (cutting the hair).

" 5. Al-Tartib, or the due order of ceremonies, as above enumerated.[1]

"The Wajibat, or requisites of Umrah, are but two in number:—

" 1. Al-Ihram, or assuming the pilgrim garb, from the Mikat, or fixed limit; and

" 2. The avoiding of all things forbidden to the pilgrim when in state of Ihram.

" In the Sunnat and Mustahabb portions of the ceremony there is no difference between Umrah and Hajj."

CHAPTER III.—OF ZIYARAT, OR THE VISIT TO THE PROPHET'S TOMB.

"Al-Ziyarat is a practice of the faith, and the most effectual way of drawing near to Allah through his Prophet Mohammed.

"As the Zair arrives at Al-Madinah, when his eyes fall upon the trees of the city, he must bless thè Prophet with a loud voice. Then he should enter the Mosque, and sit in the Holy Garden, which is between the pulpit and the tomb, and pray a two-bow prayer in honour of the Masjid. After this he should supplicate pardon for his sins. Then, approach-

---

[1] The difference in the pillars of Umrah and Hajj, is that in the former the standing on Arafat and the Tawaf al-Ifazah are necessarily omitted.

ing the sepulchre, and standing four cubits away from it, recite this prayer:—

" ' Peace be with Thee, O Thou T. H. and Y. S.,[1] Peace be with Thee, and upon Thy Descendants, and Thy Companions, one and all, and upon all the Prophets, and those inspired to instruct Mankind. And I bear witness that Thou hast delivered thy Message, and performed Thy Trust, and advised Thy followers, and swept away Darkness, and fought in Allah's Path the good Fight: may Allah requite Thee from us the Best with which he ever requited Prophet from his Followers!'

"Let the visitor stand the while before the tomb with respect, and reverence, and singleness of mind, and fear, and awe. After which, let him retreat one cubit, and salute Abu Bakr the Truthful in these words:—

" ' Peace be with Thee, O Caliph of Allah's Prophet over his People, and Aider in the Defence of His Faith!'

"After this, again retreating another cubit, let him bless in the same way Omar the Just. After which, returning to his former station opposite the Prophet's tomb, he should implore intercession for himself and for all dearest to him. He should not neglect to visit the Bakia Cemetery and the Kuba Mosque, where he should pray for himself and for his brethren of the Muslimín, and the Muslimat, the Muminín and the Muminat,[2] the quick of them and the dead. When ready to depart, let the *Zair* take leave of the Mosque with a two-bow prayer, and visit the tomb, and salute it, and again beg intercession for himself and for those he loves. And the *Zair* is forbidden to circumambulate the tomb, or to carry away the cakes of clay made by the ignorant with the earth and dust of the Harim."

---

1 The 20th and 36th chapters of the Koran.

2 These second words are the feminines of the first; they prove that the Moslem is not above praying for what Europe supposed he did not believe in, namely, the souls of women.

APPENDIX II.

THE BAYT ULLAH.

THE House of Allah[1] has been so fully described by
my predecessors, that there is little inducement to attempt
a new portrait. Readers, however, may desire a view of
the great sanctuary, and, indeed, without a plan and its
explanation, the ceremonies of the Harim would be
scarcely intelligible. I will do homage to the memory of
the accurate Burckhardt, and extract from his pages a
description which shall be illustrated by a few notes.

" The Kaabah stands in an oblong square (enclosed
by a great wall) 250 paces long, and 200 broad,[2] none of
the sides of which runs quite in a straight line, though at
first sight the whole appears to be of a regular shape.
This open square is enclosed on the eastern side by a
colonnade. The pillars stand in a quadruple row; they are
three deep on the other sides, and are united by pointed
arches, every four of which support a small dome
plastered and whitened on the outside. These domes,
according to Kotobeddyn, are 152 in number.[3] The

1 "Bayt Ullah" (House of Allah) and "Ka'abah," *i.e.* cube
(house), "la maison carrée," are synonymous.

2 Ali Bey gives 536 feet 9 inches by 356 feet: my measurement is
257 paces by 210. Most Moslem authors, reckoning by cubits, make
the parallelogram 404 by 310.

3 On each short side I counted 24 domes; on the long, 35. This
would give a total of 118 along the cloisters. The Arabs reckon in
all 152; viz., 24 on the East side, on the North 36, on the South 36,

(overleaf)

ALI BEY'S PLAN OF THE PROPHET'S
MOSQUE AT MECCAH.

Commonly called Bait Allah or God's House.

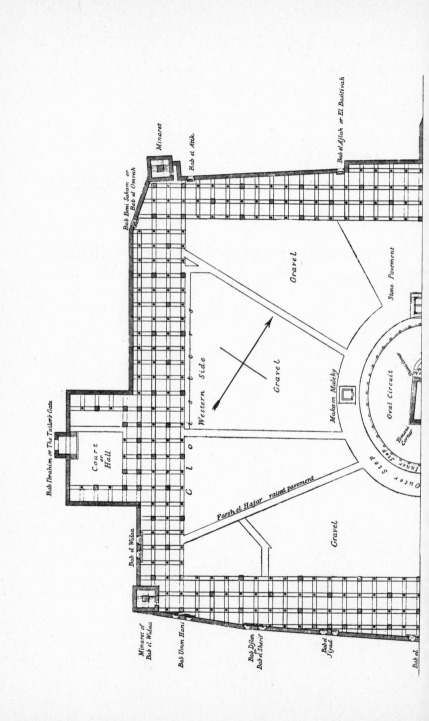

Bab Ibrahim or The Tailor's Gate

Bab Beni Saham or
Bab el Omrah

Minaret

Bab el Atik

Bab el Ajlah or El Basitvah

Court
or
Hall

C l o i s t e r s

Western Side

Gravel

Gravel

Stone Pavement

Makam Maleky

Oval Circuit

Inner Step

Outer Step

Yemani Corner

Bab el Widaa

Minaret of
Bab el Widaa

Bab Umm Hani

Bab Dijan
Bab el Sherif

Bab el
Jiyad

Bab el

Farsh el Hajar   raised pavement

Gravel

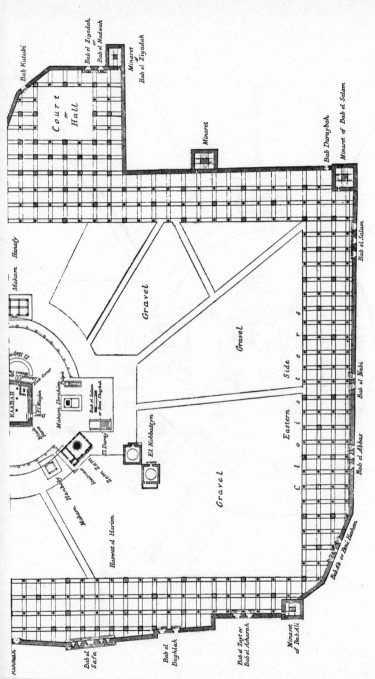

Kaabah.

Bab Kutubi

Bab el Ziyadah or Bab el Nadwah

Court or Hall

Minaret of Bab el Ziyadah

Minaret

Bab Dureybah

Minaret of Bab el Salam

R. Kiahurd sc.

Makam Hanafy

El Hayatein

KAABAH

Makam Ibrahimijeh

Door Black Stone El Maajan

Bab el Salam or Beni Sheybah

El Darej

El Kobbateyn

Gravel

Gravel

Eastern Cloisters

Bab el Salam

Makam Hanbaly

Zemzem

Bab el Nabi

Gravel

Gravel

Bab el Abbas

Hasroat el Harim.

Babes or Bni Hasham

Bab el Safa

Bab el Baghlah

Bab el Zeyt or Bab el Ashurah

Minaret of Bab Ali

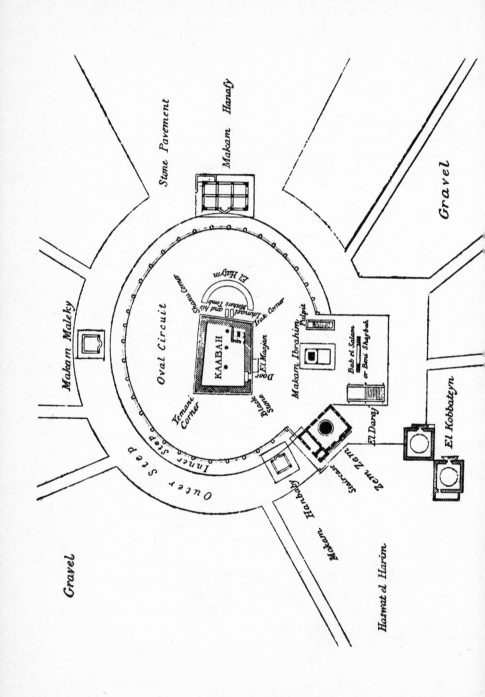

Stone Pavement

Makam Hanafy

Gravel

Makam Maleky

Oval Circuit

El Halym

Shamy Corner

and his Medīnas Tomb

Irak Corner

Yemani Corner

Black Stone

El Maajan

Door

Makam Ibrahim

Pulpit

Bab el Salam or Beni Shaybah

El Daraj

Zem Zem

El Kobbateyn

Makam Hanbaly

Staircase

Hawat el Harīm

Gravel

Inner Step

Outer Step

pillars are above twenty feet in height, and generally from one foot and a half to one foot and three quarters in diameter ; but little regularity has been observed in regard to them.   Some are of white marble, granite or porphyry; but the greater number are of common stone of the Meccah mountains.[1]   El Fasy states the whole at 589, and says they are all of marble excepting 126, which are of common stone, and three of composition.   Kotobeddyn reckons 555, of which, according to him, 311 are of marble, and the rest of the stone taken from the neighbouring mountains ; but neither of these authors lived to see the latest repairs of the Mosque, after the destruction occasioned by a torrent in A.D. 1626.[2]   Between every three or four columns stands an octagonal one, about four feet in thickness.   On the east side are two shafts of reddish gray granite in one piece, and one fine grey porphyry with slabs of white feldspath.   On the north side is one red granite column, and one of fine-grained red porphyry ; these are probably the columns which Koto-beddyn states to have been brought from Egypt, and

one on the Mosque corner, near the Zarurah minaret; 16 at the porch of the Bab al-Ziyadah; and 15 at the Bab Ibrahim.   The shape of these domes is the usual " Media-Naranja," and the super-stition of the Meccans informs the pilgrim that they cannot be counted.   Books reckon 1352 pinnacles or battlements on the temple wall.

1 The "common stone of the Meccah mountains" is a fine grey granite, quarried principally from a hill near the Bab al-Shabayki, which furnished material for the Ka'abah.   Eastern authors describe the pillars as consisting of three different substances, viz.: Rukham, white marble, not "alabaster," its general sense; Suwan, or granite (syenite?); and Hajar Shumaysi," a kind of yellow sandstone, so called from "Bir Shumays," a place on the Jeddah road near Haddah, the half-way station.

2 I counted in the temple 554 pillars.   It is, however, difficult to be accurate, as the four colonnades and the porticos about the two great gates are irregular; topographical observations, moreover, must here be made under difficulties.   Ali Bey numbers them roughly at "plus de 500 colonnes et pilastres."

principally from Akhmim (Panopolis), when the chief
(Caliph) El Mohdy enlarged the Mosque in A. H. 163.
Among the 450 or 500 columns which form the enclosure
I found not any two capitals or bases exactly alike.   The
capitals are of coarse Saracen workmanship ; some of
them, which had served for former buildings, by the
ignorance of the workmen, have been placed upside down
upon the shafts.   I observed about half a dozen marble
bases of good Grecian workmanship.   A few of the
marble columns bear Arabic or Cufic inscriptions, in
which I read the dates 863 and 762 (A. H.).[1]   A column
on the east side exhibits a very ancient Cufic inscription,
somewhat defaced, which I could neither read nor copy.
Some of the columns are strengthened with broad iron
rings or bands,[2] as in many other Saracen buildings of
the East.   They were first employed by Ibn Dhaher
Berkouk, king of Egypt, in rebuilding the Mosque, which
had been destroyed by fire in A. H. 802.[3]"

"Some parts of the walls and arches are gaudily
painted in stripes of yellow, red, and blue, as are also the
minarets.   Paintings of flowers, in the usual Muselman

---

1 The author afterwards informs us, that "the temple has been
so often ruined and repaired, that no traces of remote antiquity are
to be found about it."   He mentions some modern and unimportant
inscriptions upon the walls and over the gates.   Knowing that many
of the pillars were sent in ships from Syria and Egypt by the Caliph
Al-Mahdi, a traveller would have expected better things.

2 The reason being, that "those shafts formed of the Meccan
stone are mostly in three pieces ; but the marble shafts are in one
piece."

3 To this may be added, that the façades of the cloisters are
twenty-four along the short walls, and thirty-six along the others ;
they have stone ornaments, not inaptly compared to the French
"fleur de lis."   The capital and bases of the outer pillars are grander
and more regular than the inner ; they support pointed arches, and
the Arab secures his beloved variety by placing at every fourth arch
a square pilaster.   Of these there are on the long sides ten, on the
short seven.

style, are nowhere seen; the floors of the colonnades are paved with large stones badly cemented together."

"Some paved causeways lead from the colonnades towards the Kaabah, or Holy House, in the centre.[1] They are of sufficient breadth to admit four or five persons to walk abreast, and they are elevated about nine inches above the ground. Between these causeways, which are covered with fine gravel or sand, grass appears growing in several places, produced by the Zem Zem water oozing out of the jars which are placed in the ground in long rows during the day.[2] There is a descent of eight or ten steps from the gates on the north side into the platform of the colonnade, and of three or four steps from the gates on the south side."

"Towards the middle of this area stands the Kaabah; it is 115 paces from the north colonnade, and 88 from the south. For this want of symmetry we may readily account, the Kaabah having existed prior to the Mosque, which was built around it, and enlarged at different periods. The Kaabah is an oblong massive structure, 18 paces in length, 14 in breadth, and from 35 to 40 feet in height.[3] It is constructed of the grey Mekka stone, in large blocks of different sizes joined together, in a very

---

1 I counted eight, not including the broad pavement which leads from the Bab al-Ziyadah to the Ka'abah, or the four cross branches which connect the main lines. These "Firash al-Hajar," as they are called, also serve to partition off the area. One space for instance is called "Haswat al-Harim," or the "Women's sanded place," because appropriated to female devotees.

2 The jars are little amphoræ, each inscribed with the name of the donor and a peculiar cypher.

3 My measurements give 22 paces or 55 feet in length by 18 (45) of breadth, and the height appeared greater than the length. Ali Bey makes the Eastern side 37 French feet, 2 inches and 6 lines, the Western 38° 4' 6", the Northern 29 feet, the Southern 31° 6', and the height 34° 4'. He therefore calls it a "veritable trapezium." In Al-Idrisi's time it was 25 cubits by 24, and 27 cubits high.

rough manner, with bad cement.[1] It was entirely rebuilt,
as it now stands, in A.D. 1627. The torrent in the preceding year had thrown down three of its sides, and, preparatory to its re-erection, the fourth side was, according
to Asamy, pulled down, after the Olemas, or learned
divines, had been consulted on the question whether
mortals might be permitted to destroy any part of the
holy edifice without incurring the charge of sacrilege and
infidelity."

"The Kaabah stands upon a base two feet in height,
which presents a sharp inclined plane.[2] Its roof being
flat, it has at a distance the appearance of a perfect
cube.[3] The only door which affords entrance, and which
is opened but two or three times in the year,[4] is on the

---

1 I would alter this sentence thus:—"It is built of fine grey
granite in horizontal courses of masonry of irregular depth; the
stones are tolerably fitted together, and are held by excellent mortar
like Roman cement." The lines are also straight.

2 This base is called Al-Shazarwan, from the Persian Shadar-
wan, a cornice, eaves, or canopy. It is in pent-house shape, projecting about a foot beyond the wall, and composed of fine white marble
slabs, polished like glass; there are two breaks in it, one opposite
and under the doorway, and another in front of Ishmael's tomb.
Pilgrims are directed, during circumambulation, to keep their bodies
outside of the Shazarwan; this would imply it to be part of the
building, but its only use appears in the large brass rings welded
into it, for the purpose of holding down the Ka'abah covering.

3 Ali Bey also errs in describing the roof as "plat endessus."
Were such the case, rain would not pour off with violence through
the spout. Most Oriental authors allow a cubit of depression from
South-West to North-West. In Al-Idrisi's day the Ka'abah had a
double roof. Some say this is the case in the present building, which
has not been materially altered in shape since its restoration by Al-
Hajjaj, A.H. 83. The roof was then eighteen cubits long by fifteen
broad.

4 In Ibn Jubayr's time the Ka'abah was opened every day in
Rajab, and in other months on every Monday and Friday. The
house may now be entered ten or twelve times a year gratis; and by
pilgrims as often as they can collect, amongst parties, a sum sufficient
to tempt the guardians' cupidity.

north side and about seven feet above the ground.[1]   In the first periods of Islam, however, when it was rebuilt in A.H. 64 by Ibn Zebeyr (Zubayr), chief of Mecca, it had two doors even with the ground floor of the Mosque.[2]

---

[1] This mistake, in which Burckhardt is followed by all our popular authors, is the more extraordinary, as all Arabic authors call the door-wall Janib al-Mashrik—the Eastern side—or Wajh al-Bayt, the front of the house, opposed to Zahr al-Bayt, the back. Niebuhr is equally in error when he asserts that the door fronts to the South. Arabs always hold the " Rukn al-Iraki," or Irak angle, to face the polar star, and so it appears in Ali Bey's plan. The Ka'abah, therefore, has no Northern side. And it must be observed that Moslem writers dispose the length of the Ka'abah from East to West, whereas our travellers make it from North to South. Ali Bey places the door only six feet from the pavement, but he calculates distances by the old French measure. It is about seven feet from the ground, and six from the corner of the Black Stone. Between the two the space of wall is called Al-Multazem (in Burckhardt, by a clerical error, " Al-Metzem," vol. i. p. 173). It derives its name, the "attached-to," because here the circumambulator should apply his bosom, and beg pardon for his sins. Al-Multazem, according to M. de Perceval, following d'Ohsson, was formerly "le lieu des engagements," whence, according to him, its name, " Le Moltezem," says M. Galland (Rits et Cérémonies du Pélerinage de la Mecque), "qui est entre la pierre noire et la porte, est l'endroit où Mahomet se réconcilia avec ses dix compagnons, qui disaient qu'il n'était pas véritablement Prophète."

[2] From the Bab al-Ziyadah, or gate in the northern colonnade, you descend by two flights of steps, in all about twenty-five. This depression manifestly arises from the level of the town having been raised, like Rome, by successive layers of ruins ; the most populous and substantial quarters (as the Shamiyah to the north) would, we might expect, be the highest, and this is actually the case. But I am unable to account satisfactorily for the second hollow within the temple, and immediately around the house of Allah, where the door, according to all historians, formerly on a level with the pavement, and now about seven feet above it, shows the exact amount of depression, which cannot be accounted for simply by calcation. Some chroniclers assert, that when the Kuraysh rebuilt the house they raised the door to prevent devotees entering without their permission. But seven feet would scarcely oppose an entrance, and how will this account for the floor of the building being also raised to that height above the pavement ? It is curious to observe the

The present door (which, according to Azraky, was brought hither from Constantinople in A.D. 1633), is wholly coated with silver, and has several gilt ornaments; upon its threshold are placed every night various small lighted wax candles, and perfuming pans, filled with musk, aloe-wood, &c.[1]"

"At the north-east[2] corner of the Kaabah, near the door, is the famous 'Black Stone'[3]; it forms a part of the

similarity between this inner hollow of the Meccan fane and the artificial depression of the Hindu pagoda where it is intended to be flooded. The Hindus would also revere the form of the Meccan fane, exactly resembling their square temples, at whose corners are placed Brahma, Vishnu, Shiwa and Ganesha, who adore the great Universal Generator in the centre. The second door anciently stood on the side of the temple opposite the present entrance; inside, its place can still be traced. Ali Bey suspects its having existed in the modern building, and declares that the exterior surface of the wall shows the tracery of a blocked-up door, similar to that still open. Some historians declare that it was closed by the Kuraysh when they rebuilt the house in Mohammed's day, and that subsequent erections have had only one. The general opinion is, that Al-Hajjaj finally closed up the western entrance. Doctors also differ as to its size; the popular measurement is three cubits broad and a little more than five in length.

1 Pilgrims and ignorant devotees collect the drippings of wax, the ashes of the aloe-wood, and the dust from the "Atabah," or threshold of the Ka'abah, either to rub upon their foreheads or to preserve as relics. These superstitious practices are sternly rebuked by the Olema.

2 For North-East read South-East.

3 I will not enter into the fabulous origin of the Hajar al-Aswad. Some of the traditions connected with it are truly absurd. "When Allah," says Ali, "made covenant with the Sons of Adam on the Day of Fealty, he placed the paper inside the stone"; it will, therefore, appear at the judgment, and bear witness to all who have touched it. Moslems agree that it was originally white, and became black by reason of men's sins. It appeared to me a common aërolite covered with a thick slaggy coating, glossy and pitch-like, worn and polished. Dr. Wilson, of Bombay, showed me a specimen in his possession, which externally appeared to be a black slag, with the inside of a bright and sparkling greyish-white, the result of admixture of nickel

with the iron. This might possibly, as the learned Orientalist then suggested, account for the mythic change of colour, its appearance on earth after a thunderstorm, and its being originally a material part of the heavens. Kutb al-Din expressly declares that, when the Karamitah restored it after twenty-two years to the Meccans, men kissed it and rubbed it upon their brows; and remarked that the blackness was only superficial, the inside being white. Some Greek philosophers, it will be remembered, believed the heavens to be composed of stones (Cosmos, " Shooting Stars "): and Sanconiathon, ascribing the aërolite-worship to the god Cœlus, declares them to be living or animated stones. " The Arabians," says Maximus of Tyre (Dissert. 38, p. 455), " pay homage to I know not what god, which they represent by a quadrangular stone." The gross fetichism of the Hindus, it is well known, introduced them to litholatry. At Jagannath they worship a pyramidal black stone, fabled to have fallen from heaven, or miraculously to have presented itself on the place where the temple now stands. Moreover, they revere the Salagram, as the emblem of Vishnu, the second person in their triad. The rudest emblem of the " Bonus Deus " was a round stone. It was succeeded in India by the cone and triangle; in Egypt by the pyramid; in Greece it was represented by cones of terra-cotta about three inches and a half long. Without going deep into theory, it may be said that the Ka'abah and the Hajar are the only two idols which have survived the 360 composing the heavenly host of the Arab pantheon. Thus the Hindu poet exclaims:—

" Behold the marvels of my idol-temple, O Moslem!
That when its idols are destroy'd, it becomes Allah's House."

Wilford (As. Soc. vols. iii. and iv.) makes the Hindus declare that the Black Stone at Mokshesha, or Moksha-sthana (Meccah) was an incarnation of Moksheshwara, an incarnation of Shiwa, who with his consort visited Al-Hijaz. When the Ka'abah was rebuilt, this emblem was placed in the outer wall for contempt, but the people still respected it. In the Dabistan the Black Stone is said to be an image of Kaywan or Saturn; and Al-Shahristani also declares the temple to have been dedicated to the same planet Zuhal, whose genius is represented in the Puranas as fierce, hideous, four-armed, and habited in a black cloak, with a dark turband. Moslem historians are unanimous in asserting that Sasan, son of Babegan, and other Persian monarchs, gave rich presents to the Ka'abah; they especially mention two golden crescent moons, a significant offering. The Guebers assert that, among the images and relics left by Mahabad and his successors in the Ka'abah, was the Black Stone, an emblem of Saturn. They also call the city Mahgah—

sharp angle of the building,[1] at four or five feet above the ground.[2] It is an irregular oval, about seven inches in diameter, with an undulating surface, composed of about a dozen smaller stones of different sizes and shapes, well joined together with a small quantity of cement, and perfectly well smoothed: it looks as if the whole had been broken into many pieces by a violent blow, and then united again. It is very difficult to determine accurately the quality of this stone, which has been worn to its present surface by the million touches and kisses it has received.

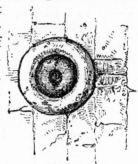

The Black Stone.

It appeared to me like a lava, containing several small extraneous particles of a whitish and of a yellowish substance. Its colour is now a deep reddish brown, approaching to black. It is surrounded on all sides by a border composed of a substance which I took to be a close cement

---

moon's place—from an exceedingly beautiful image of the moon; whence they say the Arabs derived " Meccah." And the Sabæans equally respect the Ka'abah and the pyramids, which they assert to be the tombs of Seth, Enoch (or Hermes), and Sabi the son of Enoch. Meccah, then, is claimed as a sacred place, and the Hajar al-Aswad, as well as the Ka'abah, are revered as holy emblems by four different faiths—the Hindu, Sabæan, Gueber, and Moslem. I have little doubt, and hope to prove at another time, that the Jews connected it with traditions about Abraham. This would be the fifth religion that looked towards the Ka'abah—a rare meeting-place of devotion.

1 Presenting this appearance in profile. The Hajar has suffered from the iconoclastic principle of Islam, having once narrowly escaped destruction by order of Al-Hakim of Egypt. In these days the metal rim serves as a protection as well as an ornament.

2 The height of the Hajar from the ground, according to my measurement, is four feet nine inches; Ali Bey places it forty-two inches above the pavement.

of pitch and gravel of a similar, but not quite the same, brownish colour.[1] This border serves to support its detached pieces; it is two or three inches in breadth, and rises a little above the surface of the stone. Both the border and the stone itself are encircled by a silver band,[2] broader below than above, and on the two sides, with a considerable swelling below, as if a part of the stone were hidden under it. The lower part of the border is studded with silver nails."

"In the south-east corner of the Kaabah,[3] or, as the Arab call it, Rokn al-Yemany, there is another stone about five feet from the ground; it is one foot and a half in length, and two inches in breadth, placed upright, and of the common Meccah stone. This the people walking round the Kaabah touch only with the right hand; they do not kiss it.[4] "

---

[1] The colour was black and metallic, and the centre of the stone was sunk about two inches below the metal circle. Round the sides was a reddish-brown cement, almost level with the metal, and sloping down to the middle of the stone. Ibn Jubayr declares the depth of the stone unknown, but that most people believe it to extend two cubits into the wall. In his day it was three "Shibr" (the large span from the thumb to the little finger-tip) broad, and one span long, with knobs, and a joining of four pieces, which the Karamitah had broken. The stone was set in a silver band. "Its softness and moisture were such," says Ibn Jubayr, "that the sinner would never remove his mouth from it, which phenomenon made the Prophet declare it to be the covenant of Allah on earth."

[2] The band is now a massive circle of gold or silver gilt. I found the aperture in which the stone is, one span and three fingers broad.

[3] The "Rukn al-Yamani" is the corner facing the South. The part alluded to in the text is the wall of the Ka'abah, between the Shami and Yamani angles, distant about three feet from the latter, and near the site of the old western door, long since closed. The stone is darker and redder than the rest of the wall. It is called Al-Mustajab (or Mustajab min al-Zunub or Mustajab al-Dua, "where prayer is granted"). Pilgrims here extend their arms, press their bodies against the building, and beg pardon for their sins.

[4] I have frequently seen it kissed by men and women.

"On the north side of the Kaabah, just by its door,[1] and close to the wall, is a slight hollow in the ground, lined with marble, and sufficiently large to admit of three persons sitting. Here it is thought meritorious to pray: the spot is called El Maajan, and supposed to be where Abraham and his son Ismail kneaded the chalk and mud which they used in building the Kaabah; and near this Maajan the former is said to have placed the large stone upon which he stood while working at the masonry. On the basis of the Kaabah, just over the Maajan, is an ancient Cufic inscription; but this I was unable to decipher, and had no opportunity of copying it."

"On the west (north-west) side of the Kaabah, about two feet below its summit, is the famous Myzab, or water-spout,[2] through which the rain-water collected on the roof of the building is discharged, so as to fall upon the ground; it is about four feet in length, and six inches in breadth, as well as I could judge from below, with borders equal in height to its breadth. At the

---

1 Al-Ma'ajan, the place of mixing or kneading, because the patriarchs here kneaded the mud used as cement in the holy building. Some call it Al-Hufrah (the digging), and it is generally known as Makam Jibrail (the place of Gabriel), because here descended the inspired order for the five daily prayers, and at this spot the Archangel and the Prophet performed their devotions, making it a most auspicious spot. It is on the north of the door, from which it is distant about two feet; its length is seven spans and seven fingers; breadth five spans three fingers; and depth one span four fingers. The following sentence from Herklet's "Qanoon e Islam" (ch. xii. sec. 5) may serve to show the extent of error still popular. The author, after separating the Bayt Ullah from the Ka'abah, erroneously making the former the name of the whole temple, proceeds to say, "the rain-water which falls on its (the Ka'abah's) *terrace* runs off through a golden spout on a stone near it, called *Rookn-e-Yemeni*, or *alabaster-stone*, and stands over the grave of Ismaeel." —— !

2 Generally called Mizab al-Rahmah (of Mercy). It carries rain from the roof, and discharges it upon Ishmael's grave, where pilgrims stand fighting to catch it. In Al-Idrisi's time it was of wood; now it is said to be gold, but it looks very dingy.

mouth hangs what is called the beard of the Myzab;
a gilt board, over which the water flows. This spout
was sent hither from Constantinople in A. H. 981, and
is *reported* to be of pure gold. The pavement round
the Kaabah, below the Myzab, was laid down in A. H.
826, and consists of various coloured stones, forming
a very handsome specimen of mosaic. There are two
large slabs of fine *verdi antico*[1] in the centre, which,
according to Makrizi, were sent thither, as presents
from Cairo, in A.H. 241. This is the spot where,
according to Mohammedan tradition, Ismayl the son of
Ibrahim, and his mother Hajirah are buried; and here it
is meritorious for the pilgrim to recite a prayer of two
Rikats. On this side is a semicircular wall, the two
extremities of which are in a line with the sides of the
Kaabah, and distant from it three or four feet,[2] leaving
an opening, which leads to the burial-place of Ismayl.
The wall bears the name of El Hatym[3]; and the area

---

1 Usually called the Hajar al-Akhzar, or green stone. Al-Idrisi
speaks of a white stone covering Ishmael's remains ; Ibn Jubayr of
"green marble, longish, in form of a Mihrab arch, and near it a
white round slab, in both of which are spots that make them appear
yellow." Near them, we are told, and towards the Iraki corner, is
the tomb of Hagar, under a green slab one span and a half broad,
and pilgrims used to pray at both places. Ali Bey erroneously
applies the words Al-Hajar Ismail to the parapet about the slab.

2 My measurements give five feet six inches. In Al-Idrisi's day
the wall was fifty cubits long.

3 Al-Hatim (الحطيم lit. the "broken"). Burckhardt asserts that
the Mekkawi no longer apply the word, as some historians do, to the
space bounded by the Ka'abah, the Partition, the Zemzem, and the
Makam of Ibrahim. I heard it, however, so used by learned Meccans, and they gave as the meaning of the name the break in this
part of the oval pavement which surrounds the Ka'abah. Historians
relate that all who rebuilt the " House of Allah " followed Abraham's
plan till the Kuraysh, and after them Al-Hajjaj curtailed it in the
direction of Al-Hatim, which part was then first broken off, and
ever since remained so.

which it encloses is called Hedjer or Hedjer Ismayl,[1] on account of its being separated from the Kaabah: the wall itself also is sometimes so called."

" Tradition says that the Kaabah once extended as far as the Hatym, and that this side having fallen down just at the time of the Hadj, the expenses of repairing it were demanded from the pilgrims, under a pretence that the revenues of government were not acquired in a manner sufficiently pure to admit of their application towards a purpose so sacred. The sum, however, obtained, proved very inadequate ; all that could be done, therefore, was to raise a wall, which marked the space formerly occupied by the Kaabah. This tradition, although current among the Metowefs (cicerones) is at variance with history ; which declares that the Hedjer was built by the Beni Koreish, who contracted the dimensions of the Kaabah ; that it was united to the building by Hadjadj,[2] and again separated from it by Ibn Zebeyr. It is asserted by Fasy, that a part of the Hedjer as it now stands was never compre- hended within the Kaabah. The law regards it as a portion of the Kaabah, inasmuch as it is esteemed equally meritorious to pray in the Hedjer as in the Kaabah itself ; and the pilgrims who have not an oppor- tunity of entering the latter are permitted to affirm upon oath that they have prayed in the Kaabah, although they have only prostrated themselves within the enclosure of the Hatym. The wall is built of solid stone, about five feet in height, and four in thickness, cased all over with white marble, and inscribed with prayers and invocations

---

1 Al-Hijr (الحِجْر) is the space separated, as the name denotes, from the Ka'abah. Some suppose that Abraham here penned his sheep. Possibly Ali Bey means this part of the Temple when he speaks of Al-Hajar (الحَجَر) Ismail—les pierres d'Ismail.

2 "Al-Hajjaj" ; this, as will afterwards be seen, is a mistake. He excluded the Hatim.

neatly sculptured upon the stone in modern characters.[1]
These and the casing are the work of El Ghoury, the
Egyptian sultan, in A.H. 917. The walk round the Ka'abah
is performed on the outside of the wall—the nearer to it
the better."

" Round the Kaabah is a good pavement of marble[2]
about eight inches below the level of the great square; it
was laid in A.H. 981, by order of the sultan, and describes
an irregular oval; it is surrounded by thirty-two slender
gilt pillars, or rather poles, between every two of which
are suspended seven glass lamps, always lighted after sunset.[3] Beyond the poles is a second pavement, about eight
paces broad, somewhat elevated above the first, but of
coarser work; then another six inches higher, and eighteen
paces broad, upon which stand several small buildings;
beyond this is the gravelled ground; so that two broad
steps may be said to lead from the square down to the
Kaabah. The small buildings just mentioned which surround the Kaabah are the five Makams,[4] with the well

---

1 As well as memory serves me, for I have preserved no note,
the inscriptions are in the marble casing, and indeed no other stone
meets the eye.

2 It is a fine, close, grey polished granite: the walk is called
Al-Mataf, or the place of circumambulation.

3 These are now iron posts, very numerous, supporting cross
rods, and of tolerably elegant shape. In Ali Bey's time there were
" trente-une colonnes minces en piliers en bronze." Some native
works say thirty-three, including two marble columns. Between
each two hang several white or green glass globe-lamps, with wicks
and oil floating on water; their light is faint and dismal. The whole
of the lamps in the Harim is said to be more than 1000, yet they
serve but to " make darkness visible."

4 There are only four " Makams," the Hanafi, Maliki, Hanbali,
and the Makam Ibrahim; and there is some error of diction below,
for in these it is that the Imams stand before their congregations,
and nearest the Ka'abah. In Ibn Jubayr's time the Zaydi sect was
allowed an Imam, though known to be schismatics and abusers of
the caliphs. Now, not being permitted to have a separate station

of Zem Zem, the arch called Bab es Salam, and the Mambar."

"Opposite the four sides of the Kaabah stand four other small buildings, where the Imaums of the orthodox Mohammedan sects, the Hanefy, Shafey, Hanbaly, and Maleky take their station, and guide the congregation in their prayers. The Makam el Maleky on the south, and that of Hanbaly opposite the Black Stone, are small pavilions open on all sides, and supported by four slender pillars, with a light sloping roof, terminating in a point, exactly in the style of Indian pagodas.[1] The Makam el Hanafy, which is the largest, being fifteen paces by eight, is open on all sides, and supported by twelve small pillars; it has an upper story, also open, where the Mueddin who calls to prayers takes his stand. This was built in A.H. 923, by Sultan Selim I.; it was afterwards rebuilt by Khoshgeldy, governor of Djidda, in 947; but all the four Makams, as they now stand, were built in A.H. 1074. The Makam-es'-Shafey is over the well Zem Zem, to which it serves as an upper chamber.[2]"

"Near their respective Makams the adherents of the four different sects seat themselves for prayers. During my stay at Meccah the Hanefys always began their prayer first; but, according to Muselman custom, the Shafeys should pray first in the Mosque; then the Hanefys, Malekys, and Hanbalys. The prayer of the Maghreb is an exception, which they are all enjoined to utter to-

for prayer, they suppose theirs to be suspended from heaven above the Ka'abah roof.

1 The Makam al-Maliki is on the west of, and thirty-seven cubits from, the Ka'abah ; that of the Hanbali forty-seven paces distant.

2 Only the Mu'ezzin takes his stand here, and the Shafe'is pray behind their Imam on the pavement round the Ka'abah, between the corner of the well Zemzem, and the Makam Ibrahim. This place is forty cubits from the Ka'abah, that is say, eight cubits nearer than the Northern and Southern "Makams." Thus the pavement forms an irregular oval ring round the house

gether.[1] The Makam el Hanbaly is the place where the officers of government and other great people are seated during prayers : here the Pasha and the sheriff are placed, and in their absence the eunuchs of the temple. These fill the space under this Makam in front, and behind it the female Hadjys who visit the temple have their places assigned, to which they repair principally for the two evening prayers, few of them being seen in the Mosque at the three other daily prayers: they also perform the Towaf, or walk round the Kaabah, but generally at night, though it is not uncommon to see them walking in the day-time among the men."

"The present building which encloses Zem Zem stands close by the Makam Hanbaly, and was erected in A.H. 1072: it is of a square shape, and of massive construction, with an entrance to the north,[2] opening into the room which contains the well. This room is beautifully ornamented with marbles of various colours; and adjoining to it, but having a separate door, is a small room with a stone reservoir, which is always full of Zem Zem water. This the Hadjys get to drink by passing their hand with a cup through an iron grated opening, which serves as a window, into the reservoir, without entering the room. The mouth of the well is surrounded by a wall five feet in height and about ten feet n diameter. Upon this the people stand who draw up the water in leathern buckets, an iron railing being so placed as to

1 In Burckhardt's time the schools prayed according to the seniority of their founders, and they uttered the Azan of Al-Maghrib together, because that is a peculiarly delicate hour, which easily passes by unnoticed. In the twelfth century, at all times but the evening, the Shafe'i began, then came the Maliki and Hanbali simultaneously, and, lastly, the Hanafi. Now the Shaykh al-Mu'ezzin begins the call, which is taken up by the others. He is a Hanafi ; as indeed are all the principal people at Meccah, only a few wild Sharifs of the hills being Shafe'i.

2 The door of the Zemzem building fronts to the south-east.

prevent their falling in. In El Fasy's time there were
eight marble basins in this room, for the purpose of ablution."

"On the north-east (south-east) side of Zem Zem
stand two small buildings, one behind the other,[1] called
El Kobbateyn; they are covered by domes painted in the
same manner as the Mosque, and in them are kept water-
jars, lamps, carpets, mats, brooms, and other articles used
in the very Mosque.[2] These two ugly buildings are injurious to the interior appearance of the building, their
heavy forms and structure being very disadvantageously
contrasted with the light and airy shape of the Makams.
I heard some Hadjys from Greece, men of better taste
than the Arabs, express their regret that the Kobbateyn
should be allowed to disfigure the Mosque. They were
built by Khoshgeldy, governor of Djidda A.H. 947; one
is called Kobbet el Abbas, from having been placed on the
site of a small tank said to have been formed by Abbas,
the uncle of Mohammed."

1 This is not exactly correct. As the plan will show, the angle of
one building touches the angle of its neighbour.

2 Their names and offices are now changed. One is called the
Kubbat al-Sa'at, and contains the clocks and chronometers (two of
them English) sent as presents to the Mosque by the Sultan. The
other, known as the Kubbat al-Kutub, is used as a store-room for
manuscripts bequeathed to the Mosque. They still are open to
Burckhardt's just criticism, being nothing but the common dome
springing from four walls, and vulgarly painted with bands of red,
yellow, and green. In Ibn Jubayr's time the two domes contained
bequests of books and candles. The Kubbat Abbas, or that further
from the Ka'abah than its neighbour, was also called Kubbat al-
Sharab (the Dome of Drink), because Zemzem water was here kept
cooling for the use of pilgrims in Daurak, or earthen jars. The
nearer was termed Kubbat al-Yahudi; and the tradition they told me
was, that a Jew having refused to sell his house upon the spot, it was
allowed to remain *in loco* by the Prophet, as a lasting testimony to
his regard for justice. A similar tale is told of an old woman's hut,
which was allowed to stand in the corner of the Great Nushirawan's
royal halls.

"A few paces west (north-west) of Zem Zem, and directly opposite to the door of the Kaabah, stands a ladder or staircase,[1] which is moved up to the wall of the Kaabah on days when that building is opened, and by which the visitors ascend to the door. It is of wood, with some carved ornaments, moves on low wheels, and is sufficiently broad to admit of four persons ascending abreast. The first ladder was sent hither from Cairo in A.H. 818 by Moyaed Abou el Naser, King of Egypt."

"In the same line with the ladder and close by it stands a lightly built insulated and circular arch, about fifteen feet wide, and eighteen feet high, called Bab es' Salam, which must not be confounded with the great gate of the Mosque, bearing the same name. Those who enter the Bait Ullah for the first time are enjoined to do so by the outer and inner Bab-es-Salam; in passing under the latter they are to exclaim, 'O God, may it be a happy entrance.' I do not know by whom this arch was built, but it appears to be modern.[2]"

"Nearly in front of the Bab-es-Salam and nearer than the Kaabah than any of the other surrounding buildings, stand the Makam Ibrahim.[3] This is a small building supported by six pillars about eight feet high, four of which are surrounded from top to bottom by a fine iron railing, while they leave the space beyond the two hind pillars open; within the railing is a frame about five feet square, terminating in a pyramidal top, and said to contain the sacred stone upon which Ibrahim stood when he built the Kaabah, and which with the help of his son Ismayl he had removed from hence to the place

---

1 Called "Al-Daraj." A correct drawing of it may be found in Ali Bey's work.

2 The Bab al-Salam, or Bab al-Nabi, or Bab benu Shaybah, resembles in its isolation a triumphal arch, and is built of cut stone.

3 "The (praying) place of Abraham." Readers will remember that the Meccan Mosque is peculiarly connected with Ibrahim, whom Moslems prefer to all prophets except Mohammed.

called Maajen, already mentioned. The stone is said to have yielded under the weight of the Patriarch, and to preserve the impression of his foot still visible upon it; but no hadjy has ever seen it,[1] as the frame is always entirely covered with a brocade of red silk richly embroidered. Persons are constantly seen before the railing invoking the good offices of Ibrahim; and a short prayer must be uttered by the side of the Makam after the walk round the Kaabah is completed. It is said that many of the Sahaba, or first adherents of Mohammed, were interred in the open space between this Makam and Zem Zem[2]; from which circumstance it is one of the most

---

[1] This I believe to be incorrect. I was asked five dollars for permission to enter; but the sum was too high for my finances. Learned men told me that the stone shows the impress of two feet, especially the big toes, and devout pilgrims fill the cavities with water, which they rub over their eyes and faces. When the Caliph al-Mahdi visited Meccah, one Abdullah bin Osman presented himself at the unusual hour of noon, and informing the prince that he had brought him a relic which no man but himself had yet seen, produced this celebrated stone. Al-Mahdi, rejoicing greatly, kissed it, rubbed his face against it, and pouring water upon it, drank the draught. Kutb al-Din, one of the Meccan historians, says that it was visited in his day. In Ali Bey's time it was covered with "un magnifique drap noir brodé en or et en argent avec de gros glands en or;" he does not say, however, that he saw the stone. Its veils, called Sitr Ibrahim al-Khalil, are a green "Ibrisham," or silk mixed with cotton and embroidered with gold. They are made at Cairo of three different colours, black, red, and green; and one is devoted to each year. The gold embroidery is in the Sulsi character, and expresses the Throne-verse, the Chapter of the Cave, and the name of the reigning Sultan; on the top is "Allah," below it "Mohammed"; beneath this is "Ibrahim al-Khalil"; and at each corner is the name of one of the four caliphs. In a note to the "Dabistan" (vol. ii. p. 410), we find two learned Orientalists confounding the Black Stone with Abraham's Station or Platform. "The Prophet honoured the Black Stone, upon which Abraham conversed with Hagar, to which he tied his camels, and upon which the traces of his feet are still seen."

[2] Not only here, I was told by learned Meccans, but under all the oval pavements surrounding the Ka'abah.

favourite places of prayers in the Mosque. In this part of the area the Khalif Soleyman Ibn Abd el Melek, brother of Wolyd (Al-Walid), built a fine reservoir in A.H. 97, which was filled from a spring east of Arafat[1]; but the Mekkawys destroyed it after his death, on the pretence that the water of Zem Zem was preferable."

"On the side of Makam Ibrahim, facing the middle part of the front of the Kaabah, stands the Mambar, or pulpit of the Mosque; it is elegantly formed of fine white marble, with many sculptured ornaments; and was sent as a present to the Mosque in A. H. 969 by Sultan Soleyman Ibn Selym.[2] A straight, narrow staircase leads up to the post of the Khatyb, or preacher, which is surmounted by a gilt polygonal pointed steeple, resembling an obelisk. Here a sermon is preached on Fridays and on certain festivals. These, like the Friday sermons of all Mosques in the Mohammedan countries, are usually of the same turn, with some slight alterations upon extraordinary occasions.[3]"

" I have now described all the buildings within the inclosure of the temple."

" The gates of the Mosque are nineteen in number, and are distributed about it without any order or symmetry.[4]"

Burckhardt's description of the gates is short and

---

1 The spring gushes from the southern base of Mount Arafat, as will afterwards be noticed. It is exceedingly pure.

2 The author informs us that "the first pulpit was sent from Cairo in A.H. 818, together with the staircase, both being the gifts of Moayed, caliph of Egypt." Ali Bey accurately describes the present Mambar.

3 The curious will find a specimen of a Moslem sermon in Lane's Mod. Egypt. vol. i. ch. iii.

4 Burckhardt "subjoins their names as they are usually written upon small cards by the Metowefs; in another column are the names by which they were known in more ancient times, principally taken

imperfect. On the eastern side of the Mosque there are

from Azraky and Kotoby." I have added a few remarks in brackets

Modern names.	Arches.	Ancient names.
1. Bab el Salam, composed of smaller gates or arches	- 3	Bab Beni Shaybah (this is properly applied to the inner, not the outer Salam Gate.)
2. Bab el Neby - - -	- 2	Bab el Jenaiz, Gate of Biers, the dead being carried through it to the Mosque.
3. Bab el Abbas, opposite to this the house of Abbas once stood - - -	- 3	Bab Sertakat (some Moslem authors confound this Bab al-Abbas with the Gate of Biers.)
4. Bab Aly - - -	- 3	Bab Beni Hashem.
5. Bab el Zayt ⎫ Bab el Ashra ⎭	- 2	Bab Bazan (so called from a neighbouring hill).
6. Bab el Baghlah - -	- 2	
7. Bab el Szafa (Safa) -	- 5	Bab Beni Makhzoum.
8. Bab Sherif - - -	- 2	Bab el Djiyad (so called because leading to the hill Jiyad)
9. Bab Medjahed - -	- 2	Bab el Dokhmah.
10. Bab Zoleykha - - -	- 2	Bab Sherif Adjelan, who built it.
11. Bab Om Hany, so called from the daughter of Aby Taleb	2	Bab el Hazoura (some write this Bab el Zarurah).
12. Bab el Wodaa (Al-Wida'a), through which the pilgrim passes when taking his final leave of the temple -	- 2	Bab el Kheyatyn, or Bab Djomah.
13. Bab Ibrahim, so called from a tailor who had a shop near it	1	
14. Bab el Omra, through which pilgrims issue to visit the Omra. Also called Beni Saham - - - -	- 1	Bab Amer Ibn el Aas, or Bab el Sedra.
15. Bab Atech (Al-Atik?) -	- 1	Bab el Adjale.
16. Bab el Bastye - -	- 1	Bab Zyade Dar el Nedoua.
17. Bab el Kotoby, so called from an historian of Mekka who lived in an adjoining lane and opened this small gate into the Mosque - -	- 1	
18. Bab Zyade - - -	- 3	(It is called Bab Ziyadah—Gate of Excess—because it is a new structure thrown out into the Shamiyah, or Syrian quarter.)
19. Bab Dereybe - - -	- 1	Bab Medrese.
Total - -	39	

four principal entrances, seven on the southern side, three in the western, and five in the northern wall.

The eastern gates are the Greater Bab al-Salam, through which the pilgrim enters the Mosque; it is close to the north-east angle. Next to it the Lesser Bab al-Salam, with two small arches; thirdly, the Bab al-Nabi, where the Prophet used to pass through from Khadijah's house; and, lastly, near the south-east corner, the Bab Ali, or of the Benu Hashim, opening upon the street between Safa and Marwah.

Beyond the north-eastern corner, in the northern wall, is the Bab Duraybah, a small entrance with one arch. Next to it, almost fronting the Ka'abah, is the grand adit, "Bab al-Ziyadah," also known as Bab al-Nadwah. Here the colonnade, projecting far beyond the normal line, forms a small square or hall supported by pillars, and a false colonnade of sixty-one columns leads to the true cloister of the Mosque. This portion of the building being cool and shady, is crowded by the poor, the diseased, and the dying, during Divine worship, and at other times by idlers, schoolboys, and merchants. Passing through three external arches, pilgrims descend by a flight of steps into the hall, where they deposit their slippers, it not being considered decorous to hold them when circumambulating the Ka'abah.[1] A broad pavement, in the shape of an irregular triangle, whose base is the cloister, leads to the circuit of the house. Next to the Ziyadah Gate is a small, single-arched entrance, "Bab Kutubi," and beyond it one similar, the Bab al-Ajlah (عجله), also named Al-Basitiyah, from its proximity to the college of Abd al-Basitah. Close to the north-west angle of the cloister is the Bab al-Nadwah, anciently called Bab al-Umrah, and now Bab

---

[1] An old pair of slippers is here what the " shocking bad hat " is at a crowded house in Europe, a self-preserver. Burckhardt lost three pairs. I, more fortunate or less wealthy, only one.

al-Atik, the Old Gate.   Near this place and opening into
the Ka'abah, stood the "Town Hall" (Dar al-Nadwah),
built by Kusay, for containing the oriflamme "Al-Liwa,"
and as a council-chamber for the ancients of the city.[1]

In the western wall are three entrances.   The
single-arched gate nearest to the north angle is called
Bab Benu Saham or Bab al-Umrah, because pilgrims pass
through it to the Tanim and to the ceremony Al-Umrah
(Little Pilgrimage).   In the centre of the wall is the Bab
Ibrahim, or Bab al-Khayyatin (the Tailors' Gate); a
single arch leading into a large projecting square, like
that of the Ziyadah entrance, but somewhat smaller.
Near the south-west corner is a double arched adit, the
Bab al-Wida'a ("of farewell"): hence departing pilgrims
issue forth from the temple.

At the western end of the southern wall is the two-
arched Bab Umm Hani, so called after the lady's
residence, when included in the Mosque.   Next to it is
a similar building, "Bab Ujlan" عجلان which derives
its name from the large college "Madrasat Ujlan"; some
call it Bab al-Sharif, because it is opposite one of the
palaces.   After which, and also pierced with two arches,
is the Bab al-Jiyad (some erroneously spell it Al-Jihad,
"of War"), the gate leading to Jabal Jiyad.   The next
is double arched, and called the Bab al-Mujahid or Al-
Rahmah ("of Mercy").   Nearly opposite the Ka'abah,
and connected with the pavement by a raised line of
stone, is the Bab al-Safa, through which pilgrims now
issue to perform the ceremony "Al-Sai"; it is a small
and unconspicuous erection.   Next to it is the Bab al-
Baghlah with two arches, and close to the south-east
angle of the Mosque the Bab Yunus, alias Bab Bazan,
alias Bab al-Zayt, alias Bab al-Asharah ("of the ten"),
because a favourite with the first ten Sahabah, or Com-

[1] Many authorities place this building upon the site of the modern
Makam Hanafi.

panions of the Prophet. "Most of these gates," says Burckhardt, "have high pointed arches; but a few round arches are seen among them, which, like all arches of this kind in the Hejar, are nearly semi-circular. They are without ornament, except the inscription on the exterior, which commemorates the name of the builder, and they are all posterior in date to the fourteenth century. As each gate consists of two or three arches, or divisions, separated by narrow walls, these divisions are counted in the enumeration of the gates leading into the Kaabah, and they make up the number thirty-nine. There being no doors to the gates, the Mosque is consequently open at all times. I have crossed at every hour of the night, and always found people there, either at prayers or walking about.[1]"

" The outside walls of the Mosques are those of the houses which surround it on all sides. These houses belonged originally to the Mosque ; the greater part are now the property of individuals. They are let out to the richest Hadjys, at very high prices, as much as 500 piastres being given during the pilgrimage for a good apartment with windows opening into the Mosque.[2] Windows have in consequence been opened in many parts of the walls on a level with the street, and above that of the floor of the colonnades. Hadjys living in these apartments are allowed to perform the Friday's prayers at home ; because, having the Kaabah in view from the windows, they are supposed to be in the Mosque itself, and to join in prayer those assembled within the

---

[1] The Meccans love to boast that at no hour of the day or night is the Ka'abah ever seen without a devotee to perform " Tawaf."

[2] This would be about 50 dollars, whereas 25 is a fair sum for a single apartment. Like English lodging-house-keepers, the Meccans make the season pay for the year. In Burckhardt's time the colonnato was worth from 9 to 12 piastres ; the value of the latter coin is now greatly decreased, for 28 go to the Spanish dollar all over Al-Hijaz.

temple. Upon a level with the ground floor of the colonnades and opening into them are small apartments formed
in the walls, having the appearance of dungeons ; these
have remained the property of the Mosque while the
houses above them belong to private individuals. They
are let out to water-men, who deposit in them the Zem
Zem jars, or to less opulent Hadjys who wish to live in
the Mosque.[1] Some of the surrounding houses still belong
to the Mosque, and were originally intended for public
schools, as their names of Medresa implies ; they are
now all let out to Hadjys."

" The exterior of the Mosque is adorned with seven
minarets irregularly distributed :—1. Minaret of Bab el
Omra (Umrah) ; 2. Of Bab el Salam ; 3. Of Bab Aly ;
4. Of Bab el Wodaa (Wida'a) ; 5. Of Medesa Kail (Káit)
Bey ; 6. Of Bab el Zyadi ; 7. Of Medreset Sultan Soleyman.[2] They are quadrangular or round steeples, in no
way differing from other minarets. The entrance to them
is from the different buildings round the Mosque, which
they adjoin.[3] A beautiful view of the busy crowd below
is attained by ascending the most northern one.[4] "

Having described at length the establishment

---

1 I entered one of these caves, and never experienced such a
sense of suffocation even in that favourite spot for Britons to asphixiate
themselves—the Baths of Nero.

2 The Magnificent (son of Salim I.), who built at Al-Madinah
the minaret bearing his name. The minarets at Meccah are far inferior to those of her rival, and their bands of gaudy colours give
them an appearance of tawdry vulgarity.

3 Two minarets, namely, those of the Bab al-Salam and the Bab
al-Safa, are separated from the Mosque by private dwelling-houses, a
plan neither common nor regular.

4 A stranger must be careful how he appears at a minaret window,
unless he would have a bullet whizzing past his head. Arabs are especially jealous of being overlooked, and have no fellow-feeling for
votaries of "beautiful views." For this reason here, as in Egypt, a
blind Mu'ezzin is preferred, and many ridiculous stories are told about
men who for years have counterfeited cecity to live in idleness,

attached to the Mosque of Al-Madinah, I spare my
readers a detailed account of the crowd of idlers that
hang about the Meccan temple.   The Naib al-Harim, or
vice-intendant, is one Sayyid Ali, said to be of Indian
extraction ; he is superior to all the attendants.   There
are about eighty eunuchs, whose chief, Sarur Agha, was
a slave of Mohammed Ali Pasha.   Their pay varies from
100 to 1,000 piastres per mensem ; it is, however, inferior
to the Madinah salaries.   The Imams, Mu'ezzins, Khatibs,
Zemzemis, &c., &c., are under their respective Shaykhs
who are of the Olema.[1]

Briefly to relate the history of the Ka'abah.

The " House of Allah " is supposed to have been
built and rebuilt ten times.

1. The first origin of the idea is manifestly a symbolical allusion to the angels standing before the Almighty
and praising his name.   When Allah, it is said, informed
the celestial throng that he was about to send a vice-
gerent on earth, they deprecated the design.   Being
reproved with these words, " God knoweth what ye know
not," and dreading the eternal anger, they compassed the
Arsh, or throne, in adoration.   Upon this Allah created
the Bayt al-Ma'amur, four jasper pillars with a ruby roof,

[1] I have illustrated this chapter, which otherwise might be unintelligible to many, by a plan of the Ka'abah (taken from Ali Bey
al-Abbasi), which Burckhardt pronounced to be " perfectly correct."
This author has not been duly appreciated.   In the first place, his
disguise was against him ; and, secondly, he was a spy of the French
Government.   According to Mr. Bankes, who had access to the
original papers at Constantinople, Ali Bey was a Catalonian named
Badia, and was suspected to have been of Jewish extraction.   He
claimed from Napoleon a reward for his services, returned to the
East, and died, it is supposed, of poison in the Haurán, near Damascus.
In the edition which I have consulted (Paris, 1814) the author
labours to persuade the world by marking the days with their planet-
ary signs, &c., &c., that he is a real Oriental, but he perpetually betrays himself.   Some years ago, accurate plans of the two Harims
were made by order of the present Sultan.   They are doubtless to be
found amongst the archives at Constantinople.

and the angels circumambulated it, crying, "Praise to Allah, and exalted be Allah, and there is no iláh but Allah, and Allah is omnipotent!" The Creator then ordered them to build a similar house for man on earth. This, according to Ali, took place 40, according to Abu Hurayrah, 2,000 years before the creation ; both authorities, however, are agreed that the firmaments were spread above and the seven earths beneath this Bayt al-Ma'amur.

2. There is considerable contradiction concerning the second house. Ka'ab related that Allah sent down with Adam[1] a Khaymah, or tabernacle of hollow ruby, which the angels raised on stone pillars. This was also called Bayt al-Ma'amur. Adam received an order to compass it about ; after which, he begged a reward for obedience, and was promised a pardon to himself and to all his progeny who repent.

Others declare that Adam, expelled from Paradise, and lamenting that he no longer heard the prayers of the angels, was ordered by Allah to take the stones of five hills, Lebanon, Sinai, Tur Zayt (Olivet), Ararat, and Hira, which afforded the first stone. Gabriel, smiting his wing upon earth, opened a foundation to the seventh layer, and the position of the building is exactly below the heavenly Bayt al-Ma'amur,—a Moslem corruption of the legends concerning the heavenly and the earthly Jerusalem. Our First Father circumambulated it as he had seen the angels do, and was by them taught the formula of prayer and the number of circuits.

According to others, again, this second house was not erected till after the "Angelic Foundation" was destroyed by time.

3. The history of the third house is also somewhat

---

[1] It must be remembered that the Moslems, like many of the Jews, hold that Paradise was not on earth, but in the lowest firmament, which is, as it were, a reflection of earth.

confused. When the Bayt al-Ma'amur, or, as others say, the tabernacle, was removed to heaven after Adam's death, a stone-and-mud building was placed in its stead by his son Shays (Seth). For this reason it is respected by the Sabæans, or Christians of St. John, as well as by the Moslems. This Ka'abah, according to some, was destroyed by the deluge, which materially altered its site. Others believe that it was raised to heaven. Others, again, declare that only the pillars supporting the heavenly tabernacle were allowed to remain. Most authorities agree in asserting that the Black Stone was stored up in Abu Kubays, whence that " first created of mountains " is called Al-Amin, " the Honest."

4. Abraham and his son were ordered to build the fourth house upon the old foundations: its materials, according to some, were taken from the five hills which supplied the second; others give the names Ohod, Kuds, Warka, Sinai, Hira, and a sixth, Abu Kubays. It was of irregular shape; 32 cubits from the Eastern to the Northern corner ; 32 from North to West ; 31 from West to South ; 20 from South to East; and only 9 cubits high. There was no roof; two doors, level with the ground, were pierced in the Eastern and Western walls; and inside, on the right hand, near the present entrance, a hole for treasure was dug. Gabriel restored the Black Stone, which Abraham, by his direction, placed in its present corner, as a sign where circumambulation is to begin ; and the patriarch then learned all the complicated rites of pilgrimage. When this house was completed, Abraham, by Allah's order, ascended Jabal Sabir, and called the world to visit the sanctified spot; and all earth's sons heard him, even those " in their father's loins or in their mother's womb, from that day unto the day of resurrection."

5. The Amalikah (descended from Imlik, great grandson of Sam, son of Noah), who first settled near Meccah, founded the fifth house. Al-Tabari and the Moslem

historians generally made the erection of the Amalikah to precede that of the Jurham; these, according to others, repaired the house which Abraham built.

6. The sixth Ka'abah was built about the beginning of the Christian era by the Benu Jurham, the children of Kahtan, fifth descendant from Noah. Ismail married, according to the Moslems, a daughter of this tribe, Da'alah bint Muzaz (مفاض) bin Omar, and abandoning Hᵊbrew, he began to speak Arabic (Ta arraba). Hence his descendants are called Arabicized Arabs. After Ismail's death, which happened when he was 130 years old, Sabit, the eldest of his twelve sons, became " lord of the house." He was succeeded by his maternal grandfather Muzaz, and afterwards by his children. The Jurham inhabited the higher parts of Meccah, especially Jabal Ka'aka'an, so called from their clashing arms; whereas the Amalikah dwelt in the lower grounds, which obtained the name of Jiyad, from their generous horses.

7. Kusay bin Kilab, governor of Meccah and fifth forefather of the Prophet, built the seventh house, according to Abraham's plan. He roofed it over with palm leaves, stocked it with idols, and persuaded his tribe to settle near the Harim.

8. Kusay's house was burnt down by a woman's censer, which accidentally set fire to the Kiswah, or covering, and the walls were destroyed by a torrent. A merchant-ship belonging to a Greek trader, called "Bakum" (باقوم), being wrecked at Jeddah, afforded material for the roof, and the crew were employed as masons. The Kuraysh tribe, who rebuilt the house, failing in funds of pure money, curtailed its proportions by nearly seven cubits and called the omitted portion Al-Hatim. In digging the foundation they came to a green stone, like a camel's hunch, which, struck with a pickaxe, sent forth blinding lightning, and prevented further excavation. The Kuraysh, amongst other alterations, raised the walls

from nine to eighteen cubits, built a staircase in the
northern breadth, closed the western door and placed the
eastern entrance above the ground, to prevent men entering without their leave.

When the eighth house was being built Mohammed
was in his twenty-fifth year. His surname of Al-Amin,
the Honest, probably induced the tribes to make him
their umpire for the decision of a dispute about the position of the Black Stone, and who should have the honour
of raising it to its place.[1] He decided for the corner
chosen by Abraham, and distributed the privilege
amongst the clans. The Benu Zahrah and Benu Abd
Manaf took the front wall and the door ; to the Benu
Jama and the Benu Sahm was allotted the back wall; the
Benu Makhzum and their Kuraysh relations stood at the
southern wall ; and at the " Stone " corner were posted
the Benu Abd al-Dar, the Benu As'ad, and the Benu Ada.

9. Abdullah bin Zubayr, nephew of Ayishah, rebuilt
the Ka'abah in A.H. 64. It had been weakened by fire,
which burnt the covering, besides splitting the Black
Stone into three pieces, and by the Manjanik (catapults)
of Hosayn (حصين) bin Numayr, general of Yazid, who
obstinately besieged Meccah till he heard of his sovereign's
death. Abdullah, hoping to fulfil a prophecy,[2] and seeing
that the people of Meccah fled in alarm, pulled down the
building by means of " thin-calved Abyssinian slaves."
When they came to Abraham's foundation he saw
that it included Al-Hijr, which part the Kuraysh had
been unable to build. The building was made of cut
stone and fine lime brought from Al-Yaman. Abdullah,
taking in the Hatim, lengthened the building by seven
cubits, and added to its former height nine cubits,

1 Others derive the surname from this decision.

2 As will afterwards be mentioned, almost every Meccan knows
the prophecy of Mohammed, that the birthplace of his faith will be
destroyed by an army from Abyssinia. Such things bring their own
fulfilment.

thus making a total of twenty-seven. He roofed over
the whole, or a part ; re-opened the western door, to
serve as an exit ; and, following the advice of his aunt,
who quoted the Prophet's words, he supported the interior with a single row of three columns, instead of the
double row of six placed there by the Kuraysh. Finally,
he paved the Mataf, or circuit, ten cubits round with the
remaining slabs, and increased the Harim by taking in
the nearer houses. During the building, a curtain was
stretched round the walls, and pilgrims compassed them
externally. When finished, it was perfumed inside and outside, and invested with brocade. Then Abdullah and all
the citizens went forth in a procession to the Tanim, a
reverend place near Meccah, returned to perform Umrah,
the Lesser Pilgrimage, slew 100 victims, and rejoiced with
great festivities.

The Caliph Abd al-Malik bin Marwan besieged
Abdullah bin Zubayr, who, after a brave defence, was
slain. In A.H. 74, Hajjaj bin Yusuf, general of Abd al-
Malik's troops, wrote to the prince, informing him that
Abdullah had made unauthorised additions to and changes
in the Harim : the reply brought an order to rebuild the
house. Hajjaj again excluded the Hatim and retired the
northern wall six cubits and a span, making it twenty-
five cubits long by twenty-four broad ; the other three
sides were allowed to remain as built by the son of
Zubayr. He gave the house a double roof, closed the
western door, and raised the eastern four cubits and a
span above the Mataf, or circuit, which he paved over.
The Harim was enlarged and beautified by the Abbasides, especially by Al-Mahdi, Al-Mutamid, and Al-
Mutazid. Some authors reckon, as an eleventh house,
the repairs made by Sultan Murad Khan. On the night
of Tuesday, 20th Sha'aban, A.H. 1030, a violent torrent
swept the Harim ; it rose one cubit above the threshold
of the Ka'abah, carried away the lamp-posts and the

Makam Ibrahim, all the northern wall of the house, half
of the eastern, and one-third of the western side. It
subsided on Wednesday night. The repairs were not
finished till A.H. 1040. The greater part, however, of the
building dates from the time of Al Hajjaj; and Moslems,
who never mention his name without a curse, knowingly
circumambulate his work. The Olema indeed have
insisted upon its remaining untouched, lest kings in wan-
tonness should change its form : Harun al-Rashid desired
to rebuild it, but was forbidden by the Imam Malik.

The present proofs of the Ka'abah's sanctity, as
adduced by the learned, are puerile enough, but curious.
The Olema have made much of the verselet : " Verily
the first house built for mankind (to worship in) is that in
Bakkah[1] (Meccah), blessed and a salvation to the three
worlds. Therein (fihi) are manifest signs, the standing-
place of Abraham, which whoso entereth shall be safe "
(Kor. ch. 3). The word "therein" is interpreted to
mean Meccah, and the "manifest signs" the Ka'abah,
which contains such marvels as the foot-prints on Abraham's platform and the spiritual safeguard of all who
enter the Sanctuary.[2] The other " signs," historical,
psychical, and physical, are briefly these : The preserva-
tion of the Hajar al-Aswad and the Makam Ibrahim from
many foes, and the miracles put forth (as in the War of
the Elephant), to defend the house ; the violent and
terrible deaths of the sacrilegious ; and the fact that, in
the Deluge, the large fish did not eat the little fish in the
Harim. A wonderful desire and love impel men from
distant regions to visit the holy spot, and the first sight
of the Ka'abah causes awe and fear, horripilation and
tears. Furthermore, ravenous beasts will not destroy
their prey in the Sanctuary land, and the pigeons and
other birds never perch upon the house, except to be

---

1 Abu Hanifah made it a temporal sanctuary, and would not allow
even a murderer to be dragged from the walls.

2 Makkah (our Meccah) is the common word ; Bakkah is a synonym

cured of sickness, for fear of defiling the roof. The Ka'abah, though small, can contain any number of devotees ; no one is ever hurt in it,[1] and invalids recover their health by rubbing themselves against the Kiswah and the Black Stone.   Finally, it is observed that every day 100,000 mercies descend upon the house, and especially that if rain come up from the northern corner there is plenty in Irak ; if from the south, there is plenty in Yaman ; if from the east, plenty in India ; if from the western, there is plenty in Syria ; and if from all four angles, general plenty is presignified.

never used but in books. The former means "a concourse of people." But why derive it from the Hebrew, and translate it "a slaughter"? Is this a likely name for a holy place?   Dr. Colenso actually turns the Makaraba of Ptolemy into "Makkah-rabbah," plentiful slaughter. But if Makaraba be Meccah, it is evidently a corruption of "Makkah" and "Arabah," the Arab *race*.   Again, supposing the Meccan temple to be originally dedicated to the sun, why should the pure Arab word "Ba'al" become the Hebræized *Hobal*, and the deity be only one in the three hundred and sixty that formed the Pantheon?

1 This is an audacious falsehood; the Ka'abah is scarcely ever opened without some accident happening.

APPENDIX III.[1]

SPECIMEN OF A MURSHID S DIPLOMA, IN THE KADIRI ORDER
OF THE MYSTIC CRAFT AL-TASAWWUF.

THIS is the tree whose root is firm, and whose branches are spreading, and whose shade is perpetual : and the bearer is a good man— we beg of Allah to grant him purity of intention by the power of him upon whom Revelation descended and Inspiration ! I have passed it on, and I, the poorest of men, and the servant of the poor, am Sayyid A,[2] son of Sayyid B the Kadiri, the servant of the prayer-rug of his grandsire, of the Shaykh Abd al-Kadir Jilani, Allah sanctify his honoured tomb ! Amen. A.

There is no god but Allah—Shaykh Abd al-Kadir —a thing to Allah.[3]

Sayyid A
Son of Sayyid B
of C.[4]

And of him—In the name of Allah the Merciful, the Compassionate—we beg aid.

Praise be to Allah, opener of the locks of hearts with his name, and withdrawer of the veils of hidden

1 This document is written upon slips of paper pasted together, 4 feet 5 inches long, by about 6½ inches broad, and contains altogether 71 lines below the triangle. The divisions are in red ink. It rolls up, and fits into a cylinder of tin, to which are attached small silk cords, to sling it over the shoulder when travelling or on pilgrimage.

2 The names are here omitted for obvious reasons.

3 Facsimile of the seal cf the great Abd al-Kadir. This upon the document is a sign that the owner has become a master in the craft.

4 This is the living Shaykh's seal, and is the only one applied to the apprentice's diploma.

things with his beneficence, and raiser of the flags of
increase to those who persevere in thanking him. I
praise him because that he hath made us of the people
of Unity. And I thank him, being desirous of his
benefits. And I bless and salute our Lord Mohammed, the best of his Prophets and of his
Servants, and (I bless and salute) his (Mohammed's) family and companions, the excelling in
dignity, for the increase of their dignity and its
augmentation. But afterwards thus saith the
needy slave, who confesseth his sins and his
weakness and his faults, and hopeth for the pardon
of his Lord the Almighty—Sayyid A the Kadiri,
son of Sayyid B the Kadiri, son of Sayyid
Abu Bakr the Kadiri, son of Sayyid Ismail the
Kadiri, son of Sayyid Abd al-Wahhab the Kadiri,
son of Sayyid Nur al-Din the Kadiri, son of Sayyid
Darwaysh the Kadiri, son of Sayyid Husam al-
Din the Kadiri, son of Sayyid Nur al-Din the
Kadiri, son of Sayyid Waly al-Din the Kadiri, son
of Sayyid Zayn al-Din the Kadiri, son of Sayyid
Sharaf al-Din the Kadiri, son of Sayyid Shams
al-Din the Kadiri, son of Sayyid Mohammed
al-Hattak, son of Sayyid Abd al-Aziz, son of the

Sayyid of Sayyids, Polar-Star of Existence, the White Pearl, the Lord of the Reins of (worldy) possession, the Chief of (Allah's) friends, the incomparable Imam, the Essence negativing accidents, the Polar Star of Polar Stars,[1] the Greatest Assistance,[2] the Uniter of the Lover and the Beloved,[3] the Sayyid (Prince), the Shaykh (Teacher), Muhiy al-Din, Abd al-Kadir of Jilan,[4] Allah sanctify his honoured Sepulchre, and Allah enlighten his place of rest!—Son of Abu Salih Musa Jangi-dost, son of Sayyid Abdullah al-Jayli, son of Sayyid Yahya al-Zahid, son of Sayyid Mohammed, son of Sayyid Da'ud, son of Sayyid Musa, son of Sayyid Abdullah, son of Sayyid Musa al-Juni, son of Sayyid Abdullah al-Mahz, son of Sayyid Hasan al-Musanna,[5] son of the Imam Hasan, Son of the Imam and the Amir of True Believers, Ali the son of Abu Talib—may Allah be satisfied with him!—Son of Abd al-Muttalib,[6] son of Hashim, son of Abd al-Manaf, son of Kusay, son of Kilab, son of Murrat, son of Ka'ab, son of Luwiyy, son of Ghalib, son of Fihr (Kuraysh), son of Malik, son of Nazr, son of Kananah, son of Khuzaymah, son of Mudrikah, son of Iliyas, son of

1 Or Prince of Princes, a particular degree in Tasawwuf.

2 Ghaus (Assistance) also means a person who, in Tasawwuf, has arrived at the highest point to which fervour of devotion leads.

3 The human soul, and its supreme source.

4 For a short notice of this celebrated mystic, see d'Herbelot, "Abdalcader."

5 "Hasan the Second," from whom sprung the Sharifs of Al-Hijaz.

6 Father to Abdullah, Father of Mohammed.

330   *Pilgrimage to Al-Madinah and Meccah.*

1 Dated by M. C. de Perceval about 130 years B.C.

Muzarr, son of Nizar, son of Adnan,[1] son of Ada,

son of Udad, son of Mahmisah, son of Hamal, son of

Nayyit, son of Kuzar, son of Ismail, son of Ibrahim,

son of Karikh, son of Kasir, son of Arghwa, son of

Phaligh, son of Shalikh, son of Kaynan, son of

Arfakhshad, son of Sam, son of Noah, son of Shays,

2 Thus, between Adnan and Adam we have eighteen generations! Al-Wakidi and Al-Tabari give forty between Adnan and Ishmael, which Ibn Khaldun, confirmed by M. C. de Perceval, thinks is too small a number. The text, however, expresses the popular estimate. But it must be remembered that the Prophet used to say, "beyond Adnan none but Allah knoweth, and the genealogists lie."

3 Moslems cleaving to the Neptunian theory of earthy origin.

4 Your humble servant, gentle reader.

son of Adam the Father of Mankind[2]—with whom

be peace, and upon our Prophet the best of blessings

and salutation!—and Adam was of dust, and dust

is of the earth, and earth is of foam, and foam is of

the wave, and the wave is of water,[3] and water is of

the rainy firmament, and the rainy firmament is of

Power, and Power is of Will, and Will is of the

Omniscience of the glorious God.   But afterwards

that good man, the approaching to his Lord, the

averse to all besides him, the desirous of the abodes

of futurity, the hoper for mercy, the Darwaysh Ab-

dullah[4] son of the Pilgrim Joseph the Afghan,—

henceforward let him be known by the name of

"Darwaysh King-in-the-name-of-Allah!" — hath

come to us and visited us and begged of us in-

struction in the Saying of Unity.   I therefore

taught him the saying which I learned by ordi-

nance from my Shaykh and my instructor and

my paternal uncle the Sayyid the Shaykh Abd al-Kadir[1] the Kadiri, son of the Sayyid the Shaykh Abu Bakr the Kadiri, son of the Sayyid the Shaykh Ismail the Kadiri, son of the Sayyid the Shaykh Abd al-Wahhab the Kadiri, son of the Sayyid the Shaykh Nur al-Din the Kadiri, son of the Sayyid the Shaykh Shahdarwaysh the Kadiri, son of the Sayyid the Shaykh Husam al-Din the Kadiri, son of the Sayyid the Shaykh Nur al-Din the Kadiri, from his sire and Shaykh Waly al-Din the Kadiri, from his sire and Shaykh Zayn al-Din the Kadiri, from his sire and Shaykh Sharafil al-Din the Kadiri, from his sire and Shaykh Mohammed al-Hattak the Kadiri, from his sire and Shaykh Abd al-Aziz — Allah sanctify his honoured Sepulchre and Allah enlighten his place of rest!— from his sire and Shaykh Sayyid the Polar Star of Existence, the White Pearl, the Polar Star of Holy Men, the Director of those that tread the Path, the Sayyid the Shaykh Muhiyy al-Din Abd al-Kadir of Jilan — Allah sanctify his honoured Sepulchre and Allah enlighten his place of rest! Amen! — from his Shaykh the Shaykh Abu-Sa'id al-Mubarak al-Makhzumi, from his Shaykh the Shaykh Abu 'l Hasan al-Hankari,

1 The former genealogy proved my master to be what is technically called "Khalifah Jaddi," or hereditary in his dignity. The following table shows that he is also "Khulfai" (adopted to succeed), and gives the name and the descent of the holy man who adopted him.

from his Shaykh the Shaykh Abu Faras al-Tar-
susi, from his Shaykh the Shaykh Abd al-Wahid
al-Tamimi, from his Shaykh the Shaykh Abu 'l
Kasim al-Junayd of Baghdad, from his Shaykh the
Shaykh al-Sirri al-Sakati, from his Shaykh the
Shaykh al-Ma'aruf al-Karkhi, from his Shaykh the
Shaykh Da'ud al-Tai, from his Shaykh the Shaykh
Habib al-'Ajami, from his Shaykh the Shaykh al-
Hasan of Bussorah, from his Shaykh the Prince of
True Believers, Ali Son of Abu Talib—Allah be
satisfied with him! and Allah honour his counte-
nance!—from the Prophet of Allah, upon whom
may Allah have mercy, from Jibrail, from the
Omnipotent, the Glorious. And afterwards we
taught him (*i.e.* that good man Abdullah) the
Saying of Unity, and ordered its recital 165 times
after each Farizah,[1] and on all occasions according
to his capability. And Allah have mercy upon
our Lord Mohammed and upon His Family and upon
His Companions one and all! And praise be to
Allah, Lord of the (three) worlds!

It is finished.

There is no god but Allah!

Number[2]

165.

1 Each obliga-
tory prayer is
called a Fari-
zah. The
Shaykh there-
fore directs the
Saying of
Unity, *i.e.* La
iláha illá lláh,
to be repeated
825 times per
diem.

2 *i.e.* number
of repetitions
after each
obligatory
prayer.

APPENDIX IV.

THE NAVIGATION AND VOYAGES OF LUDOVICUS VERTOMANNUS, GENTLEMAN OF ROME.

A.D. 1503.

THE first of the pilgrims to Meccah and Al-Madinah who has left an authentic account of the Holy Cities is " Lewes Wertomannus (Lodovico Bartema), gentelman of the citie of Rome.[1] " " If any man," says this *aucthor*, " shall demand of me the cause of this my voyage, certeynely I can shewe no better reason than is the ardent desire of knowledge, which hath moved many other to see the world and the miracles of God therein." In the year of our Lord 1503 he departed from Venice " with prosperous wynds," arrived at Alexandria and visited Babylon of Egypt, Berynto, Tripoli, Antioch, and Damascus. He started from the latter place on the 8th of April, 1503, " in familiaritie and friendshyppe with a certayne Captayne Mameluke " (which term he applies to " al such Christians as have forsaken theyr fayth, to serve the Mahumetans and Turks "), and in the garb of a

---

[1] I have consulted the " Navigation and Voyages of Lewes Wertomannus to the Regions of Arabia, Egypt, Persia, Syria, Ethiopia, and East India, both within and without the River of Ganges, &c., conteyning many notable and straunge things both Historicall and Natural. Translated out of Latine into Englyshe by Richarde Eden. In the year of our Lord, 1576."—(*Hakluyst's Voyages*, vol. iv.) The curious reader will also find the work in Purchas (*Pilgrimmes and Pilgrimage*, vol. ii.) and Ramusio (*Raccolta delle Navigasioni e Viaggi*, tom. i.). The Travels of Bartema were first published at Milan, A.D. 1511, and the first English translation appeared in Willes and Eden's *Decades*, 4to. A.D. 1555.

" Mamaluchi renegado." He estimates the Damascus
Caravan to consist of 40,000 men and 35,000 camels,
nearly six times its present number.[1] On the way they
were " enforced to conflict with a great multitude of the
Arabians :" but the three score mamluks composing
their escort were more than a match for 50,000 Badawin.
On one occasion the Caravan, attacked by 24,000
Arabians, slew 1500 of the enemies, losing in the conflict
only a man and a woman.[2] This " marveyle "—which
is probably not without some exaggeration—he explains
by the " strength and valiantness of the Mamalukes," by
the practice (still popular) of using the " camells in the
steede of a bulwarke, and placing the merchaunts in the
myddest of the army (that is), in the myddest of the
camelles, whyle the pilgrims fought manfully on every
side ;" and, finally, by the circumstance that the Arabs
were unarmed, and " weare only a thynne loose vesture,
and are besyde almost naked : theyr horses also beyng
euyll furnished, and without saddles or other furniture."
The Hijazi Badawi of this day is a much more dangerous enemy ; the matchlock and musket have made him
so ; and the only means of crippling him is to prevent the
importation of firearms and lead, and by slow degrees to
disarm the population. After performing the ceremonies
of pilgrimage at Al-Madinah and Meccah, he escaped to
Zida or Gida (Jeddah), " despite the trumpeter of the
caravana giving warning to all the Mamalukes to make
readie their horses, to direct their journey toward Syria,
with proclamation of death to all that should refuse so to

1 The number of pilgrims in this Caravan is still grossly exaggerated. I cannot believe that it contains more than 7000 of both
sexes, and all ages.

2 This may confirm Strabo's account of Œlius Gallus' loss, after
a conflict with a host of Arabs—two Roman soldiers. Mons. Jomard,
noticing the case, pleasantly remarks, that the two individuals in
question are to be pitied for their extreme ill-luck.

doe," and embarked for Persia upon the Red Sea. He touched at certain ports of Al-Yaman, and got into trouble at Aden, "where the Mahumetans took him," and "put shackles on his legges, which came by occasion of a certayne idolatour, who cryed after him, saying, O, Christian Dogge, borne of Dogges.[1]" The lieutenant of the Sultan "assembled his council," consulted them about putting the traveller to death as a "spye of Portugales," and threw him ironed into a dungeon. On being carried shackled into the presence of the Sultan, Bartema said that he was a "Roman, professed a Mamaluke in Babylon of Alcayr;" but when told to utter the formula of the Moslem faith, he held his tongue, "eyther that it pleased not God, or that for feare and scruple of conscience he durst not." For which offence he was again "deprived of ye fruition of heaven."

But, happily for Bartema, in those days the women of Arabia were "greatly in love with whyte men." Before escaping from Meccah, he lay hid in the house of a Mohammedan, and could not express his gratitude for the good wife's care; "also," he says, "this furthered my good enterteynement, that there was in the house a fayre young mayde, the niese of the Mahumetan, who was greatly in loue with me." At Aden he was equally fortunate. One of the Sultan's three wives, on the departure of her lord and master, bestowed her heart upon the traveller. She was "very faire and comely, after theyr maner, and of colour inclynyng to blacke:" she

---

1 This venerable form of abuse still survives the lapse of time. One of the first salutations reaching the ears of the "Overlands" at Alexandria is some little boys—

Ya Nasrani
Kalb awani, &c., &c.—
O Nazarene,
O dog obscene, &c., &c.

In Percy's Reliques we read of the Knight calling his Moslem opponent "unchristen hounde,"—a retort courteous to the "Christen hounde," previously applied to him by the "Pagan."

would spend the whole day in beholding Bartema, who wandered about simulating madness,[1] and "in the meane season, divers tymes, sent him secretly muche good meate by her maydens." He seems to have played his part to some purpose, under the colour of madness, converting a "great fatt shepe" to Mohammedanism, killing an ass because he refused to be a proselyte, and, finally, he "handeled a Jewe so euyll that he had almost killed hym." After sundry adventures and a trip to Sanaa, he started for Persia with the Indian fleet, in which, by means of fair promises, he had made friendship with a certain captain. He visited Zayla and Berberah in the Somali country, and at last reached Hormuz. The 3rd book "entreateth of Persia," the 4th of " India, and of the cities and other notable thynges seene there." The 8th book contains the " voyage of India," in which he includes Pegu, Sumatra, Borneo, and Java, where, " abhorryng the beastly maners" of a cannibal population, he made but a short stay. Returning to Calicut, he used " great subtiltie," escaped to the " Portugales," and was well received by the viceroy. After describing in his 7th book the " viage or navigation of Ethiopia, Melinda, Mombaza, Mozambrich (Mozambique), and Zaphala (Sofala)," he passed the Cape called " Caput Bonæ Spei, and repaired to the goodly citie of Luxburne (Lisbon)," where he had the honour of kissing hands. The king confirmed with his great seal the " letters patentes," whereby his lieutenant the viceroy of India had given the pilgrim the order of knighthood. " And thus," says Bartema by way of conclusion, " departing from thence with the kyngs pasporte and safe conducte, at the length after these my long and great trauayles and

---

[1] For a full account of the mania fit I must refer the curious reader to the original (Book ii. chap. v.) The only mistake the traveller seems to have committed, was that, by his ignorance of the rules of ablution, he made men agree that he was "no sainct, but a madman."

dangers, I came to my long desyred native countrey, the citie of Rome, by the grace of God, to whom be all honour and glory."

This old traveller's pages abound with the information to be collected in a fresh field by an unscrupulous and hard-headed observer. They are of course disfigured with a little romancing. His Jews at Khaybor, near Al-Madinah, were five or six spans long. At Meccah he saw two unicorns, the younger "at the age of one yeare, and lyke a young coolte ; the horne of this is of the length of four handfuls.¹ " And so credulous is he about anthropophagi, that he relates of Mahumet (son to the Sultan of Sanaa) how he " by a certayne naturall tyrannye and madnesse delyteth to eate man's fleeshe, and therefore secretly kylleth many to eate them.² " But all things well considered, Lodovico Bartema, for correctness of observation and readiness of wit, stands in the foremost rank of the old Oriental travellers.

I proceed to quote, and to illustrate with notes, the few chapters devoted in the 1st volume of this little-known work to Meccah and Al-Madinah.

CHAPTER XI.—*Of a Mountayne inhabited with Jewes, and of the Citie of Medinathalnabi, where Mahumet was buried.*

In the space of eyght dayes we came to a mountayne which conteyneth in circuite ten or twelve myles. This is inhabited with Jewes, to the number of fyue thousande

---

1 He proceeds, however, to say that "the head is lyke a hart's," the "legges thynne and slender, lyke a fawne or hyde, the hoofs divided much like the feet of a goat" ; that they were sent from Ethiopia (the Somali country), and were "shewed to the people for a myracle." They might, therefore, possibly have been African antelopes, which a *lusus naturæ* had deprived of their second horn. But the suspicion of fable remains.

2 This is a tale not unfamiliar to the Western World. Louis XI. of France was supposed to drink the blood of babes,—"*pour rajeunir sa veine epuisée.*" The reasons in favour of such unnatural diet have been fully explained by the infamous M. de Sade.

or thereabout. They are very little stature, as of the heyght of fyue or sixe spannes, and some muche lesse. They have small voyces lyke women, and ef blacke colour, yet some blacker then other. They feede of none other meate than goates fleshe.[1] They are circumcised, and deny not themselues to be Jewes. If by chaunce, any Mahumetan come into their handes, they flay him alyue. At the foot of the mountayne we founde a certayne hole, out of whiche flowed aboundance of water. By fyndyng this opportunitie, we laded sixtiene thousand camels ; which thyng greatly offended the Jewes. They wandred in that mountayne, scattered lyke wylde goates or prickettes, yet durst they not come downe, partly for feare, and partly for hatred agaynst the Mahumetans. Beneath the moun- taine are seene seuen or eyght thorne trees, very fayre, and in them we found a payre of turtle doues, which seemed to vs in maner a miracle, hauying before made so long journeyes, and sawe neyther beast nor foule. Then proceedyng two dayes journey, we came to a certayne citie name Medinathalnabi : four myles from the said citie, we founde a well. Heere the carauana (that is, the whole hearde of camelles) rested. And remayning here one day, we washed ourselves, and changed our shertes, the more freshely to enter into the citie ; it is well peopled, and conteyneth about three hundred houses ; the walles are lyke bulwarkes of earth, and the houses both of stone and bricke. The soile about the citie is vtterly barren, except that about two myles from the citie are seene about fyftie palme trees that beare dates.[2] There, by a certayne garden, runneth a course of water fallyng into a lower playne, where also passingers are accustomed to water theyr camelles.[3] And here opportunitie now serueth to

1 This is, to the present day, a food confined to the Badawin.
2 This alludes to the gardens of Kuba. The number of date-trees is now greatly increased. (See chap. xix.)
3 The Ayn al-Zarka, flowing from the direction of Kuba. (Chap. xviii).

confute the opinion of them whiche thynke that the arke or toombe of wicked Mahumet to hang in the ayre, not borne vp with any thing.   As touching which thyng, I am vtterly of an other opinion, and affirme this neyther to be true, nor to haue any lykenesse of trueth, as I presently behelde these thynges, and sawe the place where Mahumet is buried, in the said citie of Medinathalnabi : for we taryed there three dayes, to come to the true knowledge of all these thynges.   When wee were desirous to enter into theyr Temple (which they call Meschita,[1] and all other churches by the same name), we coulde not be suffered to enter without a companion little or great.   They taking vs by the hande, brought vs to the place where they saye Mahumet is buried.

CHAPTER XII.—*Of the Temple or Chapell, and Sepulchre of Mahumet, and of his Felowes.*

His temple is vaulted, and is a hundred pases in length, fourscore in breadth ; the entry into it is by two gates ; from the sydes it is couered with three vaultes ; it is borne vp with four hundred columnes or pillers of white brick ; there are seene, hanging lampes, about the number of three thousande.   From the other part of the temple in the first place of the Meschita, is seene a tower of the circuite of fyue pases vaulted on euery syde, and couered with a cloth or silk, and is borne vp with a grate of copper, curiously wrought and distant from it two pases ; and of them that goe thyther, is seene as it were through a lateese.[2]   Towarde the lefte hande, is the way to the tower, and when you come thyther, you must enter by a narower gate.   On euery. syde of those gates or doores, are seene many bookes in manner of a librarie, on the one syde 20, and on the other syde 25.   These contayne the filthie traditions and lyfe of Mahumet and his fellowes :

---

1 Masjid, a Mosque.

2 Nothing can be more correct than this part of Bartema's description.

within the sayde gate is seene a sepulchre, (that is) a digged place, where they say Mahumet is buried and his felowes, which are these, Nabi, Bubacar, Othomar, Aumar, and Fatoma[1]; but Mahumet was theyr chiefe captayne, and an Arabian borne.   Hali was sonne in lawe to Mahumet, for he tooke to wyfe his daughter Fatoma.   Bubacar is he who they say was exalted to the dignitie of a chiefe counseller and great gouernour, although he came not to the high degree of an apostle, or prophet, as dyd Mahumet. Othomar and Aumar were chief captaynes of the army of Mahumet.   Euery of these haue their proper bookes of factes and traditions.   And hereof proceedeth the great dissention and discorde of religion and maners among this kynde of filthie men, whyle some confirm one doctrine, and some another, by reason of theyr dyuers sectes of Patrons, Doctours, and Saintes, as they call them.   By this meanes are they marueylously diuided among themselues, and lyke beastes kyll themselues for such quarelles of dyuers opinions, and all false.   This also is the chiefe cause of warre between the sophie of Persia and the great Turke, being neuerthelesse both Mahumetans, and lyue in mortall hatred one agaynst the other for the myntenaunce of theyr sectes, saintes and apostles, whyle euery of them thynketh theyr owne to bee best.

CHAPTER XIII.—*Of the Secte of Mahumet.*

Now will we speake of the maners and sect of Mahumet.   Vnderstande, therefore, that in the highest part of the tower aforesayde, is an open round place. Now shall you vnderstande what crafte they vsed to deceyue our carauans.   The first euening that we came thyther to see the sepulchre of Mahumet, our captayne

---

1 Nabi (the Prophet), Abu Bakr, Osman, Omar, and Fatimah. It was never believed that Osman was buried in the Prophet's Mosque.   This part of the description is utterly incorrect.   The tombs are within the "tower" above-mentioned; and Bartema, in his 13th chapter, quoted below, seems to be aware of the fact.

sent for the chiefe priest of the temple to come to him,
and when he came, declared vnto him that the only cause
of his commyng thyther was to visite the sepulchre and
bodie of Nabi, by which woord is signified the prophet
Mahumet ; and that he vnderstoode that the price to be
admitted to the syght of these mysteries should be foure
thousande seraphes of golde. Also that he had no parents,
neyther brothers, sisters, kinsefolkes, chyldren, or wyues ;
neyther that he came thyther to buy merchaundies, as
spices, or bacca, or nardus, or any maner of precious
jewelles ; but only for very zeale of religion and salutation
of his soule, and was therefore greatly desirous to see the
bodie of the prophet. To whom the priest of the temple
(they call them Side), with countenance lyke one that
were distraught[1], made aunswere in this maner : " Darest
thou with those eyes, with the which thou hast committed
so many horrible sinnes, desyre to see him by whose sight
God hath created heauen and earth ? " To whom agayne
our captayne aunswered thus : " My Lord, you have
sayde truly ; neuertheless I pray you that I may fynd so
much fauour with you, that I may see the Prophet ; whom
when I haue seene, I will immediately thrust out myne
eyes." The Side aunswered, " O Prince, I will open all
thynges unto thee. So it is that no man can denye but
that our Prophet dyed heere, who, if he woulde, might
haue died at Mecha. But to shewe in himself a token of
humilitie, and thereby to giue vs example to folowe him,
was wyllyng rather heere than elsewhere to departe out of
this worlde, and was incontinent of angelles borne into
heauen, and there receyued as equall with them." Then
our captayne sayde to him, "Where is Jesus Christus,
the sonne of Marie ? " To whom the Side answered, " At

---

1 The request was an unconscionable one; and the "chief
priest" knew that the body, being enclosed within four walls, could
not be seen.

the feete of Mahumet.[1]" Then sayde our captayne
agayne: "It suffyceth, it suffyceth ; I will knowe no more."
After this our captayne commyng out of the temple, and
turnyng to vs, sayd, "See (I pray you) for what goodly
stuffe I would haue paide three thousande seraphes of
golde." The same daye at euenyng, at almost three a
clock of the nyght, ten or twelue of the elders of the secte
of Mahumet entered into our carauana, which remayned
not paste a stone caste from the gate of the citie.[2] These
ranne hyther and thyther, crying lyke madde men, with
these wordes, " Mahumet, the messenger and Apostle of
God, shall ryse agayne ! O Prophet, O God, Mahumet
shall ryse agayne ! Have mercy on vs God !" Our captayne and we, all raysed with this crye, tooke weapon
with all expedition, suspectyng that the Arabians were
come to rob our carauana ; we asked what was the cause
of that exclamation, and what they cryed ? For they
cryed as doe the Christians, when sodeynly any marueylous thyng chaunceth. The Elders answered, " Sawe
you not the lyghtning whiche shone out of the sepulchre
of the Prophet Mahumet[3]?" Our captayne answered
that he sawe nothing ; and we also beyng demaunded,
answered in lyke maner. Then sayde one of the old men,
" Are you slaues ?" that is to say, bought men ; meanyng
thereby Mamalukes. Then sayde our captayne, " We are
in deede Mamalukes." Then agayne the old man sayde,
" You, my Lordes, cannot see heauenly thinges, as being
Neophiti, (that is) newly come to the fayth, and not yet
confirmed in our religion." To this our captayne answered

---

1 This is incorrect. "Hazrat Isa," after his second coming, will
be buried in the Prophet's "Hujrah." But no Moslem ever believed
that the founder of Christianity left his corpse in this world. (See
chap. xvi.)

2 Most probably, in the Barr al-Manakhah, where the Damascus
caravan still pitches tents.

3 This passage shows the antiquity of the still popular superstition which makes a light to proceed from the Prophet's tomb.

agayne, " O you madde and insensate beastes, I had
thought to haue giuen you three thousande peeces of gold ;
but now, O you dogges and progenie of dogges, I will gyue
you nothing." It is therefore to bee vnderstoode, that
none other shynyng came out of the sepulchre, then a
certayne flame which the priests caused to come out of the
open place of the towre[1] spoken of here before, whereby
they would have deceyved vs. And therefore our captayne
commaunded that thereafter none of vs should enter into
the temple. Of this also we haue most true experience,
and most certaynely assure you that there is neyther iron
or steele or the magnes stone that should so make the
toombe of Mahumet to hange in the ayre, as some haue
falsely imagined ; neyther is there any mountayne nearer
than foure myles : we remayned here three dayes to
refreshe our company. To this citie victualles and all
kynde of corne is brought from Arabia Fælix, and Babylon or Alcayr, and also from Ethiope, by the Redde Sea,
which is from this citie but four dayes journey.[2]

CHAPTER XIV.—*The Journey to Mecha.*[3]

After we were satisfied, or rather wearyed, with the
filthinesse and lothesomenesse of the trumperyes, deceites,
trifles, and hypocrisis of the religion of Mahumet, we
determined to goe forward on our journey; and that by
guyding of a pylot who might directe our course with the
mariners boxe or compasse, with also the carde of the
sea, euen as is vsed in sayling on the sea. And thus
bendyng our journey to the west we founde a very fayre

1 It is unnecessary to suppose any deception of the kind. If
only the "illuminati" could see this light, the sight would necessarily
be confined to a very small number.

2 This account is correct. Kusayr (Cosseir), Suez, and Jeddah
still supply Al-Madinah.

3 It is impossible to distinguish from this description the route
taken by the Damascus Caravan in A.D. 1503. Of one thing only we
may be certain, namely, that between Al-Madinah and Meccah there
are no "Seas of Sand.'

well or fountayne, from the which flowed great aboundance of water. The inhabitantes affyrme that Sainct Marke the Euangelist was the aucthour of this fountayne, by a miracle of God, when that region was in maner burned with incredible drynesse.[1]   Here we and our beastes were satisfied with drynke.   I may not here omit to speake of the sea of sande, and of the daungers thereof.   This was founde of vs before we came to the mountayne of the Jewes.   In this sea of sande we traueiled the journey of three days and nightes: this is a great brode plaine, all couered with white sande, in maner as small as floure.   If by euil fortune it so chaunce that any trauaile that way southward, if in the mean time the wind come to the north, they are ouerwhelmed with sande, that they scatter out of the way, and can scarsely see the one the other ten pases of.   And therefore the inhabitants trauayling this way, are inclosed in cages of woodde, borne with camels, and lyue in them,[2] so passing the jorney, guided by pilots with maryner's compasse and card, euen as on the sea, as we haue sayde.   In this jorney, also many peryshe for thirst, and many for drynkyng to muche, when they finde suche good waters.   In these sandes is founde Momia, which is the fleshe of such men as are drowned in these sandes, and there dryed by the heate of the sunne: so that those bodyes are preserued from putrifaction by the drynesse of the sand; and therefore that drye fleshe is esteemed medicinable.[3]   Albeit there is

---

1 The name of St. Mark is utterly unknown in Al-Hijaz. Probably the origin of the fountain described in the text was a theory that sprang from the brains of the Christian Mamluks.

2 A fair description of the still favourite vehicles, the Shugduf, Takht-rawan, and the Shibriyah. It is almost needless to say that the use of the mariner's compass is unknown to the guides in Al-Hijaz.

3 Wonderful tales are still told about this same Momiya (mummy). I was assured by an Arab physician, that he had broken a fowl's leg, and bound it tightly with a cloth containing man's dried flesh, which caused the bird to walk about, with a sound shank, on the second day.

another kynde of more pretious Momia, which is the dryed and embalmed bodies of kynges and princes, whiche of long tyme haue been preserued drye without corruption. When the wynde bloweth from the northeast, then the sand riseth and is driuen against a certayne mountayne, which is an arme of the mount Sinai.[1] There we found certayne pyllers artificially wrought, whiche they call Ianuan. On the lefte hande of the sayde mountayne, in the toppe or rydge thereof, is a denne, and the entrie into it is by an iron gate. Some fayne that in that place Mahumet lyued in contemplation. Here we heard a certayne horrible noyse and crye; for passyng the sayde mountayne, we were in so great daunger, that we thought neuer to have escaped. Departyng, therefore, from the fountayne, we continued our journey for the space of ten dayes, and twyse in the way fought with fyftie thousande Arabians, and so at the length came to the citie of Mecha, where al things were troubled by reason of the warres betweene two brethren, contendyng whiche of them shoulde possesse the kyngedome of Mecha.

Chapter XV.—*Of the Fourme and Situation of the Citie of Mecha; and why the Mohumetans resort thyther.*

Nowe the tyme requireth to speake somewhat of the famous citie of Mecha, or Mecca, what it is, howe it is situate, and by whom it is gouerned. The citie is very fayre and well inhabited, and conteyneth in rounde fourme syxe thousande houses, as well buylded as ours, and some that cost three or foure thousande peeces of golde: it hath no walles. About two furlongs from the citie is a mount, where the way is cutte out,[2] whiche leadeth to a playne

---

1 This is probably Jabal Warkan, on the Darb al-Sultani, or Sea road to Meccah. For the Moslem tradition about its Sinaitic origin, see Chapter xx.

2 The Saniyah Kuda, a pass opening upon the Meccah plain. Here two towers are now erected.

beneath. It is on euery syde fortified with mountains, in the stead of walles or bulwarkes, and hath foure entries. The Gouernour is a Soltan, and one of the foure brethren of the progenie of Mahumet, and is subject to the Soltan of Babylon of whom we haue spoken before. His other three brethren be at continuall warre with hym. The eighteen daye of Maye we entered into the citie by the north syde; then, by a declynyng way, we came into a playne. On the south syde are two mountaynes, the one very neere the other, distant onely by a little valley, which is the way that leadeth to the gate of Mecha. On the east syde is an open place betweene two mountaynes, lyke vnto a valley,[1] and is the waye to the mountayne where they sacrifice to the Patriarkes Abraham and Isaac.[2] This mountayne is from the citie about ten or twelue myles, and of the heyght of three stones cast: it is of stone as harde as marble, yet no marble.[3] In the toppe of the mountaine is a temple or Meschita, made after their fashion, and hath three wayes to enter into it.[4] At the foote of the mountayne are two cesterns, which conserue waters without corruption: of these, the one is reserued to minister water to the camels of the carauana of Babylon or Alcayr; and the other, for them of Damasco. It is rayne water, and is deriued far of.[5]

But to returne to speake of the citie ; for as touchyng the maner of sacrifice which they vse at the foote of the mountayne wee wyll speake hereafter. Entryng, therefore, into the citie, wee founde there the carauana of Memphis, or Babylon, which prevented vs eyght dayes, and came not the waye that wee came. This carauana

---

1 This is the open ground leading to the Muna Pass.

2 An error. The sacrifice is performed at Muna, not on Arafat, the mountain here alluded to.

3 The material is a close grey granite.

4 The form of the building has now been changed.

5 The Meccans have a tradition concerning it, that it is derived from Baghdad.

conteyned threescore and foure thousande camelles, and
a hundred Mamalukes to guyde them. And here ought
you to consyder that, by the opinion of all men, this citie
is greatly cursed of God, as appereth by the great barren-
nesse thereof, for it is destitute of all maner of fruites and
corne.[1] It is scorched with drynesse for lacke of water,
and therefore the water is there growen to suche pryce,
that you cannot for twelue pence buye as much water as
wyll satysfie your thyrst for one day. Nowe, therefore,
I wyll declare what prouision they have for victuales.
The most part is brought them from the citie of Babylon,
otherwyse named Memphis, Cayrus, or Alcayr, a citie of
the ryuer of Nilus in Egypt as we have sayde before, and
is brought by the Red Sea (called Mare Erythreum) from
a certayne port named Gida, distaunt from Mecha fourtie
myles.[2] The rest of theyr prouisions is brought from
Arabia Fælix, (that is) the happye or blessed Arabia : so
named for the fruitfulnesse thereof, in respect of the other
two Arabiaes, called Petrea and Diserta, that is, stonye
and desart. They haue also muche corne from Ethyopia.
Here we found a marueylous number of straungers and
peregrynes, or pylgryms ; of the whiche some came from
Syria, some from Persia, and other from both the East
Indiaes, (that is to say) both India within the ryuer of
Ganges, and also the other India without the same ryuer.
I neuer sawe in anye place greater abundaunce and fre-
quentation of people, forasmuche as I could perceyue by
tarrying there the space of 20 dayes. These people resort
thyther for diuers causes, as some for merchandies, some
to obserue theyr vowe of pylgrymage, and other to haue
pardon for theyr sinnes : as touchyng the whiche we wyll
speake more hereafter.

1 Moslems who are disposed to be facetious on serious subjects,
often remark that it is a mystery why Allah should have built his
house in a spot so barren and desolate.

2 This is still correct. Suez supplies Jeddah with corn and other
provisions.

CHAPTER XVII.—*Of the Pardons or Indulgences of Mecha.*

Let vs now returne to speake of the pardons of pil-
gryms, for the which so many strange nations resort
thither. In the myddest of the citie is a temple, in fashyon
lyke vnto the colossus of Rome, the amphitheatrum, I
meane, lyke vnto a stage, yet not of marbled or hewed
stones, but of burnt bryckes ; for this temple, like vnto an
amphitheatre, hath fourscore and ten, or an hundred gates,[1]
and is vaulted. The entrance is by a discent of twelve
stayers or degrees on euery part[2]: in the church porche,
are sold only jewels and precious stones. In the entry the
gylted walles shyne on euery syde with incomparable
splendour.   In the lower part of the temple (that is vnder
the vaulted places) is seene a maruelous multitude of
men ; for there are fyue or sixe thousande men that sell none
other thyng then sweete oyntmentes, and especially a certayne odoriferous and most sweete pouder wherewith dead
bodyes are embalmed.[3] And hence, all maner of sweete
sauours are carried in maner into the countreys of all the
Mahumetans. It passeth all beleefe to thynke of the
exceedyng sweetnesse of these sauours, farre surmounting
thc shoppes of the apothecaries. The 23 daye of Maye
the pardones began to be graunted in the temple, and in
what maner we wyll nowe declare. The temple in the
myddest is open without any inclosyng, and in the
myddest also thereof is a turrett of the largnesse of sixe
passes in cercuitie,[4] and inuolued or hanged with cloth or

---

1 A prodigious exaggeration. Burckhardt enumerates twenty.
The principal gates are seventeen in number. In the old building
they were more numerous. Jos. Pitt says, "it hath about forty-two
doors to enter into it ;—not so much, I think, for necessity, as figure;
for in some places they are close by one another."

2 Bartema alludes, probably, to the Bab al-Ziyadah, in the
northern enceinte.

3 I saw nothing of the kind, though constantly in the Harim at
Meccah.

4 "The Ka'abah is an oblong massive structure, 18 paces in
length, 14 in breadth, and from 35 to 40 feet in height." (*Burckhardt,*

tapestry of sylke.[1] and passeth not the heyght of a man.
They enter into the turret by a gate of syluer, and is on
euery syde besette with vesselles full of balme.   On the
day of Pentecost licence is graunted to al men to se these
thynges.   The inhabitantes affyrm that balme or balsame
to be part of the treasure of the Soltan that is Lorde of
Mecha.   At euery vaulte of the turret is fastened a rounde
circle of iron, lyke to the ryng of a doore.[2] The 22 day
of Maye, a great multitude of people beganne, early in the
mornyng before day, seuen tymes to walke about the
turret, kyssing euery corner thereof, often tymes feelyng
and handelyng them.   From this turret about tenne or
twelue pases is an other turret, like a chappell buylded
after our maner.   This hath three or foure entryes : in
the myddest thereof is a well of threescore and tenne
cubites deepe ; the water of this well is infected with salt
peter or saltniter.[3] Egypt men are therevnto appoynted
to drawe water for all the people : and when a multitude
of people haue seuen tymes gone rounde about the first
turret, they come to this well, and touchyng the mouth or
brym thereof, they saye thus, " Be it in the honour of God;
God pardon me, and forgeue me my synnes." When
these woordes are sayde, they that drawe the water powre
three buckettes of water on the headdes of euery one of
them, and stand neere about the well, and washe them all
wette from the headde to the foote, although they be
apparelled with sylk.   Then the dotyng fooles dreame
that they are cleane from all theyr synnes, and that theyr
synnes are forgeuen them.   They saye, furthermore, that

vol. i. p. 248.)   My measurements, concerning which more hereafter,
gave 18 paces in breadth, and 22 in length.

1 In ancient times possibly it was silk: now, it is of silk and
cotton mixed.

2 These are the brazen rings which serve to fasten the lower
edge of the Kiswah, or covering.

3 A true description of the water of the well Zemzem.

the fyrst turret, whereof we haue spoken, was the fyrst house that euer Abraham buylded, and, therefore, whyle they are yet all wette of the sayd washyng, they go to the mountayne, where (as we have sayde before) they are accustomed to sacrifice to Abraham.[1]   And remayning there two daies, they make the said sacrifice to Abraham at the foote of the mountayne.

CHAPTER XVIII.—*The Maner of sacrificing at Mecha.*

Forasmuche as for the most parte noble spirites are delyted with nouelties of great and straunge thyngs, there-fore, to satisfie their expectation, I wyll describe theyr maner of sacrifycyng.   Therefore, when they intend to sacrifice, some of them kyll three sheepe, some foure, and tenne ; so that the butcherie sometyme so floweth with blood that in one sacrifice are slayne above three thousande sheepe.   They are slayne at the rysyng of the sunne, and shortly after are distributed to the poore for God's sake : for I sawe there a great and confounded multitude of poor people as to the number of 20 thousande.   These make many and long dyches in the feeldes, where they keepe fyre with camels doong, and rost or seeth the fleshe that is geuen them, and eate it euen there.   I beleue that these poore people came thither rather for hunger than for deuotion, which I thinke by this coniectur,—that great abundance of cucumbers are brought thyther from Arabia Fælix, whiche they eate, castyng away the parynges without their houses or tabernacles, where a multitude of the sayde poore people geather them euen out of the myre and sande, and eate them, and are so greedie of these parynges that they fyght who may geather most.[2]   The

---

1 There is great confusion in this part of Bartema's narrative. On the 9th of Zu'l Hijjah, the pilgrims leave Mount Arafat.   On the 10th, many hasten into Meccah, and enter the Ka'abah.   They then return to the valley of Muna, where their tents are pitched and they sacrifice the victims.   On the 12th, the tents are struck, and the pilgrims re-enter Meccah.

2 This well describes the wretched state of the poor " Takruri,"

daye folowing,[1] their Cadi (which are in place with them
as with vs the preachers of God's worde) ascended into a
hygh mountayne, to preach to the people that remaineth
beneath ; and preached to them in theyr language the
space of an houre. The summe of the sermon was, that
with teares they should bewayle theyr sinnes, and beate
their brestes with sighes and lamentation. And the
preacher hymselfe with loude voyce spake these wordes,
" O Abraham beloued of God, O Isaac chosen of God,
and his friend, praye to God for the people of Nabi."
When these woordes were sayde, sodenly were heard
lamenting voyces. When the sermon was done, a rumor
was spredde that a great armye of Arabians, to the number of twentie thousande, were commyng. With which
newes, they that kept the caraunas beyng greatly feared,
with all speede, lyke madde men, fledde into the citie of
Mecha, and we agayne bearyng newes of the Arabians
approche, fledde also into the citie. But whyle wee were
in the mydwaye between the mountayne and Mecha, we
came by a despicable wall, of the breadthe of foure cubites :
the people passyng this wall, had couered the waye with
stones, the cause whereof, they saye to be this : when
Abraham was commaunded to sacrifice his sonne, he
wylled his sonne Isaac to folowe hym to the place where
he should execute the commaundement of God. As Isaac
went to follow his father, there appeared to him in the
way a Deuyl, in lykenesse of a fayre and freendly person,
not farre from the sayde wall, and asked hym freendlye
whyther he went. Isaac answered that he went to his

and other Africans, but it attributes to them an unworthy motive.
I once asked a learned Arab what induced the wretches to rush upon
destruction, as they do, when the Faith renders pilgrimage obligatory
only upon those who can afford necessaries for the way. " By Allah,"
he replied, " there is fire within their hearts, which can be quenched
only at God's House, and at His Prophet's Tomb."

1 Bartema alludes to the " Day of Arafat," 9th of Zu'l Hijjah,
which precedes, not follows, the " Day of Sacrifice."

father who tarryed for him.   To this the enemie of man-
kynde answered, that it was best for hym to tarrye, and
yf that he went anye further, his father would sacrifice
him.   But Isaac nothyng feareyng this aduertisement of
the Deuyl, went forward, that his father on hym myght
execute the commaundement of God : and with this
answere (as they saye) they Deuyell departed.   Yet as
Isaac went forwarde, the Diuell appeared to hym agayne
in the lykenesse of an other frendlye person, and forbade
hym as before.   Then Isaac taking vp a stone in that
place, hurlde it at the Deuyl and wounded him in the forehead : In witnesse and remembraunce whereof, the people
passyng that waye when they come neare the wall, are
accustomed to cast stones agaynst it, and from thence go
into the citie.[1]   As we went this way, the ayre was in
maner darkened with a multitude of stock doues.   They
saye that these doues, are of the progenie of the doue that
spake in the eare of Mahumet, in lykenesse of the Holye
Ghost.[2]   These are seene euery where, as in the villages,
houses, tauernes and graniers of corne and ryse, and are
so tame that one can scharsely dryue them away.   To
take them or kyll them is esteemed a thyng worthy death,[3]

---

1 Bartema alludes to the " Shaytan al-Kabir," the "great devil,"
as the buttress at Al-Muna is called.   His account of Satan's appearance is not strictly correct.   Most Moslems believe that Abraham
threw the stone at the " Rajim,"—the lapidated one ; but there are
various traditions upon the subject.

2 A Christian version of an obscure Moslem legend about a white
dove alighting on the Prophet's shoulder, and appearing to whisper in
his ear whilst he was addressing a congregation.   Butler alludes
to it :—
     " Th' apostles of this fierce religion,
     Like Mahomet's, were ass and widgeon;"
the latter word being probably a clerical error for pigeon.   When
describing the Ka'abah, I shall have occasion to allude to the "blue-
rocks " of Meccah.

3 No one would eat the pigeons of the Ka'abah; but in other
places, Al-Madinah, for instance, they are sometimes used as articles
of food.

and therefore a certayne pensyon is geuen to nourysshe them in the temple.

CHAPTER XX.—*Of diuers thynges which chaunced to me in Mecha; and of Zida, a port of Mecha.*

It may seeme good here to make mention of certayne thynges, in the which is seene sharpenesse of witte in case of vrgent necessitie, which hath no lawe as sayeth the prouerbe, for I was dryuen to the point howe I myght prieuly escape from Mecha. Therefore whereas my Captayne gaue me charge to buy certayne thynges, as I was in the market place, a certayne Mamaluke knewe me to be a christian, and therefore in his owne language spake vnto me these woordes, " Inte mename," that is, whence art thou ?[1] To whom I answered that I was a Mahumetan. But he sayde, Thou sayest not truely. I sayde agayne, by the head of Mahumet I am a Mahumetan. Then he sayde agayne, Come home to my house, I folowed hym willingly. When we were there, he began to speake to me in the Italian tongue, and asked me agayne from whence I was, affyrming that he knewe me, and that I was no Mahumetan : also that he had been sometyme in Genua and Venice. And that his woordes myght be better beleeued, he rehearsed many thinges which testified that he sayed trueth. When I vnderstoode this, I confessed freely, that I was a Romane, but professed to the fayth of Mahumet in the citie of Babylon, and there made one of the Mamalukes; whereof he seemed greatly to reioyce and therefore vsed me honourably. But because my desyre was yet to goe further, I asked the Mahumetan whether that citie of Mecha was so famous as all the world spake of it : and inquired of him where was the great aboundaunce of pearles, precious stones, spices, and other rich merchandies that the bruite went of to be in that citie. And all my talke was to the ende

---

1 In the vulgar dialect, "Ant min ayn?"

to grope the mynde of the Mahumetan, that I might know the cause why such thinges were not brought thyther as in tyme paste. But to auoyde all suspition, I durst here make no mention of the dominion which the Kyng of Portugale had in the most parte of that ocean, and of the gulfes of the Redde Sea and Persia. Then he began with more attentyue mynde, in order to declare vnto me the cause why that marte was not so greatly frequented as it had been before, and layde the only faulte thereof in the Kyng of Portugale. But when he had made mention of the kyng, I began of purpose to detracte his fame, lest the Mahumetan might thinke that I reioyced that the Christians came thyther for merchandies. When he perceyued that I was of profession an enemy to the Christians, he had me yet in greater estimation, and proceeded to tell me many thynges more. When I was well instructed in all thynges, I spake vnto him friendly these woordes in the Mahumet's language Menaba Menalhabi, that is to say, " I pray you assist mee.[1]" He asked mee wherein. " To help me (sayed I) howe I may secretly departe hence." Confyrmyng by great othes, that I would goe to those kinges that were most enemies to the Christians : affyrmyng furthermore, that I knewe certain secretes greatly to be esteemed, which if they were knowen to the sayde kynges, I doubted not but that in shorte tyme I should bee sent for from Mecha. Astonyshed at these woordes, he sayde vnto mee, I pray you what arte or secrete doe you know ? I answered, that I would giue place to no man in makyng of all manner of gunnes and artillerie. Then sayde hee, " praysed be Mahumet who sent thee hyther, to do hym and his saintes good seruice:" and willed me to remayne secretly in his

---

1 I confess inability to explain these words : the printer has probably done more than the author to make them unintelligible. " Atamannik minalnabi," in vulgar and rather corrupt Arabic, would mean " I beg you (to aid me) for the sake of the Prophet."

house with his wyfe, and requyred me earnestly to ob-
tayne leaue of our Captayne that under his name he
myght leade from Mecha fifteine camelles laden with
spices, without paying any custome: for they ordinarily
paye to the Soltan thirtie seraphes[1] of golde, for trans-
portyng of such merchandies for the charge of so many
camelles. I put him in good hope of his request, he
greatly reioyced, although he would ask for a hundred,
affyrmyng that might easily be obteyned by the priuileges
of the Mamalukes, and therefore desyred hym that I
might safely remayne in his house. Then nothyng doubt-
yng to obtayn his request, he greatly reioyced, and talk-
yng with me yet more freely, gaue me further instructions
and counsayled me to repayre to a certayne kyng of the
greater India, in the kyngdome and realme of Decham[2]
whereof we will speake hereafter. Therefore the day before the carauana departed from Mecha, he willed me to
lye hydde in the most secrete parte of his house. The
day folowyng, early in the mornyng the trumpetter of the
carauana gaue warning to all the Mamalukes to make
ready their horses, to directe their journey toward Syria,
with proclamation of death to all that should refuse so to
doe. When I hearde the sounde of the trumpet, and
was aduertised of the streight commaundement, I was
marueylously troubled in minde, and with heauy coun-
tenaunce desired the Mahumetan's wife not to bewraye
me, and with earnest prayer committed myselfe to the
mercie of God. On the Tuesday folowyng, our carauana
departed from Mecha, and I remayned in the Mahumetans house with his wyfe, but he folowed the carauana.
Yet before he departed, he gaue commaundement to his
wyfe to bryng me to the carauana, which shoulde departe
from Zida[3] the porte of Mecha to goe into India. This
porte is distant from Mecha 40 miles. Whilest I laye

---

1 Ashrafi, ducats.   2 The Deccan.   3 Jeddah.

thus hyd in the Mahumetans house, I can not expresse how friendly his wyfe vsed me. This also furthered my good enterteynement, that there was in the house a fayre young mayde, the niese of the Mahumetan, who was greatly in loue with me. But at that tyme, in the myddest of those troubles and feare, the fyre of Venus was almost extincte in mee: and therefore with daliaunce of fayre woordes and promises, I styll kepte my selfe in her fauour. Therefore the Friday folowyng, about noone tyde, I departed, folowyng the carauana of India. And about myd nyght we came to a certayne village of the Arabians, and there remayned the rest of that nyght, and the next day tyll noone.

From hence we went forwarde on our journey toward Zida, and came thyther in the silence of the nyght. This citie hath no walles, yet fayre houses, somewhat after the buyldyng of Italie. Here is great aboundaunce of all kynd of merchandies, by reason of resorte in manner of all nations thyther, except jewes and christians, to whom it is not lawfull to come thyther. As soone as I entered into the citie, I went to their temple or Meschita, where I sawe a great multitude of poore people, as about the number of 25 thousande, attendyng a certayne pilot who should bryng them into their countrey. Heere I suffered muche trouble and affliction, beyng enforced to hyde myselfe among these poore folkes, faynyng myselfe very sicke, to the ende that none should be inquisityue what I was, whence I came, or whyther I would. The lord of this citie is the Soltan of Babylon, brother to the Soltan of Mecha, who is his subiecte. The inhabitauntes are Mahumetans. The soyle is vnfruitfull, and lacketh freshe water. The sea beateth agaynst the towne. There is neuerthelesse aboundance of all thinges: but brought thyther from other places, as from Babylon of Nilus, Arabia Fœlix, and dyuers other places. The heate is here so great, that men are in maner dryed up therewith.

And therefore there is euer a great number of sicke folkes. The citie conteyneth about fyue hundred houses.

After fyftiene dayes were past, I couenaunted with a pilot, who was ready to departe from thence into Persia, and agreed of the price, to goe with him. There lay at anker in the hauen almost a hundred brigantines and foistes,[1] with diuers boates and barkes of sundry sortes, both with ores and without ores. Therefore after three days, gyuyng wynde to our sayles, we entered into the Redde Sea, otherwise named Mare Erythræum.

---

1 A foist, foyst or buss, was a kind of felucca, partially decked.

APPENDIX V.

THE PILGRIMAGE OF JOSEPH PITTS TO MECCAH AND
AL-MADINAH.—A.D. 1680.

OUR second pilgrim was Jos. Pitts, of Exon,[1] a youth
fifteen or sixteen years old, when in A.D. 1678, his genius
" leading him to be a sailor and to see foreign countries,"
caused him to be captured by an Algerine pirate. After
living in slavery for some years, he was taken by his
" patroon" to Meccah and Al-Madinah *viâ* Alexandria,
Rosetta, Cairo, and Suez. His description of these
places is accurate in the main points, and though tainted
with prejudice and bigotry, he is free from superstition
and credulity. Conversant with Turkish and Arabic, he
has acquired more knowledge of the tenets and practice
of Al-Islam than his predecessor, and the term of his
residence at Algier, fifteen years, sufficed, despite the
defects of his education, to give fulness and finish to his
observations. His chief patroon, captain of a troop of

---

1 It is curious, as Crichton (Arabia, vol. ii. p. 208) observes, that
Gibbon seems not to have seen or known anything of the little work
published by Pitts on his return home. It is entitled "A faithful
Account of the Religion and the Manners of the Mahometans, in
which is a particular Relation of their Pilgrimage to Mecca, the
Place of Mahomet's Birth, and Description of Medina, and of his
Tomb there," &c., &c. My copy is the 4th edition, printed for
T. Longman and R. Hett, London, A.D. 1708. The only remarkable
feature in the " getting up " of the little octavo is, that the engraving
headed " the most sacred and antient Temple of the Mahometans at
Mecca," is the reverse of the impression

horse, was a profligate and debauched man in his time, and a murderer, " who determined to proselyte a Christian slave as an atonement for past impieties." He began by large offers and failed ; he succeeded by dint of a great cudgel repeatedly applied to Joseph Pitts' bare feet. " I roared out," says the relator, " to feel the pain of his cruel strokes, but the more I cried, the more furiously he laid on, and to stop the noise of my crying, would stamp with his feet on my mouth." " At last," through terror, he " turned and spake the words (la ilaha, &c.), as usual holding up the forefinger of the right hand "; he was then circumcised in due form. Of course, such conversion was not a sincere one—" there was yet swines-flesh in his teeth." He boasts of saying his prayers in a state of impurity, hates his fellow religionists, was truly pleased to hear Mahomet called sabbatero, *i.e.*, shoemaker, reads his bible, talks of the horrid evil of apostacy, calls the Prophet a " bloody imposter," eats heartily in private of hog, and is very much concerned for one of his country-men who went home to his own country, but came again to Algier, and *voluntarily*, without the least force used towards him, became a Mahometan. His first letter from his father reached him some days after he had been compelled by his patroon's barbarity to abjure his faith. One sentence appears particularly to have afflicted him : it was this, " to have a care and keep close to God, and to be sure never, by any methods of cruelty that could be used towards me, be prevailed to deny my *blessed Saviour*, and that he (the father) would rather hear of my death than of my being a Mahometan." Indeed, through-out the work, it appears that his repentance was sincere.

" God be merciful to me a
Sinner ! "

is the deprecation that precedes the account of his " turn-ing Turk," and the book concludes with,

" To *him*, therefore, *Father, Son, and Holy Spirit, Three*

Persons and *one* God, be all *Honour, Glory,* and *Praise,* world without end.   *Amen.*"

Having received from his patroon, whom he acknowledges to have been a second parent to him, a letter of freedom at Meccah and having entered into pay, still living with his master, Pitts began to think of escape.   The Grand Turk had sent to Algier for ships, and the renegade was allowed to embark on board one of them provided with a diplomatic letter[1] from Mr. Baker, Consul of Algier, to Mr. Raye, Consul at Smyrna.   The devil, we are told, was very busy with him in the Levant, tempting him to lay aside all thoughts of escaping, to return to Algier, and to continue a Mussulman, and the loss of eight months' pay and certain other monies seems to have weighed heavily upon his soul.   Still he prepared for the desperate enterprise, in which failure would have exposed him to be dragged about the streets on the stones till half dead, and then be burned to ashes in the Jews' burial-place.   A generous friend, Mr. Eliot, a Cornish merchant who had served some part of his apprenticeship in Exon and had settled at Smyrna, paid £4 for his passage in a French ship to Leghorn.   Therefrom, in the evening before sailing, he went on board " apparel'd as an Englishman with his beard shaven, a *campaign periwig,* and a *cane* in his hand, accompanied with three or four of his friends.   At Leghorn he prostrated himself, and kissed the *earth,* blessing *Almighty God,* for his mercy and goodness to him, that he once more set footing on the

---

1 Some years afterwards, Mr. Consul Baker, when waited upon by Pitts, in London, gave him a copy of the letter, with the following memorandum upon the back of it—"Copy of my letter to Consul Raye at Smyrna, to favour the escape of Joseph Pitts, an English renegade, from a squadron of Algier men-of-war.   Had my kindness to him been discovered by the government of Algiers, my legs and arms had first been broken, and my carcass burnt—a danger hitherto not courted by any."

European Christian [1] part of the world." He travelled through Italy, Germany, and Holland, where he received many and great kindnesses. But his patriotism was damped as he entered " England, his own *native* country, and the civilised land must have made him for a time regret having left Algier. The very first night he lay ashore, he was " imprest into the kings service " (we having at that time war with France); despite arguments and tears he spent some days in Colchester jail, and finally he was put on board a smack to be carried to the Dreadnought man-of-war. But happily for himself he had written to Sir William Falkener, one of the Smyrna or Turkey company in London ; that gentleman used his interest to procure a protection from the Admiralty office, upon the receipt of which good news, Joseph Pitts did " rejoice exceedingly and could not forbear leaping upon the deck." He went to London, thanked Sir William, and hurried down to Exeter, where he ends his fifteen years' tale with a homely, heartful and affecting description of his first meeting with his father. His mother died about a year before his return.

The following passages are parts of the 7th and 8th chapters of Pitts' little-known work.

" Next we came to Gidda, the nearest sea-port town to Mecca, not quite one day's journey from it,[2] where the ships are unloaded. Here we are met by Dilleels,[3] *i.e.* certain persons who came from Mecca on purpose to instruct the Hagges, or pilgrims, in the ceremonies (most

---

1 The italics in the text are the author's. This is admirably characteristic of the man. Asiatic Christendom would not satisfy him. He seems to hate the " damnable doctrines" of the " Papists," almost as much as those of the Moslems.

2 He must have been accustomed to long days' journeys. Al-Idrisi makes Jeddah forty miles from Meccah ; I calculated about forty-four.

3 Dalil, a guide, generally called at Meccah " Muttawwif."

of them being ignorant of them) which are to be used in their worship at the temple there; in the middle of which is a place which they call Beat Allah, *i.e.* the House of God. They say that Abraham built it; to which I give no credit.

"As soon as we come to the town of Mecca, the Dilleel, or guide, carries us into the great street, which is in the midst of the town, and to which the temple joins.[1] After the camels are laid down, he first directs us to the Fountains, there to take Abdes[2]; which being done, he brings us to the temple, into which (having left our shoes with one who constantly attends to receive them) we enter at the door called Bab-al-salem, *i.e.* the Welcome Gate, or Gate of Peace. After a few paces entrance, the Dilleel makes a stand, and holds up his hands towards the Beat-Allah (it being in the middle of the Mosque), the Hagges imitating him, and saying after him the same words which he speaks. At the very first sight of the Beat-Allah, the Hagges melt into tears, then we are led up to it, still speaking after the Dilleel; then we are led round it seven times, and then make two Erkaets.[3] This being done, we are led into the street again, where we are sometimes to run and sometimes to walk very quick with the Dilleel from one place of the street to the other, about a bowshot.[4] And I profess I could not chuse but admire to see those poor creatures so extraordinary devout, and affectionate, when they were about these superstitions, and with what awe and trembling they

1 Pitts' Note,—that before they'll provide for themselves, they serve God in their way.

2 Abdast is the Turkish word, borrowed from the Persian, for " Wuzu," the minor ablution.

3 Ruka'at, a bending. This two-bow prayer is in honour of the Mosque.

4 This is the ceremony technically called Al-Sai, or running between Safa and Marwah. Burckhardt describes it accurately, vol. i. pp. 174, 175.

were possessed; in so much that I could scarce forbear
shedding of tears, to see their zeal, though blind and
idolatrous. After all this is done, we returned to the
place in the street where we left our camels, with our
provisions, and necessaries, and then look out for lodgings;
where when we come, we disrobe and take of our Hir-
rawems,[1] and put on our ordinary clothes again.

"All the pilgrims hold it to be their great duty well
to improve their time whilst they are at Mecca, not to do
their accustomed duty and devotion in the temple, but to
spend all their leisure time there, and as far as strength
will permit to continue at Towoaf, *i.e.* to walk round the
Beat-Allah, which is about four and twenty paces square.
At one corner of the Beat, there is a black stone fastened
and framed in with silver plate,[2] and every time they come
to that corner, they kiss the stone; and having gone
round seven times they perform two Erkaets-nomas, or
prayers. This stone, they say, was formerly white, and
then it' was called Haggar Essaed, *i.e.* the White Stone.[3]
But by reason of the sins of the multitudes of people
who kiss it, it is become black, and is now called Haggar
Esswaed, or the Black Stone.

"This place is so much frequented by people going
round it, that the place of the Towoaf, *i.e.* the circuit
which they take in going round it, is seldom void of people
at any time of the day or night.[4] Many have waited
several weeks, nay months, for the opportunity of finding
it so. For they say, that if any person is blessed with such
an opportunity, that for his or her zeal in keeping up the
honour of Towoaf, let they petition what they will at the
Beat-Allah, they shall be answered. Many will walk round

1 Ihram, the pilgrim-garb. 2 Now gold or gilt.

3 This is an error. The stone is called Hajar Aswad, the Black
Stone, or Hajar As'ad, the Blessed Stone. Moreover, it did not
change its colour on account of the sins of the people who kissed it.

4 The Meccans, in effect, still make this a boast.

till they are quite weary, then rest, and at it again; carefully remembering at the end of every seventh time to perform two Erkaets. This Beat is in effect the object of their devotion, the idol which they adore : for, let them be never so far distant from it, East, West, North, or South of it, they will be sure to bow down towards it ; but when they are at the Beat, they may go on which side they please and pay their Sallah towards it.[1] Sometimes there are several hundreds at Towoaf at once, especially after Acshamnomas, or fourth time of service, which is after candle-lighting (as you heard before), and these both men and women, but the women walk on the outside the men, and the men nearest to the Beat. In so great a resort as this, it is not to be supposed that every individual person can come to kiss the stone afore-mentioned ; therefore, in such a case, the lifting up the hands towards it, smoothing down their faces, and using a short expression of devotion, as Allah-waick barick, *i.e.* Blessed God, or Allah cabor, *i.e.* Great God, some such like ; and so passing by it till opportunity of kissing it offers, is thought sufficient.[2] But when there are but few men at Towoaf, then the women get opportunity to kiss the said stone, and when they have gotten it, they close in with it as they come round, and walk round as quick as they can to come to it again, and keep possession of it for a considerable time. The men, when they see that the women have got the place, will be so civil as to pass by and give them leave to take their fill, as I may say in their Towoaf or walking round, during which they are using some formal expressions. When the women are at the stone, then it is esteemed a very rude and abominable thing to go near them, respecting the time and place.

---

1 Nothing more blindly prejudiced than this statement. Moslems turn towards Meccah, as Christians towards Jerusalem.

2 As will afterwards be explained, all the four orthodox schools do not think it necessary to kiss the stone after each circumambulation.

" I shall now give you a more particular description of Mecca and the temple there.

" First, as to Mecca. It is a town situated in a barren place (about one day's journey from the Red Sea) in a valley, or rather in the midst of many little hills. It is a place of no force, wanting both walls and gates. Its buildings are (as I said before) very ordinary, insomuch that it would be a place of no tolerable entertainment, were it not for the anniversary resort of so many thousand Hagges, or pilgrims, on whose coming the whole dependance of the town (in a manner) is; for many shops are scarcely open all the year besides.

" The people here, I observed, are a poor sort of people, very thin, lean, and swarthy. The town is surrounded for several miles with many thousands of little hills, which are very near one to the other. I have been on the top of some of them near Mecca, where I could see some miles about, yet was not able to see the farthest of the hills. They are all stony-rock and blackish, and pretty near of a bigness, appearing at a distance like cocks of hay, but all pointing towards Mecca. Some of them are half a mile in circumference, but all near of one height. The people here have an odd and foolish sort of tradition concerning them, viz. : That when Abraham went about building the Beat-Allah, God by his wonderful providence did so order it, that every mountain in the world should contribute something to the building thereof; and accordingly every one did send its proportion; though there is a mountain near Algier, which is called Corradog, *i.e.* Black Mountain; and the reason of its blackness, they say, is because it did not send any part of itself towards building the temple at Mecca.[1] Between

---

1 These are mere local traditions. The original Ka'abah was composed of materials gathered from the six mountains of Paradise (chap. xx.) The present building is of grey granite quarried in a hill near Meccah.

these hills is good and plain travelling, though they stand one to another.

" There is upon the top of one of them a cave, which they term Hira,[1] *i. e.* Blessing ; into which (they say) Mahomet did usually retire for his solitary devotions, meditations, and fastings ; and here they believe he had a great part of the Alcoran brought him by the Angel Gabriel. I have been in this cave, and observed that it is not at all beautified ; at which I admired.

" About half a mile out of Mecca is a very steep hill, and there are stairs made to go to the top of it, where is a cupola, under which is a cloven rock ; into this, they say, Mahomet, when very young, viz. about four years of age, was carried by the Angel Gabriel, who opened his breast, and took out his heart, from which he picked some black blood-specks, which was his original corruption ; then put it into its place again, and afterwards closed up the part ; and that during this operation Mahomet felt no pain.

" Into this very place I myself went, because the rest of my company did so, and performed some Erkaets, as they did.

" The town hath plenty of water, and yet but few herbs, unless in some particular places.   Here are several sorts of good fruits to be had, viz. grapes, melons, watermelons, cucumbers, pumkins, and the like ; but these are brought two or three days' journey off, where there is a place of very great plenty, called, if I mistake not, Habbash.[2]

1 Now Jabal Nur.
2 They come from the well-known Taif, which the country people call Hijaz, but never Habbash. The word Taif literally means the "circumambulator." It is said that when Adam settled at Meccah, finding the country barren, he prayed to Allah to supply him with a bit of fertile land. Immediately appeared a mountain, which having performed Tawaf round the Ka'abah, settled itself down eastward of Meccah. Hence, to the present day, Taif is called Kita min al-Sham, a piece of Syria, its fatherland.

Likewise sheep are brought hither and sold. So that as to Mecca itself, it affords little or nothing of comfortable provisions. It lieth in a very hot country, insomuch that people run from one side of the streets to the other to get into the shadow, as the motion of the sun causes it. The inhabitants, especially men, do usually sleep on the tops of the houses for the air, or in the streets before their doors. Some lay the small bedding they have on a thin mat on the ground ; others have a slight frame, made much like drink-stalls on which we place barrels, standing on four legs, corded with palm cordage, on which they put their bedding. Before they bring out their bedding, they sweep the streets and water them. As for my own part, I usually lay open, without any bed-covering, on the top of the house : only I took a linen cloth, dipt in water, and after I had wrung it, covered myself with it in the night ; and when I awoke I should find it dry ; then I would wet it again : and thus I did two or three times in a night.

" Secondly. I shall next give you some account of the temple of Mecca.

" It hath about forty-two doors to enter into it, not so much, I think, for necessity, as figure ; for in some places they are close by one another. The form of it is much resembling that of the Royal Exchange in London, but I believe it is near ten times bigger. It is all open and gravelled in the midst, except some paths that come from certain doors which lead to the Beat-Allah, and are paved with broad stones. The walks, or cloisters, all round are arched over-head, and paved beneath with fine broad stone ; and all round are little rooms or cells, where such dwell and give themselves up to reading, studying, and a devout life, who are much akin to their dervises, or hermits.

" The Beat-Allah, which stands in the middle of the temple, is four-square, about twenty-four paces each

square, and near twenty-four foot[1] in height.   It is built
with great stone, all smooth, and plain, without the least
bit of carved work on it.   It is covered all over from top
to bottom with a thick sort of silk.   Above the middle
part of the covering are embroidered all round letters
of gold, the meaning of which I cannot well call to
mind, but I think they were some devout expressions.
Each letter is near two foot in length and two inches
broad.   Near the lower end of this Beat are large brass
rings fastened into it, through which passeth a great
cotton rope; and to this the lower end of the covering is
tacked.   The threshold of the door that belongs to the
Beat is as high as a man can reach ; and therefore when
any person enter into it, a sort of ladder-stairs are brought
for that purpose.   The door is plated all over with
silver[2] and there is a covering hangs over it and reaches
to the ground, which is kept turned up all the week,
except Thursday night, and Friday, which is their
Sabbath.   The said covering of the door is very thick
imbroidered with gold, insomuch that it weighs several
score pounds.   The top of the Beat is flat, beaten with
lime and sand ; and there is a long gutter, or spout, to
carry off the water when it rains ; at which time the
people will run, throng, and struggle, to get under the
said gutter, that so the water that comes off the Beat may
fall upon them, accounting it as the dew of Heaven, and
looking on it as a great happiness to have it drop upon
them.   But if they can recover some of this water to
drink, they esteem it to be yet a much greater happiness.

---

1 This is an error of printing for "paces."

2 (Pitts' Note.)   Not of massy gold, as a late French author
(who, I am sure, was never there) says.   The door is of wood, only
plated over with silver; much less is the inside of the Beat ceiled
with massy gold, as the same Frenchman asserts.   I can assure the
world it is no such thing.

The door is of wood, thickly plated over with silver, in many
parts gilt.   And whatever hereabouts is gilt, the Meccans always call
gold.   (R. F. B.)

Many poor people make it their endeavour to get some of it, and present it to the Hagges, for which they are well rewarded. My Patroon had a present made him of this water, with which he was not a little pleased, and gave him that brought it a good reward.

"This Beat-Allah is opened but two days in the space of six weeks, viz. one day for the men, and the next day for the women.[1] As I was at Mecca about four months, I had the opportunity of entering into it twice ; a reputed advantage, which many thousands of the Hagges have not met with, for those that come by land make no longer stay at Mecca than sixteen or seventeen days.

"When any enter into the Beat, all that they have to do is to perform two Erkaets on each side,[2] with the holding up their two hands, and petitioning at the conclusion of each two Erkaets. And they are so very reverent and devout in doing this, that they will not suffer their eyes to wander and gaze about; for they account it very sinful so to do. Nay, they say that one was smitten blind for gazing about when in the Beat, as the reward of his vain and unlawful curiosity.[3] I could not, for my part, give any credit to this story, but looked on it as a legendary relation, and, therefore, was resolved, if I could, to take my view of it ; I mean not to continue gazing about it, but now and then to cast an observing eye. And I profess I found nothing worth seeing in it, only two wooden pillars in the midst, to keep up the roof,[4] and a bar of iron fastened to them, on which hanged three or four silver lamps, which are, I suppose, but sel-

1 This is no longer the case. Few women ever enter the Ka'abah, on account of the personal danger they run there.

2 More correctly, at three of the corners, and the fourth opposite the southern third of the western wall.

3 It is deemed disrespectful to look at the ceiling, but pilgrims may turn their eyes in any other direction they please.

4 There are now three.

dom, if ever, lighted.   In one corner of the Beat is an iron
or brass chain, I cannot tell which (for I made no use of
it) : the pilgrims just clap it about their necks in token of
repentance.   The floor of the Beat is marble, and so is
the inside of the walls, on which there is written something in Arabick, which I had no time to read.   The
walls, though of marble on the inside, are hung over with
silk, which is pulled off [1] before the Hagges enter. Those
that go into the Beat tarry there but a very little while,
viz. scarce so much as half a quarter of an hour, because
others wait for the same privilege ; and while some go in,
others are going out.   After all is over, and all that
will have done this, the Sultan of Mecca, who is Shirreef,
i. e. one of the race of Mahomet, accounts himself not too
good to cleanse the Beat ; and, therefore, with some of
his favourites, doth wash and cleanse it.   And first of all,
they wash it with the holy water, Zem Zem, and after
that with sweet water.   The stairs which were brought
to enter in at the door of the Beat being removed, the
people crowd under the door to receive on them the sweep-
ings of the said water.   And the besoms wherewith the
Beat is cleansed are broken in pieces, and thrown out
amongst the mob ; and he that gets a small stick or twig
of it, keeps it as a sacred relique.

   " But to speak something further of the temple of
Mecca (for I am willing to be very particular in matters
about it, though in so being, I should, it may be, speak
of things which by some people may be thought trivial).
The compass of ground round the Beat (where the people
exercise themselves in the duty of Towoaf) is paved with
marble [2] about 50 foot in breadth, and round this marble
pavement stand pillars of brass about 15 foot high [3] and

---

   1 It is tucked up about six feet high.

   2 It is a close kind of grey granite, which takes a high polish
from the pilgrims' feet.

   3 Now iron posts.

20 foot distant from each other; above the middle part of which iron bars are fastened, reaching from one to the other, and several lamps made of glass are hanged to each of the said bars, with brasswires in the form of a triangle, to give light in the night season, for they pay their devotions at the Beat-Allah as much by night as by day, during the Hagges' stay at Mecca. These glasses are half-filled with water, and a third part with oil, on which a round wire of brass buoyed up with three little corks; in the midst of this wire is made a place to put in the wick or cotton, which burns till the oil is spent. Every day they are washed clean, and replenished with fresh water, oil, and cotton.

" On each of the four squares of the Beat is a little room built, and over every one of them is a little chamber with windows all round it, in which chambers the Emaums (together with the Mezzins) perform Sallah, in the audience of all the people which are below. These four chambers are built one at each square of the Beat, by reason that there are four sorts of Mahometans. The first are called Hanifee; most of them are Turks. The second Schafee[1]; whose manners and ways the Arabians follow. The third Hanbelee; of which there are but few. The fourth Malakee; of which there are those that live westward of Egypt, even to the Emperor of Morocco's country. These all agree in fundamentals, only there is some small difference between them in the ceremonial part.

" About twelve paces from the Beat is (as they say) the sepulchre of Abraham,[2] who by God's immediate command, they tell you, built this Beat-Allah; which

1 The Shafe'i school have not, and never had, a peculiar oratory like the other three schools. They pray near the well Zemzem.

2 This place contains the stone which served Abraham for a scaffold when he was erecting the Ka'abah. Some of our popular writers confound this stone with the Hajar al-Aswad.

sepulchre is enclosed within iron gates. It is made somewhat like the tombstones which people of fashion have
among us, but with a very handsome imbroidered covering. Into this persons are apt to gaze. A small distance from it, on the left-hand, is a well, which they call
Beer el Zem Zem, the water whereof they call holy water ;
and as superstitiously esteem it as the Papists do theirs.
In the month of Ramadan they will be sure to break
their fast with it. They report that it is as sweet as milk ;
but for my part I could perceive no other taste in it than
in common water, except that it was somewhat brackish.
The Hagges, when they come first to Mecca, drink of it
unreasonably ; by which means they are not only much
purged, but their flesh breaks out all in pimples ; and this
they call the purging of their spiritual corruptions. There
are hundreds of pitchers belonging to the temple, which
in the month of Ramadan are filled with the said water
and placed all along before the people (with cups to drink)
as they are kneeling and waiting for Acsham-nomas, or
evening service ; and as soon as the Mezzins or clerks on
the tops of the minarets began their bawling to call them
to nomas, they fall a drinking thereof before they begin
their devotions. This Beer or well of Zem Zem is in the
midst of one of the little rooms before mentioned, at each
square of the Beat, distant about twelve or fourteen paces
from it, out of which four men are employed to draw water,
without any pay or reward, for any that shall desire it.
Each of these men have two leather buckets tied to a rope
on a small wheel, one of which comes up full, while the
other goes down empty. They do not only drink this
water, but oftentimes bathe themselves with it, at which
time they take off their clothes, only covering their lower
parts with a thin wrapper, and one of the drawers pours
on each person's head five or six buckets of water.[1] The

---

[1] (Pitts' Note.) The worthy Mons. Thevenot saith, that the

person bathing may lawfully wash himself therewith above the middle, but not his lower parts, because they account they are not worthy, only letting the water take its way downwards. In short, they make use of this water only to drink, take Abdes, and for bathing : neither may they take Abdes with it, unless they first cleanse their secret parts with other common water. Yea, such an high esteem they have for it, that many Hagges carry it home to their respective countries in little latten or tin pots ; and present it to their friends, half a spoonful, may be, to each, who receive it in the hollow of their hand with great care and abundance of thanks, sipping a little of it, and bestowing the rest on their faces and naked heads ; at the same time holding up their hands, and desiring of God that they also may be so happy and prosperous as to go on pilgrimage to Mecca. The reason of their putting such an high value upon the water of this well, is because (as they say) it is the place where Ishmael was laid by his mother Hagar. I have heard them tell the story exactly as it is recorded in the 21st chapter of Genesis ; and they say, that in the very place where the child paddled with his feet, the water flowed out.

"I shall now inform you how, when, and where, they receive the honourable title of Hagges, for which they are at all this pains and expence.

"The Curbaen Byram, or the Feast of Sacrifice, follows two months and ten days after the Ramadan fast. The eighth day after the said two months they all enter into Hirrawem, *i.e.* put on their mortifying habit again, and in that manner go to a certain hill called Gibbel el Orphat (El Arafat), *i.e.* the Mountain of Knowledge ; for

waters of Meccah are bitter; but I never found them so, but as sweet and as good as any others, for aught as I could perceive.

Pitts has just remarked that he found the waters of Zemzem brackish. To my taste it was a salt-bitter, which was exceedingly disagreeable. (R. F. B.)

there, they say, Adam first found and knew his wife Eve. And they likewise say, that she was buried at Gidda near the Red Sea ; at whose sepulchre all the Hagges who come to Mecca by way of the Red Sea, perform two Erkaets-nomas, and, I think, no more. I could not but smile to hear this their ridiculous tradition (for so I must pronounce it), when observing the marks which were set, the one at the head, and the other at the foot of the grave : I guessed them to be a bow-shot distant from each other. On the middle of her supposed grave is a little Mosque built, where the Hagges pay their religious respect.

" This Gibbel or hill is not so big as to contain the vast multitudes which resort thither ; for it is said by them, that there meet no less than 70,000 souls every year, in the ninth day after the two months after Ramadan; and if it happen that in any year there be wanting some of that number, God, they say, will supply the deficiency by so many angels.[1]

" I do confess the number of Hagges I saw at this mountain was very great ; nevertheless, I cannot think they could amount to so many as 70,000. There are certain bound-stones placed round the Gibbel, in the plain, to shew how far the sacred ground (as they esteem it) extends; and many are so zealous as to come and pitch their tents within these bounds, some time before the hour of paying their devotion here comes, waiting for it. But why they so solemnly approach this mountain beyond any other place, and receive from hence the title of Hagges, I confess I do not more fully understand than what I have already said, giving but little heed to these delusions. I observed nothing worth seeing on this hill, for there was only a small cupola on the top of it[2];

---

[1] They are not so modest. 600,000 is the mystical number ; others declare it to be incalculable. Oftentimes 70,000 have met at Arafat.

[2] The cupola has now disappeared ; there is a tall pillar of masonry-work, whitewashed, rising from a plastered floor, for praying.

neither are there any inhabitants nearer to it than
Mecca. About one or two of the clock, which is the
time of Eulea-nomas, having washed and made themselves
ready for it, they perform that, and at the same time
perform Ekinde-nomas, which they never do at one time,
but upon this occasion ; because at the time when Ekinde-
nomas should be performed in the accustomed order, viz.
about four of the clock in the afternoon, they are
imploring pardon for their sins, and receiving the
Emaum's benediction.[1]

"It was a sight indeed, able to pierce one's heart, to
behold so many thousands in their garments of humility
and mortification, with their naked heads, and cheeks
watered with tears ; and to hear their grievous sighs and
sobs, begging earnestly for the remission of their sins,
promising newness of life, using a form of penitential
expressions, and thus continuing for the space of four or
five hours, viz. until the time of Acsham-nomas, which is
to be performed about half an hour after sunset. (It is
matter of sorrowful reflection, to compare the indifference
of many Christians with this zeal of these poor blind
Mahometans, who will, it is to be feared, rise up in
judgment against them and condemn them.) After their
solemn performance of their devotions thus at the Gibbel,
they all at once receive that honourable title of Hagge
from the Emaum, and are so stiled to their dying day.
Immediately upon their receiving this name, the trumpet
is sounded, and they all leave the hill and return for
Mecca, and being gone two or three miles on their way.
they then rest for that night[2]; but after nomas, before

---

1 On the 9th Zu'l Hijjah, or the Day of Arafat, the pilgrims,
having taken their stations within the sacred limits, perform ablution
about noon, and pray as directed at that hour. At three P.M., after
again performing the usual devotions, or more frequently after
neglecting them, they repair to the hill, and hear the sermon.

2 At Muzdalifah.

they go to rest, each person gathers nine-and-forty small stones about the bigness of an hazle nut; the meaning of which I shall acquaint you with presently.

"The next morning they move to a place called Mina, or Muna; the place, as they say, where Abraham went to offer up his son Isaac,[1] and therefore in this place they sacrifice their sheep. It is about two or three miles from Mecca. I was here shown a stone, or little rock, which was parted in the middle. They told me, that when Abraham was going to sacrifice his son, instead of striking him, Providence directed his hand to this stone, which he clave in two. It must be a good stroke indeed!

"Here they all pitch their tents (it being in a spacious plain), and spend the time of Curbaen Byram, viz. three days. As soon as their tents are pitched, and all things orderly disposed, every individual Hagge, the first day, goes and throws seven of the small stones, which they had gathered, against a small pillar, or little square stone building.[2] Which action of theirs is intended to testify their defiance of the devil and his deeds; for they at the same time pronounce the following words, viz. Erzum le Shetane wazbehe[3]; *i.e.* stone the devil, and them that please him.[4] And there are two other of the like pillars, which are situated near one another; at each of which

---

1 This, I need scarcely say, is speaking as a Christian. All Moslems believe that Ishmael, and not Isaac, was ordered to be sacrificed. The place to which Pitts alludes is still shown to pilgrims.

2 (Pitts' Note.) Monsieur de Thevenot saith, that they throw these stones at the Gibbel or Mount; but, indeed, it is otherwise; though I must needs say, he is very exact in almost every thing of Turkish matters; and I pay much deference to that great author.

3 The Rami or Jaculator now usually says, as he casts each stone, "In the name of Allah, and Allah is omnipotent (Raghman li'sh' Shaytani wa Khizyatih), in token of abhorrence to Satan, and for his ignominy (I do this)."

4 The Arabic would mean stone the devil and slay him, unless "wazbehe" be an error for "wa ashabih,"—"and his companions."

(I mean all three), the second day, they throw seven stones; and the same they do the third day. As I was going to perform this ceremony of throwing the stones, a facetious Hagge met me; saith he, 'You may save your labour at present, if you please, for I have hit out the devil's eyes already.' You must observe, that after they have thrown the seven stones on the first day (the country people having brought great flocks of sheep to be sold), every one buys a sheep and sacrifices it; some of which they give to their friends, some to the poor which come out of Mecca and the country adjacent, very ragged poor, and the rest they eat themselves; after which they shave their heads, throw off Hirrawem, and put on other clothes, and then salute one another with a kiss, saying, 'Byram Mabarick Ela,' *i.e.* the feast be a blessing to you.

"These three days of Byram they spend festivally, rejoicing with abundance of illuminations all night, shooting of guns, and fireworks flying in the air; for they reckon that all their sins are now done away, and they shall, when they die, go directly to heaven, if they don't apostatize; and that for the future, if they keep their vow and do well, God will set down for every good action ten; but if they do ill, God will likewise reckon every evil action ten: and any person, who, after having received the title of Hagge, shall fall back to a vicious course of life, is esteemed to be very vile and infamous by them.[1]

"Some have written, that many of the Hagges, after they have returned home, have been so austere to themselves as to pore a long time over red-hot bricks, or ingots of iron, and by that means willingly lose their sight, desiring to see nothing evil or profane, after so sacred a sight as the temple at Mecca; but I never knew any such thing done.

---

[1] Even in the present day, men who have led "wild" lives in their youth, often date their reformation from the first pilgrimage.

"During their three days' stay at Mina, scarce any Hagge (unless impotent) but thinks it his duty to pay his visit, once at least, to the temple at Mecca. They scarce cease running all the way thitherward, shewing their vehement desire to have a fresh sight of the Beat-Allah ; which as soon as ever they come in sight of, they burst into tears for joy ; and after having performed Towoaf for a while, and a few Erkaets, they return again to Mina. And when the three days of Byram are expired, they all, with their tents, &c., come back again to Mecca.

"They say, that after the Hagges are gone from Mina to Mecca, God doth usually send a good shower of rain to wash away the filth and dung of the sacrifices there slain ; and also that those vast numbers of little stones, which I told you the Hagges throw in defiance of the devil, are all carried away by the angels before the year comes about again. But I am sure I saw vast numbers of them that were thrown the year before, lie upon the ground. After they are returned to Mecca, they can tarry there no longer than the stated time, which is about ten or twelve days; during which time there is a great fair held, where are sold all manner of East India goods, and abundance of fine stones for rings and bracelets, &c., brought from Yeamane[1]; also of China-ware and musk, and variety of other curiosities. Now is the time in which the Hagges are busily employed in buying, for they do not think it lawful to buy any thing till they have received the title of Hagge. Every one almost now buys a caffin, or shroud of fine linen, to be buried in (for they never use coffins for that purpose), which might have been procured at Algier, or their other respective homes, at a much cheaper rate; but they choose to buy it here, because they have the advantage of dipping it in the holy water, Zem Zem. They are very careful to carry the said

---

1 Al-Yaman, Southern Arabia, whose "Akik," or cornelians were celebrated.

caffin with them wherever they travel, whether by sea or land, that they may be sure to be buried therein.

"The evening before they leave Mecca, every one must go to take their solemn leave of the Beat, entering at the gate called Babe el Salem, *i.e.* Welcome Gate, and having continued at Towoaf as long as they please, which many do till they are quite tired, and it being the last time of their paying their devotions to it, they do it with floods of tears, as being extremely unwilling to part and bid farewell; and having drank their fill of the water Zem Zem, they go to one side of the Beat, their backs being towards the door called by the name of Babe el Weedoh *i.e.*, the Farewell Door, which is opposite to the welcome door; where, having performed two or three Erkaets, they get upon their legs and hold up their hands towards the Beat, making earnest petitions ; and then keep going backward till they come to the above said farewell gate, being guided by some other, for they account it a very irreverent thing to turn their backs towards the Beat when they take leave of it. All the way as they retreat they continue petitioning, holding up their hands, with their eyes fixed upon the Beat, till they are out of sight of it ; and so go to their lodgings weeping.

"Ere I leave Mecca, I shall acquaint you with a passage of a Turk to me in the temple cloyster, in the night time, between Acsham-nomas, and Gega-nomas, *i.e.*, between the evening and the night services. The Hagges do usually spend that time, or good part of it (which is about an hour and half), at Towoaf, and then sit down on the mats and rest themselves. This I did, and after I had sat a while, and for my more ease at last was lying on my back, with my feet towards the Beat, but at a distance as many others did, a Turk which sat by me, asked me what countryman I was ; 'A Mogrebee' (said I), *i.e.* one of the West. 'Pray,' quoth he, 'how far west did you come ?' I told him from Gazair, *i.e.* Algier. 'Ah!' replied he, 'have you taken so much pains, and been at so much cost, and now be guilty of this irreverent posture before the Beat Allah ?'

" Here are many Moors, who get a beggarly live-lihood by selling models of the temple unto strangers, and in being serviceable to the Pilgrims. Here are also several Effendies, or masters of learning, who daily expound out of the Alcoran, sitting in high chairs, and some of the learned Pilgrims, whilst they are here, do undertake the same.

" Under the room of the Hanifees (which I mentioned before), people do usually gather together (between the hours of devotion), and sitting round cross-legged, it may be, twenty or thirty of them, they have a very large pair of Tessbeehs, or beads, each bead near as big as a man's fist, which they keep passing round, bead after bead, one to the other, all the time, using some devout expressions. I myself was once got in amongst them, and methought it was a pretty play enough for children,—however, I was to appearance very devout.

" There   are   likewise   some   dervises   that   get money here, as well as at other places, by burning of incense, swinging their censers as they go along before the people that are sitting ; as this they do commonly on Friday, their Sabbath. In all other Gamiler or Mosques, when the Hattib is preaching, and the people all sitting still at their devotion, they are all in ranks, so that the dervise, without the least disturbance to any, walks between every rank, with his censer in one hand, and with the other takes his powdered incense out of a little pouch that hangs by his side.[1]

" But though this place, Mecca, is esteemed so very holy, yet it comes short of none for lewdness and debauchery. As for uncleanness, it is equal to Grand Cairo ; and they will steal even in the temple itself.

---

1 This is still practised in Moslem countries, being considered a decent way of begging during public prayers, without interrupting them.

"CHAPTER VIII.— *Of the Pilgrims' return from Mecca: their visit made at Medina to Mahomet's tomb there.*

"Having thus given you an account of the Turks' pilgrimage to Mecca, and of their worship there (the manner and circumstances of which I have faithfully and punctually related, and may challenge the world to convict me of a known falsehood), I now come to take leave of the temple and town of Mecca.

"Having hired camels of the carriers, we set out, but we give as much for the hire of one from Mecca to Egypt, which is about forty days' journey, as the real worth of it is, (viz.) about five or six pounds sterling. If it happen that the camel dies by the way, the carrier is to supply us with another; and therefore, those carriers[1] who come from Egypt to Mecca with the Caravan, bring with them several spare camels; for there is hardly a night passeth but many die upon the road, for if a camel should chance to fall, it is seldom known that it is able to rise again; and if it should, they despair of its being capable of performing the journey, or ever being useful more. It is a common thing, therefore, when a camel once falls, to take off its burden and put it on another, and then kill it; which the poorer sort of the company eat. I myself have eaten of camel's flesh, and it is very sweet and nourishing. If a camel tires, they even leave him upon the place.

"The first day we set out from Mecca, it was without any order at all, all hurly burly; but the next day every one laboured to get forward; and in order to it, there was many time much quarrelling and fighting. But after every one had taken his place in the Caravan, they orderly and peaceably kept the same place till they came to Grand Cairo. They travel four camels in a breast,

[1] These people will contract to board the pilgrim, and to provide him with a tent, as well as to convey his luggage.

which are all tied one after the other, like as in teams.[1]
The whole body is called a Caravan, which is divided
into several cottors, or companies, each of which hath
its name, and consists, it may be, of several thousand
camels; and they move one cottor after another, like
distinct troops.   In the head of each cottor is some great
gentleman or officer, who is carried in a thing like a
horse-litter, borne by two camels, one before and the
other behind, which is covered all over with sear-cloth,
and over that again with green broad cloth, and set forth
very handsomely.   If the said great person hath a wife
with him, she is carried in another of the same.[2]   In the
head of every cottor there goes, likewise, a sumpter camel
which carries his treasures, &c.   This camel hath two
bells, about the bigness of our market-bells, having one
on each side, the sound of which may be heard a great
way off.   Some other of the camels have round bells
about their necks, some about their legs, like those which
our carriers put about their fore-horses' necks; which
together with the servants (who belong to the camels,
and travel on foot) singing all night, make a pleasant
noise, and the journey passes away delightfully.   They
say this musick make the camels brisk and lively.   Thus
they travel, in good order every day, till they come to
Grand Cairo; and were it not for this order, you may guess
what confusion would be amongst such a vast multitude.

    " They have lights by night (which is the chief time
of travelling, because of the exceeding heat of the sun by
day), which are carried on the tops of high poles, to direct
the Hagges on their march.[3]   They are somewhat like

---

    1 The usual way now is in " Kitar," or in Indian file, each camel's
halter being tied to the tail of the beast that precedes him.   Pitts'
"cottor" must be a kitar, but he uses the word in another of its
numerous senses.

    2 This vehicle is the " Takht-rawan " of Arabia.

    3 He describes the Mashals still in use.   Lane has sketched
them, Mod. Egypt. chap. vi.

iron stoves, into which they put short dry wood, which
some of the camels are loaded with ; it is carried in great
sacks, which have an hole near the bottom, where the
servants take it out, as they see the fires need a recruit.
Every cottor hath one of these poles belonging to it,
some of which have ten, some twelve, of these lights on
their tops, or more or less; and they are likewise of
different figures as well as numbers; one, perhaps, oval
way, like a gate; another triangular, or like an N or M,
&c., so that every one knows by them his respective
cottor. They are carried in the front, and set up in the
place where the Caravan is to pitch, before that comes
up, at some distance from one another. They are also
carried by day, not lighted, but yet by the figure and
number of them, the Hagges are directed to what cottor
they belong, as soldiers are, by their colours, where to
rendezvous ; and without such directions it would be
impossible to avoid confusion in such a vast number of
people.

"Every day, viz. in the morning, they pitch their
tents, and rest several hours. When the camels are
unloaded the owners drive them to water, and give them
their provender, &c. So that we had nothing to do with
them, besides helping to load them.

"As soon as our tents were pitched, my business
was to make a little fire and get a pot of coffee. When
we had ate some small matter and drank the coffee, we
lay down to sleep. Between eleven and twelve we boiled
something for dinner, and having dined, lay down again,
till about four in the afternoon; when the trumpet was
sounded which gave notice to every one to take down
their tents, pack up their things, and load their camels
in order to proceed on their journey. It takes up about
two hours time ere they are in all their places again.
At the time of Acsham-nomas, and also Gega-nomas,
they make a halt, and perform their Sallah (so punctual

are they in their worship), and then they travel till next morning. If water be scarce, what I call an imaginary Abdes¹ will do. As for ancient men, it being very troublesome for such to alight off the camels, and get up again, it is lawful for them to defer these two times of nomas till the next day; but they will be sure to perform it then.

"As for provisions, we bring enough out of Egypt to suffice us till we return thither again. At Mecca we compute how much will serve us for one day, and consequently, for the forty days' journey to Egypt, and if we find we have more than we may well guess will suffice us for a long time, we sell the overplus at Mecca. There is a charity maintained by the Grand Seignior, for water to refresh the poor who travel on foot all the way; for there are many such undertake this journey (or pilgrimage) without any money, relying on the charity of the Hagges for subsistence, knowing that they largely extend it at such a time.

" Every Hagge carries his provisions, water, bedding, &c., with him, and usually three or four diet together, and sometimes discharge a poor man's expenses the whole journey for his attendance on them. There was an Irish renegade, who was taken very young, insomuch that he had not only lost his Christian religion, but his native language also. This man had endured thirty years slavery in Spain, and in the French gallies, but was afterwards redeemed and came home to Algier. He was looked upon as a very pious man, and a great Zealot, by the Turks, for his not turning from the Mahommedan faith, notwithstanding the great temptations he had so to do. Some of my neighbours who intended for Mecca, the same year I went with my patroon thither, offered

---

1 Pitts means by "imaginary Abdes," the sand ablution,—lawful when water is wanted for sustaining life.

this renegado that if he would serve them on this journey they would defray his charges throughout. He gladly embraced the offer, and I remember when we arrived at Mecca he passionately told me, that God had delivered him out of hell upon earth (meaning his former slavery in France and Spain), and had brought him into a heaven upon earth, viz. Mecca. I admired much his zeal, but pitied his condition.

" Their water they carry in goats' skins, which they fasten to one side of their camels. It sometimes happens that no water is to be met with for two, three, or more days; but yet it is well known that a camel is a creature that can live long without drinking (God in his wise providence so ordering it : for otherwise it would be very difficult, if not impossible to travel through the parched deserts of Arabia).

" In this journey many times the skulking, thievish, Arabs do much mischief to some of the Hagges ; for in the night time they will steal upon them (especially such as are on the outside of the Caravan), and being taken to be some of the servants that belong to the carriers, or owners of the camels, they are not suspected. When they see an Hagge fast asleep (for it is usual for them to sleep on the road), they loose a camel before and behind, and one of the thieves leads it away with the Hagge upon its back asleep. Another of them in the meanwhile, pulls on the next camel to tie it to the camel from whence the halter of the other was cut ; for if that camel be not fastened again to the leading camel, it will stop, and all that are behind will then stop of course, which might be the means of discovering the robbers. When they have gotten the stolen camel, with his rider, at a convenient distance from the Caravan, and think themselves out of danger, they awake the Hagge, and sometimes destroy him immediately ; but at other times, being a little more inclined to mercy, they strip him naked, and let him return to the Caravan.[1]

" About the tenth easy day's journey, after we come out of Mecca, we enter into Medina, the place where Mahomet lies entombed. Although it be (as I take it) two or three days' journey out of the direct way from Mecca to Egypt, yet the Hagges pay their visit there for the space of two days, and come away the third.

" Those Mahometans which live to the southward of Mecca, at the East Indies, and thereaway, are not bound to make a visit to Medina, but to Mecca only, because it would be so much out of their way. But such as come from Turkey, Tartary, Egypt, and Africa, think themselves obliged to do so.

" Medina is but a little town, and poor, yet it is walled round,[2] and hath in it a great Mosque, but nothing near so big as the temple at Mecca. In one corner of the Mosque is a place, built about fourteen or fifteen paces square. About this place are great windows,[3] fenced with brass grates. In the inside it is decked with some lamps, and ornaments. It is arched all over head. (I find some relate, that there are no less than 3000 lamps about Mahomet's tomb ; but it is a mistake, for there are not, as I verily believe, an hundred ; and I speak what I know, and have been an eye-witness of). In the middle of this place is the tomb of Mahomet, where the corpse of that bloody impostor is laid, which hath silk curtains all around it like a bed ; which curtains are not costly nor beautiful. There is nothing of his tomb to be seen by any, by reason

1 As I shall explain at a future time, there are still some Hijazi Badawin whose young men, before entering life, risk everything in order to plunder a Haji. They care little for the value of the article stolen, the exploit consists in stealing it.

2 The walls, therefore, were built between A.D. 1503 and A.D. 1680.

3 These are not windows, but simply the inter-columnar spaces filled with grating.

of the curtains round it, nor are any of the Hagges permitted to enter there.[1] None go in but the Eunuchs, who
keep watch over it, and they only light the lamps, which
burn there by night, and to sweep and cleanse the place.
All the privilege the Hagges have, is only to thrust in
their hands at the windows,[2] between the brass grates,
and to petition the dead juggler, which they do with a
wonderful deal of reverence, affection, and zeal. My
patroon had his silk handkerchief stole out of his bosom,
while he stood at his devotion here.

" It is storied by some, that the coffin of Mahomet
hangs up by the attractive virtue of a loadstone to the
roof of the Mosque ; but believe me it is a false story.
When I looked through the brass gate, I saw as much as
any of the Hagges; and the top of the curtains, which
covered the tomb, were not half so high as the roof or
arch; so that it is impossible his coffin should be hanging
there. I never heard the Mahometans say anything like
it. On the outside of this place, where Mahomet's tomb
is, are some sepulchres of their reputed saints ; among
which is one prepared for Jesus Christ, when he shall
come again personally into the world ; for they hold that
Christ will come again in the flesh, forty years before the
end of the world, to confirm the Mahometan faith, and
say likewise, that our Saviour was not crucified in person,
but in effigy, or one like him.

" Medina is much supplied by the opposite Abyssine
country, which is on the other side of the Red Sea : from
thence they have corn and necessaries brought in ships :
an odd sort of vessels as ever I saw, their sails being
made of matting, such as they use in the houses and
Mosques to tread upon.

---

1 This account is perfectly correct. The Eunuchs, however, do
not go into the tomb ; they only light the lamps in, and sweep the
passage round, the Sepulchre.

2 These are the small apertures in the Southern grating. See
Chap. xvi.

" When we had taken our leave of Medina, the third
day, and travelled about ten days more, we were met by
a great many Arabians, who brought abundance of fruit
to us, particularly raisins ; but from whence I cannot
tell.[1] When we came within fifteen days' journey of
Grand Cairo, we were met by many people who came
from thence, with their camels laden with presents for the
Hagges, sent from their friends and relations, as sweetmeats, &c. But some of them came rather for profit, to
sell fresh provisions to the Hagges, and trade with them.

" About ten days before we got to Cairo, we came to
a very long steep hill, called Ackaba, which the Hagges
are usually much afraid how they shall be able to get up.
Those who can will walk it. The poor camels, having no
hoofs, find it very hard work, and many drop here. They
were all untied, and we dealt gently with them, moving
very slowly, and often halting. Before we came to this
hill, I observed no descent, and when we were at the top
there was none, but all plain as before.

" We past by Mount Sinai by night, and, perhaps,
when I was asleep ; so that I had no prospect of it.

" When we came within seven days' journey of Cairo,
we were met by abundance of people more, some
hundreds, who came to welcome their friends and relations ; but it being night, it was difficult to find those
they wanted, and, therefore, as the Caravans past along
they kept calling them aloud by their names, and by this
means found them out. And when we were in three days'
journey of it, we had many camel-loads of the water of
the Nile brought us to drink. But the day and night
before we came to Cairo, thousands came out to meet us
with extraordinary rejoicing. It is thirty-seven days'
journey from Mecca to Cairo, and three days we tarry by

---

[1] The Caravan must have been near the harbour of Muwaylah,
where supplies are abundant.

the way, which together make us (as I said) forty days' journey ; and in all this way there is scarce any green thing to be met with, nor beast nor fowl to be seen or heard ; nothing but sand and stones, excepting one place which we passed through by night ; I suppose it was a village, where were some trees, and, we thought, gardens."

APPENDIX VI.

Giovanni Finati.

The third pilgrim on our list is Giovanni Finati, who, under the Moslem name of " Haji Mohammed," made the campaign against the Wahhabis for the recovery of Meccah and Al-Madinah. A native of Ferrara, the eldest of the four scions of a small landed proprietor, " tenderly attached to his mother," and brought up most unwillingly for a holy vocation,—to use his own words, " instructed in all that course of frivolous and empty ceremonials and mysteries, which form a principal feature in the training of a priest for the Romish Church," in A.D. 1805, Giovanni Finati's name appeared in the list of Italian conscripts. After a few vain struggles with fate, he was marched to Milan, drilled and trained ; the next year his division was ordered to the Tyrol, where the young man, " brought up for the church," instantly deserted. Discovered in his native town, he was sent under circumstances of suitable indignity to join his regiment at Venice, where a general act of grace, promulgated on occasion of Napoleon's short visit, preserved him from a platoon of infantry. His next move was to Spalato, in Dalmatia, where he marched under General Marmont to Cattaro, the last retreat of the hardy and warlike Montenegrins. At Budoa, a sea-port S.E. of Ragusa, having consulted an Albanian " captain-merchant," Giovanni Finati, and fifteen other Italians—

" including the sergeant's wife," swore fidelity to one
another, and deserted with all their arms and accoutre-
ments. They passed into the Albanese territory, and
were hospitably treated as " soldiers, who had deserted
from the infidel army in Dalmatia," by the Pasha, posted
at Antivari to keep check upon the French operations.
At first they were lodged in the Mosque, and the sergeant's wife had been set apart from the rest ; but as
they refused to apostatize they were made common
slaves, and worked at the quarries till their " backs were
sore." Under these circumstances, the sergeant discovering and promulgating his discovery that " the
Mahometans believe as we do in a god ; and upon
examination that we might find the differences from our
mother church to be less than we had imagined,"—all at
once came the determination of *professing* to be Mohammedans. Our Italian Candide took the name of Mahomet,
and became pipe-bearer to a Turkish general officer in
the garrison. This young man trusted the deserter to
such an extent that the doors of the Harim were open
to him, and Giovanni Finati repaid his kindness by
seducing Fatimah, a Georgian girl, his master's favourite
wife. The garrison then removed to Scutari. Being of
course hated by his fellow servants, the renegade at last
fell into disgrace, and exchanging the pipe-stick for the
hatchet, he became a hewer of wood. This degradation
did not diminish poor Fatimah's affection : she continued
to visit him, and to leave little presents and tokens for
him in his room. But presently the girl proved likely
to become a mother,—their intercourse was more than
suspected,—Giovanni Finati had a dread of circumcision,[2]

---

1 He describes the Harim as containing " the females of different
countries, all of them young, and all more or less attractive, and the
merriest creatures I ever saw." His narration proves that affection
and fidelity were not wanting there.

1 Mr. Bankes, Finati's employer and translator, here comments
upon Ali Bey's assertion, " Even to travellers in Mahometan coun-

so he came to the felon resolution of flying alone from
Scutari.   He happened to meet his "original friend the
captain-merchant," and in March, 1809, obtained from
him a passage to Egypt, the Al-Dorado to which all
poverty-struck Albanian adventurers were then flocking.
At Alexandra the new Mahomet, after twice deserting
from a Christian service, at the risk of life and honour,
voluntarily enlisted as an Albanian private soldier in a
Moslem land ; the *naïveté* with which he admires and
comments upon his conduct is a curious moral phenomenon.   Thence he proceeded to Cairo, and became a
" Balik bash " (corporal), in charge of six Albanian pri-
vates, of Mohammed Ali's body-guard.   Ensued a campaign against the Mamluks in Upper Egypt, and his
being present at the massacre of those miscreants in the
citadel of Cairo,—he confined his part in the affair to
plundering from the Beys a " saddle richly mounted in
silver gilt," and a slave girl with trinkets and money.
He married the captive, and was stationed for six months
at Matariyah (Heliopolis), with the force preparing to
march upon Meccah, under Tussun Pasha.   Here he
suffered from thieves, and shot by mistake his Bim Bashi
or sergeant, who was engaged in the unwonted and dangerous exercise of prayer in the dark.   The affair was
compromised by the amiable young commander-in-chief,
who paid the blood money amounting to some thousand
piastres.   On the 6th October, 1811, the army started
for Suez, where eighteen vessels waited to convey them
to Yambu'.   Mahomet assisted at ths capture of that
port, and was fortunate enough to escape alive from the
desperate action of Jadaydah.[1]   Rheumatism obliged him

tries, I look upon the safety of their journey as almost impossible, unless they have previously submitted to the rite."   Ali Bey is correct ;
the danger is doubled by non-compliance with the custom.   Mr.
Bankes apprehends that " very few renegadoes do submit to it."   In
bigoted Moslem countries, it is considered a *sine quâ non.*

  1 See Chap. xiii. of this work.

to return to Cairo, where he began by divorcing his wife for great levity of conduct. In the early part of 1814, Mahomet, inspired by the news of Mohammed Ali Pasha's success in Al-Hijaz, joined a reinforcement of Albanians, travelled to Suez, touched at Yambu' and at Jeddah, assisted at the siege and capture of Kunfudah, and was present at its recapture by the Wahhabis. Wounded, sick, harassed by the Badawin, and disgusted by his commanding officer, he determined to desert again, adding, as an excuse, " not that the step, on my part at least, had the character of a complete desertion, since I intended to join the main body of the army ; " and to his mania for desertion we owe the following particulars concerning the city of Meccah.

" Exulting in my escape, my mind was in a state to receive very strong impressions, and I was much struck with all I saw upon entering the city ; for though it is neither large nor beautiful in itself, there is something in it that is calculated to impress a sort of awe, and it was the hour of noon when everything is very silent, except the Muezzins calling from the minarets.

  ✻   ✻   ✻   ✻   ✻   ✻

" The principal feature of the city is that celebrated sacred enclosure which is placed about the centre of it ; it is a vast paved court with doorways opening into it from every side, and with a covered colonnade carried all round like a cloister, while in the midst of the open space stands the edifice called the Caaba, whose walls are entirely covered over on the outside with hangings of rich velvet,[1] on which there are Arabic inscriptions embroidered in gold.

" Facing one of its angles (for this little edifice is of

---

[1] " Black cloth, according to Ali Bey ; and I believe he is correct." So Mr. Bankes. If Ali Bey meant broad-cloth, both are in error, as the specimen in my possession—a mixture of silk and cotton —proves.

a square form),[1] there is a well which is called the well
Zemzem, of which the water is considered so peculiarly
holy that some of it is even sent annually to the Sultan
at Constantinople ; and no person who comes to Meccah,
whether on pilgrimage or for mere worldly considerations,
ever fails both to drink of it and to use it in his ablutions,
since it is supposed to wipe out the stain of all past
transgressions.

" There is a stone also near the bottom of the building itself which all the visitants kiss as they pass round
it, and the multitude of them has been so prodigious as
to have worn the surface quite away.

" Quite detached, but fronting to the Caaba, stand
four pavilions (corresponding to the four sects of the
Mahometan religion), adapted for the pilgrims ; and
though the concourse had of late years been from time to
time much interrupted, there arrived just when I came to
Meccah two Caravans of them, one Asiatic and one from
the African side, amounting to not less than about 40,000
persons, who all seemed to be full of reverence towards
the holy place.[2] "

After commenting on the crowded state of the city,
the lodging of pilgrims in tents and huts, or on the bare
ground outside the walls,[3] and the extravagant prices of
provisions, Haji Mahomet proceeds with his description.

" Over and above the general ceremonies of the
purification at the well, and of the kissing of the corner-

---

1 Ali Bey showed by his measurements that no two sides correspond exactly.   To all appearance the sides are equal, though it is
certain they are not ; the height exceeds the length and the breadth.

2 Ali Bey (A.D. 1807) computes 80,000 men, 2,000 women, and
1,000 children at Arafat.   Burckhardt (A.D. 1814) calculated it at
70,000.   I do not think that in all there were more than 50,000 souls
assembled together in 1853.

3 Rich pilgrims always secure lodgings ; the poorer class cannot
afford them ; therefore, the great Caravans from Egypt, Damascus,
Baghdad, and other places, pitch on certain spots outside the city.

stone,[1] and of the walking round the Caaba a certain number of times in a devout manner, every one has also his own separate prayers to put up, and so to fulfil the conditions of his vow and the objects of his particular pilgrimage."

We have then an account of the Mosque-pigeons, for whom it is said, " some pilgrims bring with them even from the most remote countries a small quantity of grain, with which they may take the opportunity of feeding these birds." This may have occurred in times of scarcity; the grain is now sold in the Mosque.

" The superstitions and ceremonies of the place," we are told, " are by no means completed within the city, for the pilgrims, after having performed their devotions for a certain time at the Caaba, at last in a sort of procession go to a place called Arafat, an eminence which stands detached in the centre of a valley; and in the way thither there is a part of the road for about the space of a mile where it is customary to run.[2] The road also passes near a spot where was formerly a well which is superstitiously supposed to be something unholy and cursed by the Prophet himself. And for this reason, every pilgrim as he goes by it throws a stone ; and the custom is so universal and has prevailed so long that none can be picked up in the neighbourhood, and it is necessary therefore to provide them from a distance, and some persons even bring them out of their own remote countries, thinking thereby to gain the greater favour in the sight of Heaven.[3]

---

1 An incorrect expression ; the stone is fixed in a massive gold or silver gilt circle to the S.E. angle, but it is not part of the building.

2 Ali Bey is correct in stating that the running is on the return from Arafat, directly after sunset.

3 This sentence abounds in blunders. Sale, Ali Bey, and Burckhardt, all give correct accounts of the little pillar of masonry—it has nothing to do with the well—which denotes the place where Satan appeared to Abraham. The pilgrims do not throw one stone, but

" Beyond this point stands a column,[1] which is set up as the extreme limit of the pilgrimage, and this every pilgrim must have passed before sunrise ; while all such as have not gone beyond it by that time must wait till the next year, if they wish to be entitled to the consideration and privileges of complete Hajis, since, without this circumstance, all the rest remains imperfect.

" The hill of Arafat lying at a distance of seven hours from Meccah, it is necessary to set out very early in order to be there in time ; many of the pilgrims, and especially the more devout amongst them, performing all the way on foot.

" When they have reached the place[2] all who have any money according to their means sacrifice a sheep, and the rich often furnish those who are poor and destitute with the means of buying one.

" Such a quantity of sacrifices quite fills the whole open space with victims, and the poor flock from all the country round to have meat distributed to them.

" After which, at the conclusion of the whole ceremony, all the names are registered by a scribe appointed for the purpose[3]: and when this is finished the African

---

many.   The pebbles are partly brought from Muzdalifah, partly from the valley of Muna, in which stands the pillar.

1 Mr. Bankes confounds this column with the Devil's Pillar at Muna.   Finati alludes to the landmarks of the Arafat plain, now called Al-Alamayn (the two marks).   The pilgrims must stand within these boundaries on a certain day (the 9th of Zu'l Hijjah), otherwise he has failed to observe a rital ordinance.

2 He appears to confound the proper place with Arafat.   The sacrifice is performed in the valley of Muna, after leaving the mountain.   But Finati, we are told by his translator, wrote from memory —a pernicious practice for a traveller.

3 This custom is now obsolete, as regards the grand body of pilgrims.   Anciently, a certificate from the Sharif was given to all who could afford money for a proof of having performed the pilgrimage, but no such practice at present exists.   My friends have frequently asked me, what proof there is of a Moslem's having become

and Asiatic Caravans part company and return to their own several countries, many detachments of the pilgrims visiting Medinah in the way."

Being desirous of enrolment in some new division of Mohammed Ali's army, Finati overcame the difficulty of personal access to him by getting a memorial written in Turkish and standing at the window of a house joined on to the enclosure of the great temple. After the sixth day the Pasha observed him, and in the " greatest rage imaginable " desired a detailed account of the defeat at Kunfudah. Finati then received five hundred piastres and an order to join a corps at Taif, together with a strict charge of secresy, " since it was of importance that no reverse or check should be generally talked of." Before starting our author adds some "singular particulars" which escaped him in his account of Meccah.

" Many of the pilgrims go through the ceremony of walking the entire circuit of the city upon the outside ; and the order in which this is performed is as follows. The devoted first goes without the gates, and, after pre-senting himself there to the religious officer who presides, throws off all his clothes, and takes a sort of large wrap-ping garment in lieu of them to cover himself ; upon which he sets off walking at a very quick pace, or rather running, to reach the nearest of the four corners of the city, a sort of guide going with him at the same rate all the way, who prompts certain ejaculations or prayers, which he ought to mention at particular spots as he passes ; at every angle he finds a barber, who with wonderful quickness wets and shaves one quarter of his head, and so on ; till he has reached the barber at the fourth angle, who completes the work. After which the

a Haji. None whatever ; consequently impostors abound. Sa'adi, in the Gulistán, notices a case. But the ceremonies of the Hajj are so complicated and unintelligible by mere description, that a little cross-questioning applied to the false Haji would easily detect him.

pilgrim takes his clothes again, and has finished that act of devotion.[1]

" There is also near the holy city an eminence called the hill of light,[2] as I imagine from its remarkable whiteness. Upon this the pilgrims have a custom of leaping while they repeat at the same time prayers and verses of the Koran. Many also resort to a lesser hill, about a mile distant from the city, on which there is a small Mosque, which is reputed as a place of great sanctity.

" An annual ceremony takes place in the great temple itself which is worth mentioning before I quit the subject altogether.

" I have already spoken of the little square building whose walls are covered with hangings of black and gold, and which is called the Caaba. Once in the year,[3] and once only, this holy of holies is opened, and as there is nothing to prevent admission it appears surprising at first to see so few who are willing to go into the interior, and especially since this act is supposed to have great efficacy in the remission of all past sins. But the reason must be sought for in the conditions which are annexed, since he who enters is, in the first place, bound to exercise no gainful pursuit, or trade, or to work for his liveli-

---

1 No wonder Mr. Bankes is somewhat puzzled by this passage. Certainly none but a pilgrim could guess that the author refers to the rites called Al-Umrah and Al-Sai, or the running between Mounts Safa and Marwah. The curious reader may compare the above with Burckhardt's correct description of the ceremonies. As regards the shaving, Finati possibly was right in his day ; in Ali Bey's, as in my time, the head was only shaved once, and a few strokes of the razor sufficed for the purpose of religious tonsure.

2 Jabal Nur, anciently Hira, is a dull grey as of granite ; it derives its modern name from the spiritual light of religion. Circumstances prevented my ascending it, so I cannot comment upon Finati's "custom of leaping."

3 Open three days in the year, according to Ali Bey, the same in Burckhardt's, and in my time. Besides these public occasions, private largesses can always turn the key.

hood in any way whatever ; and, next, he must submit patiently to all offences and injuries, and must never again touch anything that is impure or unholy.[1]"

*   *   *   *   *   *

" One more remark with reference to the great scene of sacrifice at Arafat. Though the Pasha's power in Arabia had been now for some time established, yet it was not complete or universal by any means—the Wahhabees still retaining upon many sides a very considerable footing, so that open and unprotected places, even within half a day's journey of Meccah, might be liable to surprise and violence."

For these reasons, our author informs us, a sufficient force was disposed round Arafat, and the prodigious multitude went and returned without molestation or insult.[2]

---

1 I heard from good authority, that the Ka'abah is never opened without several pilgrims being crushed to death. Ali Bey (remarks Mr. Bankes) says nothing of the supposed conditions annexed. In my next volume [Part iii. ("Meccah") of this work] I shall give them, as I received them from the lips of learned and respectable Moslems. They differ considerably from Finati's, and no wonder ; his account is completely opposed to the strong good sense which pervades the customs of Al-Islam. As regards his sneer at the monastic orders in Italy—that the conditions of entering are stricter and more binding than those of the Ka'abah, yet that numbers are ready to profess in them—it must not be imagined that Arab human nature differs very materially from Italian. Many unworthy feet pass the threshold of the Ka'abah ; but there are many Moslems, my friend, Omar Effendi, for instance, who have performed the pilgrimage a dozen times, and would never, from conscientious motives, enter the holy edifice.

2 In 1807, according to Ali Bey, the Wahhabis took the same precaution, says Mr. Bankes. The fact is, some such precautions must always be taken. The pilgrims are forbidden to quarrel, to fight, or to destroy life, except under circumstances duly provided for. Moreover, as I shall explain in another part of this work, it was of old, and still is, the custom of the fiercer kind of Badawin to flock to Arafat—where the victim is sure to be found—for the purpose of revenging their blood-losses. As our authorities at Aden well know, there cannot be a congregation of different Arab tribes without a

After the pilgrimage Haji Mahomet repaired to Taif. On the road he remarked a phenomenon observable in Al-Hijaz—the lightness of the nights there. Finati attributes it to the southern position of the place. But, observing a perceptible twilight there, I was forced to seek further cause. May not the absence of vegetation, and the heat-absorbing nature of the soil,—granite, quartz, and basalt,—account for the phenomenon [1]? The natives as usual, observing it, have invested its origin with the garb of fable.

It is not my intention to accompany Mahomet to the shameful defeat of Taraba, where Tussun Pasha lost three quarters of his army, or to the glorious victory of Bissel, where Mohammed Ali on the 10th January, 1815, broke 24,000 Wahhabis commanded by Faysal bin Sa'ud. His account of this interesting campaign is not full or accurate like Mengin's ; still, being the tale of an eye-witness, it attracts attention. Nothing can be more graphic than his picture of the old conqueror sitting with exulting countenance upon the carpet where he had vowed to await death or victory, and surrounded by heaps of enemies' heads.[2]

Still less would it be to the purpose to describe the latter details of Haji Mahomet's career, his return to Cairo, his accompanying Mr. Bankes to upper Egypt and Syria, and his various trips to Aleppo, Kurdistan, the

---

little murder. After fighting with the common foe, or if unable to fight with him, the wild men invariably turn their swords against their private enemies.

1 So, on the wild and tree-clad heights of the Neilgherry hills, despite the brilliance of the stars, every traveller remarks the darkness of the atmosphere at night.

2 Mohammed Ali gave six dollars for every Arab head, which fact accounts for the heaps that surrounded him. One would suppose that when acting against an eneny, so quick and agile as the Arabs, such an order would be an unwise one. Experience, however, proves the contrary.

Sa'id, the great Oasis, Nabathæa, Senna'ar, and Dongola. We concede to him the praise claimed by his translator, that he was a traveller to no ordinary extent; but beyond this we cannot go. He was so ignorant that he had forgotten to write[1]; his curiosity and his powers of observation keep pace with his knowledge[2]; his moral character as it appears in print is of that description which knows no sense of shame: it is not candour but sheer insensibility which makes him relate circumstantially his repeated desertions, his betrayal of Fatimah, and his various plunderings.

---

1 " Finati's long disuse of European writing," says Mr. Bankes, " made him very slow with his pen." Fortunately, he found in London some person who took down the story in easy, unaffected, and not inelegant Italian. In 1828, Mr. Bankes translated it into English, securing accuracy by consulting the author, when necessary.

2 His translator and editor is obliged to explain that he means Cufic, by " characters that are not now in use," and the statue of Memnon by " one of two enormous sitting figures in the plain, from which, according to an old story or superstition, a sound proceeds when the sun rises." When the crew of his Nile-boat " form in circle upon the bank, and perform a sort of religious mummery, shaking their heads and shoulders violently, and uttering a hoarse sobbing or barking noise, till some of them would drop or fall into convulsions,"—a sight likely to excite the curiosity of most men—he " takes his gun in pursuit of wild geese." He allowed Mr. Bankes' mare to eat Oleander leaves, and thus to die of the commonest poison. Briefly, he seems to have been a man who, under favourable circumstances, learned as little as possible.

APPENDIX VII.

NOTES ON MY JOURNEY.

By A. SPRENGER.

In the map to a former edition of the Pilgrimage, Captain Burton's route from Madîna to Meccah is wrongly laid down, owing to a typographical error of the text, "From Wady Laymun to Meccah S.E. 45°;" (see vol. ii. p. 155, ante), whereas the road runs S.W. 45°, or, as Hamdâny expresses himself in the commentary on the Qaçyda Rod., "Between west and south; and therefore the setting sun shines at the evening prayer (your face being turned towards Meccah) on your right temple." The account of the *eastern* route from Madîna to Meccah by so experienced a traveller as Captain Burton is an important contribution to our geographical knowledge of Arabia. It leads over the lower terrace of Nejd, the country which Muslim writers consider as the home of the genuine Arabs and the scene of Arabic chivalry. As by this mistake the results of my friend's pilgrimage, which, though pious as he unquestionably is, he did not undertake from purely religious motives, have been in a great measure marred, I called in 1871 his attention to it. At the same time I submitted to him a sketch of a map in which his own and Burckhardt's routes are protracted, and a few notes culled from Arabic geographers, with the intention of showing how much light his investigations throw on early

geography if illustrated by a corrected map; and how
they fail to fulfil this object if the mistake is not cleared
up.   The enterprising traveller approved of both the
notes and the map, and expressed it as his opinion that
it might be useful to append them to the new edition.   I
therefore thought proper to recast them, and to present
them herewith to the reader.

At Sufayna, Burton found the Baghdâd Caravan.
The regular Baghdâd-Meccah Road, of which we have
two itineraries, the one reproduced by Hamdâny and the
other by Ibn Khordâdbeh, Qodâma, and others, keeps to
the left of Sufayna, and runs parallel with the Eastern
Madîna-Meccah Road to within one stage of Meccah.
We find only one passage in Arabic geographers from
which we learn that the Baghdâdlies, as long as a thousand years ago, used under certain circumstances to take
the way of Sufayna.   Yâcût, vol. iii. p. 403, says :
"Sufayna (صفينة Çufayna), a place in the ᶜÂliya (Highland)
within the territory of the Solaymites, lies on the road of
Zobayda.   The pilgrims make a roundabout, and take this
road, if they suffer from want of water.   The pass of
Sufayna, by which they have to descend, is very difficult."
The ridges over which the road leads are called al-Sitâr,
and are described by Yâcût, vol. iii. p. 38, as a range of
red hills, flanking Sufayna, with defiles which serve as
passes.   Burton, vol. ii. p. 128, describes them as low
hills of *red* sandstone and bright porphyry.   Zobayda,
whose name the partly improved, partly newly opened
Hajj-Road from Baghdâd to Meccah bore, was the wife
of Caliph Harun, and it appears from Burton, pp. 134
and 136, that the improvements made by this spirited
woman—as the wells near Ghadîr, and the Birkat (Tank)
—are now ascribed to her weak, fantastical, and contemptible husband.

Burton's description of the plain covered with huge
boulders and detached rocks (p. 131) puts us in mind of

the Felsenmeer in the Odenwald. Yâcût, vol. iii. p. 370, describes the two most gigantic of these rock-pillars, which are too far to the left of Burton's road than that he could have seen them: " Below Sufayna in a desert plain there rise two pillars so high that nobody, unless he be a bird, can mount them; the one is called ᶜAmûd (column) of al-Bân, after the place al-Bân, and the other ᶜAmûd of al-Safh. They are both on the right-hand side of the (regular) road from Baghdâd to Meccah, one mile from Ofayᶜiya (a station on the regular road which answers to Sufayna)." Such desolate, fantastic scenery is not rare in Arabia nor close to the western coast of the Red Sea. The Fiumara, from which Burton (p. 138) emerged at six A.M., Sept. 9, was crossed by Burckhardt at Kholayç, and is a more important feature of the country than the two travellers were aware of. There are only five or six Wâdies which break through the chain of mountains that runs parallel with the Red Sea, and of these, pro-ceeding from south to north, Wâdy Nakhla (Wâdy Laymûn) is the first, and this Fiumara the second. Early geographers call it Wâdy Amaj, or after a place of some importance situated in its lower course, Wâdy Sâya. Hamdâny, p. 294, says: "Amaj and Ghorân are two Wâdies which commence in the Ḥarra (volcanic region) of the Benî Solaym, and reach the sea." The descrip-tions of this Wâdy compiled by Yâcût, vol. iii. pp. 26 and 839, are more ample. According to one, it contains seventy springs: according to another, it is a Wâdy which you overlook if you stand on the Sharât (the mountain now called Jebel Çobḥ). In its upper course it runs between the two Ḥâmiya, which is the name of two black volcanic regions. It contains several villages of note, and there lead roads to it from various parts of the country. In its uppermost part lies the village of Fâriᶜ with date-groves, cultivated fields and gardens, producing plantains, pomegranates, and grapes, and in its lower course, close to Sâya, the rich and populous village Mahâya. The whole Wâdy is one of the Aᶜrâdh (oasis-like districts) of Madîna, and is administered by a Lieutenant of the Governor of that city. Yâcût makes the remark to this description: "I do not know whether this valley is still in the same condition, or whether it has altered." Though we know much less of it than Yâcût, we may safely assert that the cultivation has vanished and the condition has altered.

At Zariba (ضريبة, Dharîba) Burton and his party put on the Ihram (pilgrim-garb). If the Baghdâdlies follow the regular road they perform this ceremony at Dzât-ᶜIrq, which lies somewhat lower down than Dharîba, to the South-east of it, and therefore the rain-water which falls in Dharîba flows in the shape of a torrent to Dzât-ᶜIrq, and is thence carried off by the Northern Nakhla. Above the station of Dzât-ᶜIrq there rise ridges called ᶜIrq ; up these ridges the regular Baghdâd Road ascends to the high-plateau, and they are therefore considered by early geographers as the western limit of Nejd. ᶜOmâra *apud* Yâcût, vol. iv. p. 746, says: "All the country in which the water flows in an Easterly (North-easterly) direction, beginning from Dzât-ᶜIrq as far as Babylonia, is called Nejd ; and the country which slopes Westwards, from Dzât-ᶜIrq to Tihâma (the coast), is called Hijâz." The remarks of Arabic geographers on the Western watershed, and those of Burton, vol. ii. pp. 142 and 154, illustrate and complete each other most satisfactorily. It appears from Yâcût that the Fiumara in which Burton's party was attacked by robbers takes its rise at Ghomayr close to Dzât-ᶜIrq, that there were numerous date-groves in it, and that it falls at Bostân Ibn ᶜÂmir into the Nakhla, wherefore it is called the *Northern* Nakhla. The Southern Nakhla, also called simply Nakhla, a term which is sometimes reserved for the trunk formed by the junction of the Southern and Northern

Nakhla from Bostân Ibn ꜤÂmir downwards, is on account
of its history one of the most interesting spots in all
Arabia; I therefore make no apology for entering on its
geography. In our days it is called Wâdy Laymûn, and
Burckhardt, vol. i. p. 158, says of it : "Zeyme is a half-
ruined castle, at the eastern extremity of Wady Lymoun,
with copious springs of running water. Wady Lymoun
is a fertile valley, which extends for several hours (towards
West) in the direction of Wady Faṭmé (anciently called
Baṭn Marr, or Marr-Tzahrân, which is, in fact, a continuation of Wady Nakhla). It has many date-plantations,
and formerly the ground was cultivated ; but this, I believe, has ceased since the Wahabi invasion : its fruit-
gardens, too, have been ruined. This (he means the
village Laymun, compare Burton, vol. ii. p. 147) is the
last stage of the Eastern-Syrian Hadj route. To the
South-east or East-south-east of Wady Lymoun is another
fertile valley, called Wady Medyk, where some sherifs
are settled, and where Sherif Ghaleb possessed landed
property.[1]" In the commentary on the Qaçyda Rod.,

---

1 Medyk is Burton's El-Mazik, the spelling in Arabic being
مضيق Madhyq. Burckhardt's account leads us to think that the
village now called Madhyq, or Wady Laymûn, lies on the left bank of
the Fiumara, and is identical with Bostân Ibn 'Amir, which is described by Yâcût as situated in the fork between the Northern and
Southern Nakhlas, and which in ancient times had, like the village
Wady Laymûn, the name of the valley of which it was the chief
place, viz., Batn Nakhla. Burton gives no information of the position
of the village, but he says : " On the *right* bank of the Fiumara stood
the Meccan Sharif's state pavilion." Unless the pavilion is separated from the village by the Fiumara there is a discrepancy between
the two accounts, which leads me to suspect that "right" is an over-
sight for "left." Anciently نخلة was pronounced Nakhlat, and, if
we suppress the guttural, as the Greeks and Romans sometimes did,
Nalat. Strabo, p. 782, in his narrative of the retreat of Aelius Gallus,
mentions a place which he calls Malŏtha, and of which he says it
stood on the bank of a river—a position which few towns in Arabia
have. The context leaves no doubt that he means Batn Nakhla, and
that Malŏtha is a mistake for Nalŏtha.

Wâdy Nakhla, as far as the road to Meccah runs through
it, is described as follows : From the ridges with whose
declivity the Western watershed begins, you descend into
Wâdy Baubât ; it is flanked on the left side by the Sarât
mountains, on which Ṭâyif stands, and contains Qarn-
almanâzil (once the capital of the Minæans, the great
trading nation of antiquity).   Three or four miles below
Qarn is Masjid Ibrâhym, and here the valley assumes
the name of Wâdy Nakhla.   At no great distance from
the Masjid there rise on the left-hand side of the Wâdy
two high peaks called Jebel Yasum and Jebel Kafw.   Both
were the refuge of numerous monkeys, who used to invade
the neighbouring vineyards.   As you go down Wâdy
Nakhla the first place of importance you meet is al-Zayma.
Close to it was a garden which, during the reign of Moq-
tadir, belonged to the Hâshimite Prince ʿAbd Allah,
and was in a most flourishing condition.   It produced an
abundance of henna, plantains, and vegetables of every
description, and yielded a revenue of five thousand Dinâr-
mithqâls (about £2,860) annually.   A canal from Wâdy
(the river) Nakhla feeds a fountain which jets forth in the
midst of the garden, and lower down a tank.   In the garden stood a fort (which in a dilapidated condition is extant
to this day, and spoken of by Burckhardt).   It was
built of huge stones, guarded for the defence of the property by the Banû Saʾd, and tenanted by the servants
and followers of the proprietor.   Below al-Zayma is
Sabûḥa, a post-station where a relay of horses was kept
for the transport of Government Despatches.   To give an
idea of the distances, I may mention that the post-stages
were twelve Arabic miles asunder, which on this road are
rather larger than an English geographical mile.   The
first station from Meccah was Moshâsh, the second
Sabûḥa, and the third was at the foot of the hill Yâsûm.
The author of the commentary from which I derive this
information leaves Wâdy Nakhla soon after Sabûḥa, and

turns his steps towards the holy city.   He mentions "the steep rocky Pass" up which Burton toiled with difficulty, and calls it Orayk.   Though he enters into many details, he takes no notice of the hill-girt plain called Sôla.   This name occurs however in an Arabic verse, *apud* Yâcût, vol. ii. p. 968: "In summer our pasture-grounds are in the country of Nakhla, within the districts of al-Zayma and Sôla."

In Wady Fâṭima, Burckhardt found a perennial rivulet, coming from the Eastward, about three feet broad and two feet deep.   It is certain that Wâdy Fâṭima, formerly called Wâdy Marr, is a continuation of Wâdy Nakhla, and Yâcût considers in one passage Nakhla as a subdivision of Marr, and in another Marr as part of Wâdy Nakhla ; but we do not know whether the rivulet, which at al-Zayma seems to be of considerable size, disappears under the sand in order to come forth again in Wâdy Marr, or whether it forms an uninterrupted stream.   In ancient times the regular Baghdâd-Meccah Road did not run down from Dzât-ᶜIrq by the Northern Nakhla which Burton followed, but it crossed this Wâdy near its Northern end and struck over to the Southern Nakhla as far as Qarn almarâzil, which for a long time was the second station from Meccah, instead of Dzât-ᶜIrq.

APPENDIX VIII.

THE MECCAH PILGRIMAGE.

HAVING resolved to perform the Meccah pilgrimage, I spent a few months at Cairo, and on the 22nd of May embarked in a small steamer at Suez with the "mahmil" or litter, and its military escort, conveying the "kiswah" or covering for the "kábah." On the 25th the man at the wheel informed us that we were about to pass the village of Rābikh, on the Arabian coast, and that the time had consequently arrived for changing our usual habiliments for the "iḥrām," or pilgrim-costume of two towels, and for taking the various interdictory vows involved in its assumption : such as not to tie knots in any portion of our dress, not to oil the body, and not to cut our nails or hair, nor to improve the tints of the latter with the coppery red of henna. Transgression of these and other ceremonial enactments is expiated either by animal sacrifice, or gifts of fruit or cereals to the poor.

After a complete ablution and assuming the iḥrām, we performed two prayer-flections, and recited the meritorious sentences beginning with the words "Labbaik Allah huma labbaik!" "Here I am, O God, here I am ! Here I am, O Unassociated One, here I am, for unto Thee belong praise, grace, and empire, O Unassociated One !"

This prayer was repeated so often, people not unfrequently rushing up to their friends and shrieking the sacred sentence into their ears, that at last it became a signal for merriment rather than an indication of piety.

On the 26th we reached Jeddah, where the utter sterility of Arabia, with its dunes and rocky hills, becomes apparent. The town, however, viewed from the sea, is not unpicturesque. Many European vessels were at anchor off the coast : and as we entered the port, innumerable small fishing-boats darting in all directions, their sails no longer white, but emerald green from the intense lustre of the water, crowded around us on all sides, and reminded one by their dazzling colours and rapidity of motion of the shoals of porpoises so often seen on a voyage round the Cape.

On disembarking we were accosted by several "muṭawwafs," or circuit-men, so termed in Arabic, because, besides serving as religious guides in general, their special duty is to lead the pilgrim in his seven obligatory circuits around the Kābah. We encamped outside the town, and, having visited the tomb of " our Mother Eve," mounted our camels for Meccah.

After a journey of twenty hours across the Desert, we passed the barriers which mark the outermost limits of the sacred city, and, ascending some giant steps, pitched our tents on a plain, or rather plateau, surrounded by barren rock, some of which, distant but a few yards, mask from view the birthplace of the Prophet. It was midnight ; a few drops of rain were falling, and lightning played around us. Day after day we had watched its brightness from the sea, and many a faithful ḥāji had pointed out to his companions those fires which were Heaven's witness to the sanctity of the spot. " Al ḥamdu Lillah ! " Thanks be to God ! we were now at length to gaze upon the " Kiblah," to which every Mussulman has turned in prayer since the days of Muhammad, and which for long ages before the birth of Christianity was reverenced by the Patriarchs of the East. Soon after dawn arose from our midst the shout of " Labbaik ! Labbaik ! " and passing between the rocks, we found ourselves in the main street of Meccah, and approached the " Gateway of Salvation," one of the thirty-nine portals of the Temple of Al-Haram.

On crossing the threshold we entered a vast unroofed quadrangle, a mighty amplification of the Palais Royal, having on each of its four sides a broad colonnade, divided into three aisles by a multitude of slender columns, and rising to the height of about thirty feet. Surmounting each arch of the colonnade is a small dome : in all there are a hundred and twenty, and at different points arise seven minarets, dating from various epochs, and of somewhat varying altitudes and architecture. The numerous pigeons which have their home within the temple have been believed never to alight upon any portion of its roof, thus miraculously testifying to the holiness of the building. This marvel having, however, of late years been suspended, many discern another omen of the approach of the long-predicted period when unbelievers shall desecrate the hallowed soil.

In the centre of the square area rises the far-famed Kābah, the funereal shade of which contrasts vividly with the sunlit walls and precipices of the town. It is a cubical structure of massive stone, the upper two-thirds of which are mantled by a black cloth embroidered with silver, and the lower portion hung with white linen. At a distance of several yards it is surrounded by a balustrade provided with lamps, which are lighted in the evening, and the space thus enclosed is the circuit-ground along which, day and night, crowds of pilgrims, performing the circular ceremony of Tawāf, realize the idea of perpetual motion. We at once advanced to the black stone imbedded in an angle of the Kābah, kissed it, and exclaimed, " Bismillah wa Allahu Akbar,"—" In God's name, and God is greatest." Then we commenced the usual seven rounds, three at a walking pace, and four at a brisk trot. Next followed two prayer-flections at the tomb of Abraham, after which we drank of the water of Zamzam, said to be the same which quenched the thirst of Hagar's exhausted son.

Besides the Kābah, eight minor structures adorn the quadrangle, the well of Zamzam, the library, the clock-room, the triangular staircase, and four ornamental resting-places for the orthodox sects of Hanafī, Shāfī, Mālikī, and Hanbalī.

We terminated our morning duties by walking and running seven times along the streets of Safā and Marwā, so named from the flight of seven steps at each of its extremities.

After a few days spent in visiting various places of interest, such as the slave-market and forts, and the houses of the Prophet and the Caliphs 'Ali and Abūbakr, we started on our six hours' journey to the mountain of 'Arifāt, an hour's sojourn at which, even in a state of insensibility, confers the rank of ḥāji. It is a mountain spur of about a hundred and fifty feet in height, presenting an artificial appearance from the wall encircling it and the terrace on its slope, from which the iman delivers a sermon before the departure of his congregation for Meccah. His auditors were, indeed, numerous, their tents being scattered over two or three miles of the country. A great number of their inmates were fellow-subjects of ours from India. I surprised some of my Meccah friends by informing them that Queen Victoria numbers nearly twenty millions of Mohammedans among her subjects.

On the 5th of June, at sunset, commencing our return, we slept at the village of Muzdalifah, and there gathered and washed seven pebbles of the size of peas, to be flung at three piles of whitewashed masonry known as the Shaitans (Satans) of Munā. We acquitted ourselves satisfactorily of this duty on the festival of the 6th of

June, the 10th day of the Arabian month Zu'lhijah. Each
of us then sacrificed a sheep, had his hair and nails cut,
exchanged the iḥrām for his best apparel, and, embracing
his friends, paid them the compliments of the season.
The two following days the Great, the Middle, and the
Little Satan were again pelted, and, bequeathing to the
unfortunate inhabitants of Munā the unburied and
odorous remains of nearly a hundred thousand animals,
we returned, eighty thousand strong, to Meccah. A week
later, having helped to insult the tumulus of stones which
marks, according to popular belief, the burial-place of
Abulaḥab, the unbeliever, who, we learn from the Koran,
has descended into hell with his wife, gatherer of sticks, I
was not sorry to relinquish a shade temperature of 120°,
and wend my way to Jeddah *en route* for England, after
delegating to my brethren the recital of a prayer in my
behalf at the Tomb of the Prophet at Medina.

In penning these lines I am anxious to encourage
other Englishmen, especially those from India, to perform
the pilgrimage, without being deterred by exaggerated
reports concerning the perils of the enterprise. It must,
however, be understood that it is absolutely indispensable
to be a Mussulman (at least externally) and to have an
Arabic name. Neither the Koran nor the Sultan enjoins
the killing of intrusive Jews or Christians ; nevertheless,
two years ago, an incognito Jew, who refused to repeat
the creed, was crucified by the Meccah populace, and in
in the event of a pilgrim again declaring himself to be an
unbeliever the authorities would be almost powerless to
protect his life.

An Englishman who is sufficiently conversant with
the prayers, formulas, and customs of the Mussulmans,
and possess a sufficient guarantee of orthodoxy, need,
however, apprehend no danger if he applies through the
British Consulate at Cairo for an introduction to the
Amīrul Haj, the Prince of the Caravan.

Finally, I am most anxious to recommend as Muṭawwaf at Meccah Shaikh Muḥammed 'Umr Fanāir-jīzâdah.   He is extremely courteous and obliging, and has promised me to show to other Englishmen the same politeness which I experienced from him myself.

1862	1278
A.D.	A.H.

الحاج عبد الواحد

(EL HAJ ABD EL WAHID.)

END OF VOLUME II.

INDEX.

Index. 427

Burial-places in the East and in Europe, ii. 183
Burma, or renegade, derivation of the word, i. 23
Burnus, i. 193
Burton, Lieut., what induced him to make a pilgrimage, i. 1   His
    principal objects, 3   Embarks at Southampton, 5   His Oriental
    "impedimenta," 5   His eventless voyage, 6   Trafalgar, 7   Gib-
    raltar, 7   Malta, 7   Lands at Alexandria, 8   Successfully
    disguises himself, 11   Supposed by the servants to be an 'Ajami,
    11   Secures the assistance of a Shaykh, 11   Visits Al-Nahl and
    the venerable localities of Alexandria, 11   His qualifications as
    a fakir, magician, and doctor, 12   Assumes the character of a
    wandering Darwaysh as being the safest disguise, 13   Adopts
    the name of Shaykh Abdullah, 14   Elevated to the position of a
    Murshid, 14   Leaves Alexandria, 16   His adventures in search
    of a passport, 19   Reasons for assuming the disguise, 22   His
    wardrobe and outfit, 23   Leaves Alexandria, 28   Voyage up the
    Nile, 29   Arrives at Bulak, 31   Lodges with Miyan Khuda-
    bakhsh Namdar, 35   Life in the Wakalah of Egypt, 41   Makes
    the acquaintance of Haji Wali, 43   Becomes an Afghan, 45
    Interposes for Haji Wali, 48   Engages a Berberi as a servant, 62
    Takes a Shaykh, or teacher, Shaykh Mohammed al-Attar, 67   The
    Ramazan, 74   Visits the "Consul-General" at Cairo, 86   Pleasant
    acquaintances at Cairo, 122   Account of the pilgrim's companion,
    Mohammed al-Busyani, 123   Lays in stores for the journey, 125
    The letter of credit, 126   Meets with difficulties respecting the
    passport, 127   Interview with the Persian Consul, 129   Obtains
    a passport through the intervention of the chief of the Afghan
    college, 131   An adventure with an Albanian captain of irregulars,
    132, *et seq.*   Departure from Cairo found necessary, 140   A display
    of respectability, 141   Shaykh Nassar, the Badawi, 141
    Hasty departure from Cairo, 142   The Desert, 144, *et seq.*   The
    midnight halt, 154   Resumes the march, 154   Rests among a
    party of Maghrabi pilgrims, 156   Adventure on entering Suez,
    159   An uncomfortable night, 159   Interview with the governor of
    Suez, 160   Description of the pilgrim's fellow-travellers at
    Suez, 161, *et seq.*   Advantages of making a loan, 165   Suspicion
    awakened by a sextant, 166   Passports a source of trouble, 168
    Kindness of Mr. West, 169   Preparations for the voyage from
    Suez, 172   Society at the George Inn, 172   The pilgrim-ship,
    186   A battle with the Maghrabis, 191   Leaves Suez, 194
    Course of the vessel, 195   Halts near the Hammam Bluffs, 197
    The "Golden Wire" aground, 200   Re-embarkation, 201
    Reaches Tur, 201   Visits Moses' Hot Baths, 203   Leaves
    Tur, 207   Effects of a thirty-six hours' sail, 209   Makes
    Damghah anchorage, 213   Enters Wijh Harbour, 214   Sails
    for Jabal Hassani, 217   Nearly wrecked, 219   Makes Jabal
    Hassani, 220   Wounds his foot, 221   The halt at Yambu',
    225   Bargains for camels, 230   An evening party at Yambu',
    232   Personates an Arab, 234   His Hamail or pocket Koran,
    239   Departure from Yambu', 241   The Desert, 242   The
    halting-ground, 244   Resumes the march, 244   Alarm of

"Inshallah bukra" (please God, to-morrow), ii. 21
Intermarriages, theory of the degeneracy which follows, ii. 84   Dr.
Howe's remarks on, 84, *n.*
Intonation and chaunting of the Koran taught in Moslem schools, i.
106, *n.*
Irak, Al-, expedition of Tobba al-Asghar against, i. 349
Iram, flood of, i. 348
Ireland, probable origin of its name, ii. 239, *n.*
Irk al-Zabyat, mountain, ii. 274, *n.*
Isa bin Maryam, reference to, ii. 274, *n.*   Spare tomb at Al-Madinah
for him after his second coming, 325
Isha, or Moslem night prayer, i. 233
Ishmael (Ismail), his tomb at Meccah, ii. 305   The two-bow prayer
over the grave of, 176
Ishmaelites, of the Sinaitic peninsula, ii. 78   Their distinguishing marks,
78
Ismail Pasha murdered by Malik Nimr, chief of Shendy, i. 138, *n.*
Ismid, a pigment for the eyes, i. 381, *n.*
Israel Benu, rule of, in Arabia, i. 345   *See* Jews
Israelites, course of the, across the Red Sea, i. 199
Israfil, the trumpet of, on the last day, i. 340, *n.*
Istikharah, or divination, ii. 23
Italians, how regarded in Egypt, i. 111
Izar, the portion of a pilgrim's dress so called, ii. 139

JA AL-SHARIFAH, the halting-ground, ii. 63
Ja'afar al-Sadik, the Imam, his tomb, ii. 40, 41, *n.*
Ja'afar Bey (governor of Suez), i. 147   Account of him, 160
Jababirah (giants), who fought against Israel, i. 344
Jabariti, from Habash, i. 177
Jahaydah, a straggling line of villages, i. 262
Jama, meaning of, i. 97
Jama Taylun, mosque, i. 96
Jama'at, or public prayers, in Al-Rauzah, i. 330, *n.*
Jami al-Sakhrah, at Arafat, ii. 192
Jami Ghamamah at Al-Manakhah, i. 395
Jannat al-Ma'ala (the cemetery of Meccah), visit to, ii. 248
Jauf, Al-, excellence of the dates of, i. 383
Jauhar, founder of the Mosque of Al-Azhar, i. 102
Jaundice, common in Arabia, i. 387   Popular cure for, 387
Java, number of Moslem pilgrims from, to Meccah, i. 179
Javelin, (Mizrak), description of the Arab, i. 237
Jazb al-Kulub ila Diyar al-Mahbub, the work so called, ii. 358, *n.*
Jabal, observations on the word, i. 220, *n.*
Jabali, the date so called, i. 401
Jeddah, slave trade at, i. 47   Price of perjury at, 47   Value of the
exports from Suez to, 178   Jews settled in, 346, *n.*   Population
of, 393, *n.*   Unsuccessful attempt of the Wahhabis to storm it, ii.
265, *n.*   Considered by the Meccans to be a perfect Gibraltar,
265   The Wakalah of Jeddah, 266   The British Vice-Consul,
Mr. Cole, 266   Different descriptions of the town, 267, 268   The
fair Corinthians at, 270   How the time passes at Jeddah, 272

452   *Pilgrimage to Al-Madinah and Meccah.*